PRAISE FOR *Best European Fiction*

"Best European Fiction 2010 ... *offers an appealingly diverse look at the Continent's fiction scene.*" **THE NEW YORK TIMES**

"*The work is vibrant, varied, sometimes downright odd. As [Zadie] Smith says [in her preface]: 'I was educated in a largely Anglo-American library, and it is sometimes dull to stare at the same four walls all day.' Here's the antidote.*"
THE FINANCIAL TIMES

"*With the new anthology* Best European Fiction 2010 *our literary world just got wider.*" **TIME MAGAZINE**

"*The collection's diverse range of styles includes more experimental works than a typical American anthology might ... [Mr. Hemon's] only criteria were to include the best works from as many countries as possible.*"
THE WALL STREET JOURNAL

"*This is a precious opportunity to understand more deeply the obsessions, hopes and fears of each nation's literary psyche—a sort of international show-and-tell of the soul.*" **THE GUARDIAN**

"*Dalkey has published an anthology of short fiction by European writers, and the result,* Best European Fiction 2010, *is one of the most remarkable collections I've read—vital, fascinating, and even more comprehensive than I would have thought possible.*" **BOOKSLUT**

"*Here's hoping to many more years of impossibly ambitious* Best European Fiction *anthologies.*" **POPMATTERS**

BEST EUROPEAN FICTION 2011

EDITED AND WITH AN INTRODUCTION BY ALEKSANDAR HEMON

PREFACE BY COLUM MCCANN

BEST EUROPEAN FICTION 2011

DALKEY ARCHIVE PRESS

CHAMPAIGN AND LONDON

ISBN 978-1-56478-600-5
ISSN 2152-6672

www.dalkeyarchive.com

Funded in part by grants from Arts Council England; the Arts
Council (Ireland); the Illinois Arts Council, a state agency; and with
support from the University of Illinois at Urbana-Champaign

Please see Acknowledgments on page 505 for additional
information on the support received for this volume

Dalkey Archive Press would like to thank "roving editor"
Roman Simić for his invaluable assistance in assembling
this second volume of *Best European Fiction*

Designed and composed by Quemadura,
printed on permanent/durable acid-free paper,
and bound in the United States of America

LOTTERY FUNDED

Contents

PREFACE **XIII**

INTRODUCTION **XVII**

[UNITED KINGDOM: WALES]
WILIAM OWEN ROBERTS
The Professionals

1

[UNITED KINGDOM: ENGLAND]
HILARY MANTEL
The Heart Fails without Warning

7

[TURKEY]
ERSAN ÜLDES
Professional Behavior

19

[SWITZERLAND]
VERENA STEFAN
Doe a Deer

31

[SPAIN: CATALAN]
MERCÈ IBARZ
Nela and the Virgins
40

[SPAIN: CASTILIAN]
ENRIQUE VILA-MATAS
Far from Here
52

[SLOVENIA]
DRAGO JANČAR
The Prophecy
71

[SERBIA]
VLADIMIR ARSENIJEVIĆ
One Minute: Dumbo's Death
90

[RUSSIA]
ANDREI GELASIMOV
The Evil Eye
96

[ROMANIA]
LUCIAN DAN TEODOROVICI
Goose Chase
107

[PORTUGAL]
GONÇALO M. TAVARES
Six Tales
121

[POLAND]

OLGA TOKARCZUK

The Ugliest Woman in the World

134

[NORWAY]

FRODE GRYTTEN

Hotel by a Railroad

146

[NETHERLANDS]

MANON UPHOFF

Desire

160

[MONTENEGRO]

OGNJEN SPAHIĆ

Raymond is No Longer with Us—Carver is Dead

168

[MOLDOVA]

IULIAN CIOCAN

Auntie Frosea

176

[MACEDONIA]

BLAŽE MINEVSKI

Academician Sisoye's Inaugural Speech

184

[LITHUANIA]

DANUTĖ KALINAUSKAITĖ

Just Things

193

[LIECHTENSTEIN]
STEFAN SPRENGER
Dust
206

[LATVIA]
NORA IKSTENA
Elza Kuga's Old-Age Dementia
220

[ITALY]
MARCO CANDIDA
Dream Diary
231

[IRELAND: IRISH]
ÉILÍS NÍ DHUIBHNE
Trespasses
240

[IRELAND: ENGLISH]
KEVIN BARRY
Doctor Sot
255

[ICELAND]
KRISTÍN EIRÍKSDÓTTIR
Holes in People
270

[HUNGARY]
LÁSZLÓ KRASZNAHORKAI
The Bill
281

[GERMANY]

INGO SCHULZE

Oranges and Angel

290

[GEORGIA]

ZURAB LEZHAVA

Sex for Fridge

311

[FRANCE]

ERIC LAURRENT

American Diary

327

[FINLAND]

ANITA KONKKA

The Clown

339

[ESTONIA]

TOOMAS VINT

Beyond the Window a Park is Dimming

348

[DENMARK]

PETER ADOLPHSEN

Fourteen Small Stories

362

[CZECH REPUBLIC]

MICHAL AJVAZ

The Wire Book

375

[CYPRUS]
NORA NADJARIAN
Exhibition
387

[CROATIA]
MIMA SIMIĆ
My Girlfriend
394

[BULGARIA]
ALEK POPOV
Plumbers
398

[BOSNIA AND HERZEGOVINA]
GORAN SAMARDŽIĆ
Varneesh
418

[BELGIUM]
FRANÇOIS EMMANUEL
Lou Dancing
436

[BELARUS]
VICTOR MARTINOVICH
Taboo
448

[AUSTRIA]

DIETER SPERL

Random Walker

462

[ALBANIA]

ARIAN LEKA

Brothers of the Blade

477

AUTHOR BIOGRAPHIES **485**

TRANSLATOR BIOGRAPHIES **499**

ACKNOWLEDGMENTS **505**

RIGHTS AND PERMISSIONS **509**

A Refusal to be Bordered

THE AMERICA OF EUROPE

The writer's proper destiny is to know where he or she comes from, confront his conscience, draw the borderline, then step beyond it. One of the deepest conundrums, and perhaps beauties, of our time is that so many of us do not know where we come from.

The concept of the global writer is a relatively new one. There has always been the Sri Lankan writer, for example, or the English writer, or the Canadian, or indeed the American. It is only in recent years that a writer like Michael Ondaatje—born in Sri Lanka, educated in England, a Canadian citizen who wrote his first novel about a black American jazz musician—was able to comfortably fit the phrase "international mongrel" into the discourse. We are increasingly familiar with our hybrid sense of nationality: that wherever we *are* can be coupled with wherever we once *were*. Writers can carry the weight of a couple of extra countries: if you put the original brick in your pocket, you can still swim the river. We're not shattered by our multiple hyphenations. We can be Irish and Argentinean, or French and Australian, or Chinese and Paraguayan, or perhaps even all of them at once.

The problem comes if you're European. What exactly is a European writer? Is there a contained geography or an accepted history in which she or he exists? Is there some sort of European voice that justifies an anthology? What does it mean, apart from the very nature of fracture, to have a literature of Europe?

Everyone knows what Europe once was—the very word opens up the charnel houses of the twentieth century—but we have an imperfect idea of what Europe currently *is*. It operates as an umbrella word, of course, but the umbrellas are inevitably carried around even when it's not threatening to rain. There's Sweden, there's Turkey, there's Macedonia. There's France, there's Germany, there's Spain. There's Luxembourg and Andorra and Vatican City and Catalonia. Some European organisations—its football authorities for instance—include Kazakhstan and Israel. (Imagine the Israelis swapping soccer shirts with the Kazakhs at a tournament, say in Sarajevo—perhaps Kafka could deal with the strange human algebra of it all.) And then there's Ireland and England, Serbia and Croatia, Georgia and Russia: long wars, short memories.

Try throwing all of these countries into the single factory chute of identity. It seems impossible, yet it has happened, and it continues to happen: the word "European" has been around a while and it is most certainly here to stay. The difficulty, for the writer at least, is knowing exactly where it begins and ends.

There's nothing new about European identity crises, of course, fictional or otherwise. Way back in 1904, Leopold Bloom, an Irish-Hungarian Jew, sat in Barney Kiernan's pub on Little Britain Street in Dublin, contemplating the idea that a nation is "the same people living in the same place." He later revises his answer to those "also living in different places." A parliamentary answer, and he gets a biscuit tin thrown at his head for his troubles. The idea is that a nation is a sort of intimate and fluctuating everywhere. It's impossible, of course, to have a nation without literature. The corresponding corollary is that it's impossible to have a literature without a nation. On the simplest level it has to come from somewhere.

The question revolves around the existence of national voices. What does it mean to have a national literature? In what ways does a writer represent a country? Is writing simply a borderless act or can we ascribe a closed-circuit origin to it? To what extent is nationality just a convenient file name to stick the writer on the shelf and soothe the nerves of the perplexed librarian?

Perhaps the term "European" is increasingly effective because of its inherent slipperiness. In eluding definition, it embraces the shifting nature of contemporary identity, this refusal to be bordered. Part of what constitutes European identity for its writers is that the literature is one of absolute variety and contention. Their identities are compound, contradictory, incomplete, even incoherent. Histories are constantly being invented and reinvented. There are forty different languages at play. There are 800 million stories to shuffle. There are as many Europes as there are words. Reality outruns definition. There is no real sense—not yet at least—of anyone wanting to draw attention to the "great European novel" in the same sense that the world anticipates, rightly or wrongly, the "great American novel," but that might be because there is still no final lockdown on what "European" actually means.

The word expands and contracts. It breathes in its own breathed-out breath. What results is a broad sense of being. On occasion, Europe expands its lungs to become a continent, and then, when necessary, it shrinks back down to its individual components. The small colonises the large, and the large rebounds upon the small. Thus Beckett is European but he's also Irish. (He might also, indeed, be French.) Danilo Kiš is Jewish and Serbian and half Hungarian and once Yugoslavian—ergo, European. And Kafka might be the most European writer of them all: his fiction lives in a constant flux.

The past is indeed all around us and this hurtling sense of ongoing identity is fabulous material for the continent's young artists. The fall of the Berlin Wall was of course no accident, either as fact or metaphor. There is a whole generation conceiving a response to 1989—and the writers in this anthology prove the point. The universal is local, brick by stolen brick. The gap in the wall gets continually bigger and the light that has a chance to break through is reason enough to keep reading. The strength of this anthology is that it gives us an idea of what is European in the broadest possible sense. Our awareness moves out concentrically from, say, Lithuania, over Paris, over Lisbon, and keeps going, reaching the shores of that imagined elsewhere.

What seems healthy—at least at first glance, and certainly in light of twentieth-century history—is that there is a lack of presumptive nationalism in the term "European." It appears, at least for now, a good deal less nationalistic than being American or Australian or even African. The growing chorus of voices that Europe has access to, the fluidity of movement from one country to the other, and the stew of languages from which it serves, makes Europe into the world's largest petri dish.

The idea would outrage most Europeans, but it is quite possible that Europe is now a dreamhouse of America, and maybe even more "American" than the U.S. itself.

Of course there are days when all of us can invent our nationality, or intranationality. For my own muddled palette—the carrier of two passports—I assume myself to be an Irishman first, a New Yorker second, an American third. There is a distant European in me also: I grew up on those Dublin roads that were financed by the EEC. W. B. Yeats said that of our conflicts with ourselves we make poetry. True enough. And, if so, of our conflicts with others, we make countries. So, by extension, of our conflict with countries, we again make ourselves. Hence the page and the words thrown against it.

COLUM MCCANN

Introduction

A year after the publication of *Best European Fiction 2010*, we can happily look back and safely say that our anthology has been a resounding success. The response of readers, reviewers, and translators—those unsung heroes of the project of literature—has been overwhelmingly marked by excitement and encouragement. The publication of *Best European Fiction 2010* exposed, like a flash of inconvenient lightning, the gaping lack at the heart of the contemporary English-language literary domain. Within weeks of its appearance, *Best European Fiction 2010* became not only necessary but inescapable—how could we have ever called ourselves a literate culture without it?

The indelibly established presence of *Best European Fiction 2010* in the Anglo-American literary universe generated a host of burningly interesting questions: Is there European writing as distinct from American (or British) writing? What is this thing called "Europe"? Do we really need translations from other literary cultures if we have writers raised in those cultures successfully writing in English? Can the American literary scene still be called isolated and insular, or be accused of not participating in "the big dialogue of literature," as was suggested by the permanent secretary of the Swedish Academy a few years ago?

All of the discussion engendered by *Best European Fiction 2010* was, I believe, fundamentally about the nature and value of knowledge (as opposed to information) transmitted between—and throughout—cultures and languages by means of translation. Despite (or because of) all the different opinions, *Best European Fiction 2010* seemed to have reignited a consensus that whatever its nature may be, such knowledge is invaluable and essential to the practice of literature, "the big dialogue" that takes place whenever a work of fiction is cracked open by a reader. There were readers who found some pieces lacking (though no two readers could agree on which); some reviewers questioned the criteria for the selections in the anthology and the overarching strategy presumably visible in such criteria (though I can assure you that the operative one was: pick the best piece in the available pile); and some Europeans may have been troubled by the conceptual flimsiness of "Europe," while some Americans may not have taken to the confrontational forms this "European" writing assumed. Whatever the objections were, what was behind them was a heartfelt enthusiasm for the project—the objections themselves became part of the big dialogue of literature. It is exactly that invested excitement that is the best measure of the success of *Best European Fiction 2010*.

Well, what now?

Well, now you have before you *Best European Fiction 2011*. If the great thing about *Best European Fiction 2010* was that nothing like it had been done before, the great thing about *Best European Fiction 2011* is that we are doing it again.

Let me, then, hasten to report that our 2011 European fiction vintage is one for the ages. This tormented anthologist had a painfully hard time picking one beautiful piece of literature over another. While reading, the anthologist was often privileged to revert to the elating state of a pure reader—only upon finishing the story would I remember that I had a cruel duty to perform and, wearing again the anthologist's tight uniform, select the volunteers for the charge at the front line of contemporary fiction.

I therefore implore you, lucky reader gripping *Best European Fiction 2011*, to read one piece at a time and not rush through this book or skim it for the purposes of informed party conversation. Whether you're reading Olga Tokarczuk's (Poland) masterpiece "The Ugliest Woman in the

World" or Hilary Mantel's (England) heartbreakingly clear-eyed "The Heart Fails without Warning"—take your readerly time, for this is a book, not a website. Enter Ingo Schulze's (Germany) mesmerizing images in "Oranges and Angel," counter the indelible melancholy in Toomas Vint's (Estonia) "Beyond the Window a Park is Dimming" with the brazen hilarity of Kevin Barry's (Ireland) "Doctor Sot." Indeed, pick any piece of fiction in this book and relish it, read it slowly, let it breathe with the lungs of common humanity.

Some years from now, you might discover this book dormant on your shelf and recognize it as a remnant of the time before e-readers, before digital entertainment flattened generations into information receptacles. You will be astonished again—I promise!—with the depth and width and beauty of human experience contained within its pages, coming from a piece of earth we arbitrarily call Europe. You will remember reading it for the first time and become overwhelmed with a sense that something great, important, and enriching was taking place in the English language, and you were there to bear witness.

ALEKSANDAR HEMON

BEST EUROPEAN FICTION 2011

WILIAM OWEN ROBERTS

The Professionals

Before then, I wouldn't really have known him from Adam. Of course I'd seen him now and then at the butcher's. But there we were together on the pavement after stop tap, him cadging a light off me.

"Fancy making a night of it?"

"Got work tomorrow." I pocketed the lighter.

"Me too."

Big bags were hanging off his eyes. We picked up a taxi by the Black Lion and ended up at a club in town. Thursday night, so quite a few students about. Mathew was taking ages coming back with the drinks so I get fed up and go over. At the bar: him and some elfin-crop woman in a full-scale domestic.

"Sorry," back he's come with the drinks slopped onto our table.

Gave me the whole caboodle, not that I'd asked. Name of Jadwiga. She was his ex-wife. From Krakow. (He was dying to light up.) Three years shacked up and no children to show for it.

"Sorry," had he given too much away? "I've done fifteen hours straight today."

A minute later he's gone and leaves his drink for dead.

Months pass and no sign of him. November last year, though, he turns up: on the front page of the *South Wales Echo*. Mathew outside a bank, his desk emptied up into a Tesco's box, Security standing guard behind him, "Stunned" and "Sulky" slapped across his forehead. The headline was BANK GOES BUST, subhead MANAGEMENT MANGLED. The lead para didn't point the finger exactly, just bolded words like **bungling**, **blame**, and **bound to happen**.

By mid May I'm in Le Garcon down the Bay for my sister-in-law's fortieth. The starter done and the main is on its way when who walks in with a blonde but Mathew. Even though he's shown to a table practically next door, he doesn't see me.

Main course digesting and I'm on my way back from the Gents: hover at his elbow. Up he looks, lost until I let him have the clues—my name, where we last met—and with a click of his fingers and a flick of a grin I'm found. But he still didn't introduce me to his date. She was in her early thirties and her face was gentle, serene, propped up on palms in an open prayer. Still, we all need a little privacy.

As our party was shuffling on our coats, Mathew's at my side.

"Listen. Not here . . . but can we talk?"

"Talk?"

"Professional thing."

A stiff nod. "Of course."

He took my card.

"Thanks."

From then on I was his weekly appointment. I feel bad pulling the wool over your eyes like this, but Mathew's not his real name, any more than Jadwiga is hers. But they are real enough people, I can tell you, it's just I'm a professional and the rules are there to be respected.

The root of his distress was this:

Mathew had been a banker and the son of one, but not the sort of banker our fathers used to beg a loan from in their best suits, more the flashy transnational deal. Money ran green in his veins with the taint of copper. Once, on the couch, he recalled dream-diving into clean, clear coins that buoyed him up like they were his best friends. Back he kept coming to the same subject like a dog to his tail.

"I got shafted." Most of the blame he shunted onto one man: we'll call him Adrian. A tad younger than Mathew, Adrian was apparently just as ambitious. "If it wasn't for that bastard I'd still be in a job. But I got shafted."

"Shafted" was the signifier, pardon my jargon. The word took him down with it and there he flailed until neither of us could stand it any more. I decided to do it by the book and go back to the original trauma. His father had been a Midas, a big man whose every next move was better than his last. At least that was the myth that was left of him, because Mathew had lost him when he was nine.

He wasn't close to his mother: hardly saw her. They were Catholics. Jadwiga was a Catholic. She divorced him, citing his long hours and Mathew's lust for money. He couldn't stand his own company, took to hanging round pubs and picking up lovers for the sake of not going home alone. He'd been promoted twice at the bank then bettered even that by moving into the high-risk world of the Hang Seng Stock Exchange to take up what I'd call authorised international gambling.

Mathew had tried for head of department. He was made for it, he said, but Adrian got it. Adrian, two years his junior, was apparently better than him. The "shafting" image was all he could see, with Adrian taking the active role, until our sessions started to go whirlpool. Things were going bottom up. Mathew didn't feel he was getting any better and now it was me who was at fault. Now it was me he was beginning to hate.

At the Heathcock one night I'm waiting at the bar when some woman, God knows who, smiles at me from over by the sofas. She was sitting with two much younger girls. As I was downing my last pint, though, it clicked: she'd been Mathew's bit at Le Garcon. I could hardly go past without saying hello, could I? She was just seeing the girls off and said she was Anna.

"Two of my PhD students," she nodded towards the door. "Clever girls."

Politics was her subject. "Thanks for helping him." She swung her bag over her shoulder.

"It's my job."

The shrink in me thought it significant that Mathew had never mentioned Anna. The way she talked about him, they were obviously pretty close. She knew all about our sessions anyway, although she respected that from my end they were confidential.

"I've tried to help him too, in my own way. Get him to see himself—his situation—in a different light; see it clearer, maybe."

" 'Different' in what way?"

"In a social context. That's what counts: not Freud."

As you'd expect, this got me going. "That's a matter of opinion."

"Not in Mathew's case."

"I disagree."

"Well, you would, wouldn't you?" Pity had caramelised her anger.

"He'll get over it," I said. "I can tell."

"I wish I could."

Next session I asked him, "Mathew, would you like to talk at all about Anna?"

"No."

"Why?"

"Don't want to."

"Why? Any particular reason?"

"'Cause I don't want to." A pause. "Leave her be. I don't want to discuss Anna. There's no point. I'd rather explore my father a bit more again . . ."

Mathew didn't come to our next appointment, nor the following one. I was getting worried so I started phoning him but all I ever got was the answering machine. The autumn nights were drawing in. By the end of November the news was full of protests against the banks in the city. Pictures of crowds in chaos, pushing and booing, windows smashed and the police like medieval infantry trying to keep a lid on things. The anger I understood: not so much the violence.

One cold morning in early December, Mathew called by.

"I haven't come to fix another meeting. Just came to settle up."

"My secretary deals with all that."

He was paler than usual, as though he had a bad cold. "I've finished with Anna."

I didn't answer straight away, just tried to curb my response in case he felt like explaining. But he just stared out of the window. The wind was rattling it but he was silent and just kept on staring out.

After a while, I asked, "How d'you feel?"

Mathew shrugged, then let his body sag a second. Our small talk filled the gap this time until I tried once more to ask him about Anna. He changed the subject with a deft, false smile. "It's not all bad news though . . ."

"Glad to hear it."

"I've given up smoking!"

"Wish I could."

He wiped his nose in his hand.

"I've found a job too."

"Congratulations!" (This *was* news.) "Around here?"

"No."

"London?"

I could see he was gasping for a fag. "You must be happy, Mathew."

"What do *you* think?" ("What a daft question!")

I kept quiet to get him to speak. Time gaped once more. "Yes, I'm happy." A smile. "Very happy."

"Good."

"Happier than I can remember. Now I know it'll all be okay." Mathew got up and stretched his hand across the desk. "Thanks for everything."

William Owen Roberts 5

"You know where to find me."

He paused at the door as though he'd forgotten to say something.

"Good luck," I said.

He gave a nod. Off he went. And that was that.

The last I heard from him was a postcard from Hong Kong wishing me a Better New Year.

TRANSLATED FROM WELSH BY GWEN DAVIES

HILARY MANTEL

The Heart Fails without Warning

September: When she began to lose weight at first, her sister had said, I don't mind; the less of her the better, she said. It was only when Morna grew hair—fine down on her face, in the hollow curve of her back—that Lola began to complain. I draw the line at hair, she said. This is a girls' bedroom, not a dog kennel.

Lola's grievance was this: Morna was born before she was, already she had used up three years' worth of air, and taken space in the world that Lola could have occupied. She believed she was birthed into her sister's squalling, her incessant *I-want I-want*, her *give-me give-me*.

Now Morna was shrinking, as if her sister had put a spell on her to vanish. She said, if Morna hadn't always been so greedy before, she wouldn't be like this now. She wanted everything.

Their mother said, "You don't know anything about it, Lola. Morna was not greedy. She was always picky about her food."

"Picky?" Lola made a face. If Morna didn't like something she would make her feelings known by vomiting it up in a weak acid dribble.

It's because of the school catchment area they have to live in a too-small house and share a bedroom. "It's bunk beds or GCSEs!" their mother said. She stopped, confused by herself. Often what she said meant something else entirely, but they were used to it; early menopause, Morna said. "You know what I mean," she urged them. "We live in this house for the sake of your futures. It's a sacrifice now for all of us, but it will pay off. There's no point in getting up every morning in a lovely room of your own and going to a sink school where girls get raped in the toilets."

"Does that happen?" Lola said. "I didn't know that happened."

"She exaggerates," their father said. He seldom said anything, so it made Lola jump, him speaking like that.

"But you know what I'm saying," her mother said. "I see them dragging home at two in the afternoon, they can't keep them in school. They've got piercings. There's drugs. There's Internet bullying."

"We have that at our school," Lola said.

"It's everywhere," their father said. "Which is another reason to keep off the Internet. Lola, are you listening to what I'm telling you?"

The sisters were no longer allowed a computer in their room because of the sites Morna liked to look at. They had pictures of girls with their arms stretched wide over their heads in a posture of crucifixion. Their ribs were spaced wide apart like the bars of oven shelves. These sites advised Morna how to be hungry, how not to be gross. Any food like bread, butter, an egg, is gross. A green apple or a green leaf, you may have one a day. The apple must be poison green. The leaf must be bitter.

"To me it is simple," their father said. "Calories in, calories out. All she has to do is open her mouth and put the food in, then swallow. Don't tell me she can't. It's a question of won't."

Lola picked up an eggy spoon from the draining board. She held it under her father's nose as if it were a microphone. "Yes, and have you anything you want to add to that?"

He said, "You'll never get a boyfriend if you look like a needle." When Morna said she didn't want a boyfriend, he shouted, "Tell me that again when you're seventeen."

"I never will be," Morna said. "Seventeen."

■

September: Lola asked for the carpet to be replaced in their room. "Maybe we could have a wood floor? Easier to clean up after her?"

Their mother said, "Don't be silly. She's sick in the loo. Isn't she? Mostly? Though not," she said hurriedly, "like she used to be." It's what they had to believe: that Morna was getting better. In the night, you could hear them telling each other, droning on behind their closed bedroom door; Lola lay awake listening.

Lola said, "If I can't have a new carpet, if I can't have a wood floor, what can I have? Can I have a dog?"

"You are so selfish, Lola," their mother shouted. "How can we take on a pet at a time like this?"

Morna said, "If I die, I want a woodland burial. You can plant a tree and when it grows you can visit it."

"Yeah. Right. I'll bring my dog," Lola said.

September: Lola said, "The only thing is, now she's gone so small I can't steal her clothes. This was my main way of annoying her and now I have to find another."

All year round Morna wore wool to protect her shoulders, elbows, hips, from the blows of the furniture, and also to look respectably fat so that people didn't point her out on the street: also, because even in July she was cold. But the winter came early for her, and though the sun shone outside she was getting into her underlayers. When she stepped on the scale for scrutiny she appeared to be wearing normal clothes, but actually she had provided herself with extra weight. She would wear one pair of tights over another; every gram counts, she told Lola. She had to be weighed every day. Their mother did it. She would try surprising Morna with spot checks, but Morna would always know when she was getting into a weighing mood.

Lola watched as their mother pulled at her sister's cardigan, trying to get it off her before she stepped onto the scales. They tussled like two little kids in a playground; Lola screamed with laughter. Their mother hauled at the sleeve and Morna shouted, "Ow, ow!" as if it were her skin being stretched. Her skin was loose, Lola saw. Like last year's school uniform, it was too big for her. It didn't matter, because the school had made it clear they didn't want to see her this term. Not until she's turned the corner, they said, on her way back to a normal weight. Because the school has such a competitive ethos. And it could lead to mass fatalities if the girls decided to compete with Morna.

When the weighing was over, Morna would come into their bedroom and start peeling off her layers, while Lola watched her, crouched in her bottom bunk. Morna would stand sideways to the mirror with her ribs arched. You can count them, she said. After the weighing she needed re-assurance. Their mother bought them the long mirror because she thought Morna would be ashamed when she saw herself. The opposite was true.

October: In the morning paper there was a picture of a skeleton. "Oh look," Lola said, "a relative of yours." She pushed it across the breakfast table to where Morna sat poking a Shredded Wheat with her spoon, urging it to-wards disintegration. "Look, Mum! They've dug up an original woman."

"Where?" Morna said. Lola read aloud, her mouth full. "Ardi stands four feet high. She's called *Ardipithecus*. Ardi for short. For short!" She spluttered at her own joke, and orange juice came down her nose. "They've newly discovered her. 'Her brain was the size of a chimpanzee's.' That's like you, Morna. 'Ardi weighed about fifty kilograms.' I expect that was when she was wearing all her animal skins, not when she was just in her bones."

"Shut it, Lola," their father said. But then he got up and walked out, breakfast abandoned, his mobile phone in his hand. His dirty knife, dropped askew on his plate, swung across the disc like the needle of a com-pass, and rattled to its rest. Always he was no more than a shadow in their lives. He worked all the hours, he said, to keep the small house going, worrying about the mortgage and the car while all *she* worried about was her bloody waistline.

Lola looked after him, then returned to the original woman. "Her teeth show her diet was figs. 'She also ate leaves and small mammals.' Yuk, can you believe that?"

"Lola, eat your toast," their mother said.

"They found her in bits and pieces. First just a tooth. 'Fossil hunters first glimpsed this species in 1992.' That's just before we first glimpsed Morna."

"Who found her?" Morna said.

"Lots of people. I told you, they found her in bits. 'Fifteen years' work involving forty-seven researchers.' "

Looking at Morna, their mother said, "You were fifteen years' work. Nearly. And there was only me to do it."

" 'She was capable of walking upright,' " Lola read. "So are you, Morna. Till your bones crumble. You'll look like an old lady." She stuffed her toast into her mouth. "But not four million years old."

November: One morning their mother caught Morna knocking back a jug of water before the weigh-in. She shouted, "It can swell your brain! It can kill you!" She knocked the jug out of her daughter's hand and it shattered all over the bathroom floor.

She said, "Oh, seven years' bad luck. No, wait. That's mirrors."

Morna wiped the back of her hand across her mouth. You could see the bones in it. She was like a piece of science coursework, Lola said thoughtfully. Soon she'd have no personhood left. She'd be reduced to biology.

The whole household, for months now, a year, had been enmeshed in mutual deception. Their mother would make Morna a scrambled egg and slide a spoonful of double cream into it. The unit where Morna was an inpatient used to make her eat white-bread sandwiches thickly buttered and layered with rubber wedges of yellow cheese. She used to sit before them, hour after hour, compressing the bread under her hand to try to squeeze out the oily fat on to the plate. They would say, try a little, Morna. She would say, I'd rather die.

If her weight fell by a certain percentage she would have to go back to the unit. At the unit they stood over her until she ate. Meals were timed and had to be completed by the clock or there were penalties. The staff would watch her to make sure she was not slipping any food into the layers of her clothes, and layers in fact were monitored. There was a camera in every bathroom, or so Morna said. They would see her if she made herself sick. Then they would put her to bed. She lay so many days in bed that when she came home her legs were wasted and white.

The founder of the unit, a Scottish doctor with a burning ideal, had given the girls garden plots and required them to grow their own vegetables. Once she had seen a starving girl eat some young peas, pod and all. The sight had moved her, the sight of the girl stretching her cracked lips and superimposing the green, tender smile: biting down. If they only saw, she said, the good food come out of God's good earth.

But sometimes the girls were too weak for weeding and pitched forward into their plots. And they were picked up, brushing crumbs of soil away; the rakes and hoes lay abandoned on the ground, like weapons left on a battlefield after the defeat of an army.

November: Their mother was grumbling because the supermarket van had not come with the order. "They say delivery in a two-hour time slot to suit you." She pulled open the freezer and rummaged. "I need parsley and yellow haddock for the fish pie."

Lola said, "It will look as if Morna's sicked it already."

Their mother yelled, "You heartless little bitch." Iced vapour billowed around her. "It's you who brings the unhappiness into this house."

Lola said, "Oh, is it?"

Last night Lola saw Morna slide down from her bunk, a wavering column in the cold; the central heating was in its off phase, since no warm-blooded human being should be walking about at such an hour. She pushed back her quilt, stood up and followed Morna on to the dark landing. They were both barefoot. Morna wore a ruffled nightshirt, like a wraith in a story by Edgar Allan Poe. Lola wore her old Mr. Men pyjamas, aged 8–9, to which she was attached beyond the power of reason. Mr. Lazy, almost washed away, was a faded smudge on the shrunken top, which rose and gaped over her round little belly; the pyjama legs came half way down her calves, and the elastic had gone at the waist, so she had to hitch herself together every few steps. There was a half moon and on the landing she saw her sister's face, bleached out, shadowed like the moon, cratered like the moon, mysterious and far away. Morna was on her way downstairs to the computer to delete the supermarket order.

In their father's office Morna had sat down on his desk chair. She scuffed her bare heels on the carpet to wheel it up to the desk. The computer was for their father's work use. They had been warned of this and told their mother got ten GCSEs without the need of anything but a pen and paper; that they may use the computer under strict supervision; that they may also go online at the public library.

Morna got up the food order on screen. She mouthed at her sister, "Don't tell her."

She'd find out soon enough. The food would come anyway. It always did. Morna didn't seem able to learn that. She said to Lola, "How can you bear to be so fat? You're only eleven."

Lola watched her as she sat with her face intent, patiently fishing for the forbidden sites, swaying backwards and forwards, rocking on the wheeled chair. She turned to go back to bed, grabbing her waist to stop her pyjama bottoms from falling down. She heard a sound from her sister, a sound of something, she didn't know what. She turned back. "Morna? What's that?"

For a minute they don't know what it was they were seeing on the screen: human or animal? They saw that it was a human, female. She was on all fours. She was naked. Around her neck there was a metal collar. Attached to it was a chain.

Lola stood, her mouth ajar, holding up her pyjamas with both hands. A man was standing out of sight holding the chain. His shadow was on the wall. The woman looked like a whippet. Her body was stark white. Her face was blurred and wore no readable human expression. You couldn't recognise her. She might be someone you knew.

"Play it," Lola said. "Go on."

Morna's finger hesitated. "Working! He's always in here, working." She glanced at her sister. "Stick with Mr. Lazy, you'll be safer with him."

"Go on," Lola said. "Let's see."

But Morna erased the image. The screen was momentarily dark. One hand rubbed itself across her ribs, where her heart was. The other hovered over the keyboard; she retrieved the food order. She ran her eyes over it and added own-brand dog food. "I'll get the blame," Lola said. "For my fantasy pet." Morna shrugged.

Later they lay on their backs and murmured into the dark, the way they used to do when they were little. Morna said, he would claim he found it by accident. That could be the truth, Lola said, but Morna was quiet. Lola wondered if their mother knew. She said, you can get the police coming round. What if they come and arrest him? If he has to go to prison we won't have any money.

Morna said, "It's not a crime. Dogs. Women undressed as dogs. Only if it's children, I think that's a crime."

Lola said, "Does she get money for doing it or do they make her?"

"Or she gets drugs. Silly bitch!" Morna was angry with the woman or girl who for money or out of fear crouched like an animal, waiting to have her body despoiled. "I'm cold," she said, and Lola could hear her teeth chattering. She was taken like this, seized by cold that swept right through her body to her organs inside; her heart knocked, a marble heart. She put her hand over it. She folded herself in the bed, knees to her chin.

"If they send him to prison," Lola said, "you can earn money for us. You can go in a freak show."

November: Dr. Bhattacharya from the unit came to discuss the hairiness. It happens, she said. The name of the substance is lanugo. Oh, it happens, I am afraid to say. She sat on the sofa and said, "With your daughter I am at my wit's end."

Their father wanted Morna to go back to the unit. "I would go so far as to say," he said, "either she goes, or I go."

Dr. Bhattacharya blinked from behind her spectacles. "Our funding is in a parlous state. From now till next financial year we are rationed. The most urgent referrals only. Keep up the good work with the daily weight chart. As long as she is stable and not losing. In spring if progress is not good we will be able to take her in."

Morna sat on the sofa, her arms crossed over her belly, which was swollen. She looked vacantly about her. She would rather be anywhere than here. It contaminates everything, she had explained, that deceitful spoonful of cream. She could no longer trust her food to be what it said it was, nor do her calorie charts if her diet was tampered with. She had agreed to eat, but others had broken the agreement. In spirit, she said.

Their father told the doctor, "It's no use saying all the time," he mimicked her voice, " 'Morna, what do you think, what do you want?' You don't give me all this shit about human rights. It doesn't matter what she thinks any more. When she looks in a mirror God knows what she sees. You can't get hold of it, can you, what goes on in that head of hers? She imagines things that aren't there."

Lola jumped in. "But I saw it too."

Her parents rounded on her. "Lola, go upstairs."

She flounced up from the sofa and went out, dragging her feet. They didn't say, "See what, Lola? What did you see?"

They don't listen, she had told the doctor, to anything I say. To them I am just noise. "I asked for a pet, but no, no chance—other people can have a dog, but not Lola."

Expelled from the room, she stood outside the closed door, whimpering. Once she scratched with her paw. She snuffled. She pushed at the door with her shoulder, a dull bump, bump.

"Family therapy may be available," she heard Dr. Bhattacharya say. "Had you thought of that?"

December: Merry Christmas.

January: "You're going to send me back to the unit," Morna said.

"No, no," her mother said. "Not at all."

"You were on the phone to Dr. Bhattacharya."

"I was on the phone to the dentist. Booking in."

Morna had lost some teeth lately, this was true. But she knew her mother was lying. "If you send me back I will drink bleach," she said.

Lola said, "You will be shining white."

February: They talked about sectioning her: that means, their mother said, compulsory detention in a hospital; that means you will not be able to walk out, Morna, like you did before.

"It's entirely your choice," their father said. "Start eating, Morna, and it won't come to that. You won't like it in the loony bin. They won't be coaxing you out on walks and baking you bloody fairy cakes. They'll have locks on the doors and they'll be sticking you full of drugs. It won't be like the unit, I'm telling you."

"More like a boarding kennel, I should think," Lola said. "They'll be kept on leads."

"Won't you save me?" Morna said.

"You have to save yourself," their father said. "Nobody can eat for you."

"If they could," said Lola, "maybe I'd do it. But I'd charge a fee."

Morna was undoing herself. She was reverting to unbeing. Lola was her interpreter, who spoke out from the top bunk in the clear voice of a prophetess. They had to come to her, parents and doctors, to know what Morna thought. Morna herself was largely mute.

She had made Morna change places and sleep on the bottom bunk since New Year's. She was afraid Morna would roll out and smash herself on the floor.

She heard her mother moaning behind the bedroom door: "She's going, she's going."

She didn't mean, "going to the shops." In the end, Dr. Bhattacharya had said, the heart fails without warning.

February: At the last push, in the last ditch, she decided to save her sister. She made her little parcels wrapped in tinfoil—a single biscuit, a few pick 'n' mix sweets—and left them on her bed. She found the biscuit, still in its foil, crushed to crumbs, and on the floor of their room shavings of fudge and the offcut limbs of pink jelly lobsters. She could not count the crumbs, so she hoped Morna was eating a little. One day she found Morna holding the foil, uncrumpled, looking for her reflection in the shiny side. Her sister had double vision now, and solid objects were ringed by light; they had a ghost-self, fuzzy, shifting.

Their mother said, "Don't you have any feelings, Lola? Have you no idea what we're going through, about your sister?"

"I had some feelings," Lola said. She held out her hands in a curve around herself, to show how emotion distends you. It makes you feel full up, a big weight in your chest, and then you don't want your dinner. So she had begun to leave it, or surreptitiously shuffle bits of food—pastry, an extra potato—into a piece of kitchen roll.

She remembered that night in November when they went barefoot down to the computer. Standing behind Morna's chair, she had touched her shoulder, and it was like grazing a knife. The blade of the bone seemed to sink deep into her hand, and she felt it for hours; she was surprised not to see the indent in her palm. When she had woken up next morning, the shape of it was still there in her mind.

March: All traces of Morna have gone from the bedroom now, but Lola knows she is still about. These cold nights, her Mr. Men pyjamas hitched up with one hand, she stands looking out over the garden of the small house. By the lights of hovering helicopters, by the flash of the security lights from neighbouring gardens, by the backlit flicker of the streets, she sees the figure of her sister standing and looking up at the house, bathed in a nimbus of frost. The traffic flows long into the night, a hum without ceasing, but around Morna there is a bubble of quiet. Her tall straight body flickers inside her nightshirt, her face is blurred as if from tears or drizzle, and she wears no readable human expression. But at her feet a white dog lies, shining like a unicorn, a golden chain about its neck.

ERSAN ÜLDES

Professional Behavior

Sooner murder an infant in its cradle than nurse unacted desires.
[WILLIAM BLAKE]

1. "BEING A TRANSLATOR is nothing like being an ordinary reader, it's the most intimate means of entering into the author's inner world."

I never really liked big talk, and was completely disgusted by the cliché Necdet Sezai Balkan kept employing in an effort to flatter me. It had been a long time since I was kicked out of the profession, I was no longer a working intellectual. But Necdet Sezai didn't need to know this, and for some reason I derived great pleasure from his thinking that I still translated.

"What translator really gives a damn about the author's inner world?" I asked.

"Don't say that, I think being a translator is really something . . . Being capable of recreating a work of art in a different language, moving so rigorously through an author's inner world, don't tell me that isn't something!"

I had left the house hoping to find a drugstore (that accepted Medicaid), but then Bahadır called and so I diverted my route to the city center. My father had been discharged from the hospital that morning and had been brought home to die in peace. There was still an hour before I was supposed to meet Bahadır at Sarmasıklı Kahve, so I wandered around Bar Street for a while. I had just decided to sit down somewhere when I bumped into Necdet Sezai. Unable to refuse his polite invitation, I plopped down across from him.

The weather was decent enough to sit outside, so they'd scattered a few tables out front. There was nothing on the table when I arrived, but then Necdet Sezai soon had an order of Mexican steak, two egg rolls, and a huge bowl of Caesar salad. Me, I just ordered a beer. After his second egg roll, Necdet Sezai ordered a beer as well.

A heated discussion was underway at a nearby table. Two young men, their ties loosened, were getting louder by the minute. Between the two sat a brunette with higher self-esteem than either, about thirty, who preferred to remain silent. One of the men, the one who looked a little less temperamental, was expressing his belief that we, as a nation, needed to adopt a more aggressive attitude; we needed to get out there and take immediate action in the world. The other, who had a prominent forehead that stuck out so far he must have had no trouble at all butting it into other peoples' business, thought instead that delivering peace and solidarity to far away countries was absolutely none of our business and that interfering with the internal affairs of other countries was in violation of international law.

I had no idea what it was precisely that had started this argument. I soon realized, however, that Necdet Sezai was no longer talking to me, but listening to the conversation at the other table. Watching the two young men—now getting really agitated—he kept rolling his eyes back and forth, like a moderator on a debate show.

Suddenly he pushed aside his empty salad bowl and announced: "Fine, but what do we gain?" He didn't look at the other table as he said this, although he was addressing them, not me. "What do we gain?"

Then, in an astounding display of agility, he grabbed his beer, rose to his feet, and lifted his glass into the air, in a single gesture, toasting the other table. He looked as if he was preparing for a long tirade. The latest version of Young Werther, vigorous but grave. Alyosha Karamazov's teacher Zosima, mortal but wise. A profile portrait of Franz Liszt playing the piano, attractive despite his long nose. The fact that he was dressed like some small-town politician hick did nothing to spoil the scene; after all, his short-sleeved green shirt and jeans almost matched.

Necdet Sezai was excellent at making ordinary events look extraordinary, no matter what the circumstances. For a moment there, the young men didn't know what to do. How were they to respond to this friendly and noble attempt of a stranger—past middle age, a venerable old uncle—trying to look and act as young as they (and who was probably a lunatic into the bargain)?

Giving in, they raised their glasses in return, hoping to appease him. What about the woman who was sitting with her back turned to us? She didn't raise her glass; she turned to Necdet Sezai and cracked a tiny smile. More effective.

"To go or not to go," said Necdet Sezai, leaning toward the other table a bit more, "to go or not to go, isn't this also a literary problem, going back hundreds of years? If we do go, what will we gain? Shouldn't we be talking about this? Or, what if we stay? What will we get if we stay?"

The three of them together gave him a look that seemed to be asking who the hell he thought he was. The lunatic was going too far now. But N. Sezai successfully read the two young men's minds and so proceeded to introduce himself:

"I'm an author . . ." he said. "I'm Necdet Sezai Balkan."

Blushing, like disciples who had come close to committing some unforgivable sin, the kids welcomed the author to their table. They even stood up to pull his chair out for him. After settling down in his seat, splaying his presence all over the place like an octopus, N. Sezai had no difficulty whatsoever in socializing with the young men and woman. He straightened his collar and tried to make his bulky body appear more slender by sitting upright.

"Guys, when graced by the presence of such a beautiful young lady, isn't it ridiculous to be wasting time talking about such trivial nonsense?"

Having been mildly scolded, the less temperamental-looking young man bought the author a beer in a bid for forgiveness; the one with the prominent forehead offered him some nuts, holding the bowl out like a bottle of cologne. Now I was left at *the other table*, all alone, drifting farther and farther away from the center of attention with every ticking second . . .

Human beings are social animals. When they don't socialize, they become savage. Perhaps I didn't start sprouting fur, but the moment I was left all alone, I became filled with the desire to dig myself down into the mud, to bury my shame. And because of this I missed a show that was really worth seeing. I failed to catch Necdet Sezai's performance as he strove to make his way through foreign territory (or how, after showing a little courtesy, after licking off the salt that the nuts had left on his bottom lip, he delicately kissed the brunette's hand). I asked for the bill.

In spite of everything, Necdet Sezai was a sympathetic man, understanding, respectful, polite. When he saw that I was leaving, he came up to me immediately and apologized exactly three times. He took out a pen from his bag and clipped it to my shirt pocket.

"In memory of today," he said, "as an apology . . ."

I felt so embarrassed I didn't know what to do; I just prayed the kids weren't watching.

Do you think this was really necessary? All things considered, it was his right, after all, to leave without notice. To head off and savannah-soothe the crude, crass islets of his heart . . .

■

I.I. TO WEAR THE "TITLE" OF AUTHOR LIKE A BADGE OF RANK is one of the most dangerous ways on earth to achieve self-satisfaction. To write is one thing, but to be a writer, an author, to live life on earth clinging to this identity is a pathology belonging more to the field of psychology than literature. And then, when these writers know their work isn't good enough, they take it all out on you, the "author's friend," that pitiful creature who has to stay fresh and interesting at all times and feed the author a steady supply of new ideas in order not to feel entirely insignificant in his presence . . .

Are you too one of those pitiful creatures? If that's the case, remain calm—no reason to panic. There's an easy way out: just admire everything you read, without question, and find a deep, underlying meaning in it all—and you're done.

During one of our Sarmasıklı Kahve sessions, Bahadır said to me, "You get all pissed off with our local authors, but then you go and take it out on foreigners!" This was months before I got fired. He was the only person I'd shared my somewhat idiosyncratic translation theory with, convinced that he wouldn't go out blabbing it to anyone else. For some odd reason.

Novels that set their supposed "readers" up for tidy, *closed* endings made me absolutely miserable. I hated all those bloodsuckers who want nothing more than to arrange their plots so as to pull off one of those perfect dénouements that leave nothing at all behind save the words making up their so-called accomplishment . . .

Let's say our protagonist is a retired police officer. If, for example, in the very first pages of the novel, the protagonist is described using such phrases as, "He was a man possessed," and "A demonic glare beamed in his eyes," and if he's given the same tired old dialogue and personality as a million other fictional cops, all the usual signifiers to indicate that this guy—that the law!—is sick, dangerous . . . well, that's when I really lose it. Thus, contrary to the expectations imposed upon the "reader," and out of pure spite, I might decide, when translating, to give our retired police officer—who at the end of the novel will chop up his neighbor with a butcher's knife after a fight over the garden fence—a chance to perform the most wonderful, the kindest deed the world has ever known.

Or, for example, I once kept a character alive until the very end of a novel, writing all his parts myself, since the "real" author had killed him off shortly after creating him, probably thinking he wouldn't contribute much to the plot. And, look, all our "readers" really liked him, and a renowned critic even wrote (in a very respected newspaper, with a very high circulation) that my creation "mirrored" both Proust's multidimensional characters and Beckett's strange and miserable parodies.

And just like I didn't approve of everyone's obsession with neat, closed endings, I also couldn't stand it when there were huge gaps left in a story. Effects like that are nothing more than buffoonish displays of incompetence—the sort of trick an author incapable of finishing off a proper essay would fall back on, under the guise of being profound. A total disgrace. (Who the hell did I think I was?) I reconstructed all the structures that the postmodernist writers I translated had deconstructed, I filled in all the gaps they had left, one by one, took out all the flashbacks I found unnecessary, changed settings, plots, dates, and sometimes even got so carried away that I'd sprinkle in a few poetic lines of my own, in raptures.

"Isn't there anyone who checks your translations, goes over them or something?" Bahadır asked.

"Of course there is. An editor who doesn't speak a word of German . . ."

I've never used any unpleasant words like "ruin," "tinker," or "rewrite" to discuss what I did when I was a translator. I think the word that best describes my activities might be "correction." Or maybe "revision" . . . or how about "polishing"? . . . But look, whichever sounds the least criminal, that's the one I'd like to go with.

I was freeing the characters of the novels I translated from the roles they had been assigned, letting them out of the cages they'd been locked inside. I was rewriting the novels, yes, making them far better and more effective than they ever could have been on their own.

However, of all the many authors whose works I "revised," there's one I find particularly noteworthy: the famous German writer Judith Wohmann. I give Wohmann the most credit. She played a major role in my ascension from translating to authorship.

"Oh wow, so Wohmann got the big prize after all," said Bahadır. "Unbelievable."

I had banished this prize thing from my mind a long time ago. All I was thinking about was starting my own work, my own writing . . .

"When you try to do something, really do it, you have to stick to it, you should never give up," said Bahadır. "I mean, if you'd shown some respect for your work, if you had just played by the rules, you'd be counting your money by now."

"You're right Bahadır, I totally agree with you. But let me ask, when did you ever stick to anything?"

"It really doesn't matter *what* you try to do, what matters is that you be persistent and never give up trying," he said. "I mean, all your complaints, all your bitterness . . . the insults . . . maybe it's just an easy way out . . ."

I.2. CHANGING THE RULES OF ONE'S PROFESSION might seem somewhat capricious, maybe even immoral. But it really depends on what sort of work you're doing. If you work at air-traffic control, well, it can and should be considered an unforgivable crime to give your pilot incorrect information, since passengers' lives are at stake. In such cases, you really are obliged to follow the rules. But if you work at a job where your decisions are of a somewhat less fundamental nature, let's say, for example, a grocer, then a little mendacity is a must. How many tomatoes in a crate do you think are actually edible? If you're a grocer, you know very well that half the crate will always be full of rotten tomatoes. Customers naturally want you to give them the edible ones, so they do their best to believe that you, as a grocer, meet their high standards: they expect some dignity, some honesty of you. Let them have their expectations. After all, that's what a customer is: an animal crouched in expectation. Never let them choose their own tomatoes. One kilo of tomatoes, please: half of it to meet your customers' expectations, the other half a mass of putrescence. For a grocer to live in this world as a mass that isn't itself rotting away, he must be faithful first and foremost to this basic law.

"They'll find out what you're up to one day," Bahadır had warned me. "Can't you stay faithful to the original even a little?"

Judith Wohmann, it was all her fault; I became completely obsessed with her. It's no exaggeration to say that I translated her entire corpus, seven novels, including her second, *The Falcon's Screech*, which introduced her to readers in our country, *The Society of Secrets* (the first edition sold out entirely), *The Homeland of a Wanderer* (the talk of the town for days and days, you must remember), and *The Number Pi: A Romance*, which is what finally won her a large female readership. Her publisher considered me an expert and sent every newly released Wohmann novel straight to me.

With every novel I took my self-appointed mandate to interpret the text however I pleased that much further. I did what I could to ruin *The Falcon's Screech*, but I completely wrecked *The Society of Secrets*. The strange thing is that no one noticed; the sales never changed. And since I saw that her readers' admiration was only increasing book by book, I lost all self-control and began to adopt all sorts of new methods. I even went so far as to sabotage the titles. Still, for whatever reason, from time to time, an author comes along before whom that mysterious community we persist in calling "readers" finds itself entirely helpless. No matter what I did, you "readers" loved Judith Wohmann.

You remember the character who kicked the bucket in the very first pages of a novel? The one I insisted on keeping alive for every one of the remaining 382 pages—the one who was declared by the critics to be nothing less than a perfect combination of Proustian and Beckettian personae? Well, you see, that was the old and miserable Colonel Enke from *The Society of Secrets* ... I don't even know why I took such a liking to that ridiculous character; maybe I just found it a bit too familiar, too much like a bad movie to have him put to death by the other members of his absurd little club for revealing their secrets to the public. His brief appearance in the novel—or rather, his brutal assassination scene, since that was all he had —was nothing more than an empty embellishment. The Colonel had no claim to being a part of the story; the plot would have clattered along with or without him.

In this respect, I thought, he was like Garfield—I mean the cat. His presence or absence made no difference to the rest of the text. Nevertheless, he felt that he had a legitimate right to sit there, to do nothing more than waste space. So Colonel Enke was a sort of literary Garfield. Yet Garfield, the original, was alive and well, despite his uselessness, his obsolescence—giving orders, playing colonel, and being well paid for the privilege.

So why shouldn't the "real" Colonel Enke live too?

Wohmann didn't agree. Enke needed to be punished. He had to be slaughtered mercilessly in the basement of the apartment building where the Society had set its trap, then stuffed in a sack and dumped into a river. The river's powerful current would sweep Enke away, pushing him out to sea, to be lost forever in its mighty, its glorious waters, somewhere near the shores of Wilhelmshaven. This was Wohmannesque symbolism and it meant: You may be a soldier, an individual who has the discipline he needs in his professional life, but if you can't keep a secret (and, according to Wohmann, not knowing how to keep a secret means not having faith in oneself, and there's no room for nonbelievers among people who've banded together for a purpose—there never could be), you'll disappear into the sea, into oblivion: not worth remembering.

And then, following the murder, their spirits raised after having banded together to expunge a parasite like Enke, the Society of Secrets worked non-stop to create new secrets and cultivate more mysteries within its ranks . . . These secrets could be quite simple and personal, or they could be about high-positioned members, or even affairs of state. The whole point was to keep secrets for their own sake. Keeping a secret means challenging the whole world. All the tragedies that have ever befallen humanity were caused by loose lips; the only thing that's kept the world intact is the existence of secret alliances, mysterious links between people or communities. Nothing should be revealed, everything should be hidden, and there should be no such thing as "common knowledge." At the end, at the very end, when all the little secrets come together, the world itself will become nothing but one big secret. And when the day comes for *that* big secret to be revealed, everything will at last be known. According to Wohmann, this was the only way to solve the numerous problems plaguing us today.

Anyway, I felt sorry for the Colonel. I just couldn't kill him off. So I didn't.

To tell you the truth, Wohmann had overdone Enke a bit; he was a busy-body, sloppy and unstable, a coward and a tattle-tale. The character was falling apart at the seams from the get-go; all soggy like a marshmallow, seeping away like a punctured sack of rice. I had to take immediate action. Incapable of keeping his big mouth shut, Colonel Enke was giving away very important secrets, including a certain critical one that might change our future forever, change all of our futures. Okay, big mistake. But was it really necessary to hammer home with such awkwardness that he would have to pay for this with his life, and from the very first page?

I translated the novel without tampering up until the page where the Colonel got slaughtered. And because I didn't have the energy to go back and make corrections (plus, of course, this would have been disrespectful to the source text, and thus to Wohmann), I only did revisions on the pages following; I kept the Colonel alive for another 300 pages, when he was supposed to leave the stage on page 82 . . .

It wasn't that difficult to find a solution to his revelation of the big secret. I made the person the Colonel blabbed to an active member of the society, which meant that the secret had now never left their community. But I still made the Colonel carry the heavy burden of his transgression until the very end of the book. All those secrets were constantly at the tip of his tongue. Congenitally unable to keep his mouth shut, he could have let out a big secret at any moment, start blabbing about the wrong things at the wrong time. But as Enke lived on, always on the verge of revealing his secrets but always coming to his senses at the very last moment, just as he was about to make the same mistake twice, the suspense in the text grew overwhelming, and so our "readers" were simply swept away.

The Society of Secrets sold more copies in this country than it did in Germany—people loved it! Wohmann had thrown in a character that no reader would be upset to see dead, using him as nothing more than a side dish. Whereas I had created a new and multidimensional character who was allowed to live on, to hit both readers and critics right where they hurt.

The honorary guest at that year's book fair was Judith Wohmann, so you can do the math yourself as to just how successful my translations turned out to be. It was right about the time when her philosophical work, *The Number Pi: A Romance*, came out. Just about everyone, serious and more pedestrian "readers" alike, remembers *The Number Pi: A Romance*. Pi (π) is said to be the ratio of a circle's area to the square of its radius, or, spelled out, three point fourteen something. But according to Wohmann's philosophy, love could have no fractions or remainders. The novel was divided into three separate chapters, was narrated by three different narrators, had three main characters, and quite surprisingly, had three different endings of which each "reader" could have their own interpretation.

My problem was that the plot of the novel left no room whatsoever for "corrections" or "revisions." Thus, I was deprived of all possible means whereby I could relieve my frustration. The structure of the novel, enslaved entirely to the number three from page one, rendered any intervention whatsoever utterly impossible. At one point I even seriously considered replacing the number three with another cardinal number, any cardinal number. Like thirteen for example, bringing in the concept of bad luck and all. But it wasn't long before I realized this was impossible. Starting from scratch with the number thirteen (writing/shaping/creating thirteen chapters/narrative perspectives/characters)[1] would have been a massively cumbersome undertaking, and the patient only had a couple of critical months left (to put it in medical terms) before Wohmann arrived. That's when I really began to pick up on how much I loathed her. I hurled curses at the one and only author who had succeeded in screwing me over; the worst things I could think of. I can say now that *The Number Pi: A Romance* was the only novel I ever translated that truly remained faithful to the original. I had, I think, been outsmarted.

TRANSLATED FROM TURKISH BY

IDIL AYDOGAN AND AMY MARIE SPANGLER

---

1 Here I attempt a new, mathematically derived technique which will come as a relief to those writers who fall prey to excessive repetition in their texts. It is called the "parenthetical equation." By confining certain expressions to parentheses rather than repeating them thousands of times, I do believe it would be possible to reduce tree consumption to far more desirable levels.

VERENA STEFAN

Doe a Deer

Until lions have their own historians, tales of the hunt
shall always glorify the hunters [AFRICAN SAYING]

When you pass the runover deer in the car, crows start squawking. The deer lies up high on a snowbank, all four legs sticking up in the air at the edge of the road, right at the spot where I come out of the woods on my snowshoes. A doe. I trudge up to her and turn her over. One side is already torn up, an eye is missing. Tracks of coyote and fox lead up to and away from the animal in all directions.

In the woods I'm illiterate. The cold preserves a script of paws, hooves, claws, of bellyfur, of tailhair which has brushed the surface layer of snow —stories of encounters, trysts, of the hunt and the chase—which I could read word for word, if I only knew how to decipher the signs. For this I need a book about animal tracks, and a bookstore, Paragraphe, perhaps, or Renaud-Bray, and the good luck to find a parking place in the snowy wastes of Montreal. And then for the book *Traces d'animaux* I also need French-German and German-English dictionaries, so I can study the signs of red fox, raccoon, skunk, porcupine, and compare their names in the three languages.

Here is the spread wing of a partridge; there are raccoon footprints in the snow. I learned these latter tracks from the raccoons themselves; one afternoon they ran by the window, one after the other, three or four of them. I went out to study their prints, the toes sharp and filigreed, the paws dainty.

Every day on my walk I read my way along the trees, past boughs that hang lower when snow has fallen, that shoot up again as soon as it melts, past the towering base of an uprooted pine, past a bend and over the frozen brook at the point where the ice will hold my weight. Under gleaming sunlight I follow the tracks of a coyote, always around midday and still with worried glances over my shoulder. Rose Ausländer's voice in my ear: my mother was once a *deah* ... the way she says *deah* in her Eastern accent.*

Years ago, in a bookstore in Rimouski, on a February day when each footstep was carved out of white or graying snowheaps, snowwalls, snowdrifts, I read that, according to Rose Ausländer, the carp in Bukowina is silent in five languages. *Elle disait d'ailleurs de cette région que la carpe s'y taisait en cinq langues.* Rimouski lay desolate under snow, ice, and fog, five hundred kilometers northeast of Montreal on the great river, which was itself covered all the way to its center with ice floes and snowdrifts. I fell silent in four languages and learned snow.

The mirrorcarp / in pepper aspic / was silent in five languages—so goes the poem, "Czernowitz: History in a Nutshell."† It would have been silent in Ruthenish, Polish, Yiddish, and German. In Czernowitz it seems there were more bookstores than bakeries, the streets were swept with dried rose bouquets, and housepets bore the names of Greek gods.

* *Meine Mutter war einmal ein Reh* from the poem: *Meine Nachtigall* (My Nightingale) by Rose Ausländer. In: *Rose Ausländer: Gedichte* (S.Fischer, Frankfurt am Main, 2001). From time to time I listen to a recording of her poetry read by herself. *Meine Mutter war einmal ein Reah,* she reads.

† Rose Ausländer: "Czernowitz: Geschichte in der Nussschale" (ibid).

The deer at the edge of the road is more disassembled every day. First the internal organs disappear, then one leg after another. In the meantime, it gets covered by snow flung up by the snowplow. Then only two ears of fur can be seen sticking out of the snowdrift, and that only if you know the spot. When the snowcover sinks again, the animal has become even more hollow, more picked apart. Day after day I trudge over there and check to see how the cadaver has changed overnight. Piece by piece it is being incorporated into something else. I imagine the coyotes racing over here, the foxes too, one after the other. Do they come singly or all at once? Do they scramble to get to the kill, snarl? First rip up the animal, then tear everything edible out of it. Nothing stays behind, nothing is wasted, nothing is buried. Hooves, ears, eyes, there's a use for everything.

Do, a deer, a female deer goes through my head, and I try as I walk on to remember the lines that follow, the ones with which English-speaking schoolchildren here learn the scales, a children's rhyme that's not in my blood, *do, a deer, a female deer, re, a drop of golden sun, mi, a name I call myself, fa, a long long way to run*, while I think about scripts in time and space, about footsteps and tracks that get covered over again, with snow or with sand. Recently I've felt the urge to improve my French and I watch the evening news on a French-speaking channel. Evenings at seven, if I so desire, *Le Monde* comes into my living room for half an hour. All the shocking news comes bubbling out of the tube in French, now as pleasantly abstract concepts that in no way encroach upon my familiar sensitivities, nor produce the least emotional reaction. To take a simple example, I read and hear L'OTAN as a random arrangement of letters with no resonance whatsoever. L'OTAN is not NATO, L'ONU is not the UN. Even *boucliers vivants* remain abstract; *human shields* by contrast hits me as close as the German *menschliche Schilde*.

If I'm really up for learning, I watch, as I do this evening, an episode of *Le grand reportage*. An installation in the desert appears on the screen, high and low wooden crosses painted pink. Not the friendly playful pink of Christo and Jeanne-Claude's wrappings. These wooden crosses commemorate the carelessly buried or simply tossed-away corpses of women and children in the desert near Ciudad Juarez. The women, all of them dark-skinned, must have been very young and pretty, and so poor that they were forced to work in one of the *maquiladoras* in the borderland between Mexico and the USA. Migrant workers who toiled in sweat shops.

Over three hundred and seventy-five women have been killed in the last ten years. The dead that were found all bore the same script on their bodies: torture, rape, mutilation, amputation. When you decipher these signs and traces, you end up with porn, presumably snuff films—i.e., torture and murder before a rolling camera—and the organ trade. The abducted women were held captive several days to two weeks, tortured, and finally, after being maimed and murdered, they were discarded. Now I have to fling open the front door and in the minus-twenty-degree cold walk a few steps up the path, count the stars that sparkle between the branches in the woods and high up in the sky. Nothing worrying me, no information, no horror—allowing the horror, the noise of information to lapse into deep freeze.

Relatives of the murdered women, mothers, aunts, sisters, cousins, grandmothers, wander the region summer and winter looking for clues. For every one of the victims they find, they put up a pink cross. High crosses for the women, low ones for the girls, a memorial of despair, terror, that has also inscribed itself in the landscape. The youngest victims are twelve years old.*

The women—who go there again and again, brushing off every thorn bush, every prickly tuft of grass, tapping the ground with their sticks, turning over stones, throwing them aside, leaving behind their own fleeting traces in the sand that just as soon waft away—don't want to accept

* A seven-year-old girl has since joined them.

the silence, their silenced-to-death daughters, sisters, mothers, cousins, aunts. What do their footprints amount to, the paths they tread in this time and place, in the desert, where no other human traces can be found?

Was it cruel for the deer? Was it run over by a car? Did an angry or frightened person fling it up onto the snowbank?

Other animals have preyed on it, gutted it, picked it clean, following the rules of the game. So one might say. That's why I'm looking for the place where the disemboweling happened. I would like it to be a place that, by human standards, is cruelty-free. I would like to know a good word for the absence of cruelty.

Living in Quebec, I've heard all the shocking news in English and French, the litanies of warscenes, Kosovo, Rwanda, Afghanistan, Palestine, Israel, Iraq, Chechnya, Congo, names of groups, factions, freedom fighters, of suicide bombers both male and female, white-collar criminals, the vocabulary of war that expands with each new war, that also insinuates into German such phrases as *collateral damage, friendly fire, humanitarian bombing, embedded journalists*, thus remaining abstract. In order to understand the real content of the news, I have to look up a deadly litany in English: *briefing, compliance, containment, defection, deployment, deterrent, quagmire, mired, cakewalk, truce, without resorting to force.*

Certainly this list is already somewhat obsolete, dating as it does from the year 2003, as the U.S. was attacking Iraq. I was sitting with an American friend in a kitchen where I felt safe, having dinner, and we turned the radio on to hear whether the U.S. had already begun to attack or not, and there was nothing else to hear since all the stations were playing the same thing, just like on September 11th and then the week after, during the memorial service. Anyone who wanted to hear or see the news around the world had to follow along with the U.S. media to see what action the U.S. was contemplating at that moment, and even before the concept had come up in the news, we were already all "embedded" in the action. Then we listened to a Canadian journalist reporting out of Baghdad at about four in the morning, the classic time for military attacks, and along with his voice, the sinister silence, of which he was speaking, entered the kitchen where we were sitting, the silence of a ghost city behind a pair of miserable sand-bags, the silence of empty streets, empty cleaned-out shops with blinds drawn. No traffic, he said, a pair of old men who've stayed behind; we're waiting, everyone is holding their breath.

Didn't I keep hoping till the very last minute that the war wouldn't happen, that the peace demonstrations around the world would see to it that there would be no war? After all, in Montreal there were a hundred and fifty thousand people in the streets. It was thirty degrees below zero and I learned to chant *So-So-So-Solidarité!* along with the natives.

Farther down along the snowshoepath stands a stocky, rotten maple tree, its main branches protruding symmetrically. Its trunk on one side is covered from top to bottom with fungus, on the other side, it's hollowed out up to my waist. The hollow is filled with ochre-colored bean-shaped scat. Here an animal sleeps, maybe several, like the bundles of flesh that hang from a maple branch in front of my window, their soft grumbling sounds waking me at dawn. Porcupines. Both places, the deercorpse and the sleepingtree, are for the animal world a meeting point, a marketplace, a newspaper stand, whereas I, loud and ungainly on my two legs, who can neither read nor understand their language, make myself an appointment in the woods, lumber over there to capture an image on film, move myself along on snowshoes through a landscape empty of humans and densely populated with trees, my destination a place where the immeasurable whiteness is interrupted by rare flecks of color, gold-yellow turds in which are stuck the needles of porcupines, or bloody ribs exposed to the sky.

After two weeks the site in the woods is almost empty. A few tufts of fur are strewn in a circle, and an ochre-colored lump of crap lies there, deep-frozen through April, while the *tourterelles tristes* announce snowmelt and spring, a promising, plaintive sound to which my body responds as it used to respond to the song of *die Amsel*, the blackbird, which is missing from the landscape here, along with its guarantee of spring. The ear here is an ear emptied of *die Amsel. Der Amsel unverfälschtes / Vokabular* writes Rose Ausländer: *the unfalsified vocabulary / of the blackbird.* That's from her "History in a Nutshell." In Quebec, spring announces itself with the call of the *tourterelles tristes*, though not that of the *Trauertauben*, as it would be called in German; for it was not the call of a *Trauertaube* that taught me spring here, when I first arrived—when the earth in the middle of April suddenly gave off heat in the places bare of snow, as if for five months a volcano had been slumbering under the ice. In the warmth the great old white pines in front of the houses grew fragrant, a *tourterelle triste* or mourning dove called and then another one; out of their soft brown-red dovebodies they sent out the springcall, and the *Frédérick* too began to call, *le bruant à gorge blanche*, the white-throated sparrow, the *Ammerfink*. Its call intensified the smell of the pines and heralded summer; on the lake you could stand in a T-shirt on the ice, still a meter thick, and listen to the glugging gurgling rivulets that ran down from the hills. It rained half the night. The whole day, thunder rumbled behind the warmth. The ice steamed up, already covered with water. Warm air escaped over it in waves. I learned that spring is sun and ice, ice and fire, light that pours out and is reflected in snow and ice, that spring is white, not green and not adorned with colorful flowers.

To snuff means to extinguish, to annihilate. I first learned this expression in Berlin, almost thirty years ago, and I've never forgotten it. There we heard for the first time that a woman had supposedly been murdered in front of a rolling camera and that a new genre of underground film had thus been launched—whether this was really the first time it happened, nobody knows. You can find plenty of tracks and traces online on this subject, of course. If you search for Ciudad Juarez or Amnesty International or violence against women or feminicide or snuff, you'll find news, reports, analyses, appeals, and images too, statements from members and affinity groups, information about solidarity actions by woman artists, feminist analyses about the mutilation of the female body, reports from delegations traveling to Ciudad Juarez for events and protests—in four languages: Spanish, English, French and German. After an hour on the net, I'm driven out of the house again, into the snow. But there are corpses here too. In Canada, over five hundred Native women have disappeared since 1985. In winter we hear in the news that once again a Native man froze in a snowbank, drunk, because no one driving by would stop for him, or because white policemen had dumped him out in the middle of nowhere, in the snow.

The desert region near Ciudad Juarez where many of the murdered women were found is known as a "labyrinth of silence." In it is contained the panicked silence that the women must have felt who arrived at work three minutes late and weren't allowed to come in. Three minutes late and the door to work, to this hard labor for four euros a day, to life, is locked, a car comes, there's not another soul on the street. In *doremifasolatido* she has only come as far as *fa, a long long way to run*, then her melody is abruptly cut short. She would give her life to be able to run a long long way, but all she has to look forward to is a horribly long ordeal and then her own murder. To want simply to live, to work, to eat, to have love, a family, to be young, to go to work, to dance on the weekends and perhaps, one day, to cross the border into the promised land, into the United States of North America. Filmmakers, politicians, businessmen, drugdealers, pimps don't even need to go to the trouble of hunting these women down in order to torture and kill them. It's enough that they're poor, young, beautiful, dark-skinned, and that they're standing in front of a locked factory door, or obliged to walk through unlit streets.

Will the Iraq war reveal itself to be a *quagmire* or a *cakewalk?* This is the question being discussed on U.S. television several weeks after the attack on Iraq. *Quagmire* is a war word dating back to Vietnam; if you're in a quagmire, it means you're stuck in the swamp or the mud. A *cakewalk,* according to Langenscheidt's encyclopedic dictionary, sixth edition, 1981, is

1. a) A grotesque dance-contest with a cake as a prize (Amer. Negro usage)

    b) A ballroom or stage dance originating in such a contest

    c) The music for such a dance

2. To dance a cakewalk.

3. To walk as in a cakewalk.

The woman who arrived three minutes too late at the locked door of a *maquiladora* and heard a car stopping beside her knew she was stuck in the mud, in a war that has never been publicly declared. The good thing about the landscape of Quebec is how empty it is of people. There are no alien thought systems polluting my mind when I walk through the woods. In winter the great cold helps to cleanse unpleasant news of its dirt. Bad news should only be broadcast in snow and ice, when the earth is frozen; not in summer, when it's permeated by moist heat, when with every step the world reminds us that it breathes and lives.

              Do: a deer a female deer
              Re: a drop of golden sun . . .

TRANSLATED FROM GERMAN BY LISE WEIL

Verena Stefan **39**

MERCÈ IBARZ

Nela and the Virgins

I neither can nor want to resist the image of the still hours, those hours that resound both in and outside of me—these are the important hours. As was said a long time ago: It's then that the world shakes its ass. Though I don't remember if that was said in Prague or at one of the sanatoriums where he'd go to recover from what he didn't want to recover from— namely, writing all night undisturbed in front of the window of his home, or at the window of the sanatorium, it doesn't matter, everywhere is home, whether it's a house that puts you up for a few days or a house you built yourself or a house that tosses you out or a house you run away from. Re- pulsively, the world shakes its ass, like a pus-oozing fat man in a cage at the circus, the circus we call life. This pain we call life: a circus. Sure. I sup- pose that it's for this that that man said if you watch and keep quiet as the world shakes its ass so obscenely, it'll reveal to you what it's really like, its sincerer side, its truth. And it does just so because it sells its ass without shame, openly, like at a circus or a cabaret. Did Kafka go to cabarets? No idea. But I do know that he didn't spend all of his time staring out of a win- dow. He also went around on a motorbike that belonged to his favorite un- cle, who by contrast was a man who really knew how to live it up. What would Kafka have seen from up on top of those wheels? He kept quiet about that. Nevertheless, there are some key differences between speeding around on an old motorbike—be it from Kafka's time or from when we were too young to care, some thirty years ago—and staring fixedly out a window, waiting for nothing the way you wait for nothing when riding a motorbike; all told, there are some key differences. The world reveals itself one way or the other, but the difference is in the things you see in it. When you stare for some time into a face, outer space, open sky, an interior patio, the street under your window, the lamppost at night or the traffic at day, you see in them more than you ever had before, you see them in another way, you see what the face, outer space, open sky, interior patio, street, lamppost, traffic all say. The speed of, say, a motorbike, turns you in toward yourself, everything goes by so quickly that your eyes, in order to stay fixed on the road and nothing else, roll back into your head, toward the inner consciousness of your body. Now that I've stopped, the still hours having kept still and quiet, I see how Valentina came to set up this strange dinner, which I say is strange because, well, you'll tell me how everyone manages to rush to the island, buzz the intercom, walk up the stairs, come in and meet up with the host, and after that look everyone there in the eye, and after that sit and dine. I see Valentina looking through a large window neither saying nor thinking anything, I see her head open like the bud of a hibiscus when day and daylight both begin, she watches the way in which Mo tells what Nela did the first day she saw the apartment, that she didn't pay any mind to either the hallway or anything else, but just sat absolutely silent on the balcony for no one knows how long, and after a few days headed up north and never returned again, breaking all ties with the island, with the entire city. Now, too, the world shakes its tail—and reveals itself. I can go on.

Three young women met on the island called the past, poured out into the city from the greater countryside. That first year in the city they didn't live together but given the frequency with which they met at some of the many small and clandestine meetings they attended, they decided to live together. They were seventeen years old. It was as though they were refugees expatriated from the towns and small cities in which they had been born, finally far from their mothers yet still in need of their tutoring, their terrifying presences. Friendships turn themselves into family. And their nostalgia for their mothers would open a wound that would last years, perhaps forever: a new perspective none of them were warned about, and with which no one was familiar. The classics teach us how to deal with homesickness. But the classics offered them something else, something they would remember for years: Everyone is dragged along by their favorite pleasure. Their favorite pleasure was to be as far as possible from their places of birth.

Virgil would have embraced those three girls with ferocious pride, though they hadn't read his poetry; they knew about him from a television commercial (from back in the black-and-white days), a commercial they barely remembered now that they'd made it out of the provinces. It was a forgetful, discourteous time: *Los veinticinco años de la paz* could do that to you. But time flies, and when they came to be teenagers they didn't feel that fear—they felt other fears, but not the type that their mothers and fathers had felt when they were young. For them, everything was new now: pop music, singles dances, advertising, plastics, the hair dryer, the transistor radio, the cassette tape, vinyl. The three of them figured out that citing classic poetry from an old TV ad wasn't exactly the cool thing to do. It wouldn't get you any credit in a test. Pretending to be educated was beside the point. If you were to quote something from a commercial, you were a reactionary—a word that caused a good deal of fear in their urbane circles. It was forbidden above all else to be a reactionary; yet, at the same time, it was constantly necessary to react. This was a paradox that none of them liked to question too deeply.

They didn't foresee ever becoming comfortable so far from their families, far and for so long. They had to learn with no net, with no strings. Yet, even coming from where they did, they ended up founding a new recruiting center, bigger than had ever been seen in the city and with as diverse a social make-up as any. These three friends were the first to break the social barrier. It was a liberating milestone that would in time become a stigma, a mark on the forehead, a pathology. For example, my father in those years would remind me time and again that I was a chosen one of the gods, and he didn't care at all how much it bothered me to hear it ... But the girls wouldn't tolerate compliance one way or another, they weren't much for any sort of idiotic conformity, be it from the right or from the left. The subject of college, among other things, made them obdurate and loyal, though to whom and to what would remain to be seen. It was the same for many of the boys, but the deepest mark this access to the temples of knowledge had was left in the young women who attended them. Whoever receives in youth the chance to change their life doesn't forget it: these girls will always recognize the vestiges of that old flame.

The city. Her. Wow, what to say? What a joy it was. Back then it was black, black like a bad thought, and so poorly lit. But what joy it was just to walk down the street, what a joy not to be recognized anywhere.

After all these years the image still remains, although of course they see her now through a much different lens: the ballast of basic anonymity both in life and at work is sold in exchange for power by those who—to each other, at least—are no longer anonymous. Such is the extraordinary makeup of the city person in charge. Now she and the others can immediately tell the difference between someone who was born in the city and someone who was not. If someone from the city is friendly, he's not in control of the situation; if he ends up feeling stifled, it's because he's from the city or hates not having been. It almost always works out that way.

City of subterranean webs emitting corrosive acids, city of never-ending unfinished business, city of hurt pride, city of the hypersensitive, city of know-it-alls, city of superegos, city of gardeners' dogs that do nothing yet let nothing go; off-kilter capital, always a touch uncomfortable and always in the dark as to whether this discomfort is caused by the past, by its spot on the map, or simply because it's exhausted itself with its own prop-aganda. Um, that list turned out rather long. But those girls, after all these years, still aren't ready to let go of the abundance and the dark beauty of their first introduction to Barcelona, this city by sea. They're still in love with a city that, as they put it, doesn't worry about exaggerated realism. It's a place for forgetting the fear that people's stares can cause. One of the first things that Isi Solís, Nela Zubiri, and Valentina Morera knew about Barce-lona was that being a virgin was a worse blemish than having been seen not participating in an assembly meeting. Nela announced this as if it were the first order of the day. It wasn't too long ago that Nela arrived at Isi and Valentina's apartment to take the place of another girl who couldn't deal with the idea that on any given day the police could show up at their door.

"We won't be virgins long!" Isi and Valentina exclaimed at the same time.

"I'm going to ask you about it again, and soon. Then we'll see."

"It doesn't have anything to do with you," Isi replied.

Nela ran her hands through her long straight hair.

Valentina agreed with Isi. It didn't have anything to do with her. Nela smiled and applied coconut cream to her lips.

And then there was me, the person telling you this story (that's what I do, it's my job). I wasn't really along for the ride, just someone who listens from time to time, someone who had dealings with the committee ... I was from a rural town as well and I was also put on notice about needing to stop doing this and needing instead to do that. I was just another girl. What a time that was. The same year that Gloria Gaynor ruled disco with her glorious "I Will Survive," and a singer-songwriter from New York named Annette Peacock, a mythic figure who turned down all sorts of offers and played instead with great musicians ranging from Mingus and Bley to Bowie, recorded a song that more than made up for my always hav-ing been just another girl and that would end up being a landmark for my era . . . it was called "My Mama Never Taught Me to Cook." And it was true: mothers weren't teaching their daughters to cook. Either they didn't know how, or had no interest in learning, or simply weren't around. Ah, Peacock's Moog synthesizer . . .

Nela was a striking beauty with slightly Asian features and held to her hard-line radical politics. She had a sexual energy that all the other girls envied, that the boys desired and feared. It was unsettling. Petite, always well dressed and made-up, everything matching, a seventeen-year-old expert of facial creams, the cause of real agitation among the politically empowered young women who acted so radically contrary to the habits of their mothers and who no longer cooked but did tend to wear Pond's creams and yet nevertheless found themselves fascinated by the sight of Nela applying her own creams from day to night. She wore her hair straight, long, and always touched-up. She was famed for being an incredible lover. You wouldn't believe the advice she'd give.

Nela's friendship with Valentina and her difficulties with Isi were both a question of basic types from day one: nothing could be done about it. When Valentina suggested that Nela come live with them, Isi shot Valentina a look. Yes, sure, she was from the assembly committee, and better her than some stranger, but . . . From Isi's point of view, Nela was about and only about superficial impressions, as though she was in advertising or was one of those sexy magician's assistants. Touches of psychedelia, pop art, leftist politics, spliffs, and sexual innuendo, but the songs of Maria Dolores Pradera when the boys weren't around . . . though Isi was partial to music with wailing guitars and sinister-sounding drumming, the voice of Janis Joplin or Jimi Hendrix winding like a snake in the walls.

Nela and Valentina went way back. They had known each other from the first year of college. Nela was a radical then, she was a quiet girl from the rural west, where Valentina was from as well. The militant political climate of the time had differing effects on people. For Nela, it brought out her best. She turned into a hard-core cheerleader for the assemblies, someone few people wanted to debate with, let alone contradict. On the other hand, for Valentina, all this activism led her to more or less take a vow of silence. They were two sides of the same coin, two forms of a life-sharing impulse that neither Nela nor Valentina knew how to get the better of. When late at night Isi would put on "All Is Loneliness," "Careless Love," or "Cry Baby," Joplin's sharp screams wouldn't let us sleep in peace.

Valentina was happy to have entered into a world a little more real, she thought, than the one she had known until then . . . but she had lost her spirit. She spent her freshman year in Barcelona in a good enough mood, going to the movies. She discovered double features and her search for double features took her all over the city where she learned along the way the names of the streets of l'Eixample and the bus and train lines. She lived near the market of Sant Antoni, which was unpredictable and lively. Sundays at the book fair she'd check out antique photographs and old magazines. But when she made it onto the assembly committee she shut her mouth, and her smile turned stale.

She realized that Nela's gravelly voice at the assemblies and meetings and the threatening tone of her suggestions were elaborate productions for the benefit of Salvador, captain of the committee, a fling that kept on going. Nela turned on the charm, which is what men need, to be charmed and to charm in return . . . I remember well the Salvador side of Nela. Isi, the most intelligent and motivated girl in our class, let them be; she even indulged their fantasies of authority, happy to use the boy's influence as though it was her own. Isi, who Valentina thought so strong, wasn't smug. Valentina watched it all unfold, confused. She just didn't get Isi, didn't understand why she bent, bent until she split in two when men were around; first Salvador, then Bat and whoever after. She saw her friend Nela disappear. Nela, who she knew—despite all of Isi's objections, despite the feelings that Salvador inspired—was really a shy and generous person. He consumed one girl after another and Valentina couldn't do a thing. She shut up to avoid disappearing like Nela or doubling over like Isi. If she just shut up perhaps she'd be able to go back to being that girl who had arrived in Barcelona happy. If she just shut up perhaps she could avoid having the words of the revolution change her like they had Nela and Isi. And so Valentina just shut up.

They used the obligatory pseudonyms when they weren't talking only among themselves, but Bat they would always call Bat. It wasn't just any old nickname but rather a matter of the effect, well calculated by him, hoping to take things in another direction entirely, that the three of them felt the day they met him. Perhaps Isi was the one who first came up with his nom de guerre, but it fit for all three of them like a tailored dress: he looked like a pop-art cartoon bat! And like that, Bat stuck. Hi Bat, they said to him the next time they saw him, which drew a laugh from him, and how he could laugh. They always shared a laugh with him during those sweet years of terror. Armoring themselves, and, above all, finding a form to live in—for Nela's sake—or, better said, *because* of Nela—as Valentina thinks now, thirty years later. Somehow there was still that bond, that old and intimate wound formed when women become friends and still see in each other the girl that once was. Nameless wounds. Nela's face lost all its tenderness and her eyes focused on the apolitical, on all the old conventional customs. Hers was a catalytic reaction, an interior convulsion that led her to believe she was an indestructible warrior—Andromeda, Joan of Arc, Magdalena, it depended on the day. Her fear would vanish if the committee supported what she was saying and the captain looked at her, pleased. Then she'd be quiet; her face perfect then, classical. She'd head to the restroom, take out her small bag of creams and subsequently reemerge looking even more precious. No one thought to call her bourgeois. She made it all look as natural as smoking. Valentina still sees her putting on her makeup. Me too. I still see her cold eyes, as though she weren't exactly making herself up, softening her look to heighten her beauty, but rather retouching the mask that allowed her to continue, to push forward. Mechanical, pleasureless gestures. Her eyes stare at Valentina from the mirror and then, yes, they become playful, taunting, friendly. Nela strikes poses like a mannequin and the two share a good laugh. To the other girls in the apartment, especially Isi, Nela is the image of conflict and freedom, hard like asphalt and so beautiful that she makes the rest of them feel small. They slept in the same room, in two bunk beds, and at times Valentina would hear her crying. One night, Nela turned over to ask Valetina if she was still a virgin. Valentina didn't see any reason to be reserved about the topic. Nela shot from her bed as though the police were knocking at the door. This has to be fixed right away! she said.

"Being a virgin is worse then being afraid of the police."

Valentina shrugged her shoulders and got up from her bunk.

"Being a virgin can make you suffer," Nela insisted.

One way to lose one's virginity, strongly considered by Nela, was the purely hygienic approach. Afterward could come the sex, the joy, the full moon . . . But it wasn't good to get carried away with losing your virginity and ending up in a relationship for the rest of your life because of it. Valentina knew that, right? How many women has this happened to in the world? It was way more interesting to plan out a deflowering sans attractions, sans sexual hunger—like an operation, just to make you feel a bit better. That way you avoid a whole host of complications. There's nothing more to expect. When all is said and done, you don't marry the surgeon who performs your appendectomy or the dentist who removes your wisdom teeth. On the other hand, heaven only knows what love is. They were all dead-set against the old, inherited forms of love that had given them life—debased by pigs and castrators all frustrated to the point of nausea. Nela said this all so easily, as though she'd just been reading the Surrealists. She had no idea who they were, and I really don't know what these three girlfriends would have said if they'd ever gotten around to reading them, back then—man, what a group they were . . . Thanks to a few newspapers and magazines, which were the mirrors of that moment, they took in as best they could what news would arrive from the frontiers. Those were tense years, tense like a traffic accident. Beds were always occupied, often with people who when they rose wouldn't say anything and wouldn't be seen again for months on end or indeed ever again. Theirs was a narrow path that had to be followed. Given all of that, the most hygienic way to lose one's virginity was to look for someone who would do it to you with no strings attached and that's it. Some asked their neighbor to do it or the first guy who passed on the street, which was an elegant and distanced sort of attitude that the oh-so-ironic postmodernists of today would have loved. The student apartments flourished: there were a ton of them; they were the breakthrough of the youth liberation movement, vestals and avant-gardists alike arrived at those most-famed loci of 1970s Barcelona. And they weren't filled with city kids, but rather with people from rural and other regional areas, and especially by young women, and our three were among them. I, your narrator, can promise you this.

The girls' and boys' apartments communicated with each other according to habit and custom, above all according to political allegiances. They also communicated due to some of the girls wanting the boys to do them the favor of deflowering them. Afterward the girls would explain it to themselves, draw conclusions, and compile lists with recommendations. One classmate—who wasn't on the committee and who, due to Valentina never saying a word, wasn't afraid of her, unlike the other girls who tended to fear the girls on the committee—told Valentina about her first time. She was a little older than the other girls in her year and so the whole virginity thing bothered her more, sort of like being the last one to get your period. One day she said enough was enough, that tonight was the night, that she would ask the first guy that went to the bar for a cup of coffee (and she said specifically a cup of coffee) if he would go to bed with her. And so it was. She didn't give any other details, she only smiled. It was the first time Valentina saw a girl actually satisfied with her first time. The first time seemed so dangerous, like being carted into the operating room. That's why Nela recommended the hygienic method. Without being aware of it, this notion fit right in with the prior generation's way of doing things. As though bodies have to fight each other before learning to dance together.

When Valentina first met Pau she christened him Sweetskin and launched right into things; whatever would happen would happen. And he, more and more certain that he should keep cool with her, spent silent hour after silent hour in American Soda by her side, quiet while love was being born; Valentina was so quiet that Sweetskin finally took her by the hand and didn't let her go again even after he heard her speak. Words wishing they could be something more spilled out of him and returned her voice to her. Day after day through Carrer del Carme until reaching La Rambla, then walking along all of Les Rambles; afternoon after afternoon at American Soda. Love's reins were tangled and unwittingly made marvelous by the art of silence and by knowing that silence too is a bond, knowing this intuitively—love becoming a sea that has no explanation save for its hushed music, only music. Nothing was said about sex nor about how they spent their nights together. Nela and Isi protested and accused, like jilted lovers. What a semester. It makes me laugh. But I'm obliged to look at things this way, since I'm the storyteller of another life, another life that was also mine. We storytellers can choose what we tell only to a certain point—after all, we were given this rare gift, we had the impertinent luck to be tellers of the ineffable. To write is to transcribe, to tell is to recount, to retell. Valentina and Pau built an intimate home for themselves, a complicated home, without knowing the foundations, confiding only in silence, who made excuses for them when they entered rooms without knocking; they wove together, one into the other, whatever the image, whatever the mask, whatever the masquerade, whatever the intention, whatever tomorrow would be. Making her way through the streets with Pau, she decided to become a photographer. In bed with Pau, all she heard was music. Heaven had made for them the choice they should have made themselves, her *I woke* him from his oblivion, the music that they heard together, it was more than music.

TRANSLATED FROM CATALAN BY ROWAN RICARDO PHILLIPS

ENRIQUE VILA-MATAS

Far from Here

1.

It is snowing in Novonikolaevsk when Andrei Petrovich Petrescov, district attorney, starts to take his gloves off in the study of his home, while the governess in charge of his twin daughters gives him alarming reports about the girls' behavior throughout the afternoon. We are at the end of a day that, for Andrei Petrovich Petrescov, has been one of frenetic activity in the midst of harsh weather, in the extreme and intense Siberian cold.

January 17, 1904. Record temperatures in the peaceful city of Novonikolaevsk. The prestigious district attorney, Andrei Petrovich Petrescov—who has just returned from a long session in the courtroom and a meeting of the Public Celebration Committee, over which he presides—feels remarkably tired. All the same, he listens attentively to what the governess, Maria Gergiev, is telling him. According to her, the twins, Olga and Vasha, had been playing hide and seek with their two older siblings, Dimitri and Seriozha, and had confused and upset the latter because they had hidden themselves among the spotless sheets of the bed that once was their parents'—the bed in the forbidden room. Naturally, no one would think to look for them there. Unable to find the girls, poor Dimitri and Seriozha—

two and three years older than the twins, respectively—had been humiliated by their little sisters, and still didn't seem to have gotten over the offence.

"Well, that will do them good. They're no angels themselves," says Andrei Petrovich Petrescov.

"And the twins, how old are they? I'm aware that this is a strange question, but I always get mixed up about the date. Every day I'm more and more overwhelmed by work. I'd like to spend more time with them, but I always get stuck in my usual routine and have to be satisfied with just reading them a story before they go to sleep."

"The girls are seven years old, sir."

"That's what I thought. Seven. They're still quite young, aren't they. I don't see the problem. I'm not one for punishments or lectures. From now on, of course, we'll lock the door to their deceased mother's room. Poor girls. They don't mean any harm."

"They may only be seven, sir, but I feel obligated to let you know that recently the girls have been restless, behaving oddly—they're becoming very strange. More and more often they have this identical, faraway look on their faces. They're only seven, but that's the age when children begin to use their reason. Olga and Vasha are indeed using their reason, but in a way that profoundly upsets me. If you don't mind my saying so, I think that—considering the unfortunate, irreparable absence of their mother—the only thing that can set things straight would be a little paternal authority. I need you to give me a hand with them, that's the truth of the matter. Your daughters seem to live up in the stratosphere."

The stratosphere! After such an exhausting day, this celestial word sounds eccentric and musical in the office of Andrei Petrovich Petrescov, who smiles as he looks at the governess discreetly, trying to make sure that a certain licentiousness doesn't appear on his face. She is a woman of forty-two, a woman who has retained an undeniable, almost categorical, physical beauty. Furthermore, she is impeccably professional. An old-school governess, with respectable professional experience in Moscow and Vladivostok.

On a number of occasions—such as today—Andrei Petrovich Petrescov has even thought about asking for her hand in marriage, even though he's never taken that step. Maria Gergiev doesn't seem to be expecting such a proposal, and so could react negatively, rejecting everything altogether, including her job, and this possibility doesn't sit well with Andrei Petrovich Petrescov. No, Maria is a professional, and it would be difficult to find someone of her stature willing to relocate to Novonikolaevsk.

At any rate, thinks Andrei Petrovich Petrescov, I still have plenty of time to ask her to marry me later on. That's what he tells himself, this district attorney who feels more alone each day, more overwhelmed by his work at the courthouse and, above all else, by his hectic family life, to which must be added that he is president of the Public Celebration Committee, which is currently preparing the events that will take place in one week to commemorate Novonikolaevsk's recently acquired status as a city—a status officially conferred by the Czar.

Andrei Petrovich Petrescov is a widower two times over. His first marriage left him with the unbearable responsibility of his two children, Anna and Mikhail, now twenty and eighteen years old, respectively: two troubled children, involved in various conspiracies, befriending dangerous subversive types who make no secret of the fact that they are enemies of the Czar. Anna and Mikhail, planning the violent overthrow of all of society's hallowed institutions in the name of equality, of happiness for all; or, failing that, at least of identical misery for all. The worst thing about it being how obvious they are about it—likely to be caught at any moment. But, then again, it's hard to deny that there's a certain ridiculousness to their cabal. What could be more ridiculous than planning the downfall of the Czar from a city as insignificant and provincial as Novonikolaevsk?

Andrei Petrovich Petrescov is constantly overwhelmed by the weight, the burden of two generations of children, two families in the same house. And no wife. Andrei Petrovich Petrescov looks again at Maria Gergiev and the idea of proposing to her comes back into his head. But finally his profound fear of her reaction sets back in, so he decides to busy himself with his paternal responsibilities. He calls his disobedient twins into the study.

In spite of the fact that his meetings at the courthouse, and especially his meetings with the Public Celebration Committee, have been extraordinarily exhausting, he will try to give some direction to the wild imaginations of his two little daughters, two girls who were born at the very moment their mother died—born at the very moment the stigma of having been bad luck to both his wives fell upon Andrei Petrovich Petrescov. Truth be told, this is another reason why he doesn't dare propose to Maria Gergiev, and undoubtedly the reason why she—who gladly agreed when he asked her to move from Vladivostok to rough Novonikolaevsk—always takes great care to keep her distance from her employer, as much distance as possible, really, because she is almost certainly afraid that fate will lead his next wife to the same misfortune that befell unfortunate wives one and two.

"They just died because they died," he'd like to tell Maria Gergiev, just like that, right now.

But he knows it's better to say nothing. In the past he would have dared to do anything. Lately however he's noticed that his pride in being a free spirit has diminished, along with his daring—as if his former courage and freedom had receded within him, corrosive, dead tissue beginning to consume his lethargic spirit.

When the governess leaves the study, the district attorney makes himself comfortable in the chair at his desk, closes his eyes, and lets his mind wander. Without knowing why, it takes him back to the spring day in 1898 when the commemoration of the first anniversary of his second wife's death took place; it was something of a special day because it coincided with the celebrated opening of the Ob River Bridge in Novonikolaevsk, an event that brought prosperity to the town, since along with the bridge they'd just finished construction of the big train station (through which the Trans-Siberian Railway would pass in the near future) and its warehouses and repair shops. A lot of the construction companies left town soon after in order to build other towns that had the potential to become urban centers, but Novonikolaevsk didn't disappear, since many people moved in from the surrounding villages thanks to the abundance of commodities that came in by the railway. And thanks to this new commerce and the creation of new businesses, the town began to transform into a small city. All that remained now was to top this all off with the grand celebrations in honor of the official arrival, one month from now, of Novonikolaevsk's status as a city.

In his thoughts, Andrei Petrovich Petrescov sees with great clarity that Novonikolaevsk could turn very quickly into the regional center for banking. The arrival of the Siberian Bank had already been announced, and others will certainly follow it. Even though his salary as district attorney is always getting better and better, Andrei Petrovich Petrescov feels that it would be wise to step down and get into the business world now knocking at the door of his splendid new city. After having been district attorney for so many years in Vladivostok, he doesn't want the same thing to happen here as happened there when the booming banks came into that city. He's been district attorney for too long, and his talent for finance demands a change. Furthermore, six children is a serious and worrisome responsibility, even more so when you take into account that the two eldest children have never given any sign of wanting to work, and have nothing but debts and ties to the world of conspiracy and crime.

All these thoughts are passing through Andrei Petrovich Petrescov's mind, punctuated with the background noise of his secret ambitions, which seem to be born of fatigue. He is engrossed in all these thoughts and on the verge of collapse—which is to say sleep—when, without even knocking at the door, Olga and Vasha enter his office laughing. Laughing, but in an infinitely serious way. They laugh and laugh and seem as though they have no intention of letting up. There's something undeniably off about their expressions. They're a little scary.

"Tekelili-lili-lo!" they repeat a number of times.

Unquestionably, thinks their father, they have created their own language, even though it doesn't seem to be very functional.

"Enough!" shouts Andrei Petrovich Petrescov finally, with an unexpected dose of paternal authority.

The girls don't seem at all intimidated and begin to mimic him as he smokes. Once again, the district attorney can't believe his eyes. They imitate him so perfectly that he almost thinks he can see the smoke coming out of their mouths.

"What's all this about?" he asks them, practically terrified.

Silence. End of the infinitely serious laughter. A powerful weariness has overtaken the district attorney. There's no fighting it off. Well, it's been a rough day. He takes off his glasses.

"Tekelili-lili-lo!"

"What's all this about? Let's see . . . Vasha? Answer me," Andrei Petrovich Petrescov declares. "Why were you laughing? Why are you being so disobedient? Do you know what disobedient means? Don't you know the story of the disobedient frog?"

"Will you tell it to us tonight?" asks Vasha.

"Daddy is a story," says Olga.

"Tekeló-lo-lo!" shouts Vasha.

"I want to ask you something," says Olga, in a faint filament of a voice.

"So ask, my daughter."

Coup de théâtre. The girls suddenly disappear, as if by magic, and while Andrei Petrovich is asking himself what the hell just happened, they reappear—laughing, again in that infinitely serious way.

Eternal return, thinks Andrei Petrovich Petrescov resignedly.

The girls again begin to imitate him smoking. "What's going on here," Andrei Petrovich Petrescov repeats to himself, disturbed. Silence. End of the infinitely serious laughter.

The aesthetic of twins, thinks Andrei Petrovich, now almost nodding off. And that's all that occurs to him.

"I want to ask you something," insists Vasha, her voice booming in her father's ears.

"What's with your voice?" he asks, finding everything increasingly strange, especially the fact that their scene keeps repeating. I must be really tired, he thinks. He wipes the sweat from his brow. Yes, without a doubt, a rough day. The Public Celebration Committee especially was what wore him out. He hardly has enough energy to eat, though that's what he needs most, and, moreover, it's what he most wants to do, urgently, at this very moment.

"It's a question about the universe," says Olga.

"Yeah, about the firmament," says Vasha.

"Why is there something?" asks Olga.

"What?" asks their father.

"Why is there something instead of nothing," explains Olga.

Andrei Petrovich Petrescov has turned pale, rigid, petrified. Disbelieving.

"Yeah. Tell us. Why is there something instead of nothing?" Vasha repeats.

Silence.

He wants to respond, "Because God made the world in seven days," but he says nothing, because he knows he's already explained this to the twins many times. In any case, if his children are talking about "something instead of nothing," then they must have started to think about those distant times in which, if truth be told, there *was* nothing; that is to say, in those remote times when there was only God. But if God was there, then there was something, there was always something, unless God himself *wasn't* there when there was nothing.

Andrei Petrovich Petrescov puts his glasses back on, a victim of his own perplexity and confusion. It's no good for you to get yourself so exhausted, he thinks. There was his operation, six months ago, and he still doesn't feel completely recovered. He's risking his health with so much activity. The operation was fantastically painful, terrifying, treacherous. Yes, he has yet to completely recuperate. He still feels fragile, vulnerable. He's sure that nothing will ever be the same in his life, and that, at any rate, he should be taking better care of his body. Lately, with so much work every day, he's been pushing it too far.

"Instead of nothing," they repeat under their breath.

When he realizes that he has become despondent, and that, as a father, he is probably making a terrible impression on the twins, he tries to reply, but recognizes that he is unable. His hectic day has left him beaten. He needs to eat something, urgently.

The twins look at him expectantly. And spectrally, because the light of the moon, entering through the window of the office, seems like it only cares to illuminate them.

"Yeah, tell us. Why is there something instead of nothing?"

"Are we, as a species, going to kill ourselves off?" he believes he hears Vasha say, now talking in a very soft voice.

"Is there life after death?" asks Olga.

He starts to wonder whether it might be true that his daughters are from the stratosphere—whether they are poor little motherless twins from this day and age or if they actually come from some far-off planet where science has deciphered the enigma of existence. What are they hiding? What do the two little girls know, but don't want to tell him? But it must be his exhaustion making him think this way, Andrei Petrovich Petrescov assumes—his tiredness is disrupting his mind and making him believe that he's been floating, for some time now, through a murky cloud, all his thoughts in a jumble. But, regardless, questions like, "Are we, as a species, going to kill ourselves off?"—if it's true that Vasha really asked him this—seem to have been formulated in the language of the future.

Could it be that his daughters are space travelers and not, in reality, his daughters? Andrei Petrovich Petrescov doesn't know what to do with his glasses, much less with his daughters.

"Yeah, tell us. Why is there something instead of nothing?" he thinks he can hear Vasha say again, again repeating herself.

He wants to have dinner and afterwards tell the girls a story and get them right to bed. Nothing sounds better. Moreover, he wants to get reacquainted with his own bed and, if it all possible, fall fast asleep as soon as possible. The twins look at him, smiling, with their stratospheric laughter. He again wonders if his daughters have chosen this hour of extreme fatigue and confusion to tell him that they belong to a superior civilization from some distant planet. But no, he repeats and repeats, I only suspect this because I'm very tired and probably about to lose my mind.

As these thoughts are all so new to him, Andrei Petrovich Petrescov is a little terrified, and so decides to ring the bell in his office, summoning the aid of the levelheaded governess.

"What is there outside of the family?"

"What is there far away from here?"

"Is there a void outside of the family?"

Following this barrage, Andrei Petrovich Petrescov feels he's been overcome by profound vertigo. When Maria Gergiev arrives, she finds him half slumped over in the chair in his office. His head drowsy, his eyelids heavy. Andrei Petrovich Petrescov recalls that yesterday he caught his two oldest children, Anna and Mikhail, repeating in unison a list of hated politicians' names, devising brutal punishments for each. Their father, the district attorney, was also included on this list. He wonders now whether he hasn't been keeping himself busy, at the Public Celebration Committee and at the courthouse—so much so that he's put his already unstable health at risk—precisely in order to forget his immense displeasure and the subsequent horrible argument this had caused.

The girls are still in front of him, with an odd look in their eyes, looking at him without really looking at him.

"Far from here," whispers Olga.

"Father, far from here, outside of the universe," says Vasha, her words broken and distant.

2.

An hour later dinner is interrupted by two inspectors banging at the door, sent by the police department to respectfully inform Andrei Petrovich Petrescov that his son Mikhail has been accused of belonging to the rebel faction under the command of the traitor Kirov and is in custody at the jail in the basement of the police station. Even though he had been expecting something like this, the news was crushing for Andrei Petrovich Petrescov. Desperation. He just isn't strong enough to carry such a heavy family burden. And Anna? She also hangs around with that damned Kirov's gang, as some good friends have already let him know. But it seems that Anna hasn't been arrested. Where could she be? It would be best if he found her soon, before things get worse. He feels a certain tenderness for Anna, though in reality this affection is so minimal that it hardly makes the least difference. Of course, Andrei Petrovich Petrescov can't feel even this amount of affection for Dimitri and Seriozha, who won't stop fidgeting at the table and who, at this moment, are bombarding each other with breadcrumbs in an attempt to recover their sovereignty, lost earlier that afternoon in the embarrassing episode with the twins. As for the twins, with them it's not a question of affection at all—just of knowing how to overcome the stupor that they provoke in him every time he witnesses them behaving as if they were sent from a nameless star in some unknown constellation . . .

At this very instant, the twins are rolling their eyeballs around their sockets before the astonished stares of the two inspectors, whom they have just asked, undoubtedly at the worst possible time:

"Mr. Policemen, why is there something?"

"What?"

"Yes, Mr. Policemen, why is there something instead of nothing?" says Vasha.

It looks like this day is never going to end for Andrei Petrovich Petrescov, honorable citizen of Novonikolaevsk, who is not very optimistic about discharging his responsibility to raise six ungrateful children, or indeed about the task now set before him, namely, the horrendous prospect of going to police headquarters to give some initial legal assistance to his subversive son.

There's no way to undo this, no way. Dinner has suffered an inopportune interruption. And Andrei Petrovich Petrescov has to put his gloves and coat back on and leave with the inspectors.

The copious snow stuns him with its sudden whiteness when he walks out into the open air. "Why is there something instead of nothing?" Andrei Petrovich Petrescov asks himself in desperation. "If instead of six ungrateful children, I had none, everything would be better," he thinks as he cleans off his glasses.

The sight of the snow enters the consciousness of Andrei Petrovich Petrescov together with an ancient desire for escape, from childhood, from the days when he wanted to be invisible. These very precise dreams of invisibility have been with him for as long as he's had a memory, a yearning to be invisible and to move freely among other beings, who likewise turn out to be ethereal.

"The ideal: a precise dream," thinks Andrei Petrovich Petrescov. Then, at the next breath: "What better ideal than invisibility, the most precise of all my dreams?" On the other hand—how to make oneself invisible with six kids, jobs as district attorney and president of the Public Celebration Committee, fragile health, and an enormous house in the center of the city?

In the slow rhythm of the carriage that transports him to the police station, Andrei Petrovich Petrescov ponders the fact that by this coming July, after thirteen years of hard work, the Trans-Siberian will pass through the Novonikolaevsk train station. The Trans-Siberian, as everyone refers to it, stretching ten thousand kilometers, will connect Moscow with the Russian Pacific coast—with Vladivostok, to be more specific, the city where Andrei Petrovich Petrescov lived for a few years, and to which he always says he doesn't care to return.

"Novonikolaevsk," he whispers to himself, as if this word sums up all of his problems.

In the slow rhythm of the carriage, the overwhelmed district attorney passes by the façade of the future Trans-Siberian station, thinking about how vulgar his two sons, Dimitri and Seriozha, are. He is horrified at their repulsive mediocrity and the fact that they look like so many other gray citizens of Novonikolaevsk, as alike as two drops of water. When they grow up, Dimitri and Seriozha will be nothing more than a couple of idiots, just like the majority of people in this burgeoning Siberian city. The impoverished spirit of the region has infected Dimitri and Seriozha, and you could say that they represent the present state of mind of Andrei Petrovich Petrescov: a present that somehow also includes Anna and Mikhail, and their own, somewhat bloodthirsty, ideals. And further down the road there was the future to worry about, undoubtedly represented by his stratospheric twins.

Oh, poor Dimitri and Seriozha, stuck between the revolution of their older siblings and the futurist Novonikolaevsk of the girls. And while Andrei Petrovich Petrescov is thinking about all this he arrives at the police station and slowly climbs down from the carriage with a horrible fear of slipping on the snow, which would thus add one more misfortune to this exhausting day—a finishing touch.

"Where's Anna?" he asks Mikhail when, after a great deal of protocol and statements made, he is finally able to spend a few seconds alone with him.

"You'll never see her again," says his son, with a contemptuous look on his face. "She's going to sacrifice herself for the Cause."

"What cause?" asks Andrei Petrovich Petrescov, horrified.

"The Revenge of the People. We're going to assassinate reactionaries until we achieve the total downfall of the State. Police officers, high-court officers, and corrupt ministers will no longer exist . . . we'll execute any attorney who isn't on our side."

"You want to become a criminal," says Andrei Petrovich Petrescov remorsefully. "The only thing I can understand is that you want to be a murderer. As for the rest of it, I don't understand a word. You belong to some gang and, even though I can kind of imagine what that means, I can't even guess at what that could possibly mean to *you*. All I can understand is that you want to be a murderer and that you're even capable of killing your own father in the name of your gang. Is that right?"

"Not exactly," Mikhail limits himself to saying, arrogantly.

After some futile negotiations, Andrei Petrovich Petrescov realizes that his influence with the police isn't enough to lessen the serious charges brought against his son and the Kirov gang, and so he ends up taking the painful trip back home wondering where his daughter, Anna, could be hidden. The police had been courteous with him, nothing more, allowing him to see his son and then putting a horse-drawn carriage at his disposal. But the favors stop there. Back at his house, Andrei Petrovich Petrescov senses that his extreme fatigue has now reached the point where it will prevent him from getting any real sleep. He decides to light up a cigar in his office, and simultaneously recalls the startling imitation of himself smoking that, two hours earlier, his twin daughters had performed. His eyes are like two headlights in the middle of the deep Novonikolaevsk night when he wonders if the twins have been able to get to sleep without hearing a story from him. The house is silent, everyone is asleep, except for Suvorin, the butler.

"Suvorin, Anna didn't come home, did she?"

"No she didn't, sir."

"Oh, Suvorin," he says, exhaling a potent mouthful of smoke. "God has been a little hard of hearing as of late. I've been pleading with the Almighty for Anna to come back to the path of the righteous, but it's no use."

"You don't know how sorry I am, sir."

Andrei Petrovich Petrescov has once again proven that he can't hold a conversation with a single other person in this world, can't tell his problems to anyone, much less to Suvorin, no matter how much he trusts him, because Suvorin, well trained, will always respond:

"No, sir."

"You don't know how sorry I am, sir."

"Yes, sir."

Andrei Petrovich Petrescov is alone in the night and in the world, with a whole family in his care. He is an isolated and at heart very lonely person. Perhaps he could only breathe if he dared to step out into the empty space that must exist—thinks Andrei Petrovich Petrescov, suddenly putting out his cigar in the ashtray—outside of his family. But how do you step into that empty space? And how is it possible that empty space could replace the happiness that a family supposedly provides?

"I'm going to make sure the twins were able to get to sleep without my bedtime story."

"Yes, sir."

"Good night, Suvorin. You can go to bed."

"Thank you, sir."

As he walks down the long hallway of the west wing of his house, he feels his loneliness more acutely than ever, but also, curiously, finds himself enjoying it. This pleasure is absolutely new to him, and it seems to be directly connected to the sorrow of walking alone down this familiar hallway. Continuing along the corridor, he immerses himself so deeply in an analysis of this newfound pleasure that he ends up feeling as though he is entering into an unknown land, a space where the limits of his capacity for thought can be found. It's as though he has arrived at a point beyond which one can think no further. He has another, though fleeting, attack of vertigo, as if he were walking along the passage that leads to the empty space outside of all human families, starting with his own. It's true that, ever since his operation, he has felt, day by day, a strange expansion of the nooks and crannies—or, rather of the cells—in his brain.

He's read a lot about cells—not revolutionary cells like the Kirov group, which to him are a mystery—for a number of years. He was always fascinated by the work of Robert Hooke, who in 1665 introduced the term "cell"—inspired by the cells in a monastery—in his book *Micrographia*, written after the tedious observation of plates of cork under the microscope, in which he discovered a series of alveoli that were, in reality, empty cavities, delimited only by the cellular walls of the cork: dead tissue.

Andrei Petrovich Petrescov is contemplating these empty cavities, delimited by cellular walls, as he walks down the hallway that dead-ends— it's only the far end of the hallway, but it seems to him the boundary of his mind as well—at the silent bedroom of Olga and Vasha, the twins. He enters this bedroom in such a state of nervous agitation that any story in the world would seem inadequate to his excitement. The girls, with smiles frozen on their faces, appear to be asleep. And Andrei Petrovich Petrescov looks at them for a while, observes them, trying to find some physical features that he can identify as being specifically his, belonging exclusively to the Petrescovs. He looks and looks again, and even starts to imagine them flying through space, traveling daily from some distant star to drop in at the house of the district attorney of Novonikolaevsk, where they pretend to be his daughters. Thinking they can't hear him, Andrei Petrovich Petrescov tells them a story:

There was once a man who always thought about his two frozen wives, dead, both of them buried in iron coffins under snow-covered mountains, both of them in the old cemetery of a city in which all of the families made up a gloomy, uniform, dead, interwoven tissue. This man is your father, who has always been nothing more than a character in a story, but also the district attorney of the high courts of Novonikolaevsk, twice a widower and father of six children from two marriages who greatly complicate his life. He is a man who was operated on just a few months ago and is putting his illness behind him as best he can, and who—having heard that some tribes in the equatorial jungle in Africa believe that when a sick person is cured he must change his name to a new one—is thinking of changing his name this very night. He is a man who tells his daughters a story every night, like this one, like the one I'm telling right now to you both, both fast asleep. Today's story tells us that there was once a district attorney of the high courts of Novonikolaevsk who went about his life disillusioned because his two eldest children had turned into murderers in some revolutionary cell, his third and fourth children were complete idiots, and his two youngest daughters were eccentric and strange and had been sent to Earth by some mysterious race from a distant star. Caught between revolution, mediocrity, and a sidereal future, the district attorney of Novonikolaevsk worked like a slave every day, to the point of collapse, in order to keep his ungrateful family going. Even if he was absolutely exhausted, he told his daughters a story every night, while in his mind the novel idea of leaving it all behind, changing his name, and starting a new life far from Siberia grew stronger every day. He was the one with a true project for a revolution in Novonikolaevsk. And then, one day, January 17, 1904, in the dark of the night, feeling infinitely weary, but unable to even shut his eyes, while he watched his poor little sleeping daughters, he decided to leave the family home in silence and head on foot to the doors of the *Daily News* of Novonikolaevsk, to wait until the arrival of the first employees and write out a notice, a notice that would occupy a discrete corner of a single page of the newspaper the following day, a notice that would declare that it is more necessary than ever to set in motion the revolution desired by the enemies of Christian society, that society erected on the foundation of selfish families, and take the first step toward a more just and fraternal society of lone individuals. "I, an isolated being who will breathe henceforth surrounded by space that is as empty as it is distant from any sort of Christian family, hereby summon all citizens who likewise desire to unite and establish the fraternal Society of Solitary Fathers," is how the announcement would read, which they would never allow to be printed, of course, but which, at the very least, he would have had the nerve, the courage, the good sense to write down.

That's how his story ended. The district attorney stayed quiet for a moment and ended up adding, merely for the pleasure of saying it:

"Novonikolaevsk."

On this day, January 17, 1904, Anton Chekhov debuted *The Cherry Orchard* in Moscow. It would be his final dramatic work. But Andrei Petrovich Petrescov never knew of this, and though he had certainly heard of Chekhov, who was already well-known in Russia, this was only information gleaned from books. Andrei Petrovich Petrescov couldn't have known that this January 17 would go down in history as the day of the final Chekhov premiere. Just as Andrei Petrovich Petrescov couldn't have known that my grandfather Maurice had chosen that day to come into the world, to be born in a country house in Massiac, not too far from Clermont-Ferrand, France.

I think it would be nice of us to see Andrei Petrovich Petrescov as merely a character in a story, which is what he really wanted to be, and how he wanted to be seen by posterity, as he told his daughters Olga and Vasha on that day, believing that the two were asleep, when, in reality, Vasha was awake the whole time, listening in silence to that story whispered in the middle of a pathetic and profoundly provincial and forgettable night in Novonikolaevsk.

Many years later, Vasha would remember, word for word, this story that, whispered in the nocturnal silence, aspired in vain to dissolve into nothingness. Around 1914, exiled in Berlin, Vasha recounted it as such—as a story—to her closest friend, my grandfather Maurice, who counted me among his grandchildren, me, to whom this story has been transmitted almost intact, faithfully passed down through a delicate family chain that has saved from oblivion the almost precise memory of the noctambulatory words of that district attorney from Novonikolaevsk who one night wound up wishing he were merely a character in a story and the founder of a more just society, composed of solidary, solitary men.

His story has reached our time, has reached me, safe from incalculable deformations. And today I'm just another link in the chain, merely passing it along so that solitary men of the future can take up the task of organizing themselves, just as the father of my grandfather's Russian friend wished to. I've told his story with a scrupulous respect for his desire to spend his life as nothing more than a character in a story. A Russian story, I'd like to add, while sitting here comfortably on the terrace of this bar in Malibu, under a striped umbrella, in the middle of a tropical heat wave. I'm wearing magenta pants, shoes in a cherry shade of leather, and a casual shirt that looks like a thin blue pajama blouse. I don't dress very stylishly—I'm American, and, honestly, it's very hot today and I'm not in the mood to put on a jacket and tie. I turned thirty recently and I feel a subtle and strange nostalgia for the snow, perhaps because I have never, in my whole life, seen any. Sometimes I believe I can feel raindrops slide shakily down my brain cells, which is just as gloomy a prospect as the dead, interwoven tissue within which all the families of Malibu wend their way: families buried their whole lives in iron coffins, relaxing in the sun on the Pacific beaches, where, in a matter of seconds, a simple Bloody Mary transports me—as it's doing right now—to paradise.

TRANSLATED FROM CASTILIAN BY RHETT MCNEIL

DRAGO JANČAR

The Prophecy

1.

One peaceful August morning, on the inner door of a bathroom stall, Anton Kovač saw an inscription that made his blood run cold. The loud echoes of commands and the clomping of thick-soled boots against asphalt could be heard from the distant parade ground—the mustering ground was called "the circle," although it was hard to figure out why when it was shaped like a large square; the new recruits were practicing marching under the hot sun. Here in stall 17 it was cool and quiet, just as it was in the whole row of empty stalls that had recently been cleaned. Anton Kovač was an "old soldier," which meant that he had only about a month to go before his tour was up. He worked in the library and was no longer required to drill, which was why he didn't begrudge himself the luxury of sitting on the toilet in the middle of the afternoon reading a newspaper. He hadn't read the inscriptions on the bathroom walls for a long time. When he was still a "pheasant"—that's what new recruits were called, no one knew why—he'd eagerly read the vulgar thoughts, the names of girls from far-off places, those bitches who were sleeping around while the guys here were pissing blood, groaning about the number of days left to serve, all the messages liberally ornamented with drawings of sexual organs. Since he was a professional reader, a librarian, he'd thought for a while about jotting down the most inspired graffiti and putting together a small anthology of bathroom literature, which is to say an anthology of all the yearning for civilian life, an anthology of jealousy, melancholy, quickly formed petty hatreds, conceits, mockeries, and comments. But he soon dropped the idea. The Balkan military vocabulary was colorful and varied, but it had one ancient leitmotiv, *fucking*, sometimes used literally but more frequently allegorically. Everybody was fucked, from mothers and sisters to brothers and grandfathers, from dogs and cats to abstractions such as sadness and joy, from trees to objects; someone had even written: *Fuck your home address.* Thus, the quantity and monotony of all this bathroom creativity had eventually begun to bore him. And that's why, when he was able to spend a few minutes in that space, once he was no longer a pheasant, he returned to the usual civilian bathroom reading material: the newspaper. He never took a book into the stall; that seemed improper somehow, and not just because he was a librarian. He was a passionate reader for whom books, at least the majority of books, were receptacles of great spirituality, chalices of wisdom, vessels of intoxication—whereas newspapers were simply not.

When he lifted his glance from his newspaper that August day he saw the new inscription amid the drawings and the graffiti; it did not lack the well-known leitmotiv, but its message was so unheard of, so blasphemous, so dangerous that, again, the blood ran cold in Kovač's veins. Almost by the wall, on the right-hand side of the door, in blue pen in uneven letters and in Serbo-Croatian, someone had written something that Anton Kovač would never forget, and that he would translate into Slovenian years later:

> *You'll eat grass, King of Yugoslavia*
> *Donkeys will fuck your fat ass.*

2.

His first thought was: get out of there. Get out of this place as quickly as possible. It seemed he was hearing the hellish ticking of a time bomb that would end his life. He was about to fly out the door when he stopped himself. If anyone saw him coming out of stall 17, he would be a suspect. He listened carefully. He could hear nothing from the corridor except the dripping of water from a broken faucet. And the beating of his heart, which was now up in his throat. From the circle outside he could still hear terse commands and the pounding of boots on asphalt. It sounded like bursts of machine-gun fire: the pheasants didn't know how to march yet. Marching should sound like a single step, not like machine-gun fire—that's how sheep walk. A single step—he recalled the motto written on the barracks wall: *We are all in step.* A new command brought the marching in the circle to a halt. He heard the young corporal telling the recruits how to move their feet, that they should bang their boots onto the ground *so that your balls fall out.*

Anton Kovač walked to the aisle with the sinks; it was empty. He would have preferred to run, but he calmly washed his hands and then forced himself to walk slowly and lazily, as if to let everyone know that an *old soldier* was passing by, always moving at his own pace, with straps loose and his cap stuck into his belt and not on his head. He avoided the yawning man on guard duty who was dozing against the gun rack.

When he entered the library he yawned himself, as though nothing exciting had happened in his boring soldier's life for a long time. And he let himself relax. For the moment it seemed to him that he was safe. The senior officer who ran the library was fiddling with the dial of the crackling radio set, and his colleague, Professor Rotten, who like him was finishing out the last month of his tour, was typing away.

"How goes it, Anton? Did you finish reading the paper?" Rotten asked without even looking up.

Anton Kovač wanted to ask him to walk over to the shelves in order to tell him what he had just read. Recently he'd become quite friendly with this professor, this Belgrader who'd been nicknamed Rotten. Both of them were finding their last month of service hard to take; they'd gone into town together a couple of times to listen to a café singer in a short skirt and get a bit drunk. Rotten was a serious young man, a quiet academic with impeccable military and library discipline. He sometimes loosened up on Sunday trips into town, and would silently down a few shots of brandy. It seemed to Anton Kovač that it would be all right to tell him about the horrifying thing, the time bomb that was waiting in the cool quiet of stall 17. But at the last moment he decided against it. If two people know something, everyone does.

"Fine," he said, "just fine, as always."

He sat down at his desk and began to write book titles down on catalogue cards. "It's hot," said the sergeant, who turned off the crackling radio, walked over to the window, and opened it. The pheasants were still out there, endlessly thumping the asphalt with their boots.

"Sing!" called out the corporal down there on the circle. The lone, pure, and resonant voice of a single young pheasant cried out a song to the rhythm of the marching boots: the "Hymn of the Artillerymen":

> We're artillerymen
> The army has called
> To guard all our borders
> And Marshal Tito

And the chorus of recruits shouted out the refrain:

> Tito's a marshal
> A genius is he,
> He's in command
> Of our splendid army.

Anton Kovač asked himself how many times he had sung that song before he'd mastered the art of marching. A hundred times? So many times, in any case, that he no longer thought about the meaning of those words. Now he suddenly knew how arrogant they were, how horribly at odds they were with what he had read a little while earlier. And he thought about the courageous lunatic who had dared to write the bathroom verse. Anyone who could do that could as easily place a bomb in the barracks.

3.

He slept badly, every time the duty officer in the big bunkhouse woke a new soldier for watch duty he would bolt upright. In a half-awake doze he saw an invisible hand writing letter by letter on the bunkhouse wall the words: *You'll eat grass, King of Yugoslavia* . . . The other half of the couplet was so coarse that Anton Kovač didn't allow himself to see it; instead he'd blink his eyes and try to think of other things. The second half of the horrifying graffito, that vulgar expression of hatred toward the Supreme Leader, was by itself more or less harmless, as its tone was in keeping with all the variations on penetration immortalized on those walls, from top to bottom. Anyone could have written it. But there was something mysterious about the "grass." He recalled a bad joke he had heard once in a bar: a beggar is sitting by a road along which big-shot government officials are traveling, and he's eating grass. A first official stops and gives him a ten, a second comes along and gives him even more money, and then the white-uniformed Marshal pulls up in his black Mercedes. Instead of giving money he asks: "Why don't you go eat away from the road, where it's clean and fresh?" No, no good. *You'll eat grass* . . . Why grass? And if we all know who the King of Yugoslavia must be, why did the author resort to such a fancy, archaic tone? *You'll eat grass, King of Yugoslavia.* Maybe it meant, "You'll be killed with your face in the grass"? Anton Kovač had terrible thoughts that night. And the worst of all was that he might be suspected of writing the couplet himself. He usually used stall 17 because it was the cleanest. Now he knew why. Anyone who had been there even once must have avoided it thereafter. Only he was stupid enough to keep going in there every morning. Like a murderer who keeps returning to where he's hidden the body, until at last he's found out. Kovač imagined that he was already under suspicion. Of course, *anyone* could be under suspicion, but if anyone could be suspected or even accused, then that anyone might easily be him. It was only after four A.M., when the last soldiers returned from guard duty, that he managed to catch a couple of hours of sleep before reveille. In the morning he looked, against his will, to see if anyone would go into stall 17. No one did, at least while he was watching.

4.

He spent the next few days in the library in a state of incessant, low-level anxiety. He sensed that something was going to happen: an officer from the counterintelligence service would open the door, step inside, and ask: who wrote *that*? But nothing of the sort happened. Peace and quiet reigned in the library. The officer spun the radio dial as he always did when he was there; either that or he was off taking care of his own affairs. Kovač's friend Professor Rotten was the silent type, generally bent over his papers. In those August days he was already preparing his university classes. He kept a copy of the Old Testament underneath a pile of papers and would pull it out and begin taking notes as soon as their officer closed the door on his way out. Rotten was preparing to teach a seminar on biblical themes in world literature in the fall semester.

Rotten's real name was Milenko Panič, but at that artillery base in southern Serbia, no one remembered this anymore—everybody called him Professor Rotten, or even more frequently, just Rotten. He had received his new name soon after joining the army. He'd still been a pheasant, no more than a month into his service, when once, during the morning muster, Major Stankovič came to a halt in front of him and fixed his eyes on the open button of the left-hand pocket of Panič's shirt. Two pens were sticking out. Major Stankovič was a gruff but pleasant man whose large, heavy frame might have made him look dangerous to some—indeed, like a pit bull preparing to attack—but in fact he was a good-natured sort, always ready for a joke. And so the soldiers liked him.

Even so, however, Panič was ill at ease when the Major stopped in front of him.

"What's that?" the Major asked, pointing to the two pens. Panič shrugged his shoulders and the major shifted his eyes to those of his young corporal, standing at his side, who was now paralyzed with terror at having to answer for the undisciplined appearance of his men.

"I said, 'What's that?' " the Major repeated.

Panič replied stoutly: "Two pens, Comrade Major!"

Silence fell. This wasn't a good answer; everyone could see that there were two pens, and the Major could easily get angry. But he did not get angry; he just stared at Panič for a time.

"I see. For a minute there I thought they were some sort of military decoration," he said slowly.

Then he chuckled, the relieved corporal laughed, and the whole long row of soldiers joined him.

"What do you do in civilian life, soldier?"

"He's a professor," the corporal answered.

"I asked him," said the Major.

Panič looked around somewhat abashed as about a hundred soldiers and several officers waited for his answer. He explained that he was a classical philologist, he'd studied Latin and ancient Greek.

"And what on earth do you need *them* for?" the Major asked.

Panič did not reply.

"Those languages are dead and buried—rotting in the ground!" the Major guffawed, and all the soldiers in the ranks joined him so loudly that the walls of the barracks echoed. Panič blushed. Rotting—that is to say, decayed—languages were unnecessary, comical, like the first, rotten Yugoslavia that had to collapse so that the new socialist Yugoslavia could appear. Panič wanted to say that it wasn't proper to speak this way about Latin and Greek, about subjects to which he had chosen to devote his entire life. But he realized he had no desire to hear any other jokes from the bemused Major. He swallowed his saliva. Satisfied with himself, Major Stankovič continued to walk along the row of soldiers while professor Milenko Panič just stood there among the men, alone and humiliated, a professor of rotten languages.

By the afternoon he had become *Professor Rotten*, and by the evening, when some of the men wanted to needle him still further, he had become just *Rotten*, and Rotten he remained.

He never became reconciled to this new title, which gave him no end of trouble. Anyone saddled with that sort of nickname—which, worst of all, he received in public, to the general amusement of his fellow soldiers—automatically becomes the target of daily mockery, over familiarity, pranks. Who doesn't know how to take apart a gun? The professor of decaying languages. Who'll wash the latrines this morning? Professor Rotten. And the angrier he let himself look, the more fun everyone had with Professor Rotten. One night they even made him do "the bicycle." This was a favorite nighttime trick of soldiers. You stick a piece of paper between the toes of a sleeping person and light it on fire. When the flame gets close to the skin, his leg begins to twist, and the closer the flame gets to his toes, the faster he pedals. Only when the pain gets really bad does the person finally wake up, bewildered, and look around in amazement at all the laughing faces. Rotten had had to put up with the bicycle on a number of occasions, precisely because he was a professor of rotten languages. He was only able to get a bit of relief when he and Anton Kovač were assigned to the library. There he threw himself into his studies. And every time the officer who ran the library and its piles of Marxist scholarship, partisan historiography, and patriotic literature walked out the door, Rotten would pull his copy of the Vulgate from his heaps of papers and lose himself eagerly in the mysteries of the text. This shortened the hours and days that remained before the end of his tour; with every page he turned he got closer to his home and farther from the laughingstock called Professor Rotten.

His calm was infectious. For a few days Anton Kovač still trembled every time the door to the library opened, but then, alongside the tranquil Professor, he soon got back to his usual routine, waiting for his demobilization. Gradually he began to forget about the dangerous writing in the bathroom, and he also stopped waking up at night to see the invisible hand writing letters on the bunkhouse walls. On his morning visits to the bathroom, which he could not avoid completely, he noticed that no one ever used stall 17. One afternoon he marshaled his courage and opened the door to that stall. The message was still there. He leapt away as though from a snake.

5.

August turned into September and only fourteen days were left to their tour. On Sunday he and Rotten went into town, did some drinking and listened to gypsy music. With the sound of trumpets echoing in their heads they returned to the base in a petulant mood. It was their penultimate Sunday.

And now the penultimate Monday began. It began with the sound of running down the hallways and sharp commands that cut through Anton Kovač's head, which was still a bit hazy thanks to Sunday's brandy and gypsy trumpets. He squirmed through the pile of bodies that were looking for their boots in the corridor and headed for the toilets. The bathroom was locked and the guard who stood in front of the door said that the plumbing was out of order and that he should use the bathrooms in another part of the base. Anton Kovač knew the plumbing was fine, and that anyway when something really went wrong with it, no one ever thought to post a guard at the door. He headed for the library, but he met Rotten on the way.

"The library's closed," he said, "we've all got to line up outside."

"What's going on?" Anton Kovač asked cautiously.

"What's going on?" Rotten said, "Some nasty shit's going on, and only two weeks before we get out of here."

They tightened their belts, quickly laced up their boots, and at the last minute Anton Kovač took the two pens out of Rotten's shirt and stuffed them in his pants pocket. It wouldn't be good to have good-humored Major Stankovič stop in front of him again this morning. Then, amid the crowd of men stampeding in the corridor and hopping down the stairs, they made their way out onto the parade ground.

There was an ominous silence on the circle as the last of the men rushed to join their units. A group of officers, led by Major Stankovič, emerged from the officers' quarters. The duty officer called out: *Attenshun!* The Major's heavyset form, which usually radiated goodwill and good humor, now seemed gloomy and dangerous. He walked up to the small podium on the field and the other officers ranged themselves behind him. An intelligence officer, a captain, tried out the mike: one, two, three, testing. Then he withdrew, leaving room for the commanding officer. The Major stepped slowly to the microphone, biting his upper lip, and for a few moments it seemed that he was trying to decide what he should say. A cold September wind from the nearby hills blew over the heads of the silent soldiers.

"We are the Yugoslav People's Army," the Major said in a soft voice that the loudspeakers made almost metallic.

"We guard this country and its laws. Our supreme commander is Marshal Tito, who led this army triumphantly through the Balkans in so many bloody battles for liberty and victory."

He fell silent, allowing the soldiers to digest these phrases.

"And yet, in this army there are people who do not respect what we all hold most holy. Even worse, people who are prepared to sabotage brotherhood, unity, and our freedom."

The breeze carried his words to the last rows of soldiers. Hands behind his back, he took a couple of steps on the podium.

"We no longer have kings," he continued unexpectedly. "Kings fell along with the old, rotten Yugoslavia."

He looked at his intelligence officer, who was as white as a sheet. And he spoke as if that officer was directly responsible.

"Counterrevolutionary graffiti has appeared in our barracks—that is all that I can say for now. Anyone who could write the sort of thing we've found—" and Anton Kovač knew very well what the Major would say next: "—anyone who could write that sort of thing would be just as capable of planting a bomb in the barracks. Or turning his gun on one of his comrades. We will not allow this. We will track all such men down, and all those who protect them, and we will court-martial every last one. You will receive further instructions in your units."

The duty officer called out: at ease.

6.

The investigation began. To start with, the soldiers of each unit were asked to sit at the desks in the barracks classroom. A young corporal with supple, twitching fingers placed a piece of paper and a pen in front of each soldier. He lit a cigarette and recited a prepared speech that each man was meant to copy down word for word. It was an old fairy tale that begins with a description of a grassy field across which rides a man on a donkey, and there are other donkeys around eating grass. Then a king goes by accompanied by his retinue—meaning that the words "grass," "king," "Yugoslavia," "donkeys," and "eat," were all used on a number of occasions. And every time Anton Kovač got to one of those words, his hand shook. You shouldn't shake, he thought, because a handwriting expert will be asked to come in and determine whose hand shook while writing the word "donkey." Professor Rotten, completely calm, was sitting right next to Kovač and writing down the sentences the corporal was dictating—dictating very slowly and with frequent repetitions, since not everyone in the room could write very well. Anton Kovač wondered how many of the guys knew what was going on. Stall 17 was clean and empty, after all; everyone avoided it. He wondered whether Rotten knew, and he was sorry he hadn't confided in him. At least then the Professor could have testified that Kovač was innocent. No one who wrote those words would possibly call attention to himself by asking a friend whether he had seen them too. But then, the intelligence officer would ask why Kovač hadn't reported what he'd seen. Perhaps you don't love Marshal Tito as much as everyone else? And in fact Anton Kovač did not love him. Anyone who loved him would have nothing to fear. He would have quickly reported that hostile and disgusting bit of doggerel. But Kovač had remained silent, and therefore had become an accessory.

That night, the horrible inscription appeared again on the bunkhouse wall, and in his rambling dreams it seemed to him that his eyeballs were broiling in his head, that he could not hide from the words that his own eyes were projecting into the night.

7.

The next day there was no more talk about uncovering counterrevolutionary individuals or groups on the base. At breakfast Kovač heard they'd arrested an Albanian they'd found in possession of live ammunition that he had apparently stolen while on guard duty. Someone said he'd be put before a firing squad, bang, right on the spot. But Anton Kovač knew that this was just the usual gossip young soldiers bandied about to pass the time faster. At the circle, just before the morning muster, they heard that an unscheduled military exercise was being organized. This sounded a lot more likely. But still no one said anything about why the investigation was happening at all.

An intelligence officer came by the library in the morning and asked everyone whether they'd seen anything unusual, any soldier who was behaving strangely. He asked what books had been taken out recently and who had taken them. The officer in charge of the library was clearly more frightened than either of his two assistants, and he answered quickly. Nothing could happen here because he never left the library. The officer looked Anton Kovač in the eye and asked him how frequently *he* left the library and whether he ever went to the bathroom. I do go, he said, heart beating quickly, but always with the sergeant's permission. The sergeant confirmed this and that satisfied the intelligence officer. Then he took some sheets from the pile of papers that lay in front of Professor Rotten. Anton Kovač knew there was a Bible underneath. Rotten was calm, gloomy, motionless. When the officer removed the final sheet there was nothing underneath. The Professor had removed the Old Testament and his notes in time. Anton Kovač relaxed. They really didn't need a new scandal because of a Bible on the premises. There was enough going on already.

In the evening there was a surprise drill; the company was turned out in full uniform and under a cold rain blown in by the mountain winds forced to march some ten miles to the rifle range. There they had to put on gasmasks and hurl themselves into a swamp. They didn't get back to the base until the next morning and all fell right into bed. But at ten A.M. they were up again practicing their marching to the "Hymn of the Artillerymen." No one was allowed to stay in the classroom or the library. Anton Kovač began to think that the ten days that separated him from the end of his tour would last forever. He knew that in exceptional circumstances the term of military service could even be extended.

8.

The sun came out again at noon, and during the rest period he lay in the grass behind the mess hall, stretching his sore legs that were no longer used to marching. He lit a cigarette, looked up at the clouds, and wished he could escape from what was coming, perhaps tomorrow. He imagined the heavyset Major Stankovič walking across the circle, leaning toward him and saying: "*Civilization* is waiting for you in the depot—you are dismissed." "Civilization" was another word that wasn't too clear to the Major: here it meant civilian clothes that had been sent from home. But those were only pleasant midday thoughts brought by the clouds that rushed into the Balkans from the valley of the Morava River on their way either to the Aegean or the Black Sea.

At five in the afternoon they were again chased out onto the parade ground. They marched around the circle and sang: *Tito's a marshal, a genius is he . . .* And the more the boots crunched the more Kovač asked himself: Who wrote the bathroom poem? Who will be unmasked? And although no one had ever told the company what the investigation was all about, and although none of the soldiers had ever admitted to seeing anything untoward on the bathroom walls, Anton Kovač sensed that the words that had so haunted him were flashing too before the eyes of each of the marching men. It was like when someone can't stop laughing at a funeral: at every step, some letter from the bathroom walls shone on the circle. For every "Marshal" they sang there was the grass that the King of Yugoslavia would eat. For every "genius" there was the donkey who would fuck the King in his ass (a terrible thought), or rather in his *fat* ass (an even more terrible thought). During the guard duty he had to serve once again by the armory where the 155 mm cannons were kept, as the stars were just winking out in the sky and the first light was coming over the mountaintops, Kovač wished that the culprit would be found. Let him be captured at last to put an end to all this uncertainty, let him be caught and brought before a court-martial. Later Anton Kovač would be ashamed of having had such thoughts—a court-martial was no joke, but at the time he was such a nervous wreck that he would have been glad to see the idiot strung up, sent to jail, anything. After all, thanks to the "poet," he was still stuck on the base. Rotten would miss a semester if not a whole year. How was it possible, Kovač thought angrily, how was it possible for this unknown writer to issue such a brazen challenge inside this army, this fearsome army—feared by everyone, even by the citizens of its own country, who also loved it precisely because they feared it, just as they feared and simultaneously loved its Commander, Marshal, genius.

9.

Although it seemed to him that he would never get away, it turned out that Kovač was able to leave the base only a few days later than scheduled. It seemed the investigation had begun with the men about to be discharged before moving on to the wider population. There were quite a few soldiers at the end of their tours, so things got held up. For Anton Kovač, all the years he'd spent at the base now felt as though they'd passed faster than these final days in southern Serbia, when it seemed to him that every hour lasted an eternity. Particularly because he had been so afraid of it, the graffiti lodged itself deep into his memory. Only once did he tell his friends

about what had happened to him in the far south. The story was a big success, but he never repeated it—his friends had laughed hardest at the fact
that it had been him, Anton Kovač, sitting there terrified, holding a newspaper (the Belgrade daily *Politika*, in fact), his pants around his ankles.
People are malicious; they like nothing more than to laugh at someone
else's misfortune, incompetence, or general unhappiness, as for instance
when they are made to do "the bicycle." Who could really understand Anton Kovač and his distress in those last days of his tour? And so he was
happy to forget the whole thing—he *wanted* to forget it. And besides, there
were new things to worry about: the world was out of joint for a while. The
Marshal died and soon after so did the country itself. The army that was
supposed to protect it collapsed, and so no one marched on the circle
singing the "Hymn of the Artillerymen" anymore. When Anton Kovač
saw burning Balkan villages on the television screen and heard the roar of
155 mm cannons he sometimes thought about the officers of that glorious
and triumphant army. Where were they now, what uniforms were they
wearing? He recalled the young corporal with the supple fingers—where
was he lighting cigarettes now?—the lazy sergeant from the library—he
was probably retired—and then Major Stankovič—whose soldiers was he
commanding, to whom was he lecturing from his podium? But it was all
so far away, and when the wars were over it all became even farther away
and more nebulous, sinking deeper into the mists of memory.

One day on television Anton Kovač saw a man with earphones on his
head sitting in front of a tribunal and denying that he was guilty of killing
civilians. His face seemed somehow familiar. Then the camera showed
that same man in uniform. He was heavyset and his sleeves were rolled
up. With a pleasant chuckle he was telling some miserable civilians that
nothing would happen to them. A group of officers and soldiers was standing near him and then they forced those people onto some buses with their
bundles. Anton Kovač suspected he'd seen that face before . . . was it not

the good-natured, though sometimes sullen and dangerous, Major Stankovič? Back at the base his hair had been black, but now it was gray. And then, for the first time in years, as if an enormous wave was washing over him, the whole set of events, in every detail, came back to Anton Kovač. He was not at all bothered by the clips on television; he was shaken by that old fear from the cold corridors of the army base far in the south.

In the middle of the night, half asleep, he again saw the invisible handwriting on the wall. And he thought that the bathroom inscription had been some kind of prophecy. A prophecy? *Mene, mene, tekel* . . . ? Now Anton Kovač was wide awake. He got up, got dressed, and in the middle of the night went to the library where he worked as a cataloguer. He turned on all the lights in his office and all the lights in his head went on as well. He searched for a Bible, he knew where *mene, tekel* appeared. In the Book of Daniel an invisible hand wrote *Mane, Thekel, Phares*—as it is translated in the Vulgate. Anton Kovač rifled the pages with a shaking hand: ". . . and his heart was made like the beasts, and his dwelling was with the wild asses, they fed him with grass . . ." The King of Babylon was kicked out of his palace, he had to live among donkeys, eat grass, and he had an animal's heart . . . And it went on: ". . . all people, nations, and languages, trembled and feared before him," the Babylonian King—"whom he would he slew; and whom he would he kept alive; and whom he would he set up; and whom he would he put down." The King of Babylon, Anton Kovač thought, of course, of course, that was the message, the King of Yugoslavia was the King of Babylon . . . "Then they brought the golden vessels that were taken out of the temple of the house of God which was at Jerusalem; and the king, and his princes, his wives, and his concubines, drank in them. They drank wine, and praised the gods of gold, and of silver, of brass, of iron, of wood, and of stone." And now, now he saw him, the professor of rotten languages walking down the corridor in the middle of the night or perhaps in the middle of his workday in the army library with his ballpoint pens stuck in his shirt pocket. He greets the guard in the corridor nonchalantly, goes into the bathroom, down to the end of the row of stalls, he sees that no one is around, undoes his belt just in case, and takes out his pen . . . "In the same hour came forth fingers of a man's hand, and wrote over against the candlestick upon the plaister of the wall of the king's palace: and the king saw the part of the hand that wrote . . . And this is the writing that was written, *mene, mene, tekel, upharsin.*" Which means, as Professor Rotten knew very well: "God hath numbered thy kingdom, and finished it. Thou art weighed in the balances, and art found wanting. Thy kingdom is divided, and given to the Medes and Persians." And he also knew the fate that the King of Babylon had been promised in the Book of Daniel: ". . . they fed him with grass like oxen, and his body was wet with the dew of heaven." How Anton Kovač had hated that fat and dissolute king, and how his friend, that silent librarian, professor of rotten languages, had hated him too. He wrote a prophecy about him on the walls of a bathroom in southern Serbia, he couldn't do it except in the vulgate, so to speak, mostly to avoid being caught but also so that all would understand. To write something as terrifying as *mene tekel* could only have been done in those days in the form chosen by his quiet friend Professor Milenko Panič, who could escape from himself only after he'd had a few brandies.

Anton Kovač turned off the lights, closed the library door, and headed into the night. He drove around the dark streets of Ljubljana for a long time. Maybe his friend hadn't hated the King of Babylon, he thought, maybe he was just getting some revenge for his petty humiliation, for the fact that he had become the professor of rotten languages, the much-mocked Professor Rotten. Maybe he just wanted to send the base a message translated from one of his "rotten" languages into their living, soldier's dialect. Anton Kovač looked into the rearview mirror: I have gray hair, and you have gray hair too, Professor Rotten, somewhere in Belgrade or wherever you are, and Major Stanković also has gray hair, I saw him on television. Your mysterious prophecy was indeed horrible, Rotten, and true. But all has passed; today all those ancient kingdoms and their armies no longer interest anyone, and by tomorrow we too will be forgotten and no one will understand our stories.

TRANSLATED FROM SLOVENIAN BY ANDREW WACHTEL

VLADIMIR ARSENIJEVIĆ

One Minute: Dumbo's Death

(60) For the last two years he hadn't budged from this dark corner in the Calle de Colón (59) no one bothered him or drove him away, he became a kind of attraction, a black mark in an otherwise faultless city (58) tourists came every day to take his photograph, they turned off their well-worn route through La Rambla (57) bent down, leaned their hands on their knees and stared at him, talking him over in low voices (56) cameras clicked, flashes flared, lenses hummed (55) art students sat down opposite him with their legs crossed, tucked their feet under their buttocks (54) and took out pads and sketch books and drawing materials, pencils, charcoal, and felt-tipped pens, rapid sketches came into being (53) and the city dogs sniffed him and slunk away in horror without his being aware of anything (52) and once he even ended up on a postcard, though he was oblivious to this, and it was, thank goodness, only a parody made by one of the students (51) in that picture he was lying on the cold stone like a log, like a heap of dead flesh (50) vomit had slid down his rough cheek, followed by thick snot (49) colored with red strands of bloody spit, forming a little puddle on the pavement (48) while above his head there was a shiny sign in several European languages (47) "WELCOME TO GLORIOUS BARCE-LONA!"

■

"He always was ugly, honest to God," that's what his drunken mother said way back in nineteen eighty-four, in front of family and friends gathered to celebrate his twelfth birthday, shrugging her shoulders with an unusual mixture of love and revulsion as she surveyed the bony face, imposing nose, and small, sunken eyes of her only son, "but how did he get to be so flop-eared, that's what no one knows!" Everyone round the table roared with drunken laughter. And, indeed, Hasan's ears were so huge that even in his first year at primary school in his native Sarajevo someone called after him, "Hey, there goes Dumbo!" And it stuck, like a mask that he was never able to pull off, while mocking voices round him echoed, *Dumbo, Dumbo, Dumbo, Dumbo* . . .

(46) and now it was the summer of the year two thousand and it was raining continuously, the sky had suddenly opened **(45)** and now it was pouring, pouring, it had woken even Hasan from his eternal sleep **(44)** he raised his heavy head to watch the fat drops of rain falling onto the world outside his shelter under the colonnade **(43)** and then dropped it back feebly into his own vomit—that soft, tepid pillow which dispersed at once under the pressure **(42)** until his cheek finally met the cold stone once again **(41)** just beside the broken-down wheelchair in which Aurelio was snoring loudly **(40)** hunchbacked Aurelio with his bearded face covered with a layer of several years of filth and a horrible waxed hood **(39)** Aurelio who had somewhere along the way lost his left arm and both his legs **(38)** the one true friend he had left in this world

Swimming had been all that interested Hasan in life. In Sarajevo, that city of non-swimmers, he felt like a bird among moles. "Do you realize, Dumbo, that around seventy percent of your contemporaries would sink like stones in this pool!" his trainer, fat Charlie, said to him sometime in nineteen eighty-seven—Charlie was the only person he didn't mind calling him that name. "Well, you've got to swim for all of them, understand?"

And: "Come on, Dumbo, faster!" he shouted at him in nineteen eighty-nine, "faster, damn you! Sixty seconds, bah! Sixty fucking seconds! When you break that barrier, kid, that's your ticket to the championship, and then who knows—maybe the Olympics." And: "Barcelona, Dumbo, remember that, Bar-ce-lo-na!" he promised him in nineteen ninety-one. But nothing came of it: Hasan never did manage to swim the hundred-meter backstroke in under sixty seconds. That same year, war broke out in Croatia; Dubrovnik and Vukovar were in flames; and then, in ninety-two, in the spring, just before the Olympics, war came to his native city. But by then everything had gone to hell anyway, so why shouldn't the plans and ambitions of Hasan Halilović—unfortunately known as Dumbo—go along for the ride?

(37) "Aurelio, you're the ugliest damn sight in this city, *cabrón*," said Juan, *Mexicano* (36) who kept coming and going on his crutches and had now stopped here to shelter from the sudden downpour recently unleashed upon the city (35) "you're the ugliest damn sight in Barcelona, *pendejo*, you ought to get a pension," (34) he added in his singsong, drunken accent, laughing squeakily until Aurelio pushed his head out of its hood (33) looked at him with twinkling eyes that gleamed by contrast with his dark face and started to laugh himself (32) toothlessly and hoarsely—what did he know, but it was funny anyway (31) *ha ha ha ha*, his lungs hurt when he laughed but he couldn't stop himself (30) "Hasan, Hasan!" he yelled, but how could Hasan hear him or see him or respond (29) his eyes had rolled back, his head was lying in smelly, crusty vomit, bloody snot was trickling down his rough cheek (28) just like on the postcard *welcometo-barcelona* (27) "No, no, no, *germà*," yelled Aurelio then and turned back to Juan, "*Mira Hasan!* Take a look at Hasan!"

He entered the war innocent. The Chetniks shelled Sarajevo day and night. Charlie vanished from the city—it was only then that Hasan realized that

Charlie was a Serb. Hasan's mother was terribly worried about him and begged him to stay at home. But, since there were no more training sessions, Hasan was going stir crazy. Uncontrollable energy built up in him. He didn't care whether he was killed, and he wasn't killed—but his mother was killed when a shell flew in through a cellar window and exploded. Hasan spent the rest of the war in a unit of the Bosnian Army, mainly in positions around the city. Among his fellow soldiers he was known for his cold, merciless cruelty. No one dared call him Dumbo any longer. Once he found a stopwatch on a Chetnik prisoner. Just like the one fat Charlie had. He looked more closely at the body crouching on the floor—why, it really *was* Charlie. Wasting away, pale, with fear in his eyes. His mouth full of blood, he moaned something unintelligible, something that sounded like "Dumbo" to Hasan. "Goddamn it," muttered Hasan through clenched teeth. He killed him quickly, in a rush of revulsion. Afterward he thought, maybe it wasn't Charlie. He kept the stopwatch. Just before the end of the war, in the twenty-third year of his life, he fucked a woman for the first time. A young war whore, already worn out. Later he didn't remember anything except that she stank of other soldiers.

(26) "Hasan, Hasan!" Aurelio kept calling, then yelling, yelling, *ha ha ha ha*, his lungs were already burning (25) and he waved that blue stump of his that had been sewn together so badly that it looked as though it would burst at any minute (24) open up and the whole of him would pour out of it making a messy puddle on the asphalt (23) a perfect meal for the packs of city dogs that Aurelio fed in any case with the remains of the scraps he was given every day (22) by the owners of local restaurants, because Aurelio was—at least insofar as was possible (21) in his situation, of course —generous, though exclusively so toward those who had by his extremely immodest assessment (20) sunk even lower than himself, like Hasan, and Aurelio was right . . . because even if (19) someone had taken poor Hasan in, bathed him and cleaned him up, then gotten him treatment, treated

him **(18)** for all his illnesses, those numerous colonies of bacteria and viruses which had colonized **(17)** his sick, collapsing body, the ulcers and pimples and rashes and hives **(16)** which had overwhelmed him like Job, even if someone had cared for him and knocked him into shape until **(15)** he became something like a man again, Hasan would probably continue to be the ugliest damn sight in the whole of Barcelona **(14)** but Hasan no longer cared about that because Hasan no longer cared about anything **(13)** his face was just a mask it was impossible to take off **(12)** while he himself, under that mask, was simply a pure white empty chrysalis

He left Sarajevo as soon as he had a chance. He took a few things with him including that old stopwatch of Charlie's. He saw that he wasn't in control of his destiny and let the current carry him and it carried him through refugee camps all over Europe. He spent the most time in Denmark, picked pockets there, got used to heroin and alcohol, cheated his way to a fake passport, and one very ordinary evening in Copenhagen fucked a Ukrainian whore, the Balkan way, in a blind alley, pressing her back into a rough wall. A year later, he already looked like a wreck. He attributed this to the bad dope he was buying but he was afraid of an illness whose name he did not even dare pronounce. His body was decaying fast. He collected all the money he could raise and traveled to Barcelona. There he went through some terrible withdrawal symptoms on a park bench; the next night was even worse, and then on the third he was brutally attacked by some locals—they kept kicking him in the head, took everything he owned, and left him to squirm and writhe, like a worm, while the stopwatch kept ticking helplessly in his pocket—the only thing in the world he had left. He was taken up, battered as he was, by a group of vagrants. They gave him water to drink and a filthy waxed blanket to pull around him. *What's your name?* they asked him. *¿Cómo te llamas? Com et dius?*

For a long time he could not remember, and then it finally came to him: Hasan Halilović Dumbo.

The one and only.

■

(11) and in the meantime the downpour had stopped just as suddenly as it began (10) *"Pues Juan, por favor, mira a Hasan, hermano!"* said Aurelio once again to the barely interested Juan (9) switching from Catalan to Spanish in the hope that he would understand him better, and coughed and literally jumped in his wheelchair (8) while Juan, after examining Hasan carefully, jerked on his crutches (7) and without a single word turned and hastily fled from some sudden danger visible only to him (6) (for all his drunkenness he had seen what was still escaping Aurelio: that Hasan was no longer breathing and that his eyes were glassy and lifeless) (5) and while Aurelio was wiping all those flowing tears from his own eyes and bending over Hasan and nudging him with his stick (4) although there was no longer anyone there under it, no one other than a dead body (3) Juan disappeared round a corner and was lost in the crowd of tourists and shoppers that was once again milling under the eaves, among the stalls, colonnades, cafés, restaurants, shops, and doorways (2) and, pushing and shoving, slowly but persistently, like a solemn procession on a frieze or fresco

(1)

making its way along

(0)

La Rambla

TRANSLATED FROM SERBIAN BY CELIA HAWKESWORTH

Vladimir Arsenijević 95

ANDREI GELASIMOV

The Evil Eye

"It's good you called for me," said old Potapikha, fussing over her magical dough. "Because nowadays it's Kuzmich they ask for. As if only his spells work. But who, I'd like to know, set things right with Zubov's bride's belly? And who fixed Makarov's boy's hernia?"

Potapikha pounded away at her wonderworking dough in a wooden tub and from the effort of it and having to stoke the stove in summer, she quickly broke out in a sweat and pulled off her high-collared black jacket of thick shiny cloth. Petka didn't know what it was called. What he did know was that for a long time old lady Darya wanted one like it, but old man Artem just couldn't put together the money to head off to Krasnoka-mensk for it, so old lady Darya had to be patient for now.

"And what's this one doing here?" asked Potapikha, squinting in Petka's direction. "We don't need a stranger watching."

"He's Valerka's friend," Valerka's mama answered softly. "Let him sit a while."

"Well, watch out, that's a dark eye he's got. Don't you see it? That kind puts the worst hex on you."

Valerka's mother looked at Petka in alarm.

"He'll hex someone for sure," old Potapikha added.

"I'll close my eyes," Petka said quickly. "I'll go sit over there. Under the table. You can't see me from there."

"Do, Petka," Valerka's mother asked. "You never know what can happen."

"It's not that you never know—you can bet something will," Potapikha confirmed, turning white as an undershirt, like a strange snowman, in the stuffy, dusky room. "Go on, get under the table."

It was dark in the house since Valerka's mama and Potapikha had closed the shutters ten minutes before.

"Light in this sort of thing gets in the way," Potapikha had announced from the doorway. "Where there's light there's sickness."

And she also ordered the rooster removed from the yard so he wouldn't start crowing.

"Because if he crows, the whole thing's over. Up in smoke."

So they locked the rooster in the bathhouse. Two scraggly chickens, who by some miracle had held out till Victory Day and weren't eaten up during the last spring of the war, came over right on the heels of Valerka's mama and tried clumsily to fly onto the vent to peek inside.

"Kill the speckled one for me later," said Potapikha, looking thoughtfully at the hens jumping around near the bathhouse.

She always took a hen as payment for her services.

Petka hadn't expected that Valerka would be so sick. But Valerka was now lying on a wide wooden bed and his mother, beside herself with fear, was pacing around with a towel in her hands, unable to keep still.

"Better sit down," Potapikha said to her finally. "Or my dough won't rise."

"What do you mean? How's that my fault?" Valerka's mama asked in dismay. "Why my fault?"

"Well, who else then? The little fellow's sitting under the table. Down there he's got no chance to hex anyone."

"All right," said Valerka's mama, and Petka saw how her feet came to a stop near a stool. Next to old Potapikha's feet, those feet behaved very timidly, and looking at them it was obvious they were waiting for something. If Petka hadn't known where this table was—the table he was sitting under, squeezing his eyes shut (and at times, just in case, even covering them with his hands)—he'd have thought Valerka's mama's feet were the visitors, not old Potapikha's. She stood solidly, like a landing barge, with half its hull grounded on the shore, while Valerka's mama kept shifting around, holding her breath, and shuddering intermittently, lifting now one foot now the other onto the wooden crosspiece of the stool.

"Will he die?" her voice asked softly.

"Who? The little one? No, he won't," old Potapikha's voice answered.

Her slippers, cut from felt boots, which she didn't take off even in such heat, turned toward the stool. She moved all at once, in one piece. Like a real ship.

"What are you talking about—die? Where'd that come from? He's too young. His ass ain't even rounded yet."

Valerka's mama's feet froze for an instant then dropped together from the crosspiece to the floor.

"Is that so?"

Petka knew those ankle boots well. Valerka's mama had bought them when Valerka's father's "Killed in Action" notice came. At first she sat a long time in the hall and looked at the holes in the wood and at the spider web—she didn't even notice that the postman, Comrade Ignat, had said good-bye and left quietly. Then she hid the notice behind the mirror, put Valerka's things together, and set off with him for Krasnokamensk. From there Valerka came back wearing these very same boots. Here in Atamanovka none of the kids had anything like them. Not even all the grown-ups walked around in real leather boots. There were felt ankle boots, knee-high boots, slippers. Now suddenly leather boots turned up. But Valerka didn't take care of them at all. He got them all scuffed in just one winter so the other kids would take him along to play. And his mama didn't scold him. When the boots wore down, she began to use them herself.

Once she came to school in them to see the teacher, Anna Nikolaevna. She asked the teacher to point out where Stalingrad was on the map. She looked at the place, covered it with her palm, stood a while like that, and then said, "Thank you."

Either she was thanking Anna Nikolaevna or the entire big map of the Soviet Union.

Staring at these broken-down boots and having forgotten what could happen when his eyes were open, Petka noticed that the string which Valerka's mama used to lace the left boot was coming loose and that it would soon open wide like a hungry little cuckoo's mouth. Petka extended his hand carefully from under the table, trying to tie up the string, but Valerka's anxious mother unexpectedly moved again and stepped on the same fingers that had been smashed in a recent fight. Petka let out a hiss and instantly old Potapikha's head swung down under the table. It was easier for her to bend over than to turn around.

"*Whaat?*" she asked suspiciously. "What's all this hissing?"

Obviously she had decided that Petka in his malice had invented a new, vocal version—as yet unknown to her—of the evil eye. She was clearly furious, but Petka immediately squeezed shut his eyes again and even covered his mouth with both hands. Potapikha, after giving it some thought, softened up a bit.

"Well, go on, instead of just sitting there like a dunce, go catch me some roaches. But don't you kill them now, just press down on them a bit. Put them in this matchbox here. Mind, don't come up out from under the table."

And Petka began his hunt.

There weren't many roaches because roaches live where there's at least something left to eat, but leaving aside Valerka himself and Valerka's mama, there was nothing left. There just couldn't be. They hardly had enough for themselves. Any crumbs were swept up carefully into palms and, in full view of the disconsolate roaches, carefully deposited into mouths. Like coal in the mine near Krasnokamensk. One scoop—and it's in the trolley.

So Petka didn't spot his prey right away. Especially since he kept squinting. He believed just as strongly in the evil eye as he did in Marshal Zhukov. Someplace deep in his heart there even flickered the suspicion that the Germans lost the war because he, Petka, had hexed their Hitler. That's not to say, of course, that our troops didn't fight fiercely and that, all in all, they're not the best troops in the world ... but still, Petka too had done all he could.

Sometime around a year ago, in old lady Darya's hayloft, he had begun scratching out dirty words about Hitler. At first just to amuse himself, but soon he discovered with astonishment that for each word he scratched our troops took big cities.

Once, having decided to take a chance and put this thrilling coincidence to the test, he quit writing his curses, but regretted this almost immediately. In the newspapers and those reports "From the Soviet InfoBureau," the very same words began to repeat, over and again, like a broken record: "Stiff Enemy Resistance ... Heavy troop losses ..." Scared out of his wits, Petka then crawled back into the hayloft where he spent a feverish, sleepless night. He scratched and scratched dirty words about Hitler with a nail, all along the wooden walls, and by the next morning Comrade Levitan announced on the radio at the village council office that the troops of the Second and Third Ukrainian Fronts, under the command of Marshals Malinovsky and Tolbukhin, had—after sustained fighting—completely wiped out a 190,000-man segment of the German Army Group South and liberated the city of Budapest.

Racing back from the village council, Petka lovingly surveyed the fruits of his night's labor, then collapsed in the hay and slept through to the middle of the next day. There wasn't a happier person than he in the entire Soviet Union. Except for Marshals Tolbukhin and Malinovsky. But Petka didn't mind sharing his happiness with them.

A hundred ninety thousand Fritzes for one night's work—not bad for a kid with a nail in a hayloft.

And so Petka believed in the evil eye.

It was for precisely this reason that he was scared to so much as stick his hand out from under the table when the roach he'd been tracking scurried away to the middle of the room. That's how sorry he felt for Valerka.

He sat patiently with the matchbox old Potapikha had given him, rustling it quietly, opening and closing it to interest the runaway roach and lure it back under the table. Petka wasn't sure that roaches responded to the rustle of matchboxes, but he had no other options.

"Come here, Hans," he whispered. "Crawl over here, filthy little Adolf."

The roach picked up Petka's rustle, hesitated, but then realized what this rustle might mean for him, and shot across the room toward Valerka's bed.

Petka cursed and stretched out on the floor.

From there he could see the whole bed, a rumpled pillow and Valerka's hand hanging down, lifeless, like a regimental banner that has fallen to the enemy. Useless. Looking at Valerka's hand, it somehow occurred to Petka that he'd never seen dead birds. He'd seen plenty of birds that had been killed, but birds that died like people—slowly, from old age or illness—that he'd never come across. Because if they'd died naturally, then they should be lying around somewhere. After all, you wouldn't fall from heaven anywhere but to earth. But neither in Atamanovka itself nor around it had Petka ever seen dead birds on the earth. Only the ones killed by cats or kids. And so it seemed they flew to another place to die. Or they didn't die at all.

"Bring him a bucket," said old Potapikha. "Can't you see—the little one's getting upset. He's about to throw up."

Valerka's mama's feet tramped off into the entrance hall and returned. The wooden bucket banged the floor next to the bed.

"Hey," said Potapikha. "I've got the same kind at home. I bet Artem made it."

"I don't know," answered Valerka's mama and sat down again on the stool.

She really didn't know. And couldn't know. It was Petka who had dragged this bucket over when he and Valerka had seriously considered sneaking off to the front. They didn't make it, however. They'd waited too long for it to warm up. They didn't understand then that it got warmer much later in Atamanovka than in Germany.

"Go on, hold him tighter," said Potapikha. "Can't you see him shaking all over?"

Petka stuck his head out from under the table to have a look at what they were doing with Valerka, but old Potapikha's broad back, hunched over the bed, blocked his view.

Over her head Valerka's hand, thrust upward, was swaying. He seemed to be drowning. This hand, flung toward the ceiling from somewhere under the water, was reaching for the air with all its might.

"Hush now, hush now," Valerka's mama repeated through her white lips, pressing down on him harder and harder, trying to restrain his hands.

"Hold him tighter!" Potapikha hissed at her. "Even tighter."

"They'll smother him," thought Petka, and almost crawled out from under the table.

He had always suspected that old bats like Potapikha smothered little kids in secret. Why else would so many of them have died in the past two years? He would swear to it, even in the name of Comrade Stalin—there was something mean in the eyes of these Atamanovka ladies.

"Hey, you! Get back under there!" shouted Potapikha, who, God knows how, had detected Petka's movement behind her back.

"Hush now, hush now," Valerka's mama said again, speaking not to Valerka, but to Petka, who was sitting on the floor, gaping in fear.

Because she'd turned around, Petka finally was able to catch sight of Valerka. He was lying on his side, his face wrinkled and his eyes clamped shut. A huge paper funnel was stuck in his ear. At first it had seemed to Petka that old Potapikha was hoping to finish Valerka off by ramming an aspen stake into his head, but then he realized it was only a newspaper.

Actually, the most terrifying thing was yet to come. As if in some ghastly dream about fascists who simply couldn't be killed, old Potapikha took some matches from the stool, lit them, and carried her flames to the opening of the paper funnel. The fire leaped down towards Valerka's head. He opened his eyes, his jaw dropped wide without a sound, and Petka saw a stream of white smoke curling out onto the pillow from this open mouth.

"Ah-ah-ah!" Petka finally heard Valerka's scream. "Ah-ah-ah!" Valerka kept screaming, and his thin voice reminded Petka now of singing, now of weeping.

Old Potapikha's methods seemed a little strange to many people in Atamanovka. As for Petka, he didn't understand them at all. She treated red spots with sparrows' droppings, angina with kerosene, herpes with a mixture of tar, copper vitriol, hot sulfur, and unsalted pork fat. That sort of fat was the hardest to find, so Potapikha wasn't always successful with herpes. On the other hand, if a dog scared someone, Potapikha would immediately fumigate the victim with smoke from a burned mixture of thistle and the same dog's fur, with the result that the victim was never afraid of anything else again.

Once when Petka caught a bad cold and for some reason his legs became numb, old Potapikha had had him bundled up tightly, put in a haystack rotted from summer rain, and kept there exactly three days. In a weakened state, Petka peered out anxiously from the haystack, dozed off, sweated, and fouled himself, but at the appointed time, his legs did indeed begin to come back to life. Of course, later on he strongly suspected that they had gone numb simply from hunger and that while he was sitting in the haystack, old Potapikha had suffered a fit of generosity and so kept shoving buttered pancakes into the hay. But it was only Petka who had doubts. After this incident, old lady Darya came to believe unconditionally in Potapikha's powers, and when it was necessary, for example, to wean old man Artem off the bottle, she went straight to her.

"Eh?" said Potapikha, peering under the table. "Did you collect some? Or did you fall asleep there, you little shit?"

Petka silently held out the matchbox.

"Is that all!" She was holding the crushed roach with two fingers, as if about to poke it in Petka's face.

"There weren't any more," Petka grumbled. "I barely caught that one."

"Caught it? Is that what you think! Look what you did to it—you mashed it all up! And I need a whole one! And not one, but a dozen!"

"Well, there weren't any more."

"Look at him, still talking back. Wait, you're going to get it!"

She jabbed the hand with the roach in Petka's direction but he dodged it and nipped her on the wrist.

"He bites, the son of a whore!" old Potapikha informed Valerka's mama, who also peered solicitously under the table.

"Please don't bite, Petka," she begged. "We have to look after Valerka. Can't you see he's not doing well?"

"But why is she . . . ?"

"I'll show you 'why' right away!" said old Potapikha, rubbing her bite. "Come out of there this minute!"

"I won't!"

"Hand me a knife," Potapikha said to Valerka's mama. "I've got to check his hair. Sure, it's not so good without roaches, but lice will work too."

A minute later Petka was sitting on the stool in the middle of the room and old Potapikha was scraping around in his hair with the knife. Again he covered his eyes, this time not from fear of hexing Valerka, but from pleasure. Whether it was because his mama had gotten so tired from work lately or just forgotten about him altogether, she hadn't checked his hair for some time now. Someone scratching with a knife along his scalp always felt good.

"Looks like we're done," old Potapikha said finally and Petka, with great regret, opened his eyes.

"Do I have to go back under the table? I can't see anything from down there."

Potapikha hesitated, but then waved her hand:

"All right, stay put. If I've got to, I'll cast the spell against the evil eye. You know, yours don't seem so dark after all, now. Come on, get over here."

She dragged him to a chink in the shutters from which a ray of light was falling, narrow as a razor, placed his face under the tickling, warm sun, and Petka went blind for a moment.

"No-o-o," old Potapikha drawled from the teary darkness. "How are they dark? No, they're not dark at all. What sort of trick have you been playing on us, you little shit?"

"I didn't play any trick on you," said Petka and blinked so that his eye would tear.

Then he sat quietly in the corner, watching how old Potapikha cooked up pies from the dough into which she'd carefully folded all the lice she had found, plus the crushed roach, and how Valerka was eating these pies and then throwing up into the bucket, with old Potapikha bent over him repeating, "Now, now, this'll be over soon, this'll be over soon, darling"— and then watching how she left the yard with a little speckled hen under her arm, its neck already wrung and dangling like drunken Grandpa

Artem's tassle, and how she kept going farther and farther down the street to her grandchildren who were probably tired of waiting for her, and how she began quietly to sing her favorite song:

> *I'll be da-an-cin' reels,*
> *I'll be put-tin' on my shoes,*
> *Gonna kick up my heels,*
> *Higher than them stools.*

TRANSLATED FROM RUSSIAN BY SYLVIA MAIZELL

LUCIAN DAN TEODOROVICI

Goose Chase

I was a child, growing up at my grandparents', and one day someone stole the seven geese we had left to roam in the lane. On our street in front of everyone's yards there were patches of grass, and the villagers were in the habit of letting their geese or ducks roam free. It wasn't a problem; they never got mixed up. Geese and ducks have a herding instinct, if you can call it that with poultry: they loiter in groups near the yard where they were reared. What's more, perhaps because they assumed that some mad goose or some mad duck might nevertheless abandon its group and wander off, the peasants used to paint a mark on the wings of their property. Ours had a kind of red comma painted on the right wing, a bit like the famous Nike logo, although at the time I didn't know what the Nike logo looked like, and I doubt my grandparents knew either. But there were also geese that wore a blue cross, and others a yellow dot. Or stranger markings, even. One of our neighbors, for example, painted a little fir tree on each of his sixteen geese. With green paint, of course. Another aroused his neighbors' indignation, including my grandmother's, by painting a phallus on the wings of his geese, in brown paint. Grandma was angry because I was only eight and I shouldn't have been exposed to that sort of thing, and so she made a complaint to the militia, along with some of our other neighbors. And the man then had to pluck the feathers of those eight geese emblazoned with a brown phallus on their left wing, and in its stead he painted a square, also brown, on their right. That neighbor hated us, because a square made no sense to him, but he hadn't been able to come up with anything better at the time, because the militiaman insisted on seeing the entire operation through, the plucking of the shameful feathers and the repainting of the birds, and it all happened within the space of about half an hour. And so our neighbor didn't have time to think up anything clever, especially seeing as he was under threat of a hefty fine, though there was no law on the books banning the painting of phalluses on geese. I know this because the neighbor, as he was plucking the feathers, said he wanted to see a copy of that law, and the militiaman explained to him, calmly at first, then with less patience, that in our village *he* was the law. And in the end he even started swearing and waving his truncheon at the phallus-painter menacingly.

Grandfather too started cursing one day when he saw that our geese with their Nike mark were nowhere to be found. And he began to go from house to house, looking for them. I followed, more out of curiosity than anything else, although he let me tag along because he imagined that I, at the age of eight, must have had better eyes, and thus could spot things that he, at the age of sixty, would be unable to. In the end, it did turn out to be a good thing that he took me along. Because, while he was in a neighbor's yard, I stayed in the lane, bouncing up and down the rather deflated ball I'd brought from home so as not to get too bored during the search. And as my grandfather was talking to the neighbor in the yard, a gap-toothed, hare-lipped friend of mine came up. I told him our geese had been stolen and he said:

"I fink I know who shtole them. They were on the corner of the street." He pointed to the place. "And that Gypshy who stole our ball that time when we were playing football on the pitch by the railway shtation turned up," he added. "Honest. He was holding a shwitch and I shaw him driving the geesh up there to the water tower. I don't know if they were yoursh, but they had marks and I even thought, what the hell, gypshies don't mark their geesh."

I went into the yard after my grandfather to call him outside. Grandfather told me to leave him in peace because he had things to discuss with the neighbor. Then I explained to him that I had picked up a lead, and he abruptly broke off his discussion with the man and went outside. And my gap-toothed, hare-lipped friend told my grandfather the same story, which infuriated him no end. From my friend's description Grandfather realized that he knew the Gypsy in question: he was the son of somebody or other, I can't remember who.

The water tower was on the street that led to where the gypsies lived, up on the hill. No one had the courage to go up there, because back then it seemed the gypsies somehow lived in another world. Even the militia didn't pay them any mind. The village militiaman, the same one who had yelled at the neighbor who'd painted phalluses on his geese and threatened him with his truncheon, always used to say that the gypsies weren't his problem, that they should form their own militia if that's what they wanted, but he wasn't going to get involved. My grandfather wasn't afraid, though, and this was because he had many friends among the gypsies, what with him being a conductor on the train and all. *Chief conductor*, even, as he used to say. And over the years he had let many of the gypsies in the village ride the train for free. They respected him, and when they saw him they would say: "Long life to you, Mr. Chief, sir!" They respected him not only because he had let them travel without a ticket in the past, but also because they still had need of him, inasmuch as there were still a few years left until he retired. Once, when a neighbor's cow vanished, a neighbor who was a friend of Grandfather's, the old man had gone into the gypsies' neighborhood all by himself and come back leading the cow by a rope, only two hours later. The gypsies respected my grandfather.

Now he was cursing, though, because it was a matter of our very own geese, not some neighbor's cow. And he told me to go home, because he was going to go and fetch the geese himself. But I didn't want to. Grandfather got angry with me too then, and said he would give me two smacks on the ass if I didn't obey. But I—because it was something that had worked for me before—just went up to him and hugged him, like this, from the side. I clasped my arms around his belly and begged him to take me with him. My grandfather was fond of me, after all, and so he said only this:

"Listen, I'll take you, tadpole. But don't you budge from my side, or else I'll smack your ass ten times, not two! And don't you say a word, don't you get to talking with the gypsies . . ."

The truth is that my grandfather never smacked me, not even once, let alone twice or ten times. But he was always threatening me, and, though I have no idea why, sometimes I would even get afraid. I think now it was maybe because of his voice. Grandfather had a powerful voice. It always seemed like, if he said something, he was bound to follow through.

■ ■ ■

We entered the Gypsy neighborhood. Rickety houses, which up until then I had only seen from a distance. It somehow smelled odd even in the street, a pungent smell of oldness and damp. I was, I must admit, amazed at what I saw and I was thinking about how I would boast to all my friends that I had been down the gypsies' street and about how I would tell them about all the things they'd never seen. At the same time, I was proud of my grandfather, because the other children's grandparents or parents would never have had the courage to go there—let alone hand in hand with their children or grandchildren.

Somewhere in front of us, on the right, we saw a few men and women gathered in a yard. I thought that must be where we were going, because my grandfather kept looking at them as we drew closer. But at the house right before, my grandfather stopped in front of an old fence, whose slats were largely rotten, broken, or missing, and unfastened the latch of the little gate. He went into the yard, dragging me behind him. In the yard, instead of a dog, there was a rather skinny pig, which was rooting with its snout under the doorframe. The door was crooked, hanging from a single hinge, and the pig kept thrusting its snout under, and the door was rattling around as though about to fall off at any moment. My grandfather aimed at kick at the pig, which squealed, looked at him, but didn't budge. And then my grandfather gave it another kick. The pig moved aside, squealing again, and I laughed. It was funny how the pig glared at my father from where it decided to settle, about six feet away. Then my grandfather knocked at that door which was barely hanging from its hinge, and I thought it was sure to fall off. It didn't fall off; it opened. And in the doorway appeared a Gypsy with wisps of white hair poking out from under his hat. He said:

"Well . . ."

And my grandfather greeted him.

"Long life to you," he said.

"Ah," went the old Gypsy. "Long life to you, Mr. Chief, sir!"

Then the man fell silent and looked at Grandfather, and Grandfather seemed somewhat embarrassed. He didn't know how to begin.

"Well?" went the Gypsy.

"Er," said my grandfather, "won't you come out so that we can talk?"

The Gypsy looked toward the yard next door, where we could see the men and women gathered, nodded his head, took off his hat, brushed it off, then put it back on his head, and looked at Grandfather once more.

"I'll come out," he said.

Grandfather stood aside, the old Gypsy came out and pulled his door shut behind him, after which he pointed to a log on the ground. Grandfather sat down, and I sat down beside him. And the old Gypsy looked around him, trying to find something, and at last he saw the upright log nearby, the one used for chopping wood, with an axe leaning on it. And on the log, as well as on the axe-head, there were traces of blood, but the old

Gypsy went and brought the log over. He placed it in front of ours, and sat right down on top of the blood.

"Well," said he, "what's it to be, Mr. Chief, sir? You ain't just here to pass the time of day, eh?"

"No," Grandfather shook his head. "I have chores to do at home."

"Well?"

"Look here," my grandfather scratched the top of his head, "someone told me something about your kid."

"Well?"

"I have seven or so geese," began my grandfather. "And today I couldn't find them."

The old Gypsy frowned. He put his hand on his head, on his hat, then took it off.

"Someone said that he saw your kid bringing them this way."

The old Gypsy stood up. He went like this, with his hands—as though to say "what the hell am I supposed to do now?," and in one hand, as I said, he was holding his hat. Then he flung his hat onto the ground, into the dust. And the skinny pig went up to the hat, snuffling around it with its snout. And the old Gypsy gave the pig a kick in the belly, but with such fury that the pig took off at once, squealing like it would drop dead. After that, the man went into the house.

I looked at my grandfather; I pulled his sleeve to make him look at me.

"What is it?" I asked him. "Why did he go back inside?"

"Shut up," my grandfather said.

And no sooner had he said that than the door which was barely hanging from its hinge moved again, and from behind it emerged the old Gypsy, dragging by his coat that other Gypsy who had stolen our ball that time when we were playing football on the pitch by the station. They came to a halt in front of us, and the old Gypsy whacked the young Gypsy across the back of the head.

"Ow, Papa!" he howled. "Why you hitting me?"

"You fucking halfwit," his father said, "them geese you pinched was the Chief's! Them you took?"

And he whacked him over the head again and kicked his behind. I was starting to get scared, and so I squeezed my grandfather tightly by the hand, then I felt my grandfather squeeze my hand back and I was reassured.

The old Gypsy kept on hitting his son, and his son kept bawling and saying: "Stop hitting me, Papa!" At one point, between two blows, the kid looked at me with so much hatred that it froze my insides and once again I squeezed my grandfather's hand, and he squeezed mine back and I was reassured. In the end, the old Gypsy calmed down or else he just got tired—but in any case he gave the young Gypsy one more clout across the nape and sent him into the house. Then he wiped the sweat from his brow, looked around him, spat, and bent down to pick up his hat. And then he came over to us and sat down on the blood-smeared stump once more.

"Well," he said, "I didn't know, Mr. Chief, sir. That's all. So what can I do now?"

"Well," said my grandfather, "give them back to me and we'll forget it."

The Gypsy put his hat on, disheartened.

"I'll give you them," he muttered. "But there's only five."

"Only five? I just told you that I have seven."

"That's as many as you had," said the old Gypsy. "On my life, yes, that's as many as you had."

"Well, then?"

"Well, then . . . I cut two, 'cause I didn't know they was yours, Mr. Chief, sir. Look," he pointed down at the stump on which he was sitting: "I cut them."

Fresh blood had recently trickled down the log, and the old Gypsy was pointing at it with his finger, by way of proof, and we followed his finger, looking.

"Two?" asked my grandfather, amazed.

"But how was I to know, damn it!" said the old Gypsy, and then he looked toward the house: "I could wring his neck, I could!" Then to us: "I didn't know, Mr. Chief, sir. My woman made us fried meat and soup, it's still cooking on the stove, so it is."

"But two?" my grandfather repeated, still amazed.

The old Gypsy waved his hands again. Grandfather sighed.

"Well," he said, "I'll take back the other five. And we'll sort it out somehow with the other two."

I had begun to relax, especially given that it really did seem, from the old Gypsy's expression, that he was sincerely sorry—so I was convinced that the whole affair would sort itself out. Except that, just as I had begun to relax, there were screams from the neighboring yard, the one where all the people were gathered. And we all turned in that direction. My grandfather rose and looked over the old Gypsy's head. I looked around the old Gypsy to the side. And the old Gypsy swiveled his head.

Two burly gypsies were dragging a third into the yard next door, and the prostrate third had taken quite a beating. They were all about a hundred feet away, but it was clear how severely he'd been hurt. And then, the two who were carrying him let him fall into the dust. One of them bent down and ripped the hurt man's shirt off. Then the other produced a whip, the sort you'd use to drive horses, and started lashing the fallen Gypsy's back. My fear was back. And because, leaning sideways, I'd had to let go of my grandfather's hand, I quickly reached out and squeezed it. Then my grandfather said to me:

"Listen, what are you looking at, anyway? Haven't you got anything else to look at? Go on, look at that pig instead!"

The pig was standing quietly next to our log, with its snout raised, sniffing the air. The old Gypsy stood up and said to my grandfather:

"Well, let's move away some. It's none of our business."

And he dragged the blood-smeared log over to the wall of his house.

"Look," said my grandfather, "if you just give us the geese, we'll be on our way. And we'll talk later about some sort of arrangement for the missing two."

"Sit, Mr. Chief, sir," said the old Gypsy, a note of compassion in his voice now. "You've not come at a good time. Now's not the time to be going into the lane driving a gaggle of geese, you know."

Then Grandfather stood up too and pulled me over to the wall. We both leaned against it.

"Do you have a cigarette, Mr. Chief, sir?" the old Gypsy asked my grandfather, as soon as he had sat back down on his log.

"I do," said Grandfather.

And he pulled out a packet of Mărășeștis, extracting a cigarette with two fingers, which he then gave to our host. Soon there was one between his own lips as well. My grandfather didn't smoke. Or rather he smoked very rarely. He always kept a packet of Mărășeștis on him, and he would smoke one of the cigarettes now and then, but not at all often. Only when he did. And, as I said, he only rarely did. Now he pulled a box of matches from his pocket, and lit his Mărășești. Then he held the lighted match to the old Gypsy's Mărășești. And they both began to smoke.

"But what's all that there?" asked Grandfather, pointing at the yard next door.

Whence could be heard the cracks of the whip and the howls of the one being whipped.

"Well, our folk," said the old Gypsy.

I leaned forward a little and again looked into the yard next door. The fallen man was still being whipped on his back. He was howling.

"Not my business," the old Gypsy went on. "His kin are giving him a licking. If he's done wrong, that's what he deserves," he added.

Grandfather pulled my head toward him.

"What are you doing? Haven't you got anything better to look at? Look at the pig," he said.

I looked at the pig. It had come up to the old Gypsy, who gave it a kick in the rump.

"Scram," he told the pig and spat at it. "Get going, damn you."

Then he took another puff on his cigarette, and the pig went away.

"But what happened?" insisted Grandfather.

"I wouldn't like to say," said the old Gypsy, "with your boy around, Mr. Chief, sir. I wouldn't like to say. He was tried, is all."

"Tell me," said Grandfather. "The boy's old enough."

"Well, what can I say? If he couldn't keep his *pelenghero* in his pants!"

"Aha," went Grandfather, but I understood nothing. "And they tried him, did they? Isn't a man allowed to go out once in a while and . . ."

He made a sign.

"Well, that he is!" said the old Gypsy. "But not with our married women . . ."

"Aha," said Grandfather, and I began to understand, vaguely, how things stood. "And they caught him?"

"Worse," said the old Gypsy. "He was drunk on a few bottles of *mol* and got to bragging. Said she was seventeen years old. Didn't say which. Well, we've four married women of seventeen, none others. Them four there."

The Gypsy pointed with his finger. Grandfather leaned forward. I leaned forward too. In the doorway there were, indeed, four Gypsy women, who were looking at the man on the ground. They weren't weeping; they weren't afraid. They were just standing there. And the one on the ground was no longer howling, he was just lying there, and it was plain—even from a hundred feet away—that he was covered in blood.

"Not one of them said it was her. And now the women's kinfolk and his kinfolk, they're beating him so that he'll tell. Me, I'd tell, 'cause I wouldn't lose my own hide for the sake of some slut. But he's crazy. He'll make them beat him till he tells.

"What will happen to him if he doesn't tell? How long will they beat him?"

"Till he tells."

"What if he won't tell? They'll end up beating him to death."

"Well, that's his misfortune. If he's crazy and won't tell."

"And what'll happen to her if they find out who she is?"

"Well!" went the old Gypsy and waved his hand like this. "Well," he added. "We have a law. Her husband hangs her by his own hand."

"Aha," went Grandfather.

"It's none of our business," said the old Gypsy and tossed away his Mărăşeşti, trampling it with his worn-out shoe. "But you can't be leaving now with them geese."

The old Gypsy sucked his gums and nodded.

"Don't know why the hell he don't tell. But it's none of our business, is it?"

"No," agreed my grandfather.

"We have to reckon up for them two geese."

"Then," said Grandfather, "I'll put it to you like this: you'll send your boy to work two days in my field for each goose. Potato picking."

The old Gypsy again took his hat in his hand. He scratched his head.

"He's lazy . . ."

"Lazy or no, I'm telling you this is how we'll make our peace," my grandfather said.

"Four days?" asked the Gypsy.

"Yes."

"Got another cigarette?"

The old man took out the packet of Mărăşeştis again. He extracted a cigarette with two fingers and handed it to the old Gypsy. Then he took the box of matches from his pocket, lit one, and held it to the cigarette between our host's lips.

I leaned forward again. The two burly men had lifted the fallen Gypsy off the ground. Now they were dragging him to the house. They stood him up against the wall. But the accused slid down and fell on his rump. Then he fell sideways, scraping the wall, next to the feet of the four women who were in the doorway. One of the burly gypsies kicked him in the guts, and the other kicked him right in the face. I closed my eyes for a moment, waiting to hear his cries, but there was nothing. Then I opened them and saw that the first burly Gypsy, the one who had kicked him in the guts, had pulled out a knife. And he said something to the women, waving the knife back and forth in front of their faces. They flinched somewhat, but didn't answer. Then, the burly Gypsy tossed the knife in the air and caught it by the handle, blade down. And he leaned toward the Gypsy fallen at the women's feet.

My grandfather said, "What the hell are you doing? Look at that pig, how funny it is."

He pulled me by the coat. The pig was sprawled on the ground next to the log, rubbing its back against it. I was quite frightened and didn't find the pig at all funny now. But I went on watching it, in silence, because my grandfather wouldn't let me look into the yard next door.

The old Gypsy was silent. And he smoked his Mărăşeşti staring at the ground. But now and then he would suck his gums and spit. At one point he started to cough, with a rattle in his throat, and I looked up at him. His Adam's apple was quivering oddly, it would move up his throat, come back down, then move up again as he coughed. As though it were a ball sliding up and down under his old skin: up-down-up-down. As though it were alive, in fact. A mouse trapped under a carpet. And after he had done coughing, he asked Grandfather for yet another cigarette, and he gave him one, making exactly the same gestures as before. And the old Gypsy smoked the third cigarette in silence. But now and then he would turn his head and gaze into the other yard. Then, after he tossed away the third cigarette, he stood up and said to my grandfather:

"I think you can leave now, Mr. Chief, sir. Let me give you the geese."

He stood up and my grandfather followed him to the coop. I wanted to come too. But my grandfather barred my way with his hand.

"You stay here," he said. "Wait here with the pig and I'll be back right away."

But the pig had vanished somewhere. The door of the house was wide open and I suspected that the pig had gone inside, because there was nowhere else it could be. And then I took a step forward, moving away from the wall, and I looked into the yard next door.

But there was no one there. At least, no one standing. There was only the accused, no one else. He was lying stretched out in front of the door. The others had left. I took a few steps forward, going over to the fence. The beaten Gypsy's face was still covered in blood, I could see that. And not only his face. His upper body was all furrowed with red lines; there was blood clotting all over his body. I couldn't get a closer look because the geese driven by my grandfather were honking behind me now, and he shouted:

"What the hell are you doing over there? I told you to stay with the pig by the house."

"But the pig's gone," I said.

Grandfather looked and saw for himself that the pig was no longer in the yard. Behind Grandfather came the old Gypsy. Grandfather was holding a switch and driving the geese, and they were honking. They were unruly and wouldn't form a line to go through the gate. And so I went to one side and helped Grandfather to drive them properly.

"Just you wait and see what a smack on the ass I'm going to give you for not listening," my grandfather said.

The old Gypsy opened the gate and the geese went out into the lane. I went out after them, but Grandfather stopped in front of the gate and shook the old Gypsy's hand.

"So it's settled, four days, as we agreed," said Grandfather.

The old Gypsy nodded.

"I'm sorry, Mr. Chief, sir," he said. "Don't be angry, I didn't know they was yours."

"All right, no great harm done," said Grandfather. "Let's forget it."

"Well, long life to you, Mr. Chief, sir," said the old Gypsy.

Grandfather saluted him, raising two fingers to his temple. Then he began to drive the five geese along the lane. I walked in silence alongside, now on one side, now on the other, so that our geese wouldn't stray off. Then we left the gypsies' neighborhood, and before us rose the water tower. And it wasn't until then that my grandfather spoke.

"What's on your mind, tadpole?" he said.

That's what he used to call me, tadpole.

TRANSLATED FROM ROMANIAN BY ALISTAIR IAN BLYTH

GONÇALO M. TAVARES

Six Tales

THE INGENUOUS COUNTRY

Sadness was so prevalent that people were paid to smile. Amid the city crowds, plainclothes men watched for the few smiling citizens that happened to pass by and, discreetly, ordered them to stop.

They introduced themselves—"We're with the government," they said—and then asked to see the smiler's ID. They took down his or her name and address.

At the end of the month, these smiling citizens received a check. Their payment arrived with a document that read, for example, "During the month of February you were observed smiling in the street three times."

Well then, in a very short time the emotional climate of the country was completely transformed by this practice. Whether because of their greed or simply because the payments had actually changed their temperament, in two years' time the country became known for "the impressive and unflagging optimism of its citizens," as one international news agency put it.

The state smile subsidies ended shortly thereafter, but since no one ever informed the citizens of this, they all retained their stupid, repugnant, inadequate, useless, meaningless smiles.

THE OLD MAN

Since he didn't have enough time to actually read them—he was gradually, week by week, going blind—the old man at least wanted to read the titles of all the books in the biggest library in the world. If the essence of a book is contained in its title, he would then, by reading every title in the catalog, have absorbed the essence of the entire library.

He began on the first of January at eight in the morning. He started with the North Wing.

With his head tilted to one side, then to the other, and back again—like he was out of his mind, or at least suffering from some sort of palsy—he read each title off the spine of each book.

To reach the highest shelves he climbed up the steps of a metal stepladder provided for that very purpose.

Exhaustively meticulous, he dragged the stepladder along with him on his rounds so that not a single book, on whatever shelf, would escape his notice.

Yes, he was exhaustive—he didn't miss a single book—but it was slow work. It wasn't until June that he reached the South Wing of the library, and he wasn't getting any younger: he was now almost blind. At this pace he would probably never get through the second wing of the library. Death and total sightlessness were approaching side by side.

The librarians and patrons both cheered him on during his final days, and some even helped him move his ladder.

"I'm about to go completely blind," the old man said again and again. But everyone understood this to mean, "I'm about to die."

But the old man was still able to read, albeit with increasing difficulty. He now read like a child just learning to sound out words: letter by letter.

He arrived at the last book in the library. He read the title with extraordinary difficulty. Afterward he sat down in a chair, breathing heavily. Instinctively, people began to clap: employees and patrons of the library displayed their admiration for his incredible achievement, for his perseverance.

The old man stayed in his chair.

And there he remains, without moving, seated in precisely the same position. There are those who say he's so happy, he just can't die.

THE DANCE

They believed it. That dancing with someone wasn't simply a series of movements more or less coordinated between two people. Far from it.

Dance wasn't a merely physical relationship, but a spiritual one, they said. Moving through dance steps with a partner was like sharing in some final, definitive act.

It was as if, they said, at its best, that dance began a sort of osmosis between dancers, in which two were transformed into one: their substances, their minds becoming equally balanced, so that in the end no imbalance could remain. It wouldn't be possible for a couple to dance "harmoniously," as they say, without this intimate circulation of intangible elements taking place between the partners.

If one person is considerably more irritable than the other, in the end this doesn't make much difference: one partner might gain, as it were, a few grams of a negative characteristic, while the other would lose those same few.

Thus, they saw dance as an elegant means of correcting intellectual, physical, moral, economic, cultural, behavioral, and other types of imbalances.

The truth is, however, that when people realized the effect that their dances were having, they stopped dancing entirely. No one wanted to lose to their partners whatever uniqe admixture of qualities they believed they possessed. (People are generally so pleased with at least one part of themselves that they naturally assume they'll be on the losing end of any such exchange, no matter who their partner is.) Some dancers were afraid of losing some of their intelligence, others didn't want to lose any of their strength, others their money, others their culture.

Couples no longer danced. Only solo dancing remained. One or another dancer still going through their steps, as if for old time's sake, in front of a mirror.

THE ANTHEM

Five men from different countries started singing their national anthems all at the same time. Thus: five different songs, five different languages, five rhythms.

Such chaos could only confuse anyone who happened to hear it.

Words from one language mixed with the words of another, rhythms from the different songs careened toward one another and collided like solid objects, finally retreating.

At times it seemed that a word from one language was actually sabotaging the words of another.

It became clear that, deep down, this was a war of voices, rhythms, and words.

Five songs behaving like five armies.

Soon, other songs were added to this sonorous conflict. Passersby belonging to any other country joined the choir. They couldn't tolerate hearing their own national anthem left out of the mix.

We were in a fairly cosmopolitan city. In a matter of hours, more than six-dozen singers were there on that busy sidewalk, each one singing his anthem.

For those who passed by without paying much attention, the noise sounded something like the screams that rise from the earth after an aerial bombardment.

But suddenly all the singers all shut up. And in a few seconds the situation changed completely.

Now silent, they could very well have all come from the same country. The fight was over.

"Silence is quite calming," thought an old woman who still liked to try and take notice of what went on around her.

But although they were now silent, the singers weren't still.

Each one was moving to take the loaded gun out of their pocket. This would, they were sure, resolve the dispute.

THE MOTHER AND HER THREE CHILDREN

The mother walks alone, already headless and looking for her three children. She is in the backyard; her head was chopped off, and the blood that flows out creates a trail, an itinerary, which will be essential if her three children are to find her. The mother would like to find her three children herself, but she is headless—and thus this task is beyond her.

The mother runs around headless in the backyard and a number of chickens edge away from her, look up, and fail to recognize this human being-shaped thing.

The backyard is big and the woman who got her head cut off continues to proceed, step by step, a little like she's been blindfolded. Yes, it is like the children's game, "Marco Polo"—but this woman wasn't blindfolded, as we hope to make clear, her head was cut off with an axe. She goes along calling for her children (but how can she yell?) and all of a sudden: she is lost. The headless woman is lost in what is most certainly a labyrinth, and in this labyrinth she keeps passing a wide variety of animals: goats, pigs, chickens, a horse—you know, animals. Two pigs are copulating, but the headless woman doesn't see them.

The three children have entered the labyrinth as well and follow their mother's trail of blood.

The mother knows that the blood she leaks onto the ground is also the only way she will be able to find their way out of the maze, later on. Because of this she is afraid to bleed too much too quickly, but she knows she can't stop bleeding. Sometimes she raises her right hand up to her neck, to the spot where her head was sliced off, and scoops out, with her hand, a little of the blood, which she then trickles on the ground deliberately. The smell of blood is thick and intense; it will be easy for her to follow it back later.

But the three children, following behind her, clean the blood off the ground as they call out to her. The youngest of the children is the last, and it is his responsibility to wipe away even the slightest trace of their mother's blood. It's a mess, what a shame, the oldest child had said. Shame, shame, repeated the middle one.

They call out for their mother, but their mother doesn't hear. She has no head, she can't hear a thing. (Though we remain confused as to her ability to yell without a head.) Up ahead she calls out for her children; the children hear something up ahead and continue to follow the trail of blood.

At some point the mother's voice started to become clearer. The three children ran on. At front, the oldest; at the rear, the youngest. All of a sudden mother and children find each other. The mother has no head, and the oldest child screams, the middle one cries, and the youngest trembles.

The mother, even without her head, tries to calm them. She asks them if they saw her head somewhere along the way.

They reply that they didn't.

But they want to know how all of this happened.

How was it cut off? asks the oldest.

Who cut it off? asks the middle child.

Why? asks the youngest child.

The mother responds:

With an axe.

It was your father.

Because he wanted to have more space on the bed.

The children sit in silence for a few moments, but then the oldest child screams, the middle one cries, and the youngest trembles.

While they go on in this fashion, a sudden flash of lightning, followed by thunder, right above the labyrinth, frightens them all; the light and sound are impressive.

All of them go silent out of fear and look up, including the mother, who can't do much more than flex the piece of her neck that's still intact.

Taking advantage of the momentary calm, the mother again asks:

Did you see my head?

How big was it? asks the oldest.

How much did it weigh? asks the middle one.

Are its eyes open? asks the youngest.

This size, says the mother, her hands above her neck, miming the exact size.

More than seven kilos, that's what it weighed.

And yes, its eyes are open.

If my head sees you, it will recognize you. Please, go find it.

The three children immediately turn around and run off to find the head. The oldest child runs the fastest, the middle one a little slower, and the youngest the slowest. The middle one looks back and thinks about returning to wait with his mother, but seeing his younger brother following him, he continues to press on.

The youngest looks back and thinks about returning to wait with his mother, but seeing that his two older brothers are still running ahead, he does the same. Let's go, let's go! says the oldest, up ahead.

The three of them run for three days and three nights, until, at the beginning of the fourth day, right at sunrise, they find themselves in front of their mother's head, which is on the ground in the backyard. They had already left the labyrinth behind, and now introduced themselves to the head of their mother:

I am your oldest son.

But their mother's head does not recognize him.

I'm the middle one.

But their mother's head does not recognize him.

I'm the youngest son.

But their mother's head does not recognize him.

Their mother's head does not recognize any of them. The oldest son screams, the middle one cries, the youngest one trembles.

But after their sadness they become angry. The oldest insults the head of their mother, the middle one spits at it, and the youngest kicks it.

They abandon the head and decide to return to the labyrinth and reunite with their mother's headless body—the body that recognized them.

They enter the labyrinth at great speed, but soon slow down.

It's this way, says the oldest.

No, it's this way, says the middle one, pointing to another path.

It's this way, says the youngest, pointing to a third.

It is impossible to know the right way. They themselves, out of shame, had cleaned the blood that indicated their mother's path, and now they don't know which way to go. There was no sign of her trail left to follow.

After discussing it, each one chooses to go his own way.

The three of them decide that whoever finds their mother will yell out so that the others can hear. The others will then follow the voice—and then we'll all end up together, they say.

Thus decided, each one takes off on his own path at great speed, calling out for their mother.

The oldest yells.

The middle one yells.

The youngest yells.

The oldest son finds their headless mother's body.

She is still able to mumble: I've lost a lot of blood.

She is dying.

The oldest son tries to yell out, but nothing comes out. Not a sound. He is mute. Or is pretending to be.

Now free from his brothers, he kneels down over the body of his dying mother.

THE COIN

Vass Kartopeck bent over to pick up the coin for the second time.

"Did it again!" the young woman with him shouted.

And laughed.

In one sense, Vass Kartopeck was sick. Annoying blotches marred his features below his eyes and along his neck, which compelled him to constantly rub at his rash in order to soothe what he called "a disquieting enthusiasm on the part of my face."

On a night some time ago, a few months back, the young woman, after they had made love, began, with a certain controlled perversity, to count his dark blotches: one, two, three, four . . .

But only after they made love.

"You're rich, sir!" she teased, "More than fourteen blotches!"

Kartopeck wiped at them incessantly with his right hand, especially the blotches right below his eyes.

At his last appointment, which his mother had attended as well, the doctor had told him: "They're blotches, nothing more, what do you want me to do? If you believe that looking good is really the only sign of good health, then you are indeed sick, sir. If not, forget about it. The blotches are unsightly, of course, but there are some people without any blotches who are much uglier than you."

At this point, Kartopeck helped his mother out of the examination room. She didn't understand any of it; she had long since lost the minimum faculties necessary to live on her own. *A man with a scarred face is helping a senile woman cross the street*, thought Kartopeck, trying to distract himself from the stares of the old men watching their progress.

Days later, his face's "enthusiasm" worsened: the blotches burned now, if *calmly*, with a gentle flame, said Kartopeck.

Despite this, the young woman wouldn't stop making fun of him. Though he'd remunerated her quite generously, she wouldn't stop trying Mr. Kartopeck's patience. First, she counted the coins he had given her, putting them in a little stack: one, two, three, four, five . . . When the stack fell over—which happened a number of times—the young woman started counting all over again: one, two, three, four . . . There were fourteen coins.

The counting of the coins was followed—after a short break—by the counting of the blotches on Kartopeck's face, and then by the young woman's victorious and obscene smile.

"Eleven blotches," she said first.

And then, seconds later, "Fourteen little coins!" And again she smiled at Mr. Vass Kartopeck.

Kartopeck wore unsophisticated clothes. It was clear that he didn't let the city have an excessive influence on the way he dressed. Other elements of his personality proceeded from this preference. Or else had caused it. Kartopeck rarely went to the city center. Whenever he did, he couldn't help but feel uneasy. This usually led to a diatribe about the horrible demands city life makes on its citizens.

It sometimes seemed as though the crowds were made up of people furtively making the same useless gestures over and again. These were men attempting to resist the ubiquitous disorder of their lives and likewise ignore the fact that they couldn't control the ceaseless onslaught of time— the century and this one insignificant day both ticking along whether they liked it or not—by burying themselves in the constant tumult of the city and its myriad rituals, for instance raising their arms, fingers out-stretched, in order to attract the attention of the fastest means of trans-portation. But no, this wasn't a form of resistance: these were merely the movements of bodies more accustomed to acquiescing than to demand-ing. Thus thought Vass Kartopeck, who, in his particular little world—an insignificant sort of world to those busy people, to be sure—was accus-tomed to giving orders.

The doctor saw him again. Only six months had passed, and meanwhile something had occurred that is absolutely relevant to this account: the death of Kartopeck's mother.

Kartopeck entered the doctor's office with the young woman, and the two of them sat down to wait. The receptionist recognized him. After a quick glance, she asked, "Is it worse?"

"Yes," he replied.

The blotches had increased in size, and now an ashlike color—unheard of in the medical field—spread out from the center of each individual blotch. Since she was trained to deal with things that would disgust lay-men, the receptionist didn't lapse into the usual grimace that people tended to make when first surprised by that face. It had indeed taken on, let's say, a monstrous appearance. It was as if Kartopeck's facial abnormal-ity had, after an initial period of hesitation, evolved into an altogether different form, one no longer fit for civilized society. Kartopeck's face had become horrendous, indecent. It was like he was assaulting the people who saw it. Kartopeck couldn't have caused a greater moral affront to any spectators if he had stripped naked there in the middle of the waiting room, in front of all the other patients. The ugliness of his face had be-come metaphysical. It was a sin, not just a physical blemish.

The young woman who was with him certainly didn't go unnoticed ei-ther. The way she dressed revealed two things: that she wasn't from the city, and that she was a prostitute. She couldn't stop fidgeting in her seat, adjusting her skirt in an absurd gesture of modesty, which in any case came across as feigned, since it was accompanied by a provocative stare that swept across the entire waiting room and challenged everyone in it. Being there made her feel beautiful.

The discomfort that the couple caused for everyone else quickly reached a crisis point. With some made-up excuse, one of the older women who was waiting to see the doctor got up and left.

"Where's your mother?" asked the receptionist.

"She died," responded Kartopeck, who was already on his feet, ready to be called. "Two months ago," he added.

The receptionist lowered her eyes. Now she'd made matters worse by being indiscreet.

Then it was finally Kartopeck's turn. His young woman stayed in the waiting room, at the doctor's request.

She smiled at everyone now. It flattered her that the doctor had addressed her specifically.

"Your face is much worse!" the doctor announced.

And they sat down.

"But I have your analyses here," he continued. "There is no medical problem, here. You, Mr. Kartopeck, are not sick. This is clearly an external problem, and I mean entirely external, there's no trace of any abnormality within your organism itself, nor is there any reason to suspect that whatever is on your face is making its way inside. Sure, it's unpleasant to be deformed, but on the medical side of things all we can do is recommend some products to help relieve the irritation. You're not going to die a single minute earlier just because your face has developed this . . . difficulty."

Kartopeck was relieved: in the past few weeks he had come to the conclusion that his blotches must be the equivalent of a death sentence. He had even practiced the courageous way that he would respond to the words that he was certain he'd hear: *You only have six months to live!*

So, the doctor's reassurances were received more or less like a victory.

The rest of the examination was quick. Before the doctor opened the door for him to leave, Vass Kartopeck—wanting to show his gratitude—shoved his right hand into his pocket and pulled out a coin, which he held out to the doctor. The doctor refused to accept this token by shifting his weight away from Kartopeck and, doing his best not to laugh, smiling apologetically:

"One doesn't really tip doctors," he said. "At least not in the city. Keep it for yourself."

Vass Kartopeck, embarrassed, shut his hand around the coin: he was a yokel, he told himself, nothing but a yokel! And once again, he'd made this quite clear. I'm an imbecile, he mumbled to himself.

"Best wishes," said the doctor, to both Kartopeck and the young woman.

In the middle of the street, no more than two hundred meters from the spot where the precise center of the city was marked on the street, Kartopeck dropped his coin for the second time.

"Again!" exclaimed Kartopeck, irritated.

And the young woman laughed.

TRANSLATED FROM PORTUGUESE BY RHETT MCNEIL

OLGA TOKARCZUK

The Ugliest Woman in the World

He married the ugliest woman in the world. As a widely known circus impresario, he made a special trip to Vienna to see her. It wasn't a premeditated act at all—it never occurred to him beforehand that he might make her his wife. But once he had seen her, once he had weathered the first shock, he couldn't tear his eyes away from her. She had a large head covered in growths and lumps. Her small, ever-tearing eyes were set close under her low, furrowed brow. From a distance they looked like narrow chinks. Her nose looked as if it was broken in many places, and its tip was a livid blue, covered in sparse bristles. Her mouth was huge and swollen, always hanging open, always wet, with some sharply pointed teeth inside it. To top it all off, as if that wasn't enough, her face sprouted long, straggling, silken hairs.

The first time he saw her she emerged from behind the cardboard scenery of a traveling circus to show herself to the audience. A cry of surprise and disgust went rolling over the heads of the crowd and fell at her feet. She may have been smiling, but it looked like a woeful grimace. She stood very still, conscious of the fact that dozens of eyes were staring at her, avidly drinking in every detail, so that the audience members could describe this face to their friends and neighbors or to their own children, to be able to summon it up again, as they compared it with their own faces in the mirror—and then breathe a sigh of relief. She stood patiently, perhaps with a sense of superiority, as she gazed over their heads toward the roofs of the houses beyond.

After a lengthy silence, swollen with astonishment, someone finally shouted: "Tell us about yourself!"

She peered into the crowd, to the spot where the voice had come from. She was searching for the person who had said it, but just then a stout lady ringmaster ran out from behind the cardboard wings and answered on behalf of the Ugliest Woman in the World: "She doesn't talk."

"Then you tell us her story," the voice requested, so the stout lady cleared her throat and started speaking.

After the performance, as he drank a cup of tea with her by the little tin stove that heated the inside of the circus trailer, he found her to be quite clever. Of course she could speak, and make perfect sense too. He observed her closely, wrestling with his own fascination with this freak of nature. She could see right through him.

"You thought my speech would be just as bizarre and repulsive as my face, didn't you?" she asked.

He didn't answer.

She drank her tea in the Russian manner, pouring it from a samovar into small cups with no handles, nibbling at a sugar lump between each sip.

He quite soon found that she spoke many languages, but apparently none of them too well. Now and then she shifted from one language into another. It was no cause for surprise—since early childhood she had grown up in the circus, in an international troupe full of grotesques of every possible stripe, never in the same place twice.

"I know what you're thinking," she said again, looking at him with those puffy little animal eyes. After a short silence she added: "Anyone who hasn't got a mother hasn't got a mother tongue either. I use many languages, but none of them is my own."

He didn't dare reply. Suddenly she had begun to get on his nerves, though he wasn't sure why. She was making witty remarks, she was coherent and specific—not at all what he'd been expecting.

So he bid her farewell, and to his astonishment she gave him her hand—a very feminine gesture. The gesture of a lady, in fact; and a perfectly lovely hand it was, too. He bowed down toward it, but didn't touch it with his lips.

As he lay on his back in his hotel bed he was still thinking about her. He stared ahead into the damp, stuffy hotel darkness—the sort of deep dark that invited his imagination to kick into gear. He lay there wondering what it must be like to be her, what it felt like from inside, how the world might look through eyes like a pig's eyes, what it must be like to breathe in air through such a misshapen nose—did she even smell the same things as normal people? And what would it be like to touch a body like that every day while washing, or scratching, while doing all the usual little things?

Never once did he feel sorry for her. If he had sympathized with her, he never would have thought of proposing.

Some people used to tell this story as though it were an unhappy love affair, saying that his heart had somehow gazed directly into hers, and that he'd fallen in love with the sweet-natured angel he saw inside her, despite her repulsive face. But no, it was nothing of the sort—that first night after meeting her he simply couldn't stop imagining what it would be like to make love to such a creature, to kiss her and undress her.

He hovered around the circus for the next few weeks. He would leave and always come back again. He gained the trust of the manager, and negotiated a contract for the troupe in Brno. He followed them there, and the circus people began to regard him as one of their own. They let him sell the tickets, then later he took over from the fat lady ringmaster—and it has to be said he was good at this job, warming up the audience before the shoddily painted curtain was raised.

"Close your eyes," he cried. "Especially women and children, because the ugliness of this creature is hard for sensitive eyes to bear. No one who has seen this freak of nature is ever able to fall asleep in peace again. Some people have even lost their faith in the Creator . . ."

At this point he hung his head, seemingly leaving this sentence incomplete, though in fact it wasn't—he didn't know what else to say. He figured the word "Creator" put everything in its proper light. Some people might lose their faith in this Creator, looking at the woman waiting behind the curtain, but he himself had become convinced of the opposite: if anything, the Creator had demonstrated His existence by singling the impresario out, bestowing this opportunity upon him. The Ugliest Woman in the World. Some idiots fought duels and killed each other over beautiful women. Some idiots gave away their fortunes at a woman's whim. But he was not like them. The Ugliest Woman engaged his affections like a sad, domesticated animal. She was different from all other women, and she even provided him financial opportunities into the bargain. If he made her his wife he'd be set apart—special. He'd have something other people didn't have.

He started buying her flowers—not special bouquets, just cheap little bunches wrapped in foil with a flimsy tissue paper bow; or he'd give her a cotton neckerchief, a glossy ribbon, or a small box of pralines. Then he'd watch, hypnotized, as she tied the ribbon round her forehead, and instead of being an adornment, the colorful bow would become a horror. And he'd watch as she sucked the chocolates with her oversized, bulging tongue, causing brown saliva to form between her wide-spaced teeth and dribble down her bristle-coated chin.

He liked to look at her when she didn't know he was watching. He'd sneak off in the morning and hide behind the tent or the trailer, he'd sneak off in order to lurk nearby and watch her for hours on end, even through the cracks in the wooden fence. She used to sunbathe, and while she did she'd spend ages slowly combing her straggly hair, as if in a trance, plaiting it into skinny braids and then immediately undoing it again. Or else she would crochet, the needles glittering in the sunlight as they stabbed at the noisy air of the circus. Or, in a loose shirt, with her arms bare, she would launder her clothes in a washtub. The skin on her arms and upper chest was covered in pale fur. It looked pretty. Soft, like an animal's.

He needed this spying, because day by day his disgust was lessening, melting in the sun, disappearing like a puddle on a hot afternoon. Gradually his eyes were growing used to the painful asymmetry of her, the broken proportions, all her shortcomings and excesses. Sometimes he even thought she looked ordinary.

Whenever he began to feel uneasy, he told them all he was going away on important business, that he had a meeting with so and so—and he'd mention a stranger, or, for contrast, a well-known name. He was making deals, he was holding talks. He'd polish his boots, wash his best shirt, and set off on his way. He never went far. He'd stop in the nearest town, steal someone's wallet, and get drunk. But even then he was never free of her, because he'd start talking about her. He couldn't do without her, even during these escapades.

And the strange thing was, she had become his most valuable possession. He could even pay for wine with her ugliness, when he wanted—and, more than that, he could mesmerize beautiful young women by describing her face, women who told him to go on talking about her even later in the evening, when they were lying beneath him naked.

When he got back he would always have a new story about her ugliness ready to tell the crowd—well aware that nothing really exists until it has its own special story. At first he made her learn them by heart, but he soon realized that the Ugliest Woman wasn't good at telling stories: she spoke monotonously and burst into tears at the end, so he started telling them for her. He'd stand to one side, point his hand toward her, and recite: "The mother of the unfortunate creature that you see before you, whose appearance is so terrible for your innocent eyes to bear, lived in a village on the edge of the Black Forest. And there, one summer's day, as she was picking berries in the woods, she was hunted down by a savage boar, who attacked her in a frenzy of mad, bestial lust."

At this point he invariably heard muffled, horror-stricken cries, and some of the women, who'd already wanted to leave, would start tugging at their reluctant husbands' sleeves.

He had several other versions:

"This woman comes from a land cursed by God. She is the descendant of an evil, heartless race who showed no mercy to a sickly pauper, for which Our Lord punished their entire village with this terrible hereditary ugliness."

Or: "This is the fate that befalls the children of fallen women. Here you see the fruits of syphilis, a terrible illness that punishes impurity unto the fifth generation!"

He never felt guilty. Any one of these might well have been true.

"I don't know who my parents were," the Ugliest Woman told him. "I've always been like this. I was found at the circus as a baby. No one can remember what came before."

When their first season together was at an end and the circus was traveling in a lazy curve back to Vienna for its annual hibernation, he proposed to her. She blushed to the roots and trembled. Then she quietly said, "All right," and gently rested her head on his arm. He could smell her fragrance —it was soft and soapy. He endured this moment, then drew back and began to tell her his plans for their life together, listing all the places they would visit. As he paced about the room she kept her eyes fixed on him, but was sad and silent. Right at the end she took him by the hand and said she'd like the exact opposite —for them to settle somewhere in the sticks, and never have to go anywhere or see anyone. And that she would cook, and they'd have children and a garden.

"You'd never be able to cope with it," he retorted indignantly. "You grew up in the circus. You want, you *need* to be looked at. You'd die without people's eyes on you."

She didn't answer.

They were married at Christmas, in a tiny little church. The priest who conducted the ceremony almost fainted. His voice trembled as he recited. The guests were people from the circus, because he told her he didn't have any family and was just as alone in the world as she was.

When they were all drowsing in their seats, when all the bottles were empty and it was time to go to bed (even she was tipsily tugging at his sleeve), he told everyone to stay and sent for more wine. He couldn't get drunk, though he was trying as hard as he could. Something inside him remained absolutely alert, tensed like a string. He couldn't even relax his shoulders or cross his legs, but sat there bolt upright, his cheeks flushed and his eyes gleaming.

"Let's go now, my love," she whispered in his ear.

But he clung to the edge of the table, as if pinned to it by invisible tacks. The more observant guests might have assumed he was simply afraid of being intimate with her, naked—afraid of the obligatory post-nuptial intimacy. Was that in fact the case?

"Touch my face," she asked him in the darkness, but he wouldn't do it. He raised himself above her on his hands so that all he could see was her silhouette, a little lighter than the darkness of the rest of the room, a faint patch with no distinct edges. Then he closed his eyes—she couldn't see it —and took her, like any other woman, without a single thought in his head, as usual.

■

They began the next season on their own. He had some photographs of her taken and distributed them worldwide. The bookings came by telegraph. They had numerous appearances and traveled first class. She always wore a hat with a heavy, gray veil, from behind which she saw Rome, Venice, and the Champs-Élysées. He bought her several dresses, and laced up her corset himself, so when they walked down the crowded streets of the cities of Europe, they looked like a proper human couple. But even then, during the good times, he still had to escape from time to time. That's just the sort of man he was: the eternal runaway. A sort of panic would suddenly rise in him, an unbearable anxiety attack. He'd start sweating and choking, and so take a wad of cash, grab his hat, and run down the stairs, soon finding himself, unerringly, slumped in one of the dives near the port. Here he'd relax, his face would go slack, his hair would get ruffled, and the bald patch usually hidden under his slicked-down locks would emerge insolently for all to see. Innocently and joyfully he would sit and drink, letting himself ramble on, until finally some persistent prostitute would rob him blind.

The first time the Ugliest Woman reproached him for his behavior, he punched her in the stomach, because even now he was afraid to touch her face.

He no longer told stories about syphilis or the boar in the woods when they did their routine. He had received a letter from a professor of medicine in Vienna, and nowadays he liked to present his wife in scientific terms:

"Ladies and gentlemen, here we have a freak of nature, a mutant, an error of evolution, the real missing link. Specimens of this kind are very rare. The probability of one being born is about as miniscule as the likelihood of a meteor hitting this very spot as I speak!"

Of course they used to visit the university professor once in a while. At the university they posed for photographs together, she sitting and he standing behind her, with his hand on her shoulder.

Once, while the Woman was being measured, the professor had a word with her husband.

"I wonder if this mutation is hereditary?" he said. "Have you thought about having children? Have you tried? Does your wife . . . er . . . ? Do you in fact . . . er . . . ?"

Not long after, perhaps unconnected with this discreet exchange, she told him she was pregnant. From then on he was a man divided. He wanted her to have a child just like herself—then they'd have even more contracts, even more invitations. If the need arose he'd be guaranteed a long liveli-hood, even if his wife died along the way. Perhaps he'd become famous? But then at once he'd have the thought that the child would be a monster, and that he'd really rather rip it from her belly to protect it from her poi-sonous, defect-infested blood than see it doomed to a life like hers. And he had dreams that he was that son in her belly, imprisoned there, damned to be loved by such a woman, and that by confining him inside herself she was gradually changing his face. Or else he'd dream he was the wild boar in the forest, violating an innocent girl. He'd wake up in a sweat and pray for her to miscarry.

Her belly gave the audience courage, and made it easier for them to forgive her monstrous ugliness. They started asking her questions, which she would answer shyly in a quiet, unconvincing way. Their closer acquain-tances began to make bets on what sort of child she'd have and whether it would be a boy or a girl. She took it all as meekly as a lamb.

In the evenings she sewed baby clothes.

"You know," she would say, stopping for a moment and fixing her eyes on a single faraway spot, "people are so fragile, so alone. I feel sorry for them as they sit there in front of me, staring at my face. It's as if they them-selves are empty, as if they have to take a good look at something, fill them-selves up with something. Sometimes I think they envy me. At least I'm something. They're so lacking in anything exceptional, so lacking in any specialness of their own."

He winced as she said it.

She gave birth in the night, without any fuss, quietly, like an animal. The midwife only came to cut the umbilical cord. He gave her a wad of bills to make sure she didn't spread any stories too early. His heart thumping, he lit all the lamps at once, to be able to give the thing a close inspection. The child was horrible, even worse than the mother. He had to close his eyes to keep from retching. Only much later did he satisfy himself that the newborn child was a girl, as the mother had proclaimed.

So here's what happened: he went into the dark city, it was Vienna, or maybe Berlin. Light, wet snow was falling. His shoes trailed pitifully over the cobblestones. He felt divided inside again—happy, but at the same time desperate.

He drank and remained sober. He daydreamed and felt afraid. When he came back several days later, he had ideas for their itinerary and promotional engagements all ready. He wrote to the professor and arranged for a photographer to call, who with hands shaking through flash after flash of magnesium recorded the monstrous ugliness of both creatures.

As soon as winter ends, as soon as the forsythia blooms, as soon as the cobbles of the great cities are dry, he thought. Petersburg, Bucharest, Prague, Warsaw, farther and farther, all the way to New York and Buenos Aires ... As soon as the sky stretches tight above the earth like an enormous azure sail, the whole world will be bewitched by the ugliness of wife and daughter, and will fall before them on its knees.

At more or less this point he kissed her on the face for the first time ever. Not on the lips, no, no, but on the brow. She looked at him with brightened eyes, almost human. Then the question returned—the question he could never ask her: "Who are you? Who are you? Who are you?" he kept repeating to himself, failing to notice when he started asking this question of others as well, even himself in the mirror while shaving. It was as though he had discovered a secret—that everyone is in disguise, that human faces are just masks, the whole of life one big Venetian ball. Sometimes he drunkenly fantasized—because he never allowed himself this sort of nonsense when sober—that he was removing the masks, and with a gentle crackle of glued-on paper they were revealing . . . what? He didn't know. It began to bother him so much that he couldn't bear to be at home with her and the child. He was afraid that one day he'd give in to his bizarre temptation and start trying to scratch the ugliness off her face. His fingers would rummage in her hair, seeking out the hidden edges, the straps and the strips of glue. So he'd slip out for a drink and then think up the next itinerary, design the posters and draft new telegrams.

But in early spring came the terrible epidemic of Spanish flu, and mother and child both fell ill. They lay beside each other in a fever, breathing heavily. From time to time out of some panic-stricken instinct she would cuddle the child to her, trying to feed it in her delirium, not understanding that it had no strength left to suck and was dying. And when it finally died, he gently took it and laid it on the edge of the bed, then lit a cigar.

That night the Ugliest Woman briefly regained consciousness, only to start sobbing and whining in desperation. It was more than he could bear —it was the voice of the night, the sound of darkness, straight from the blackest abyss. He covered his ears, until finally he grabbed his hat and ran, but he didn't go far. He walked up and down beneath the windows of his own apartment until morning, and in this way he helped her to die as well. It happened quicker than he could have expected.

He shut himself in their bedroom and looked at both bodies; suddenly they seemed heavy, burdensome, substantial. He was surprised how much the mattress appeared to be sagging beneath them. He had no idea what to do now, so he told no one but the professor; drinking straight from the bottle, he sat and watched as the twilight gradually effaced the contours of the motionless shapes on the bed.

"Save them," he pleaded incoherently once the professor had arrived to perform a postmortem.

"Have you gone mad? They're no longer alive," the man snapped.

Afterward the professor handed him a piece of paper and the widower signed it with his right hand, taking the money with his left.

But that same day, before vanishing into the port, he helped the professor to transport the bodies by carriage to the university clinic, where soon after they were secretly stuffed.

For a long time, almost twenty years, they stood in the chilly basement of the building, until better times came and they went to join the main collection, including Jewish and Slavonic skulls, two-headed babies, and conjoined twins of every possible race and color. They can still be seen today in the storerooms of the Pathologisch-Anatomisches Bundesmuseum—a glass-eyed mother and daughter, frozen still in a perfectly dignified pose, like the remnants of some new, unsuccessful species.

TRANSLATED FROM POLISH BY ANTONIA LLOYD-JONES

FRODE GRYTTEN

Hotel by a Railroad

He stood by the window smoking. If he went back to the indoor pool now, maybe he could still catch a glimpse of the girls. They had gotten into the water just as he and his wife were getting out. He had suggested that they get a cup of coffee in the restaurant beside the pool. You could sit there and look at the bathers. But his wife wanted to go back to the hotel.

Are you hungry? he asked without turning around.

No. Are you?

Not really. We're going out to eat tonight I suppose?

Do you have someplace in mind?

No.

She sat in the armchair behind him reading a book. After they had gotten back from the pool, she had complained about the heat and taken off her dress. It irritated him when she went around half-naked like that. There was something carefree and unseemly about it, as if she had given up and just couldn't be bothered anymore.

What do you feel like doing tonight? he asked.

What do you mean?

Maybe we could do something special since it's our last night.

Yeah. I suppose we could.

He decided to go back if a train passed before he had finished his cigarette. The room began to shake every time a train approached. It was a vibration that increased in strength right up until the train was visible from the window for a few seconds. Then the trembling subsided and the room was quiet again. He had tried to work out the system behind the train schedule, how long it was between departures, but hadn't figured it out.

He had looked at the trains and concluded that they seemed different depending on what time of the day they passed. The morning train carried individuals, people on their way to school or work; something was about to commence, something was about to begin. The night train carried groups of people, the darkness creating a fellowship, the light in the cars gathering together those who sat there. At night he stood at the window with an entirely different feeling. Different things were at stake. People were on their way toward peace or pleasure.

He stubbed his cigarette out against the window frame and threw away the butt. No train had passed. He turned to his wife. She looked ridiculous in that pink slip.

I'm going down to buy a pack of smokes, he said. Do you want anything?

Get me a Coke, she answered without looking up from the book.

Anything else?

No.

He stood in the doorway waiting. She didn't take her eyes from her book. He remained standing longer than was natural, but still she didn't look up. It struck him that you could stop looking at people, you could just refrain from looking at people, and in the end get exactly what you want.

Out in the corridor he regretted having said that he was going down to reception. It made it impossible for him to go back in and get his coat. He was dressed in a shirt and pants and a sleeveless sweater. The weather was warm but he felt naked without a coat. There was something temporary about not wearing a coat, something unfinished that he disliked.

The hotel had gone downhill since they were there last. He had warned his wife when they booked their room but she had insisted that they stay at the same place as on their honeymoon. Back then they could hardly afford to go, and she had gotten a little loan from her parents. The hotel facade was still grand, but the years hadn't been kind to the interior. He imagined the facade hid rooms that had suddenly lost their content. It was like a person who had changed character—not an organic aging, but brutal and unexpected.

After they had checked in, she had complained about the place.

What did I tell you? he asked triumphantly.

It's so sad, she had answered.

We should have stayed somewhere else.

Don't start.

When he was on the stairs down to reception, the train thundered past. I'm cheating, he thought, I'm a cheat. The entire hotel vibrated. That shuddering and shaking was perhaps what he remembered best from their honeymoon, the initial shock when a train made the building tremble, while the staff hardly seemed to notice. And then he remembered how they had made love, he remembered days that had been full of appetite and waste. They had gotten out of bed and dressed themselves only in order to undress and go back to bed again.

He nodded to the fat guy at reception.

Ran out of cigarettes, he said, as if he needed to explain why he was on his way out.

We have cigarettes, Fatty called out after him.

He stopped and gesticulated.

I need a couple of other things too, he said.

All right, smiled Fatty.

The sun washed over him. For a few seconds it was as though he neither knew who he was nor where he was going. Gradually his vision returned. Shadows flickered across buildings and asphalt. The afternoon sun burned patiently. Gothenburg had also changed. He couldn't explain it, but it wasn't the same city. Maybe it was just his memory that had failed him; the distance in time had opened up a rift that the days here couldn't close.

He walked back to the pool as quickly as he could. There were fewer people in the water than an hour ago; all the same he couldn't see the two girls. They must have gotten out. He bought a cup of coffee and sat down by the window where you could look into the pool area. The girls had moved in the water in a natural way that had appealed to him. One had short hair and wore a light blue swimsuit. The other had long, dark hair and a red bikini. The straps of her top had slipped down, exposing a clean expanse of skin.

He sipped at his coffee and felt disappointment, but relief as well, that the girls had gotten out. He yawned. He'd been woken last night by noise from the neighboring room. At first he'd thought they were fighting in there, because it seemed like someone was breaking up the furniture. Then he had realized that they were making love. He had lain awake listening to the woman's groans. He had wondered if his wife had also been woken by the noise. She lay with her back to him, but the deep breathing that sleep brings was absent.

He could have reached over and kissed her, but he had lain still until it was quiet in the neighboring room. Finally he had fallen asleep, before being woken by someone down on the street talking. At breakfast he had examined the other guests, wondering which of them was staying in the room next door. He hadn't been able to make any of the people in the breakfast room fit with the sounds of the night before.

The girls came up from the changing room by the time he had finished his coffee and decided to return to the hotel. They looked different now after having dressed and dried their hair. The blonde one was wearing a beige summer dress. The dark one was wearing jeans and a T-shirt. He hesitated a moment before he got up from the table and followed them out into the street.

Suddenly Gothenburg was closing in on him. The city snatched at him with cars and bulldozers. A bus lurched past. His head shrank and seemed to be without contour. He had no idea what he was going to do. All the same, he viewed the girls as a gift, something he had to take care of and look after as best he could.

Calm descended as he walked along the pavement. He strode and dropped back, strode and dropped back fifty or sixty meters behind the girls. It was as if the sunlight helped him breathe and his heartbeat fell into the same rhythm as his steps. He was following his initial impulse without pondering the alternatives.

He crossed the street and saw the girls disappearing into the Liseberg Amusement Park. He bought a ticket and followed them in. He and his wife had been there earlier in the week. The funfair had actually been even more of a disappointment than the hotel. They had gone in the middle of the day, and the sunlight exposed the place in a merciless way.

Inside, the girls stopped at one of the restaurants and sat down. He positioned himself at the table beside them. He looked at them while they ate ice cream and wondered which he liked best. He had had so little time in the pool that he hadn't been able to decide. He would have gone for the dark one instinctively, but right now he thought that the blonde one had something calm and clear about her.

The girls spoke loudly about boys, as if to impress the people around them. Their chatter was very grown-up, but it was interrupted all the time by giggling and laughter. He tried to listen to what they were saying, maybe catch their names or find out if they lived here in town. He sat there and wondered how old they were. He concluded it was best not to know.

Suddenly the dark one looked straight at him. Her glance was sharp and inviting, as if she was aware of the power she had over him. Then she looked away and continued licking her ice cream. He remained seated without thinking. His head couldn't manage to hold onto anything. He only felt a faint murmuring in his skull.

Three boys stopped at the girls' table, but fortunately they moved on quickly. The girls drank Coke and fiddled around on their phones. After a while they strolled over to the roller coaster. He followed and studied their movements, first in the line, later up in the car, high above the earth. He heard them screaming as they rushed down toward the ground in the red cars.

While the girls tried other attractions at the funfair he sat on a bench in the shade and squinted over at them. He wondered if they had noticed him following them. A lot of girls enjoyed that, even when they hadn't realized they were being trailed. He had reached the conclusion that there was no such thing as a one-sided pleasure; both parties had to enjoy it. On holiday last year, for instance, he and his wife had made love, and when she happened to say that it had been lovely, he'd seriously considered making it clear to her that this would be the last time that they would have sex.

He tried to remember if they'd actually had sex after that, but he wasn't quite sure. He hadn't gone near his wife this week, even though a hotel room is almost an invitation to be intimate. He'd read an article about how much sexual intercourse took place in a hotel in an average twenty-four hour period. Someone had calculated how many kids you could expect to be conceived in a normal hotel room per year as well. He couldn't recall the exact number, but he remembered being surprised at it.

On the bus downtown he stood three or four meters behind the girls. The dark one smiled teasingly at him at regular intervals. She could actually be the type of girl that likes to be followed, one of the ones who liked to know he was there, to feel the hold she had over him. In the window he saw his reflection appear and disappear. A face that came and went. He wondered what the girl saw when she looked at him. Who was he? What errand was he out on? He himself saw a man without a coat. He saw a balding head, a forehead with wrinkles, and a graying moustache.

When they got off the tram at Göta Place, the girls hugged each other and laughed. The blonde girl's hand rested on the dark girl's backside while they walked along the pavement. Then her hand slipped further down, as if they were lovers. They laughed and giggled again. It was a game, an intimate act in the middle of a crowd.

The one following them was the only person who had seen what they did. He stopped in the sun, feeling how grateful he was. What he had seen wouldn't happen again, wouldn't be repeated. He had been the only witness to an almost perfect act.

He followed them down streets, in and out of shops, into a new café, out onto Kings Street where they met two other friends. The whole time he stayed at a suitable distance; the whole time he hunted for more acts of intimacy. He was happy with the choice he'd made; he had a talent for this, choosing the right girls, finding girls who were sensitive to a situation like this.

In a clothes shop on Fredsgatan, the girls disappeared into the same changing room. They undressed, tried on different tops, and looked in the mirror together. The dark one glanced at him, but just as he was going to maneuver himself into a perfect position, he was disturbed by a pushy saleswoman.

Can I help you with anything? he heard a voice behind him say.

He turned around.

No, thank you, I'm just looking.

He thought he had shaken the woman off with that reply, but the fat lady stuck to him. It must have been because he seemed out of place. He was the only male customer in the shop.

Are you looking for underwear for your wife? the saleswoman asked.

Yes, something for my wife.

We've got so many nice things for the autumn. Would you like to follow me?

The fat saleswoman led him in the opposite direction from where the girls were changing.

What are her vital statistics? She asked. Is she the sporty type or more feminine?

She talked nonstop and showed him underwear without him even managing to affect interest. Finally he just said thank you and that he'd think about it a little. He had to think it over a little. He'd think about it a little more.

He waited for the girls outside the shop. Several women passed by while he stood there. He watched them with that melancholy that always came over him when he saw beautiful women walk through a city: Look at her, she's so beautiful, she's so beautiful, and I am never going to see her again. But he felt sure about the two girls. He'd made a good choice.

Ten minutes later they both came out with one shopping bag each. Out on the street they hugged one another and stood talking for a moment before they each went their separate ways. The dark one disappeared down Fredsgatan. The blonde one was preparing to cross the street in the direction of the canal.

This was a situation he hadn't considered. He had thought of them as a unit the entire time, not as two individuals who could suddenly part company. He had to decide quickly before he lost both of them.

He chose the blonde.

He nearly lost her too, but ran down the street so that he caught up with her again at the canal. She crossed Gustav Adolf's Square and then walked along Harbor Street East. He wondered if he had made the wrong choice. Maybe the dark one was better looking after all, but the blonde one had stood waiting for a green light, so all in all it was easiest to follow her.

They walked down streets where the sun had disappeared. Soon it would be dusk. There was something wistful about the girl when she was alone, something vulnerable that hadn't been there when she walked together with her friend. She walked as if she had some kind of secret. Now that he had gotten used to it, he liked this turn of events. He had made a choice. He had chosen the blonde.

Frode Grytten 153

At a set of traffic lights he came so close to her that he could see the freckles on her arms. He looked at her in profile and thought she was perfect. He had definitely made the right decision. She turned for a moment and looked right at him. He knew from the glance that she knew he was there, she knew what was going on. He felt his heart beat faster. Now it was just him and her.

It's a lovely evening, he said.

Yes, it is, she said nodding.

They continued down toward Queen's Square and he almost felt happy. He could walk like this all evening, all night, he could walk all day tomorrow, he could follow her to the ends of the earth.

He lost her down by the main railway station. A group of tourists got between them at the front entrance. The tourists were dragging a load of suitcases behind them and he really had to restrain himself from cursing at them. He turned and ran in one of the other doors. When he finally got inside, the girl was out of sight. He looked for her at the ticket counter, in the café, at the newsstand, and on the platforms.

She was gone.

She was perfect and he had lost her. She was the most beautiful girl he had ever seen, and now she was gone. A sense of disappointment flared up inside him. He felt that the day had let him down. He had invested in this day and he hadn't gotten anything in return.

He bought a beer and sat down at the pub in the concourse. Every day was a series of these kinds of losses, some more serious than others. He knew that someday his luck would change. Someday he'd follow someone who knew the game as well as he did, a girl who after a while would stop and look at him: You're following me, aren't you?

And then she'd say that he should follow her all the way home.

He noticed how hungry he was. It was half past eight, and he hadn't eaten since lunch—he had just sat and watched the girls eat. He glanced at the placard for the *Evening Post* at the newsstand: *Rude, nude, and wild.* He wondered what he was going to say to his wife when he got back to the hotel. There was nothing to say.

Every man's life is a mystery, he thought, it's as simple as that. That's what he could tell her. That's what he'd say. Where have you been? she'd ask. Every man's life is a mystery, he'd reply.

He went to the toilet to take a leak. It was the kind where you had to pay five kroner to get into the cubicle. He usually put off going to public toilets for as long as he could. When he was ten, he had been on a trip into the city with his mother, and when they were going to take the train home, he had gone into the men's toilets while she waited outside. When he was finished, he hadn't been able to open the door.

The panic still flared up inside him, the fear of closed doors, anxiety about anything that was locked; the fear of never being able to get out again. He had hammered and kicked but he hadn't gotten out. Finally he had stepped up onto the toilet seat and climbed over the side of the cubicle. As he had climbed over he had looked down into the other stalls. He could still picture all those grown-up men lined up with their trousers around their ankles.

Out in the concourse he found a phone and rang directory assistance. He got the number to the hotel. He rang up and asked to be put through to room 207. The receptionist asked him to hold the line. He stood looking at what people had written on the phone box.

Someone had scrawled in blue marker: *Håkon 4 Ever* and *My liddle puddy cat.*

Yes? she said on the other end.

It's me.

Hello?

It's me.

Hold on.

She was gone. He heard her turning down the volume on the TV. Then she was back again.

What's happened? she asked.

Nothing.

You said you were going down to reception to buy cigarettes. That was seven hours ago.

They didn't have the brand I wanted.

They've got that brand everywhere.

He heard her breathing into the receiver. He said nothing. He could picture her, standing in the hotel room in the same slip that she had on when he went out.

You know what? she said. I can't take this anymore.

What?

This.

What do you mean?

I don't want to know any more.

What do you mean by more?

I don't want to know any more, do you understand? I've tried to help you.

You can't help me.

I don't know what else I can do.

There's nothing to do.

He realized that this was developing into one of those telephone conversations that he'd always remember, like some sort of curse, a catastrophic moment in which everything is reduced and bent into sentences he wouldn't forget.

Are you leaving me? she asked.

I don't know, he said.

You're not coming back, are you? It hit me when you left without a coat. If you had put your coat on, you would have come up again.

Why's that?

Because that would have been you. If you had put on your coat, it would have been you. It was another man who went out the door.

It went quiet. He waited. He thought he heard the sound of a train going past, but he wasn't sure if the sound was coming from the telephone receiver or from the station around him. He pictured her again: her face, her mouth, her shoulders, her breasts, her thighs. All the things that were beyond his reach now.

What happened to us? he asked.

I don't know.

Yes, you do.

Nothing in particular happened.

Didn't it?

No, something in particular doesn't always happen. Things don't always break or fall to pieces.

Why's that?

Maybe it's just something that fades and becomes something else, like the seasons. Do you know what I mean?

Yes.

Are you coming back?

He didn't answer at first. He swallowed. The line was quiet.

Are you waiting for me? he asked.

I'm here in the room, she said.

He hung up.

Afterward he bought cigarettes and sat down on a bench. He'd finish his cigarette and then go back to the hotel. They were going back home tomorrow. Everything would be like before. He stood up and felt a white twinge in his head. He sat down again. He'd just sit a little longer and then he'd go back to the hotel.

He caught sight of the blonde girl in a line over at the newsstand. She'd bought a Coke. He had lost her, but now she was here again. Now she'd returned. In some miraculous way he had gotten another chance. His eyes welled up with tears as he stood and followed her down the steps to the railway track.

The girl disappeared into one of the trains.

He waited a few seconds and then he got on as well. He managed to find a seat three rows behind her. He didn't know if he needed to have a ticket or if he could buy one from the conductor. Maybe the girl would get off before the conductor even turned up. He'd see how it went; in any case he couldn't get off and buy a ticket now.

It was almost dark outside, the kind of darkness that comes in late summer, when the warm days end in a soft, black moan. It was that time of the day when parents had put their kids to bed, when the TVs were turned on, when people poured themselves a glass of wine and leafed through the newspaper. He wanted to be inside those bright, blurry rooms on the other side of the carriage window. He wanted to be there doing ordinary, everyday things.

Like the salesman he had seen the first night at the hotel, a man in one of the other rooms who had been unpacking wedding dresses. He had stood at the window and seen the salesman unpacking one dress after the other. The man had spread the dresses out on the floor and on the bed, had hung them up and then let them unfold, like it was snowing in the room. This sight had moved him to tears.

There was a little jerk and the train started to move. Now it was too late. The girl sat there reading a magazine. He studied her and realized that he liked everything about her. She hadn't noticed that he was back. It was quiet in the carriage; he only heard the muffled sounds that come from people being squeezed together, face to face, back to back.

He looked down at his hands. His right hand still held the pack of cigarettes, his left hand rested on his pants. It was odd; he thought his hands looked very young, as if they belonged to another, younger man. Yet another mystery, that he had such young hands.

The train had picked up speed now.

He wasn't sure what direction it was going in, but he thought they'd soon reach the area near the hotel. He leaned toward the window and shielded his eyes from the interior light so he could look out. Everything disappeared behind them at high speed. When they passed the hotel, it went so fast that he couldn't see if there was anyone standing at the window in their room. It didn't matter. In any case, she'd feel the tremor from the train as it thundered by, out in the darkness.

TRANSLATED FROM NORWEGIAN BY SEÁN WILLIAM KINSELLA

MANON UPHOFF

Desire

The winter was cold, with frost on the pane. The chill forced its way in through cracked window frames. The girl, quiet by nature, had just turned fifteen. A lot was happening to her that winter. Sometimes she sat in the bus and picked at her cuticles till the skin tore. Then she stared at the slowly welling, thickening drop of blood as it trickled down at an angle.

She liked fairy tales, but not the ones with happy endings. The Little Mermaid dissolving into foam amid the waves, the Snow Queen who kissed a child's heart to ice, and the Red Shoes, which forced Karen to dance upon her mother's grave—these interested her.

But that winter she read no fairy tales. In her older brother's room—where it was warmer than anywhere else in the house—she pored over a book called *The Geisha*. The cover had a charcoal drawing of two young women: Lucille and Amaryllis. The writer wanted to make love to both of them, preferably at the same time. Lucille and Amaryllis weren't upset by this. The girl was sure she'd think that was terrible—you can only surrender yourself to one person.

On a Saturday night in January, at the club where they only let her in because she'd made herself look years older, an Oriental-looking man bought her a drink. She'd been standing under the disco ball for hours, in a white blouse and tight jeans, but he had just come in. He was much older than she was. His hair shone, and the girl thought his narrow eyes were mysterious. The way he gave her the drink, his hand momentarily brushing the back of hers, frightened her. She couldn't take her eyes off him.

A little later, when she saw his nails, gleaming dimly like the inside of a shell, she knew she would go with him.

At two o'clock they left the club. Cars drove off honking and girls collapsed giggling into their boyfriends' arms. The doorman tapped his gold-braided hat and watched as they turned the corner.

The strange man and the girl walked through the center of town without a word. With each step her curiosity grew: not so much about this man, but about herself.

They crossed a bridge and walked out onto a lawn. The air was cold. It's not true that someone else can burn you with their heat, but the touch of his soft palm against hers burned anyway. In the grass, wet from melted patches of snow, they lay down. Up close, her nose buried in the worsted of his coat, she tried to find her way past all his strange smells to a smell she knew. Water was soaking through her clothes. Her teeth started chattering and the blood drained out of her face. She worried that her lipstick would dry and her mascara would run, and he'd think she was a child.

"It's too cold here," the man said. He helped her to her feet. Her hair was wet. There was grass on her coat and jeans.

He asked her to go home with him, and she said "yes," following the same urge that drove her to tug at the translucent skin around her nails in the bus and watch the lines of welling blood. The excitement grew in her. She felt she was swelling and drawing the darkness of night up into her, like a flower does sweet water. On the town square she imagined she was no longer in any normal city—she was in a world of glass and stone, where she and the man were the only two warm animals. The thrum of distant cars sounded like bumblebees. Drops of rain began rolling slowly over her cheeks, down her neck, and the walk went on and on and on.

Manon Uphoff 161

"Have you been in Holland long?" the girl asked at last.

"No," the man said. "Only two years. And I don't know if I'm going to stay."

They turned down a side street. The girl thought about her parents' house, her brother's room with the book about the geisha lying on the bed. How there, in that room, you could hear her mother's breathing. About her little sister, who would be asleep now, thumb moistly in her mouth—and the Barbies and the horse on the floor.

"Do you live by yourself?" she asked.

"No." A smile crossed the man's face. "Here we are." They stopped in front of a blue door and he pulled a key ring out of his pocket. There were colored cords of silk hanging on it.

"I don't live by myself. There are a lot of people upstairs—we'll have to be quiet."

She followed him cautiously up the dark stairs.

The cloth of coats scraped against her cold cheeks. The man put a key in the lock.

The girl stood behind him. Over his shoulder she looked into the room and the light. Rows of metal beds stood left and right, with men sitting on all of them, except one. There was laughter and mumbling, and faces turned toward her. With narrow eyes they looked at her.

"Welcome!" one of them said. His skin was yellowish and dry. He had a magazine in one hand. On the glossy cover lay a naked woman, legs spread, eyes closed in ecstasy.

He read from right to left and slapped the page teasingly as she walked past.

The man held her hand and led her into the far corner of the room. In front of his bed was a black curtain attached to metal rails—like in a hospital.

"Don't be afraid," he said, pushing the curtain aside carefully. Little tufts of grass fell from her coat onto the gray blanket. He closed the curtains and fastened them with a safety pin. The laughter from the room grew louder.

"They won't do anything," the man said as she sat on the bed and counted the beats of her heart. He played calmly with her fingers.

"Before long they'll sleep and leave us alone. Women almost never come here."

They waited until it was quiet and they could hear the soft snoring of people in peaceful sleep. A little lamp was burning. It was so low that the shadows it cast on the wall were large and wide.

"How old are you?" he asked. "Fourteen? Fifteen?"

She didn't answer.

"You've made yourself look older than you are."

She felt his lips approach her throat, and then a sudden hard bite that made her list sideways, like a boat after a hard gust.

"Girl," he said. His hand was a fish gliding up under the cloth, across her skin. He pulled the blouse up over her head, his nails ticking against her nipples. His mouth searched for hers and his tongue slid in like an oyster. The saliva in his mouth tasted sweet and warm.

He pushed her under the blankets and pulled on the zipper of her pants, which jammed until he broke it.

"I'll do it," the girl whispered. In a panic, she pulled the stiff material down as fast as she could.

"Soft," he whispered. He held a little fold of her belly in his mouth, rolling it between his sharp teeth.

"I don't know him," the girl thought. "He's a stranger. I don't know him."

A few times that winter, in the warm city bus to school, she had pushed the stop button too early, on purpose. One time she'd been with her father.

When the doors opened with a hiss, he made her get out—because the driver would expect her to.

That's just how it would be with this man.

"You're soft, still. A real girl." He petted her breasts, almost in surprise. "I think it's lovely that you're white."

She *was* white. When she looked down, his head was like a black stone between her legs. His lips were pressing against her pubic hair and his tongue slid in slowly. She wanted to stop him. A stranger ... but a warm and dark glow made her belly heavy, her legs heavy, and she closed her eyes—following the path of the heat.

"Don't stop," she said, startled at her sudden desire, her craving to hold onto this heat. "Just keep doing that." Her pelvis pushed up and she ran her hands through his stiff dark hair, forcing his head down harder, as if she were a nut with a hard shell, and now that the shell was cracked, power and rage came pouring out, and a wanting, a wanting that frightened her.

The heavy strands of his hair fell across her fingers.

"Keep doing that," she said again, but he stopped. She heard the crackling of paper, a rustling. His elbow jabbed her suddenly and sharply in the side.

"I'm going in you," he said, bending over her, enveloping her. "Don't be afraid. Don't yell or scream."

She saw his shoulders where the muscles bunched together, and the pounding of the vein in his neck. The mouth with the full red lips. She tensed her own muscles, but he was faster than she'd thought. A flaming white pain and a sharpness between her legs. With all her might she tried to pull back, but his mouth bore down on hers and his back and limber hips arched over her like a net.

"Don't fight," he said. "Don't fight."

But the pain, which stabbed harder now that she had tensed all her muscles in panic and pushed up her pelvis to force him off, made her stronger. She bucked so hard that he shot out of her. Hipbone cracked against hipbone.

"Don't!" he said. "What are you doing? It's going to happen *anyway!*"

"No!" the girl said, feeling a sudden powerful rage. "You have to fight too!"

He grabbed her by the waist and pushed her back on the sheet.

"You're scared," he said. "But don't be scared." With a hard lunge he went back in her and grabbed her buttocks hard with his fingertips.

"It hurts!"

She dug her nails into his back and pulled down hard. The skin began swelling under her fingers right away, and she saw his eyes pinch shut in pain. She pushed her mouth against his and bit into his lower lip. Lukewarm blood dripped into her mouth. He looked at her with dark gleaming eyes. There were beads of sweat on his forehead.

"You have to fight too."

There was squeezing, growling and thrusting. His hands and hers were everywhere, and everywhere her nails left clawing stripes that filled with red, but he didn't remove himself from her, and the flaming feeling between her legs remained. Even though she bucked her hips and hissed words she'd never used before.

Slowly the burning ebbed away and the heaviness disappeared. He was still in her. She had braced herself for new pain, but he moved only slightly, or not at all. Very calmly. Obliquely. Suddenly she heard her own moaning, and she gushed out like water on a stone floor. He went on, moving in her like a young animal.

"Woman," he whispered in her ear. "Now you're a woman."

The girl took her hands off his back and looked. The man's blood was deep under her nails and he was swathed in an odor she'd never smelled before. There was sweat on his shoulders and his stomach moved up and down. His lower lip was thick and swollen where she'd bitten it.

To her own surprise, she wasn't tired. The pain was gone and she didn't know whether she was happy or frightened, furious or proud.

He lay down beside her, sighing.

"I'm not tired," the girl thought, pulling the white sheet up over herself. "I'm not tired."

The stripes on his back were white and his hand reached for hers across the sheet, but she pulled her hand back and looked. At his shiny hair. The darkness of night. The rips in the curtain fastened with a safety pin. At the little lines of clotted blood. His cock lying limp across his thigh, which she dared look at only now. The condom leaking out slowly on the sheet.

And when he was rested and went into her again, her fingertips pushed hard against his ass, setting the rhythm for him to go in. She bit his throat, sniffing up his smells, and cupped his neck in her hand, as though she was holding a kitten.

The next morning they hardly spoke. He woke up, kissed her, went to sit on the edge of the bed, and quickly and silently put his clothes on. The light from outside was struggling through the window.

"Where are you going?" she asked, feeling around between the sheets for her underwear.

"Work," he said. "I have to go to work. What are you going to do? Will I see you again tonight? Will you come to me tonight?"

"No," the girl said. "I won't come back here anymore."

"You're a woman now," he said. "I'd like it if you came here tonight." But she shook her head.

Ten minutes after he went away, she left the room. The men were sleeping in their beds, breathing quietly, their backs hunched under the gray blankets. The magazines were lying open on the floor.

Outside it was chilly, but the sun was already shining weakly. She searched her coat for a bus ticket. She found one and waited for the bus that would take her home.

■

At the house, her mother was sitting at the table with a cup of coffee. The lady from next door across from her.

"Well? Did you have fun at your girlfriend's?" she asked. "Did the two of you go out dancing?"

"Oh, no," she said. "It was kind of late. We didn't really feel like it."

She left the room and climbed the stairs. The door to her brother's room was open a crack. He hadn't come home. The book about the geisha, with the picture of Amaryllis and Lucille on the cover, was still lying on his bed. Their firm breasts with nipples touching. The girl closed the door and turned the key in the lock. She pulled her torn jeans and panties down carefully over her shaking legs. There wasn't much blood, just a little dark spot. The sheet in his room had been worse. She looked at the spot on the cotton and at her pubic hair curling up. She thought about the Little Mermaid, who had traded her beautiful singing voice for real human legs. The pain that had cut into her at every step—and how she had turned to foam on the sea.

She thought about the Ice Queen in the solitude of her cold palace, where every human heart froze at once. She thought about the angel Gabriel, standing before the doors of the church with a flaming sword, waiting—for the little girl who danced and danced, her feet in red shoes, across her mother's grave, and on and on and on. Until her feet were cut off, and she found rest. But didn't get the shoes back.

"At least I fought," the girl said out loud to herself, pulling up her panties and jeans. The zipper's copper-colored teeth stuck out crookedly.

TRANSLATED FROM DUTCH BY SAM GARRETT

OGNJEN SPAHIĆ

Raymond is No Longer
with Us—Carver is Dead

They were drinking juice. Watching TV. The old set could only pick up two channels. She was expecting to give birth by the end of the week. He was an accountant at a sock and underwear factory.

"Perhaps I'll go round to Vladimir's," he said.

His wife was leafing through the newspaper and did not raise her head.

"Perhaps?" she said a minute later.

It had been raining for three days without letting up. He had read that especially painful births were seventeen percent more common in humid weather. Medically unproven but true. He believed in statistics. And hoped the statistics would bypass them this time.

"The phone number's on the fridge. If anything happens—just call."

"Do you have to tonight?"

"What do you mean have to?"

"Do you have to go out?"

"You know where I'm going. What's the problem?" he said as he put on his coat.

He had no idea where to go. The only thing he knew for sure was that he usually ended up at Vladimir's. Vladimir lived alone and went to bed late.

She supported her back with her hand as she walked. She went with him to the door so she could lock it afterward. Her full belly looked healthy. At the hospital they said hers was a "textbook pregnancy."

She believed the doctors and liked their "bookish" comparison. She straightened the collar of his coat and said:

"Bring me a book. Let Vladimir choose. I want to read something exciting. Okay?"

"Of course," he said, checking his umbrella.

She kissed him on the cheek and locked the door twice.

The stairway stank of urine. The rain wouldn't stop for the rest of the week, he thought, and looked up—the sky was the color of a dead TV screen.

He would stroll along some neighboring streets and then take the boulevard to Vladimir's. He would not have to avoid the puddles. He had good, watertight American boots. His socks would stay dry. The socks made by his company bled dye when they were wet. You had to keep them dry.

When he went round the corner he thought of the baby and tried to imagine how it would look. But he could only picture pale skin and helpless arms waving. An unborn child—a nameless being, he thought as he entered the drugstore. He would buy a bottle of whiskey for Vladimir and try to stay sober tonight.

"Twenty, please."

He searched through his wallet—he only had fifteen.

"I'll put the whiskey back then," he said.

"You'll have to," the cashier said, punching the buttons of the cash register.

If the baby came on Thursday, it would be born on their wedding anniversary. Double luck, he thought as he left the shop. But he still didn't feel real joy. That was probably normal *the first time*. He thought everything would change when he saw the baby, when he held it in his arms and called it by its name. He looked to the left and then to the right, down the street.

There were no crowds downtown that day. So much water, he thought, it had to run off somewhere. He skirted the largest puddles and chose the sidewalks under the eaves. The wind snapped two ribs of the umbrella, opening it became impractical. He would have coffee in the bar on the other side of the street and wait for the weather to calm a bit.

"Your face, sir," the waiter said, pointing to his own face.

"What's wrong with my face?" he asked, perplexed.

"There's blood on your face."

He touched his nose and looked in embarrassment at the blood on his fingers. Now it made sense—the metallic taste in his mouth in the last few minutes.

"It's my blood pressure," he said and pulled out his handkerchief. "Sometimes I just start bleeding," he said.

They brought him napkins. Lots of napkins.

In the bathroom only one bulb was working. As he washed himself with cold water a man and a woman were arguing. They paid him no mind.

"You could at least have asked. I was the father."

"You pig."

"That's murder!"

"It's my business."

"Is that so?"

"It sure is."

He turned off the tap and wiped his hands with the last napkin.

"You think our child is just your business!"

"Yep, it was inside me, and it ain't no more. Simple enough?"

Instead of answering, the man slapped her hard in the face. As he was headed back to the table he heard a second slap.

He finished his coffee and waited for the two to come out. Maybe he should have done something. He was sure he would never hit his wife. He loved his wife and knew hitting her would destroy him.

It began to thunder. Every explosion made the image on the TV screen above the bar disappear. Humphrey Bogart and Ingrid Bergman were blanketed in electronic snow. The waiters swore.

First the man came out, then several minutes later the woman. She was leafing busily through a smallish bundle of bank notes. Large dark glasses covered her face. He saw them once again the same evening, arm in arm under an umbrella and staring into a store window full of TVs. The central screen was the focal point for their two faces, now drawn into smiles. Before continuing off down the street the woman adjusted her hair. The man waved at the camera in the window and they walked off again in silence.

Vladimir's apartment was on the fifth floor, just round the corner. Vladimir was a writer. He was forty-three and wore his age like an old man. He was divorced and had a daughter. Little Ines lived in another town with her mother and came to visit once a month.

He knocked, and behind the door heard a "Coming!" and then an amiable "Hello! Roll on in."

They shook hands and patted each other on the back. Vladimir took him by the arm and led him into the dining room.

"Sit down. I'll be with you right away," he said.

He sat down and looked at the books scattered over the table. Piles of books. Instinctively he wanted to turn on the television, but his friend had voluntarily relinquished his TV.

"I'm much better known as 'the man without a TV' than I am as a writer. Shocking, isn't it?" he sometimes commented.

Vladimir rummaged in the kitchen, there came the clink of glasses.

"A sad night, old friend," he came back with two glasses and a bottle of whiskey.

"The greatest among us is no more. The great text tamer. The prince of the short story. The baron of metonymy . . ."

"Cut the crap. Who are you talking about?"

"You really don't know?"

Vladimir poured the whiskey and pronounced solemnly: "Raymond is no longer with us—Carver is dead.

"Oh, and so I don't forget: your beautiful wife called," he added.

"What? Are you out of your mind? Why didn't you tell me right away? Give me the phone. She's pregnant, you know!"

Six.

Two.

One.

He thought of the little yellow cot in the corner with the designer bedcover they spent ages choosing.

Five.

Eight.

Four.

"Come on, come on, come on, for God's sake!" he stamped his foot impatiently. The phone rang seven times. He worried he was going to be late for the birth. That she was in the hospital already or perhaps still there in the apartment, on the floor, unconscious.

But then her voice came, a sleepy "Hello?"

"Is it you?" he yelled.

"Sure it's me. What's up?"

"You're okay? And the baby? Everything okay?"

"Everything's okay. Why?"

"Just say that again, please."

"*Everything's okay*, I said. What's wrong?"

He put his hand over the receiver. Vladimir stood leaning against the doorpost with his glass of whiskey and wide inquisitive eyes.

"Everything's okay. False alarm," he said with relief and put the receiver back to his ear. She asked why he had gotten so worked up, she didn't understand. She had called to ask Vladimir about a book. He said he'd send "a good, dead American writer."

"Carver died today, I guess?" he asked.

"Yes, he did."

She said it was interesting to read someone when you know that the author—far away in America—is still lying in an open coffin.

"And a wave of sadness, strange and strong, rolls in from across the ocean."

"You weren't there when I called," she said.

"No. I stopped for a coffee on the way."

"Did you get wet?"

"A bit."

"Ha! I can feel the baby moving. It tickles."

"That's normal. It'll be coming soon."

"Please don't come back too late. I want the book. And you're not so terrible yourself," she said cheerfully.

"I'll be right back," he said and reached for his glass of whiskey.

Carver was in his pocket. Before he left he had one more glass with Vladimir and drank to his health. There was an *American way of life*, and there was also an American way of death, he thought. It wasn't good that the summer had begun with such unpleasant weather. Warm, boring rain. She couldn't go outside, that dampened the mood a bit. So far they hadn't had any serious arguments. He thought the two of them would have a harmonious, easygoing marriage. A little more money would remove all misunderstandings. But it was good like this too, he thought, as he looked up from the street at the window of their rented apartment. They hadn't bought curtains yet. All of a sudden he felt sorry that he had left her alone. He wouldn't do it again. At least not at night. She had to be relaxed and feel secure. He couldn't give her the Carver tonight for the same reason. Carver's stories were unsettling. They radiated a particular kind of anxiety. They were too much like real life, he thought.

She unlocked the door, put her arms around his waist, and hugged him.

As she kissed him on the cheek he felt her belly against his stomach. He wasn't sure he liked the feeling. And her face was moist. As though from tears.

Usually she watched television before going to bed. She turned off the lights and lay down on the couch. The freshly whitewashed living room was bathed in the flashes from the TV screen. Hues of red and green danced on the objects, on her face. The bright reflections of film explosions glistened in her eyes. The cool inexorability of the cathode tube.

"Did you bring the book?" she asked.

"Sorry, I forgot it. Your call threw me," he said, going into the kitchen.

"I felt it in your coat pocket. Why the lie?"

"Listen, I don't want you to read Carver tonight."

She went into the hall and got the book.

"It's cold and wet around the edges," she said.

"I'm afraid it's like that inside as well. Cold and wet," he said.

She sat down and began turning the pages.

"Please, leave it on the table."

Ignoring him, she began to read the first lines.

"Leave the book, for goodness sake. You don't need that agitation, neither you nor the baby," he said, getting loud this time.

He thought Carver's stories would have a negative influence. But he wasn't sure how. There was a brilliant vagueness and a queasiness to them that he couldn't grasp. He sat down next to her, but she turned away.

"I'm going to the bedroom. I'll read there. Good night," she said and got up.

He also got up.

In the near-dark he worked on her fisted fingers with one hand. With the other he gripped the book. She felt Carver slipping away from her.

"No!" she yelled just as her hands came loose. Today she would read. She would have this damn book.

She caught one of the covers and a dozen pages and leaned back.

But he would not let go. He felt the book slipping out of his hands and he pulled back very hard.

In this manner, the issue was decided.

TRANSLATED FROM MONTENEGRIN BY WILL FIRTH

IULIAN CIOCAN

Auntie Frosea

Because of the heavy shopping bags, crammed full of squash and pota-
toes, Auntie Frosea's hurried pace looked more like a penguin's waddle.
The woman was running, she was out of breath, and sweat beaded her furrowed brow. She had to get back home quickly. There wasn't a minute to
spare. A neighbor overtook her, calling out as she went, "Faster, Frosea,
faster, it's just about to start!" She shivered with fright. What if she was
late? She paused for a few moments to catch her breath, under a billboard
that read, "ПЕРЕСТРОЙКА! ГЛАСНОСТЬ! ДЕМОКРАТИЗАЦИЯ!"
(Perestroika! Glasnost! Democratization!) And then she resumed her gru-
eling race against time. A man with a bottle of brandy tucked under his
arm burst out of a grocery shop, jumped into a car and sped off. A mother
was dragging along a tearful, obstinate little girl behind her, yelling at her
to hurry up. From the window of a block of apartments, an elated housewife shouted down to her husband, beating carpets in the yard, to drop
everything—because "it's starting!" Every passerby was rushing home.
Soon the streets were deserted, as at the dead of night. Something out of
the ordinary was in the air. The city, exhausted by its anguishing wait, was
yearning for the moment of deliverance.

When at last Auntie Frosea reached her own apartment block, there
wasn't a soul to be seen. The silence was almost total. The only sound was

the squeaking of a swing from which a little girl had leaped but a minute before, impelled by an irresistible desire. With a feeling of foreboding, Auntie Frosea climbed the stairs, her eyes bulging. The handles of her huge, over-laden shopping bags cut into her calloused palms. She shoved open the front door of her apartment with her shoulder and, drenched in sweat, burst into the tenebrous hallway, where shoes, sandals, and boots of varying ages all lay in a heap. Sprawled in an armchair, her husband was goggling at the television screen. On hearing the noise in the hallway, the man yelled, annoyed: "What kept you, woman? *Isaura's* started!" Auntie Frosea winced: she had missed some precious moments in the never-ending drama of *Isaura the Slave Girl*! All of a sudden she felt real resentment toward her husband, a malice such as she had never experienced in all their long marriage. She looked at the man with muted hatred. Why, she asked herself, was she always the one who had to do the shopping? Why was she the only one who had to lug heavy bags across town? And, entering the room, she raised her voice at her husband for the very first time, shocking him into silence: "Why don't you ever lend me a hand, Vova? Why am I the only one who has to go out and buy the groceries?"

■ ■ ■

When, one rainy afternoon in the autumn of the year 1988, the first Latin American soap opera ever to be broadcast on Soviet television came to Auntie Frosea's attention, she was suffering from a terrible toothache. But the plot of the soap opera was so gripping that, by the end of the episode, it had taken the ache away—better than any painkiller could. Never in her life had Auntie Frosea seen anything so enthralling. Never had she felt such unease after watching something on television. She had been moved. It was as if a ray of sunlight had pervaded her entire being. Soviet films no longer mattered. There were still those Indian films, of course. They were an old passion of hers. But in this Latin American soap opera, *everything was different*: the music was more exuberant, the vegetation more luxuriant, the atmosphere more dramatic, the stories more authentic, and the relationships between the characters far more complicated. Soon she could also add that the soap operas drew out their suspense far more deliciously, endlessly postponing their always unpredictable finales. Her soul ached with pity for Isaura the Slave Girl, a beautiful and diligent girl exploited by a hard-hearted landowner named Leoncio. The master not only treated her badly, not only humiliated her, but also made distasteful advances toward her. But Isaura had strength of character and refused to sleep with this exploiter, because she was in love with a free man, Tobias, against whom the jealous, tyrannical Leoncio bore a grudge. After every episode, Auntie Frosea would feel the need to share her overwhelming reactions with her friends. In the yard outside the apartment block she would meet with Viorica Ionovna and Olga Leonovna and they would talk for hours on end about Isaura. Other housewives of that period of political transition would also linger there talking about this and that, but Auntie Frosea was always simply horrified at the sufferings of the Brazilian slave girl:

"Poor Isaura! How can she live in slavery like that? How can she put up with the cruelty of that bandit Leoncio?" she would whisper, wiping away her tears.

"That's right, Frosea. The poor suffering girl ..." Viorica Ionovna sighed, in chorus with Auntie Frosea's lament.

Olga Leonovna, on the other hand, liked to play devil's advocate. "You shouldn't grieve for her so much! She isn't all that badly off ... You keep going on about slavery. What use is it that I'm free if I've never been farther away than Koblevo? Have I got the money to go off to Brazil? No, I haven't. And even if I had, would the authorities let me?"

Auntie Frosea looked puzzled: "What are you going on about, Olga? Haven't you got any idea what it means to be a slave? It's true we don't live in the lap of luxury, but at least we're free. What with perestroika and all, you're free to say whatever you like now, more or less ..."

At this point there intervened an implacable old woman, a war veteran, who was convinced that Gorbachev was an agent provocateur working for the Americans.

"This perestroika will be the ruin of us! We'll end up envying Leoncio's slaves! Just you wait and see! It won't be long now!" she warned them, and this brought the conversation to a dead halt.

The most harrowing episode was the fourteenth. The cruel Leoncio had laid a trap for Tobias. Isaura's lover let himself be caught and was burned to death in an abandoned building. Tobias's death was an injustice that cried to the heavens for vengeance! How could he have been so gullible! Why did he have to die? Why did Auntie Frosea have to be parted from such a beloved character? There were other episodes to follow, but Auntie Frosea just couldn't imagine how the story would go on without Tobias. That night, Auntie Frosea couldn't sleep. She tossed and turned until dawn, irritating her husband no end. He had to get up early to go to the factory and in his mind he cursed the reckless hero of the soap opera for ruining his night. After her husband, his eyes bloodshot, left the house in the morning, slamming the door behind him, Frosea jumped out of bed and telephoned Viorica Ionovna.

"What's Isaura going to do now? How do you think she'll be able to go on living without Tobias?"

Viorica Ionovna had also been deeply upset by the untimely death of Isaura's lover. "Oh, Frosea, it's a real catastrophe. She was devastated, poor thing. Did you see the look on her face? And you know . . . I'm afraid there might be worse to come . . ."

"What do you mean?"

Viorica Ionovna fell silent for a few seconds, finally saying in a strangled little voice, "Frosea, I'm afraid Isaura is going to give in to Leoncio . . ."

Auntie Frosea gasped. The thought that Isaura might end up rolling in the hay with Tobias's murderer was utterly unbearable.

But what frightened Auntie Frosea even more were Olga Leonovna's theories. The latter not only found Viorica Ionovna's sinister supposition plausible, but also had the deep-seated conviction that Isaura shouldn't play so hard-to-get: "A shame about Tobias dying. But let's be honest, Frosea, he was a bit puny, he was a bit of a weed compared to Leoncio. I don't see how Isaura could have loved him. Don't take this the wrong way, but I think that Isaura would be stupid not to go for Leoncio now. He's tall, the bastard, and he's got beautiful eyes . . ."

"But . . . don't you see that he just wants to sleep with her? Don't you understand that he's not going to make her his wife?" Auntie Frosea blurted out.

Yes, Olga Leonovna understood, but she couldn't see a more alluring alternative on the horizon.

Auntie Frosea kept thinking all day about the choice Isaura was going to have to make. While trying to guess the intentions of the unhappy slave girl, she forgot all about making supper. Then, when she remembered and started bustling about the kitchen, her mind wandered and she burned the steaks. Tired and hungry, her husband got home shortly before Episode Fifteen was about to start—an episode that promised to be enlightening in many respects. He quickly went to the kitchen, saw the charred meat in the pan, and started screaming his lungs out: "Where's my goddamn dinner, you stupid bitch?" Auntie Frosea jumped as though catapulted from the armchair where she was awaiting the beginning of the episode. She felt guilty. She told her husband she would fry him some eggs right away and tried to explain that the death of Tobias was to blame. Uncle Vova's eyes widened and he yelled, "You stupid woman! What do you mean, you bitch? You expect me to eat eggs after I've worked like a pack mule all day? Can't you understand, you stupid bitch, that the actor's not dead? It was the character that died, woman!"

Auntie Frosea bowed her head. She could not and would not distinguish the actor from the character he played.

■ ■ ■

Auntie Frosea, Uncle Vova, and their son Valeriu had lived all their lives in a dowdy, forty-two square meter apartment. Their block had been built in 1953, the year of Stalin's death. The building turned thirty-five the year that Auntie Frosea discovered Latin America and Valeriu came home after finishing his military service. Like every other *stalinka*, the place was decrepit before its time, but Auntie Frosea was content: To have an apartment in Chişinău, even a dowdy one, was no mean feat! The misfortunes of Isaura had reinforced this conviction. In comparison to the sufferings of the Brazilian slave girl, Auntie Frosea's problems were trifles. Yes, her husband had grown quite petulant lately, and sometimes he would even get plastered and yell at her to go fuck herself, but it wasn't as if you could compare those minor excesses with the ferocity of the diabolical Leoncio. Auntie Frosea knew that her husband was essentially a good and kind-hearted man. Yes, their dowdy flat had become even more cramped after Valeriu brought home a pregnant wife in the 1990s, and especially after their son was born, whom Auntie Frosea took charge of so as not to jeopardize the young parents' studies. But Isaura didn't even have a shed to call her own! Yes, after she had chanted "Unification, Moldavians!" for days on end along with Olga Leonovna and the thousands of other people demonstrating in the city's main square, Auntie Frosea felt like she had been duped by the "Romanianizers" who had consigned the economy to oblivion. And yes, sometimes the family didn't even have enough money for food, and so for half a year Auntie Frosea had sold tins of fish on the street corner, which she'd bought at a lower price from a shop on the other end of town. The lugging of those tins from one part of the city to another came to an abrupt end one rainy autumn day when, carrying two fully laden shopping bags, Auntie Frosea bent double with pain and collapsed into a huge puddle. In the ambulance on the way to the hospital they diagnosed her with a run-of-the-mill slipped disk. But—did the slaves on the plantation have it any better under the lashes of the whip? True, the factory no longer paid Uncle Vova's wages on time and in the end they even declared him redundant, though he hadn't yet reached retirement age. But Leoncio's slaves could never even dream of wages and pensions!

And so Auntie Frosea was content. When she thought about the lives of Isaura, Maria, and Leticia, and then about the lives of the female characters in the other Latin American soap operas, Auntie Frosea saw the truth: she was outrageously lucky. There was, it's true, one minor problem: the seemingly never-ending soap operas would occasionally come to a real conclusion, and for a few days Auntie Frosea would feel adrift. But a new serial would always begin in time and Auntie Frosea would recover her spirits and her optimism. Everything was fine! Perhaps it would have been like a wonderful fairy tale if Isaura, Maria, and Leticia had been able to overcome their fate, but for some reason this was impossible—so Auntie Frosea could always find comfort in commiserating with them.

But then, one day, a doubt nevertheless stole into her mind. She remembered Isaura's friend—Januaria the cook, a black woman who slaved in the kitchen from dawn to dusk and who used to comfort Isaura. Strangely enough, even though she was a slave, even though she toiled away, Januaria was serene and meek. She hated Leoncio, but she would never dream of defying him. She used to tell Isaura to be patient, because *one day* all would be well. What strange advice! What inexplicable resignation! Auntie Frosea was puzzled. How could this woman be so reconciled to her fate? I mean—it would have been easy for her to put poison in the landowner's food and rid them all of the cruel oppressor! But Januaria did nothing. It was the height of absurdity. Was she afraid of the consequences? Or perhaps . . . Was it that she liked the life of a slave? That really would take the cake! There must be something else to it, but Auntie Frosea couldn't quite understand what . . .

■　■　■

One evening, going out onto the balcony to look for a basin among the piled-up junk there, Auntie Frosea glanced down into the yard. Outside it was cold and muddy. People had ensconced themselves in their houses. A bearded tramp was rummaging in a heap of garbage. A crow cawed sadly in a bare tree. The block of apartments opposite looked like a barracks before reveille. Everything was gray, colorless.

And, all of a sudden, Auntie Frosea was struck by a revelation. She understood why those South American landscapes so caught her eye: they *contained no gray*. The colors of the New World were vivid, striking! Isaura's world—with its azure ocean, its exotic fruits, its shady palm trees, its zany parrots and beaches bathed in blinding sunlight—was enchanting! No, Moldova, with its long, cold winters, couldn't compete with the New World. And then, almost immediately, Auntie Frosea found herself facing what seemed a logical contradiction: How could slavery exist in such a paradise? How could man exploit his fellow man in the midst of such beauty? It was a blatant contradiction, one that Auntie Frosea could not comprehend, however hard she tried. She liked Brazil, but slavery horrified her. After much cogitation, Auntie Frosea saw the light: Isaura and all the other slaves belonged to a bygone world. There was no slavery in Brazil nowadays! But for a good few years now Auntie Frosea had lived with the certainty that Isaura was her contemporary, that the slave girl's sufferings had some sort of relevance for the present day. What's more, Auntie Frosea had even been watching the shows about contemporary Latin Americans—the characters in modern dress—through the lens of Isaura's plight. For some inexplicable reason, *all* the wronged heroes of the soap operas had been "slaves" to Auntie Frosea. This fresh revelation bewildered her. Isaura had escaped Auntie Frosea, slipping back into another time. It was unacceptable. Isaura had to belong to the same age as her, to the same moment— she had to stay put, had to stay suffering.

Auntie Frosea couldn't bear to see her slave go free.

TRANSLATED FROM MOLDOVAN BY ALISTAIR IAN BLYTH

BLAŽE MINEVSKI

Academician Sisoye's Inaugural Speech

Sisoye was finally made a member of the Macedonian Academy of Arts and Sciences.

He just needed to deliver his inaugural speech and he would at last be admitted to those hallowed halls.

But on the day this was supposed to take place, something entirely un-predictable happened, as we shall mention in the **EPILOGUE**.

Yet when one knows the end, one should also know the beginning.

INTRODUCTION

The sun had just risen above Mount Petelino and the air was already puls-ing with excitement on the morning of the day Sisoye was to hold his speech. It was not yet officially summer and the nights were still brisk; dew gleamed like sugar crystals on the pine trees and on the lawn in front of his building. Satisfied with himself as never before, Sisoye opened his bed-room window wide, breathed deeply, and watched the atoms wandering along Einstein Boulevard and turning into little pine needles, the tiny flies that hovered around the garbage bins, and the droplets of dew that glinted on the grass. One of the main points of his speech was to be that when we die and no longer operate as mass in motion—and we are only in motion because we all have souls—our atoms dissociate, as when you scramble a Rubik's Cube; they depart and reconfigure elsewhere, for example in the tip of a leaf, in the eye of a woman in love, or as part of a droplet of dew. "Who knows what Slavko Sivakov will turn into, after he and those other senile academicians from his macabre little clique prevented me from becoming an academician for ten whole years . . ." Sisoye thought and smiled, winking as if making jokes with an invisible companion, and he tossed his head to make a drooping strand of hair return to place. He patted down said hair in the same motion as if smacking a fly on his forehead, and once again his head resembled that of an intellectual.

Since it was still too early to leave for the Academy, he stayed at the window and calmly inspected his suburb, even looking over to the gardens of the illegal settlement that stretched most of the way up to the huge cross on top of the hill. He also studied the other part of the hill that was sliced like a watermelon by the cement works at its base. The morning was so completely still that he could hear the chatter from the settlement that had no water supply or sewage system, but also the hum of the dewdrops as they ran down pine needles or seeped into the grass.

Apart from atoms, which were his particular professional purview, Sisoye also loved to interpret sounds and signs in space, particularly birds in flight, the barking of dogs—the secret pathways of dreams . . . He believed that if the front door creaked, or a west-facing window, or if you accidentally broke some household object, someone in the family would die; if a hen crowed like a rooster and peeked in through your door, someone in the family would die; if a raven circled over your house, like that one wheeling over that house there, the one with the stone wall, someone *there* would soon die; while if a raven cawed in the morning, whoever heard it first would have bad luck, or else there would be some misfortune in his house; owls, ravens, and cuckoos were all birds of ill omen; cuckoos were especially dangerous, particularly their first call in the morning, Sisoye said to himself, looking through a cloud of his condensed breath at the illegal settlement opposite. When a dog howled like a wolf at sunset with its nose pointing toward the sun, this certainly portended evil—and then death, disaster, or other misfortunes were in store; Sisoye trembled at the thought. Just then, the pigeon that visited his windowsill every morning looking for crumbs flew up: "If you dream of a pigeon killed and trussed, someone close to you—or you yourself—will die a sudden death; on the other hand, if you dream of flying, someone close to you will die; while if you dream of someone *else* flying, diving down from up high and hitting something on the way, that person will certainly die," Sisoye whispered, as if speaking to the pigeon; he gave a start then and looked around to make sure no one had heard him; he couldn't have people saying that he, an academician, had started talking to himself. Down below on the sidewalk, in the precious shade of the Japanese cherry trees brought along with their soil from so far away, people were now walking around. They were going to work early, like in the old days, or perhaps they were sleepwalkers with open eyes, dreaming of rusty factory gates. But now Sisoye stepped back from his window and hid in the dark of the room; after a while he reached out to crumble some bread for the pigeon. As he watched the people rushing past his building, apparently knowing where they were going, he remembered that one should always have a bite to eat in the morning before leaving the house: "If someone hears a cuckoo—at almost any time—and if they're hungry at that moment, someone in their family will die . . . or, if he lives alone, the person who heard it will die." Sisoye yawned as he watched a roaming cuckoo trying to land on the top of the pine in front of the building; then he ate up the bread that remained in his hand, left the window, crossed himself (although he didn't believe in God, only in atoms), and got dressed. Despite being single now, his apartment was immaculate and orderly, and he always had a vase of flowers and a bowl of fruit on the table. Now there were three bananas and one orange in the bowl. As a widower without any children (although for years he tried unsuccessfully to adopt), he had got used to laying out his own clothes for the next day. Right after sunset, as he read the stars and listened to the birds settling down in the trees for the night, he always went over his plans for the next day and what clothes he ought to prepare. Whatever he decided to wear he put out on the clothes hanger in the hall, so in the morning everything was ready—he just needed to get dressed, spruce himself up, put on his hat, take his briefcase (with his papers on the movement of atoms), and leave for the Institute of Strategic Studies . . . same as every morning for the last forty years. Although the two old barracks where the Institute was located—speckled with jackdaw droppings—were in the same suburb as his apartment, he always used to drive to work. There had been two cars in his life: first a Moskvich, then a Lada. But in the last few years, with gasoline becoming so expensive and Russian cars getting about the same mileage as tractors, he never bothered taking the Lada out of the garage. Now he only used its trunk to store preserves for the winter: he put jars of stewed peaches there so they wouldn't freeze if the season was too severe and the cold came in through the cracks in the roof. Now he closed the heavy, wooden door of his apartment (his name plaque didn't say "Academician" yet), checked three times that it was locked, and recorded this in the little notebook that he habitually carried in the left-hand pocket of his coat; he did this to avoid having to leave the bus at the third or fourth stop to go back and ensure that he had indeed locked the front door. Using the notebook for his brilliant ideas was already an everyday habit, but now it had replaced his memory entirely. When he wrote in the notebook that the door was locked he saw that he had noted the night before that his inaugural speech was already in his briefcase, and this made him smile with satisfaction; he blinked and went down the stairs from the fourth to the first floor. As far as we're concerned, at present, Sisoye left for the Academy in good time, ready to create a sensation with the speech he had been preparing for precisely six months.

THE SPEECH

The Great Hall of the Academy of Arts and Sciences was filling up; Academician Slavko Sivakov was not in the audience, as far as Sisoye could tell in a cursory glance from the rostrum; several other elderly members of the Academy were also absent—probably because they wouldn't be able to find their way home afterward without help, Sisoye consoled himself. The President, Secretary, and a dozen other prominent academicians sat in the front row. Among them, leaning forward with a pendulous belly that wobbled between his knees, was Sisoye's chief mentor and friend, Prežihov, and next to him Trepetlika dozed with a plastic bag on his lap. It was getting noisy in the hall since many of the academicians had now seen one another and were exchanging anecdotes about their youth and snippets of biographical information; Sisoye cleared his throat loudly several times, the babble died down, and his speech could finally begin. Now, I happen to know—as I myself prepare this text about Sisoye—that his speech was meant to begin with the assertion that nothing in the universe is more enduring than its atoms. Atoms exist in abundance, of course, and in Sisoye's view it is quite significant that they are indestructible—an atom can never be destroyed. Since they are so long-lasting, atoms can move to other locations and traverse thousands of kilometers; they know all the languages in the world and all the secrets of nature. "Every single atom that each of *you* contains has passed through multiple stars and been part of millions of organisms on its way to become part of you," Sisoye said. "In other words, dear colleagues, all of you, all of us, are only reincarnations, and ephemeral ones at that. When we die, our atoms will dissociate as when you scramble a Rubik's Cube; they will go off to seek new configurations in other places, becoming part of a leaf, or the eye of a woman, or a tiny droplet of dew. None of us know if we bear within us an atom of a fly that died a thousand years ago or an atom from the pumpkin that the wife of Kosan, the scribe of the Macedonian King Vukashin, baked between her torrid thighs in 1366. Atoms do not die," Sisoye stressed. "Half a million atoms placed in a row would only be as wide as a human hair," he added, unconsciously patting down that disobedient strand on his head. "When we know all this it is easy to grasp that every living creature is the product of a single idea, and it is the fate of all living things to turn into nothing. Except for bacteria . . ." he added, "bacteria will still be here when the sun dies; this is their planet, and we are only here because they let us share it with them." He stood on his toes so the audience could see the handkerchief perching jauntily in the breast pocket of his coat. "Bacteria existed for billions of years without us, but we can't survive a single day without them," he continued without looking at his notes under the green lamp on the rostrum. "Why not? Because microbes, for example, provide us with the very air we breathe. Who taught the lion, when it has fever, to treat itself by eating monkey? The atoms of a physician that have become part of the lion, of course! The key to life is to be found in the atoms that dissociate and go off to seek new uses after each of us expire," Sisoye said, and took a quick gulp of mineral water; it sloshed in his glass and a little splashed out. Someone in the upper rows burst out laughing, but no one joined in, so he cleared his throat and fell silent again. The audience in the hall was largely still attentive; only a few of the older academicians in the center were dozing, shaking their heads as if in disagreement with everything Sisoye said. He went on undeterred: "Therefore, dear colleagues, if we are descended from monkeys, and monkeys in turn from bananas, which came first—the chicken or the egg?" Now there were guffaws, as if from nowhere; the upholstered chairs in the hall creaked and all the birds that had been sitting on the frosted-glass dome above them suddenly took flight. Since Sisoye had been studying the theses of his inaugural speech for years, he knew with certainty that something like this would happen when he reached that sentence, so he made a calculated pause; taking another sip of the mineral water that by now had gone flat, and, although the hubbub had not quite subsided, he added calmly: "If monkeys are descended from bananas, then we ourselves are very closely related to fruit, and therefore to vegetables as well. It is important to note that half of the chemical functions that take place in a banana are identical to those in a human being. This can be readily verified by simple laboratory analysis, and proves that all life is one, or rather that all the life in the universe is based on a single idea, whoever might have originated it," he concluded and coughed into the white handkerchief from his breast pocket. Many people in the audience thought he had finished, and there was some muffled applause, but Sisoye picked up his folder, took two steps to the left of the rostrum, and surveyed the hall with a quick, cynical glance: "All of you sitting on chairs are actually not sitting on them but floating about one hundred millionth of a centimeter above them—your electrons and those of the chair fiercely resist any greater intimacy!" he announced. And just at that moment it seemed that the gap between the chairs and the academicians' bottoms began to grow and the academicians started to float first above their seats, then over the rows where they had been sitting, ascending higher and higher; they passed through the square concrete frame of the ceiling, which the frosted-glass dome rested on, rose even higher, penetrated the glass, and disappeared like shadows into the cloudy sky above the Academy.

APPENDIX

Academician Sisoye opened his eyes and was about to thank his audience, but there was no one in the Hall. He could hear only a strange chuckling in the second row, somewhere on the right behind the ornately carved column. Perplexed by the emptiness of the hall, Sisoye headed toward the door on the left, turned around . . . and then saw him, leaning back in the upholstered chair behind the column, wiping his thick glasses with his necktie, and laughing sweetly—his greatest antagonist, Academician Slavko Sivakov. He is as indestructible as atoms, Sisoye thought.

EPILOGUE

After Sisoye's death, the Institute of Strategic Studies at the Academy entrusted me to look after the estate of our colleague, who, unfortunately, as you know, never managed to give his inaugural speech. Among the notes that I found in the sandal box under his dining-room table I discovered a short letter that amounted to his will: it stipulated that his mortal remains be buried in his native region, in the Sveta Petka Monastery, and that "my coffin as well as the cushion holding my medals and decorations be taken to the specified eternal resting place on Uncle Erdo's handcart." The investigating magistrate's report states that Sisoye died while eating a banana, but the autopsy confirmed that cause of death was acute myocardial infarction—in other words, a heart attack. The records confirm that his inaugural speech lay on the table in front of him, as well as a vase, a bowl containing two bananas and one orange, and a brief story he had written about his oration, which shows that he had been going over the event in his mind up until his final moments. His only error was that he wrote that I would be sitting in the second row behind the ornately carved column on stage right. I was actually sitting in the front row between Academicians Prežihov and Trepetlika; the latter asked jokingly several times if making people wait was inherent to the human condition or was simply part of our national will toward self-destruction. By then the hall was full and the audience was waiting patiently for Sisoye's inauguration to begin—but our fellow academician was already dead.

BIBLIOGRAPHY

In compiling this text, I used Sisoye's speech and the notes found in his apartment; I often referred to Bill Bryson's *A Short History of Nearly Everything*, underlined here and there with a yellow pencil, as well as the books that stood neatly ordered in two columns of ten on Sisoye's desk in his kitchen. I noted that he had been an avid reader of Harry James Cargas, Dion Scott-Kakures, Frederick Ferré, Ronald Miller, and Richard Popkin; my own book on the ethical aspects of aesthetics was also there, among many others.

ACKNOWLEDGEMENTS

Now at the end—or is it perhaps the beginning?—I would like to thank my colleagues at the Institute of Strategic Studies, who read my work even at the manuscript stage and made useful suggestions. Without them, this text would not be what it is. I would also like to thank my loving, patient, and incomparable wife Savka Sivakov, who encouraged me to persevere and complete this project. Sincere gratitude to Tacko Najstej in Paskvelija, the monks from the Sveta Petka Monastery, and to Uncle Erdo for lending me his handcart, in which I took our deceased colleague to his grave at such an ungodly hour. And of course many thanks to you as well, because you are paying attention to me as though I exist, though I know I don't.

TRANSLATED FROM MACEDONIAN BY WILL FIRTH

DANUTĖ KALINAUSKAITĖ

Just Things

I am a teacher of Lithuanian language and literature. Recently I asked my senior class to write an essay on the topic of "Things" (the idea was suggested by my son: "All the things around us seem so distant now . . . it's as though they no longer exist . . ."). I wanted them to write about the most common things—an orange, a pair of shoes, a hand towel. The idea was to write about the quiet essence of the things you use every day and surround yourself with, but which you never really pay attention to. Almost all my students, however, wrote about "soshal" inequality. About the things that they would like to own, but couldn't.

One student wrote the following: "Her daughter-in-law has a salon in the center of Vilnius while her son works at growing company, where of course he's the director. He has a country home filled with tile and hardwood floors. And her other son has a house with a pool, a sauna, a bar, three dogs, a cat, a chinchilla, an iguana, and the devil knows what else. But all we have is a kitten named Raisin that we found under a bridge."

Under the Soviets, when the cultural elite talked about spiritual wealth and the state of society in general, they had much to say about this variety of possession—possession of things, possession of wealth. Back then it meant the betrayal of your spiritual values. In articles that professed to analyze "the interaction between literature and contemporary reality," critics warned of "the increasing danger of our developing a cult of material goods," noting that there was a real threat that "love of things" might "replace the love of man," quite commonly turning man into a "slave of things." "Things are impervious to human warmth," etc.

Ideologies have changed. The "cult of material goods" has been officially sanctioned, and the "greedy materialist consumer" has been entirely rehabilitated. Only the things themselves remain innocent. As the years go by, one even manages to convince oneself that they are in fact permeable—if you yourself, for whatever reason, haven't already lost all your own humanity—to human warmth and coldness, to crime and punishment, to this world and the next, to everything.

I won't pretend to be ambivalent about "material goods." I like things. I find them interesting. They are the sowers of discord, but also act as peacemakers—like fungi that, with their long microscopic threads, have managed to interweave themselves into our human interactions. Things are like fragments, which nonetheless can unspool a sense of wholeness. Or else, we feel that wholeness has managed to squeeze itself into one component part. Into some black coat that's already been reversed at least once and whose shiny lapels, cuffs, and pocket flaps are touched up with a piece of coal before you head off to an important engagement . . . Things: the signs of fate and all fate's prophets. Archives or depositories, hiding places or artifacts. Things in the attic unnecessary to anyone, living out their final incarnations: nobody will ever take them anywhere again. Life after life.

It's quite true that after death, people take up residence in things. When I look in the mirror with the chipped corner, which has a picture of Riga on the other side, or at a jackknife (price: two rubles, ten kopeks), or at a chess piece, the white rook, or at these Peponen pumpkinseed-oil capsules available at any pharmacy, I know—without any recourse to divination— that these are my father. This rosary with finger-worn prayer beads, and a note from a neighbor who was leaving on a trip: "Dogfood in the greenhouse. Wish us luck!" My aunt died during that trip. On my desk, the thorn-apple cocoon emptied of its contents by rain and wind—that's me when I temporarily "take my leave." And my parents' house, which no longer exists. The dyed lock of hair in the jewelry box with the secret bottom is not "a keratinized epidermal skin cell" as the encyclopedia says, but Vilmutė.

Vilmutė was from another town, and while receiving treatment in Vilnius, she stayed at my place. We cut off those locks of her hair in the kitchen, following her doctor's suggestion (because they would fall out anyway), after we'd filled a pot with stuffed cabbage. Joking around (back then we still joked around a bit), we each decided to keep a lock for ourselves, "as souvenirs." Vilmutė's friend, also a junior, having dyed his hair orange, the color of hope, gave up his studies in that other city and moved in with us, sleeping on an inflatable mattress. He put a lock of his hair into the pages of his physics textbook. Vilmutė's cousin, also a student, pressed his lock into the pages of his address book. My son, then a sixth grader, with no idea why anyone would want a lock of human hair, tied his lock with a string and hung it from the table lamp. I was shocked. When I looked at it, I saw the sad, drooping mustache of a Jew sentenced to death. I told my son that the locks were souvenirs and must be preserved. We found a place for ours in the box I kept my pewter ring in—the box with the secret compartment.

Vilmutė's parents were divorced. Her father was a musician. When drunk, he'd turn expansive and generous, and the world became his stage. One day while observing a solar eclipse through an X-ray of his wife's lungs, it occurred to him that he was suffocating in his own home, where nobody understood him. That's when he decided to sell his two saxophones and buy a cottage in the country. Worn out by all the city noise and constant bickering with his wife in their common but unshared apartment, he was now a happy man, with nobody nagging him, able to sleep until noon and shave his beard outdoors using the shard of a broken mirror. He kept a goat, and with it (because it never got bored or interrupted him), he would discuss his many existential dilemmas. Sometimes he would go back to the city, to his former home, because one room still belonged to him there. He'd heard about Vilmutė's diagnosis, but he never knew what city or to what hospital she'd been admitted—nor what her temperature was, what she was eating, or if she was eating at all. In fact, he was annoyed when his wife's relatives would force him to concern himself with such matters, forcing them "through the eye of the needle of banality!" His relationship with his daughter—well, it was intense. Spiritual. He couldn't care for her or help her in any way because he'd suffer too much in the process. He couldn't endure it. He'd die himself. And so, just to feel that he was contributing to the cause, he'd leave some farm-fresh apples on the table in the foyer. But his daughter, coming back from the hospital after chemotherapy, usually found that these had already rotted in her absence. If she still hadn't come home by the time of his next visit, the bowl of rotten apples would so infuriate her father that he would break everything in sight.

Vilmutė melted like butter, however, and little by little forgave everyone. Even her father, because he really did love her, after all—it was just that his love was trying to find some new means of expressing itself, and it hadn't had any luck so far. And then she forgave Paris, though she had been condemned to never see it. And the little black dress with spaghetti straps. Her peach-colored lipstick. With her belongings in a plastic shopping bag from Maxima, she went from hospital to hospital. Already visiting the foreign clinics when her doctors still had hope, "in theory," one evening she quietly asked her mother to bury her in the cemetery next to her grandparents. To plant snapdragons there, because "their mouths are happy." She promised to look after them all "from the other side." On her last day, having tidied up her things, she told them what to give to whom, and then she washed up and brushed her teeth. She prepared herself like someone who'd lived for ninety years, for whom death had not appeared unexpectedly but was just one more little hill in the map of her mind.

During the funeral, Vilmutė's father—a tragic figure by nature—wailed, truly wailed, clinging to the shoulder of his own mother, an old woman, because, as usual, he had arrived "a tiny bit late." To try and salvage something of the vent, he poured some dirt from his daughter's grave into his mitten (where does he keep that dirt now—in a bottle? a bottle with a false bottom? did he spill it while drunk?), but, not having been invited to the funeral dinner, he disappeared soon after. To the horror of his parents, Vilmutė's friend dropped out of school and dyed his hair black, but fortunately only for a short while. Vilmutė's mother ("I am, but I'm not!") had already cried out all her tears. Yes, you can run out of tears. I know a woman who seemed to have been singled out for suffering: she lost her father, then her mother, and then her only son—who was hit by a truck while trying to change a tire on the side of the road—and now spends all her time taking care of her mother's sister, whose legs are swollen like balloons. The old lady wets her bed and yanks at her caregiver's hair and spits porridge in her face whenever she's being fed. The woman's eyes are all cried out by now: they're as dry as gravel. In order to be able to cry her feelings out like most people, she would need an operation on her tear ducts. Obviously, that's out of the question. So she's forced to make do with fake tears. Which she nevertheless has to buy. They cost thirteen litas, seventy-five cents. There's always a vial full of tears in the fridge. She often asks her husband, "Bronius, where did you put my tears? Is it time for me to buy new tears already?"

When people start dying around you—and once you turn forty, that's pretty much unavoidable—you start to notice what happens to the things the departed have left behind. These objects are valuable, after all: juicers, dishes, bedding, towels ... frequently with price tags still hanging off them, having been kept for "special occasions." These leftovers are distributed to relatives like prizes. The most loyal things, however, the things most deserving preservation—the things used so often as to become irreplaceable, almost second skins—tend to get thrown out when their owner dies: not worth anything to anyone. Dentures, shaving implements, bandages, a container for kidney stones, underwear, shoes shaped by one's own feet . . . all are sent off to their ends in the garbage can—for bums perhaps to discover and use again. Things carry away our entire lives, piece by piece. As if we'd never even existed.

Those on their way out of this world have to leave their things behind, whether they like it or not, even though their possessions made up a large part of themselves. The living, on the other hand, hold onto their things tightly, as if they won't ever have to die. And they accumulate even more the longer they live. Yet, everything that is accumulated and warehoused sucks up life's oxygen. But to have only as much as one needs requires superhuman strength. Perhaps the things themselves won't let go of us? Perhaps they're manipulating us according to their own evil ends? Over there, a moth-eaten rug inherited from a deceased relative has pitted brother against brother. And a pair of cousins is beating up one another over a small handheld eggbeater, worth no more than a few litas. I read somewhere that things follow the same social patterns as human beings: they seek revenge, hold grudges, lie, quarrel, and kill. And this is especially true of tables, wallets, and knives. My friend's uncle, who left for America, sold all his family's gold and silver in a time of need, but he kept and cherished his most ordinary kitchen knife. He's certain that he only made it because of that knife. It's true, little knives have always had to shoulder the heaviest burdens and be party to the most difficult tasks. Look how much they figure in stories of poverty, fear, hope, making a (comfortable) living, and death. But most often it's the violins and pianos that really go bad. At my house, everyone sighed with relief when four men pulled our Ukrainian piano out onto the stairwell on a greased hide. I decided to sell it when I heard my son tell his new Internet girlfriend over the phone: "If you really want to know more about me, I'll start with the worst: I play the piano . . ."

To get rid of what you don't need anymore, the things that suck up your life's oxygen, is an enormous relief. That's probably why we've found ourselves with less and less decoration in our homes—the winds of time have whisked all the clutter away from our contemporary, minimalist interiors. Accordingly, I categorize homes as "hard" or "soft." "Hard" ones are furnished with nothing more than what is needed by someone exhausted by the stressful tempo of contemporary life: lots of clean, empty space. No irritants to assault the psyche. The past has been surgically removed. Blinds. Halogens (operating-room lighting). Silent, creeping constructions. Laminated flooring. Plastic ceiling tiles. Euphorbia and chamaedorea. Cacti. A computer. One hundred percent functional. True, such blinding newness sometimes affects homeowners in a strange way: they feel like guests in their own homes. That's why the rich spend such outrageous sums of money to send their designers to London to learn how to falsify the marks of time, to age things stylishly: to retouch the walls and furniture with a patina of time—even the lighting fixtures—to soften the kitchen mirror with the suggestion of steam, to graze the sink with rust. For the "soft" homes, there's no need to invest in age. Time does all the redecorating for free. In the cluttered halls of these homes, things no longer serving any purpose rise high in piles all mired in sentimental sap—no one makes a move to toss them out. Sparrows make their nests on the windowsills, and no-longer-fashionable geraniums become overgrown. Doors creak. The floorboards make their own footsteps.

Sometimes, if you're home alone, a metaphysical wind blows out of some dark corner. It brings in with it—through what tunnels?—the smell of the other side, the smell of grayness, and the hairs on the back of your neck stand up. In the "soft" homes, all the voices, footfalls, and dust need to settle somewhere—so they creep into the drapery and shades. Spiders are never at a loss for places to weave their lacy blankets—and there are always plenty of those unfortunate spiders to feed to the green salamander named San Sanych who came here in a box of oranges from Spain. There's always something to break: the framed and glassed Chardin *Grace before the Meal* that hung on the wall for twenty years has a fatal fall at two o'clock in the morning and shatters. That probably means something.

Nonetheless, during a person's life, things do vanish of their own accord—in diminishing concentric circles around you—and this has nothing to do with fads or fashion. You have no choice in the matter. It's a banal comparison, but does a tree in autumn choose to drop its leaves around itself in a ring? First to go is the gold sequin matron of honor dress. And the formal suit with white pinstripes and the hankie in its pocket. Ties. Hats and hat pins. Sixty place settings and as many champagne flutes. You won't have to borrow any from your neighbors, though. All sixty of your relatives, friends, and acquaintances have died or forgotten you—only one or two visit you now. The fishing net and bamboo spin-cast rod. Shish kebab skewers, pruning shears, the electric juicer, the meat grinder, the sausage maker, the shovel, the hammer you kept under your bed (for protection). Finally the thimble, spools of thread, pens, knitting needles, checkers, photographs, toothbrush and toothpicks—because there's nothing left to pick—until only "hard" minimalism remains in your newly narrowed circle: chamber pot, eyeglasses (held together with wire), the pressed-glass tumbler. It's too heavy for your X-ray of a hand to lift, but that's why, perched at the edge of the table, it doesn't tip over when the green love bird swoops down to get a drink. Yes, you share your last sips with a bird . . . But this person hasn't yet turned into a thing. If he keeps his wits about him, if he pays attention to what goes on, he can be a real prophet till the end of his days . . . he can see through walls, he can hear the unheard "Forward!" shouted by time. He knows what his relatives will say before they've said it. They putter about him, but he's a "thing unto himself." A rock that will not be moved until it's good and ready.

But it's a different story entirely when a person actually becomes a thing. Officially he still has a passport and an identification number, a pensioner's certificate, a line in the census taken by the Republic of Lithuania, and, during elections, a vote. But, unofficially, he's a thing. An old suitcase with a checkered lining, once upon a time taken to Petersburg or Bauska and later used to transport Clapp's Favorites, fruit that practically melts in your mouth, to the market. Now it's in the attic under a heap of rags, wrapped in a dusty scrap of fur. Such a person, lost in time and space, living in his children's apartment on the ninth floor, wakes up at three in the morning (for his children, it's night) and goes to feed the pig and the chickens. He goes out to do his "feeding" every half hour, every day, sometimes even more often. Or he ends up somewhere strange, and when he's there, he has "bowel movements" (anyone who's ever been to the hospital has heard doctors ask during their morning visits: "When was your last bowel movement?"), and in his mind's eye there are no more hills, dales, or steep slopes, only plains. That's when the relationships between the children of these old folks (God's little birds) become sorely tested: "If you force me to take Dad, I'll lock him in a closet—I have no other place to put him." Or: "If you won't agree to take Mother, I'll just leave her on the doorstep—in the morning you'll find a nice little present."

But that's not even all. Not too long ago I read a story in the paper about an accident on the German Autobahn that killed three Lithuanians. Young, attractive, traveling around Europe. They were returned to Lithuania in zinc coffins. When their relatives—and later the court-appointed forensics expert—opened the coffins, they were horrified. The dearly departed had been thrown into the coffins like logs, "uncomfortably," with their arms broken and legs twisted, already disintegrating, faces rotting (they had not been refrigerated), probes still in their mouths, taken directly from the intensive care unit. Their relatives immediately tried to take the German authorities to court—to protect the right of the dead to their dignity. But the pragmatic German burial laws dismissed their claims: a body being transported has the same status as an object; which is why you can't file a suit on its behalf—at least not seeking redress for an insult to its dignity. Theft or destruction of property ... now that would be another story. In other words, don't go looking for something you never had. You got back what you sent out: things. We apologize for the poor quality of the objects on their return. For their depreciated value.

You wake up in a cold sweat when your blood pressure is up and you imagine what will become of you after death. Your hair, your nails, your skin. Where will you go? What kinds of states, situations, or deceptions still await you? If your faith is limited to what you can see and touch, most likely you'll come back as a thing: a remote control for a television, a Siemens telephone, a pen, a potato peeler, a lavender sachet. An aromatherapeutic bar of soap.

I like things. I guess I'm a slave to things. I like the very physical essence of things. Their texture. Their roughness, their coarseness ... A close up of Amélie's hand reaching into a bag of slippery peas in that movie ... her hand could be mine. At my friend's house, I open up her old kitchen cabinet without permission and breathe in the scent. It's not the scent of pearled barley or buckwheat in three-liter jars, but of a past world long gone. That world, I'm guessing, is made up of bags of wool and a patch of muslin, a dark green bottle of turpentine, a dry cough, bread wrapped in cheesecloth, nutmeg and cardamom, heart medicine, and, in a secret corner of the cabinet, a gold ring—but that's another story—which, because of carelessness, had been sold to my friend along with the cabinet. Her husband had worked long and hard on the piece when they first bought it from an old lady: squirting a special mixture into each termite hole he could find. Thus embalmed, it survived the old lady and her daughter—the ring's owner—and the orchard, which was leveled, and the village, whose name everyone has already forgotten. At another friend's house, I secretly dig my nail into her Malaysian hardwood table (it's only *called* hardwood: it's soft as butter). Damn my oversensitive sense organs! I must smell everything, touch everything with my fingertips . . .

Besides that, I find it hard to part with things. It's harder than I'd like for me to throw the things I can easily do without down the garbage chute. I am especially fond of little things. All kinds of knickknacks, short stories, wisdom that can be summed up in one sentence. I could write an entire treatise about the smallness of things. But smallness is more palatable for the Chinese, because they have such tiny fingers. Lithuanians, though . . . My father told me how his father, my grandfather, many years ago in the village whose name everyone has forgotten, was repairing a watch that he had taken apart on the kitchen table. This big-nosed guy named Peredavi ius stopped by the cottage and spent some time chatting. When he was ready to leave, Grandfather suddenly noticed that a tiny watch piece was missing—probably a spring. The whole family fell silent, concentrating, Peredavičius along with them, searching for that spring in the pots and pans, in the cracks between the floorboards, in the bucket of ashes; they even studied the garbage. After about two hours of hunting, Peredavičius, to his great surprise, found it under the nail of his ring finger, big as life. "What a little shit," he said on his way out, as if he had been offended or tricked by someone . . .

In the oppressive heat of the afternoon, as I look at the pumpkins, squash, and zucchini, all scattered in the matte-gold dust, I realize that the very soul of summer is locked in those seeds. The poplar bonsai is dropping its yellowing leaves: on its miniature shoulders, it balances time's cosmic turn from autumn to winter. From my ninth-floor apartment window, the silver Mazda looks like a wrinkled piece of aluminum foil after the accident. The wasps' nest under the ceiling of the woodshed, like a water-soaked Japanese paper lantern . . . That's more or less how I wanted my students to look at things. But they wrote only about *having* them. To have this, that, and the other thing. To have things is also what my son wants. Since his earliest days, I've been trying to teach him to appreciate the intangible —in the absence of this, that, or the other thing—which is impossible to buy or to own. For example, the golden threads of a good story. Metaphors and metonyms. Beauty itself without any possession. Especially beauty invisible to the naked eye. I teach him to cherish small things. In the way that Arundhati Roy's protagonists cherish them in *The God of Small Things*: "They laughed at ant-bites on each other's bottoms ... At the minute spider who ... camouflaged himself by covering his body with bits of rubbish —a sliver of wasp wing. Part of a cobweb. Dust. Leaf rot. The empty thorax of a dead bee." And so on. But inevitably the time will come when one's child will want big, serious things. It's his God-given, human right to have a Lamborghini, or at least a Harley Davidson. The kind of car that, when you press a button, instantly turns into an office; from its depths emerge a computer, a modern telephone, a chilled bottle of champagne, silver goblets, and even a naked woman.

In moments of crisis, I go to my friend's house in Markučiai. She's a heartless cynic, but that helps me. Last time when she was upset and I showed up saying, "I just want to kill myself," she immediately gave me a cold compress. Now wearing jay-feather earrings in the deepening darkness, she puffs on her pipe, her anger fermenting. Furious, she demands that I lie down and she rubs my back with coarse salt. While rubbing, she says: "Your everyday ontology, the dead bee's empty thorax, and all those quiet essences are just full of shit. You have to give your son the best of everything, and that's that. Instead of crying and feeling sorry for yourself, hold your head up. Damn it, you're a teacher, a specialist, you should be sparkling with ideas! About how to marry him off to the daughter of a Mafioso or the head of the customs office! Then your little Vytautas will *have* his Harley Davidson, and after your chin is covered in whiskers and you're suffering from gout, you will *have* a peaceful old age, covered up in a fringed shawl." I know my cynic is right as usual. But for me, like for all mothers, it's uncomfortable to go "forward." I look around my "soft" home. I go out "feeding": I feed an autumn fly to my San Sanych.

I look around my pantry and bookshelves. A little bit of everything, all sucking up the oxygen of my life. Lots of sentimentality, but nothing worth passing on in my son's hope chest. Not even a porcelain dinner service for twelve with an oversized soup bowl. Not even silver candlesticks made up of eleven parts each. Not even any family heirlooms: a great-great-great-grandmother's gold incisor or a pair of scissors for trimming candle wicks. Of course there's no sign of any Fabergé eggs. Instead, I've got my thorn-apple cocoon, into which I escape in moments of weakness. The time, I know, will come . . . when I will remain in it for eternity. For now, just in case, I keep my chin up and fill the cocoon with something intangible. Secretly—if we are successful—I hope that my son will be able to sneak it into the customs office director's house . . . like contraband.

TRANSLATED FROM LITHUANIAN BY JŪRA AVIŽIENIS

STEFAN SPRENGER

Dust

▪

In Burgenfeld in Lower Bavaria a group of medical practitioners and therapists met in Wittelsbacher Castle every second Wednesday evening during the winter to experiment with the continuing developments in Family Dynamics since Bert Hellinger. The participants arrived with suggestions about what should be discussed that evening and during preliminary talks came to an understanding about approach. The range of topics was wide: everything from historical events to the question of future energy supplies to the existence of metaphysical presences was examined to the last detail. The basis for the group's "performative mimesis" was the theory of morphic resonance postulated by Sheldrake, which states that the growth, behavior, and mentality of living beings are influenced by the experiences of their ancestors by way of a shared, location-and-time dependent field.

One of the field studies of the Burgenfeld Circle concerned itself with the question of which stage in evolution emotion began. The biologists, physiologists, and neurologists all agreed unequivocally on this point, giving an answer quite familiar to the other participants: below humans and the higher animals, there can be no emotion. Therefore, in order to be able to measure emotion on an incremental scale, moving step by step from a wholly emotionless state to the level of human beings, the researchers attempted to establish a baseline of zero emotion by examining ordinary household dust. The results were astonishing: counter to all of their assumptions, the Burgenfeld Circle in fact detected a really quite considerable level, indeed an abundance, of emotion in the stuff, necessitating a revision of their entire emotional hierarchy . . .

■ ■

Frau H.'s studio was located in the attic of an industrial building; a paint factory, a carpenter, and a metal-worker occupied the three floors below. Never having expected that the attic might be used for anything besides storage, the owners had—for ease of maintenance, as well as to minimize the noise level in the neighborhood—installed an enormous air compressor there, rather than putting it outside; all the various tenants used it in their daily operations. So Frau H. shared her loft with a device that came to life with a loud clacking of its return valve every time someone in the workshops below drew compressed air, and it continued to clang, bang, and whistle until the system returned to full compression, which cacophony imposed random pauses in speech and thought upon Frau H. and any guests. Additionally, it happened that the vibrations of the device kicked up all the industrial dust that appeared in the poorly insulated loft and so spread it throughout the entire space with incredible efficiency. Yet, the compressor wasn't the only piece of machinery that made its presence known in Frau H.'s studio: the motor of the freight elevator had its housing on the roof and howled and shook inside Frau H.'s head whenever goods or materials were transported between the floors. Frau H. was not only able to "take" all this, however, but indeed was endowed with the ability to lose herself in the noises as soon as she walked into her studio—having developed a kind of patience with or perhaps consideration for this technic-pneumatic pandemonium, despite its being quite enough to drive any other artist (not possessed of Frau H.'s unique temperament) out of their mind. Frau H. saw the arrhythmic alarum of the machinery as her fair share of the abuse that man committed against man. The studio, she understood, was her expiation. Beyond this, she never gave the noises much thought.

Frau H. often sought the far away. Not its stillness, but its action, its hectic pulse.

Once, after returning to her studio loft in E. after several months abroad, she found that a thick layer of dust had formed on her work table —a large, propped-up slab of black Formica—and all strips and leaves of paper she'd left lying on it. Because Frau H. was already looking ahead to her next project, she began to remove the papers without dusting the table beforehand. The compressor sprang to life as she worked, and her eyes widened in wonder as she took in the sight of bright dust flecks flocking onto the dark Formica slab, gradually whitening the clean black spaces, the rectangle and square shapes left by her efforts to tidy up.

■　■　■

"Do you hate your instrument?" tour manager Brandstetter asked when he finally got the opportunity in W. to confront Klubka after a concert. The evening before, the third violin had decided to disappear into the night immediately after the final applause had died down. He hadn't come back— still wearing his concert tux—until the rest of the orchestra was in bed. This time Brandstetter had lain in wait for Klubka at the artists' entrance of the W. municipal concert hall and then tugged on the violinist's sleeve after following him to the neighboring Havana Club. Klubka didn't resist, accepted the proffered cigar and Cuba libre, and afterward observed in silence as the barkeeper, who'd had to open a new bottle of Havana Club Anejo Especial for Brandstetter's drink, let the first drops of rum fall to the teakwood floor.

"Ah," Klubka said, "the *lágrima*."

"The what?" the tour manager asked. He wanted to come to the point with Klubka quickly. He still had eight points on his daily to-do list to cross off after this.

"The ritual of tears," Klubka said. "For the orishas. In gratitude that they came over the sea with the slaves. It's difficult for gods to cross the big water."

The tour manager looked at Klubka, uncomprehending.

"Forget it," said Klubka. "In answer to your question: no, I do not hate my instrument."

■　■　■　■

The emotion discovered in the Burgenfeld dust plunged the group of researchers into embarrassed confusion: they knew that type and composition of this emotion had to be explored. After all, once a morphogenetic field is tapped, it must be exhausted then and there, or else continue to have influence in unknown ways from that point on. Nonetheless, they were understandably afraid of what they might find—was it possible that they might discover a new means of precisely measuring all emotion that would render their previous research into human psychology obsolete? One of them too expressed his fear that they might discover in the dust the source of the existential "ennui," the entropic querulousness occurring so frequently in men of their age; while another made clear that he'd been raised a Catholic, speculating that it was possible they had all stumbled onto the concrete and omnipresent manifestation of evil in the form of this ever-present dust. So they moved out of the great hall in which they usually held their symposia and into the wood-paneled hunting room nearby to take a much-needed break and fish for dust-related information on their Blackberries and iPhones—something that the UMTS antenna in the castle tower, which also provided the whole city's 3G coverage, facilitated within seconds:

+ *Dust is a result of the divisibility of matter* + *The dust particle is the smallest object the human eye can detect* + *In terms of size, proportionally, a sin-*

gle unit of household dust represents the halfway point between a subatomic particle and the planet Earth + Memento, homo, quia pulvis es, et in pulverem reverteris + Household dust results from an attritive mixture of dead insects, particles of human skin, and cloth fibers + Dust mites, which feed on particles of human skin, live in household dust, discharge feces twenty times per day, and produce a new generation every three weeks +

"Oh dear," commented Gerlinde (Hawaiian massage, Constellation Work, past-life regression) who had pulled that last gem from the web. "Dust eats people."

The symposium chair, Sonja (systemic assemblies, life coaching, angels), sprung from her leather chair, visibly anxious, and said with forced cheer—trying to set a good example—"Let's find out!" The group followed her halfheartedly back into the great hall and prepared themselves for an exacting analysis of the emotion of dust.

■   ■   ■   ■   ■

Frau H. gazed wide-eyed at the dust tableau on her table because in her absence the very work had come into being toward which she had been striving for years and had only ever caught sight of, caught hints of, in flashes of intuition. She had tried to scratch it out of copper plates, to coax it out of mixtures of water and egg and limestone and pigment, to sift it out of the grain of enlarged photographs. In all of these projects, the merest hint of the sought-after something had become perceptible, but Frau H. wanted more. And she *did* more: making herself sick in order to experience again the gritty fever dreams of her childhood illnesses, curious if the same swirling, milling, cascading cataracts that the young girl's brain had known how to produce would now return ... But no, there was only lethargy. She set off stun grenades in the basement, having discovered in her research that sudden, overwhelming sensory experiences can affect the brain's vision centers to such an extent that you lose the depth and sharpness and color provided by your photoreceptor cones for weeks on end, having to make do with nothing more than the grainy black-and-white night vision of your rods—a slow and indistinct form of vision that might help her to approach the effect she sought. Instead of giving herself perpetual night vision, however, Frau H. suffered hearing loss, and could only go out into open air with dark sunglasses for quite a while after. Also, she got horrible sweating attacks, leaving her body dripping wet, as though she were trying to sweat out the grenade's effects.

Asked what the hell *it* could possibly be, the thing that she'd been searching for so doggedly in her eye and brain, she only knew what *it* wasn't: it wasn't smooth, or clear, or new, or segregated; it wasn't an image, some material, or an object. Was it only, God help her, some new way of seeing she was after?

"No," she said, "Or, if so, then that's only the way in which it will reveal itself."

And now it had revealed itself.

■ ■ ■ ■ ■ ■

"But you don't clean your violin anymore!" Brandstetter said to Klubka.

Klubka pulled his little leather pouch of violin resin out of his pocket and laid it on the bar next to his cigar butt, all burned out in the expensive-looking ashtray. Brandstetter sighed to himself: again it was time to hear a little lecture.

"Colophony," Klubka said, "is gleaned from pine resin distilled in steam such that the turpentine volatizes and the colophony remains."

These lectures always occurred in instances when the orchestra's musicians felt that they were being called to duty as guardians of culture, while he, in their eyes, was just a stupid little bookkeeper happy to run himself ragged seeing to their needs.

"You add galipot, Venetian turpentine, beeswax, or mastic to it according to the area of application. You apply it to the violin bow so that stiction arises between the bow hair and violin string. The colophony bonds the bow hair to the violin string; the hair pulls the string in the stroke's direction from the at-rest position."

Which is exactly what the tour manager's musicians were constantly trying to do to him: pull him out of his at-rest position. Their salaries were too low, the hotels too dingy, cars too uncomfortable: complain complain complain. He never had a moment's rest, thanks to these arrogant penguins.

"If the resistance of the string is greater than the stiction, then it rebounds. That's okay, because the speed of the bow's motion across the string generates warmth and the colophony changes from an adhesive to a lubricating film, in which the string can safely slide back into place. If the heat from friction dissipates, the colophony hardens again and fuses the bow hair and string together until frictional heat arises again. Stick, slide, stick."

Before the tour Brandstetter had done some research and made out index cards for every instrument. He knew that you needed cleaning sheets with a magnesium layer for the keys of woodwind instruments so that the player's spit doesn't clog the keys and leave the thing making ugly kissing noises in concert. He knew that trombonists were discussing a new lubricant that didn't have to be mixed from two substances, but was also considered a little too "monotonous." And he knew that after concerts a violinist ought to cleanse his violin of colophony dust with a cloth and a mild cleaning agent and that Klubka had not done this since the beginning of the tour. Because of this, the *fortissimi* kicked up so much dust from the violin section you might as well have been sitting in a construction site. Of course, his colleagues had complained—Klubka would set off someone's allergies, everyone's clothes were getting dirty, complain complain complain. And that's why he was sitting there with Klubka, playing with his Cuba libre and looking for an opportunity to suggest Klubka clean his violin.

"Stick, slide, stick," Klubka repeated slowly, as if savoring the meaning and hidden meaning of each individual word. "There's something to that."

So there you have it, Brandstetter thought tiredly, another hurrah for the lecture circuit.

"It's like in life," Klubka continued. "A person wants to stick to something no matter what. A woman. A kid. An instrument. But you always slide away. Or it slides away from you. Even if you think you've got a good hold on it—the woman because of marriage, the child because of its dependency, the instrument because it's safe in its case. But you lose the inner adhesion. Because the resistance is too great."

"Yes," Brandstetter said, and remembered the story one of the violas had told him: Klubka's son had drowned years ago and Klubka had never gotten over it. So that was it: Klubka was having a crisis. He would—Brandstetter snuck a look at his watch—listen for twenty more minutes, saying "yes" and "I understand" before finally being able to turn his attention to the day before yesterday's medical expenses, when one of the musicians had urgently demanded special medicinal herbs at half past midnight, despite everyone's being in perfect health.

■　■　■　■　■　■　■

Though the great hall of Wittelsbacher Castle had underfloor heating, it was cooler than the hunting room. Some of the researchers pulled their cardigans tighter while others nestled into their pullovers. Through a glass roundel the crescent moon gleamed on the western horizon, almost bent to a circle by the old and uneven glass. A cold January wind rustled in the ivy on the outer wall. Sonja, the chair, let her eyes wander from face to face. "We'll establish the components of dust individually, then we'll bring in a stand-in for emotion"—she nodded towards Maja (Bach flower remedies, chromotherapy)—"and we'll see where it goes. Agreed?"

The circle nodded.

"I need stand-ins for dead insects, human dandruff, and cloth. Oh, and for mites. Can you do mites, Georg?"

Georg (grief counseling) nodded and over-exaggeratedly scratched his left armpit. The group laughed, thankful for comic relief, and pushed their chairs back to the wall while Sonja posted the stand-ins in the newly opened space in the middle of the room. She pointed to each and told her stand-ins firmly: "You are now Dead Insects, you are now Dandruff ..."

The stand-ins closed their eyes and concentrated on their performance energies. The moods of Cloth, Dandruff, and Dead Insects, respectively, were neutral; while Mites, according to Georg, were feeling "fit as a fiddle, restless, and smug."

"Now move according to your impulses," Sonja told them.

The dust components huddled together in a group while Emotion with arms crossed over her chest and an unfocused gaze made loops and circles around them.

"Where do you belong?" Sonja asked her.

"I belong to dust but not to any of its individual parts here."

"Something is missing," Dead Insects suggested.

"Yeah," said Dandruff, "the most important thing is missing."

"Ahaaa," said Sonja, looking now at the circle of people sitting and watching the performance. She asked Winnibald (bodywork):

"Could you be the most important thing that's missing?"

"Of course," Winnibald said.

Winnibald had hardly stepped onto the stage when the other stand-ins turned to him and smiled; Emotion beamed and moved next to him.

"Are you material or immaterial?" the assembly leader asked him.

"Immaterial."

"From the Schools of Light or the Schools of Darkness?"

"Schools of Light."

"Is your function to learn or to teach?"

"More to act as a sort of ... remainder." Winni rumpled his forehead.

"I am that which remains when you have understood. Something exhausted, empty, but free." He closed his eyes. "Cinders. No, finer. Ash. Fly ash. Finer than air. When someone has understood something, something disperses. One part floats away upward. I am the part that sinks back. To the Earth. But invisible. The invisible remaining waste."

"I'm ashamed and grieving," said Emotion with tears suddenly rolling down her cheeks.

"For what?"

"For the many erring paths. The tears. The sorrow. The violence. The blood."

"What do you mean by that?" Sonja asked.

"For a few it's passed," sobbed Emotion, "but so many are still stuck in it. It's so . . . shameful."

All the other stand-ins were crying now too.

Sonja stared at Emotion, turning after a long pause to her seated colleagues: "I can't make sense of this anymore. Can someone help me out?"

The circle too was full of confused looks. Gerlinde spoke up:

"It appears that there is an additional, hitherto unknown component of dust," she said haltingly, "a sort of spiritual cinder. Or ash. Invisible, but with a heavy emotional weight. It appears that this emotional weight is shame."

She cleared her throat, stared into space for a moment, and then said so softly that only those next to her could hear: "It seems that dust is ashamed of people. For what they do. How they do it."

■　■　■　■　■　■　■　■

With regard to her Formica epiphany, Frau H. did something at once very smart and very dumb: She reached for her camera, loaded it with 3200 ASA black and white film, and set about taking pictures of the dust tableau from all sides: with macro, normal, and wide-angle lenses and from varying distances.

This was very smart because she managed thus to break her epiphany into smaller and smaller pieces and so provide herself with material that would last the next few years of her life and career.

This was very dumb because she would spend these next few years struggling desperately to conjure back the epiphany's entire and monstrous wholeness, profundity, and value.

This was very smart because she understood in the emotional rush of the first sighting that any attempt to represent the wholeness of her experience would only be destined for failure.

This was again very smart because Frau H. had for a long time chosen ceaseless action and restlessness over stillness and contemplation, which to her meant failure. Movement, decisiveness were what fueled her as an artist—epiphany or no epiphany.

This was very dumb because Frau H. had condemned herself to the position of photographic middleman: someone who might taste the thing itself but never be fully satisfied, never truly receive the dust gift she'd worked so hard to be worthy of—with every muscle fiber, with every neuron—in the years leading up to this day.

This was again very dumb because Frau H. failed to perceive the true meaning of the epiphany that had come unto her, which was not, as Frau H. thought, that she had been chosen to bring the beauty of dust to the world, but rather that she, Frau H., was just as whole, as profound, and as valuable, as the epiphany itself.

■ ■ ■ ■ ■ ■ ■ ■ ■

Brandstetter was convinced that you only really see what other people are like when they're having a crisis. How a person behaves at the bottom of the barrel—whether that person gets drunk, overeats, starves himself, yells, goes quiet, starts fights, runs away—shows you the sort of stuff that person is made of. Klubka, well, Klubka became a hermit when in crisis: withdrew, ruminated, lost sight of the practical. Hermit crises were difficult because they were slow and persistent. No end in sight. Brandstetter would have to set about fighting the symptoms one at a time.

"I like this song," Klubka said, indicating the Cuban song playing in the bar. "Old men who meet once a week, drinking rum, smoking, playing music, singing. Relaxed, worn out, thankful for every day they still have. I should move to Cuba. Klubka in Cuba, hah."

Brandstetter hadn't been paying attention to the music, and he didn't start now, but it was good that Klubka was talking again. "Do you speak Spanish?" Brandstetter asked.

"A bit. Took some continuing ed courses," Klubka replied.

"Nice language," said Brandstetter.

"Yeah, isn't it? Good string tension. Taut and elastic at the same time. I like it a lot." And then, after a pause: "God thinks in Spanish."

"*Viva*," Brandstetter said and nudged Klubka, "Want another one?"

"God thinks, but he doesn't speak." Klubka pressed his temples. "Clever. You have to lure Him out, you know? But not with prayer. That's useless. Believe me."

Brandstetter signaled the bartender, pointed to his empty glass and raised two fingers. The bartender nodded.

"You lure Him out by showing that you know how He thinks," Klubka said. "This, for example," Klubka raised the leather pouch of violin resin, "is typical God. First there's the forest, then we come along. Then there's the resin. And with resin, culture begins. Because you can glue things with resin while in nature there's no such thing as gluing. Resin makes flint points and sticks and birds' feathers into arrows. *Viva*."

"*Viva*," said Brandstetter and decided to put off doing the expenses for the day before yesterday's concert until tomorrow. Today, "The World According to Klubka" was on the program. And they were still stuck on colophony.

"God's saying something there. Even if He's not talking. He says 'Whoever wants to know what I think, considers the resin.' So I consider the resin. And what have I found out? It's everywhere. At its lowest point as the pitch rubbed on pigs to remove their hair before slaughter. In the middle as the soldering agent in electronics. At its highest point as violin resin in music. God's saying something here." Klubka winked knowingly. "Do you want to know what, Brandstetter?"

"Of course," said Brandstetter, tired.

"And do you know why I'm going to tell you and only you?"

"Yeah," said Brandstetter. "No."

"Your name."

"Gerolf?" asked Brandstetter.

"Brandstetter."

"Okay."

"*Brandstetter*, German for 'fire-starter,' the one who goes into the forest and burns himself a clearing so he can settle down there and work."

"Aha," Brandstetter said.

"That's someone who understands."

"Sure," Brandstetter said and felt alcohol and exhaustion taking the life out of him. He had to bring things to close here soon.

"God says: the resin is like Me. At the lowest point, at the highest, and in the middle. And so I draw Him out."

"With the colophony on your violin?"

"With the colophony on my violin."

"That's smart," Brandstetter said slowly. "But isn't God even closer to you when He can stay in . . . that leather pouch, next to you, up against your body?"

Klubka winked at Brandstetter again, put the colophony away, stood up, smoothed his concert tux, and bent down to Brandstetter's ear.

"It has to kick up dust, Brandstetter. That's the trick. God only comes when dust is flying."

Klubka left the bar, smiling, elated.

At least their talk had done some good for someone, Brandstetter thought. God only comes when dust is flying. It's been Operation Desert Storm from the beginning.

"Can I tell you a secret?" Brandstetter asked the bartender. The bartender raised his left eyebrow and looked at his customer with a shifting mixture of patience and weariness.

"Orchestra tours are a real bitch," Brandstetter said, shuddering. "And this time a double, please."

TRANSLATED FROM GERMAN BY DUSTIN LOVETT

NORA IKSTENA

Elza Kuga's Old-Age Dementia

The languid afternoon light of autumn envelops Greenwich Village. There is silence, peace, and a certain strangeness in the air. In New York, once called New Amsterdam, this network of narrow streets, crowded with the houses and warehouses, meanders haphazardly. Fortunes are told for five dollars on Bleecker Street, a polished, pre-packaged Tibet, India, or Nepal ready to cast an Eastern third eye on the inhabitants of the Village: their artists' delusions, all the fantasies of Gotham. The happiness of gay men is in full parade on Christopher Street. Small yellow flowers grow in beds and pots along Horatio. They smell like chrysanthemums and look like balls of butter. A man with a pale, flower-yellow, illness-ravaged face sits on some steps.

"Elza," he calls out and waves with a wasted, almost transparent hand.

Elza Kuga is sitting in her "coach." Her coachmen tend to change often. But for some time now she's been pushed around by Nebucadnecaria of the Ivory Coast.

"Call me Nabuco, ma'am!" she had screamed into Elza's ear the first time they met. They're like night and day—Elza with her white tuft of hair and Nabuco with her head topped by a shiny black tower fashioned of a hundred small braids.

Elza waves back at the flower-yellow man.

"I wonder what his name is," Elza thinks. She no longer remembers how many years these Village scenes have slid by her eyes. She's like a small dog being taken for a walk—though a dog whose walker doesn't yet need to bring scoop or bag in case of any unforeseen accidents. When that day comes, Elza will move to an old folks' home, where, when she needs some fresh air, she'll be pushed out onto the balcony or into the yard.

Elza asks Nabuco to stop beside the yellow flowers. She reaches out her thin hand to pluck one. The flower-yellow man smiles weakly at her. Elza's coach moves on. She brings the blossom to her nose and draws in its fragrance. In this brief moment, through her time-eroded memory, the scent draws out some sort of echo, some distant reverberation that she almost certainly recognizes. She wants to reach it but cannot.

. . . a yellow flower is a yellow flower is a yellow flower, it has the fragrance of a yellow flower, the fragrance of a yellow flower, the fragrance of a yellow flower . . .

In Elza's lap rests a rust-colored, dog-eared little book. She flips it open, puts the flower in it, closes it tightly, then holds the book with both hands. Two young men are strolling on the opposite side of the narrow street; one has something resembling a dog's collar around his neck, while the other has him on a short leash. The two appear very much in love, happy, demonstrating publicly their good-natured dependence upon each other.

Elza closes her eyes and turns her old face toward the tender autumn sun. She is and the sun is. The two of them speak to each other without words. Not even half a word is needed for them to understand one another. The sun is Elza's father, who carries her to her wet nurse, because her mother was destined to never rise from her birthing bed. The sun is her lover, who, having kissed her breasts, goes off to war never to return. The sun is her home, which she knows by name—"sun."

When they stop at a tiny intersection, Elza opens her eyes. A slender young man in black jeans, with a baby in kangaroo-pouch draped around his chest, is crossing the street. An old Labrador hobbles behind him, its back legs in a wagonlike contraption. The dog lumbers forward, stiffly moving its unencumbered front legs and weakly lifting its head to look at its master with sad, trusting eyes. The trio inch across the intersection.

Someone is knocking at Elza's heart, asking her to open the door, wanting to see what's hidden inside. Elza herself can no longer enter. "England is locked, the key is broken." God only knows why this fragment of an old nursery rhyme is going through her head. Time has rusted the hinges of her heart.

If Elza had children, would they lead her along like the young man his old Labrador, or would they whisk her away somewhere, out of sight? So that their children need not see feeble old age with its sad trusting eyes and its back legs locked into a wagonlike contraption, Elza thinks. Elza refuses to continue this train of thought. Elza is Elza is Elza. She will die in Greenwich Village, she will be turned to ashes and buried somewhere in the middle of Gotham. She will mingle with the crowd of thousands of fallen souls who have got stuck in chimneys en route to heaven. There will be a place commemorating her passing. A spare patch of earth in a carefully mowed lawn among stone crosses and other markers. It seems to Elza that it would be only proper for there to be some burial mounds around as well. But why?

Nabuco guides "the coach" expertly through the door of an Italian eatery. On noticing the new arrivals, a man behind the counter calls out happily:

"Elza, Elza, *mozzarella fresca, mozzarella fresca . . .*"

Elza smiles at him and nods in agreement. The lively Italian, knowing well the answer, turns to Nabuco.

"No mozzarella for me," Nabuco says, a warning note in her voice.

"*Salmone a la griglia,*" the Italian tempts her.

"Let it be," Nabuco sings out in a throaty voice, crooning the popular song.

The delighted Italian rushes into the kitchen, returning after a while with take-out containers full of food.

Enticed by the smell, Nabuco pushes Elza forward enthusiastically. The slow-motion frames flickering in front of Elza's eyes accelerate as well.

... people, buildings, dogs, sidewalk cafes, squirrels, the golden-coin leaves of a maidenhair tree, pigeons, short Puerto Rican flower vendors, faded rose petals in gutters, discounted book piles on sidewalks, antique tea services, fresh chocolate cakes, mannequins—transparent virtual lovers with shaved heads in shop windows ...

Elza hurries on. What will flash past her eyes in her last moments? Elza senses that in that brief instant she will suddenly remember everything. The faded contours will all be sharpened, her phantoms filling out with bright, natural colors. Their voices will sound clearly.

Elza will be handed a mug of hot chocolate, she will be advised to blow on it, and just to make sure, asked to tie on a bib. A bunch of yellow flowers will be bought for her in the quiet, spring-touched city. Elza will talk and think in one and the same language. Elza will make love twice. In warm, yellow leaves and in a war-destroyed house with a torn-off roof. Over the shoulder of her beloved she will see rain clouds. Beyond them it will be thundering. Noises empty of the evil intent behind mankind's own thunder. It will thunder in order to rain, and rain in order to make things grow. As nature intended. Without hate. With love. Peace of thunder on earth and goodwill toward Elza, because a beloved heart is knocking at her door. And then Elza will be alone. Elza will be Elza will be Elza.

Nabuco brakes suddenly. The escalator of thoughts and images stops abruptly in Elza's head. The idling of her "coach" returns her to reality. Nabuco opens a low gate and, bending down, pushes Elza into a small garden. In the trees, bushes, and flowers, autumn plenty is battling with premonitions of decay. Nabuco guides Elza's "coach" toward a bench at the farthest corner of the garden. Then she enacts a long-practiced ritual. She takes the rust-colored book, still tightly closed to make sure that the yellow flower does not slip out, from Elza. She lays out serviettes and places the container of food on Elza's lap. Finally Nabuco settles herself comfortably on the bench opposite Elza.

They begin their meal. The noises of the city beyond the garden wall sound like the foghorn of a boat on a distant sea. A gray squirrel jumps on the bench. Elza grimaces at the honey-grilled salmon, gnaws delicately on a small chunk of white cheese. A pigeon spoiled by urban luxuries lands heavily. A thirsty wind blows over a plastic water glass. A hungry bush throws purple leaves at the diners. The sun snuggles up to the feast like a pregnant cat.

Keeping the same silence, Nabuco removes all vestiges of the meal, tidies and smoothes out the blanket around Elza's knees, settles herself more comfortably on the bench, and opens the rust-colored little book.

"Sanskrit lesson," she says in a practiced voice.

In caring for the solitary people of Gotham, Nabuco has come to know dozens of forms of senility and folly. She has had to participate—in all seriousness—in a secret conspiracy against the Arabs, has had to help dress a prima donna each evening for a nonexistent performance, has had to make certain to lead a pug dog to pee in a despised neighbor's flower bed, be the single audience for one-man song and dance shows, dye gray hair to a fiery red or a pitch black, help announce the end of the world, and paste up slogans against communists, against genocide, for equal rights, against abortion, for celibacy, against, for, against, for . . .

Thus, Elza's "Sanskrit lessons" seem perfectly acceptable to Nabuco. Elza doesn't talk much, and that's a help too. Elza gives Nabuco pocket money and pays for their lunch. Elza isn't high-handed, fussy, or cantankerous. Nabuco senses that Elza's thoughts fly with golden wings.

"*Deva—Maya*," Nabuco diligently deciphers in a loud voice.

"*Dieva māja*," Elza responds.[1]

1 Latvian for "God's house."

Elza hasn't ever had the opportunity of meeting God. She has lived without God. It turns out, in fact, that she has been godless. She's heard about divine revelations that have changed lives. About the fog suddenly being lifted, about the light descending upon the supplicant, about the red dot painted in the middle of a forehead that comes alive like a third eye to bring enlightenment, to see past the material world. The door to God's house does not open for everyone. How does one become worthy of the key?

One morning, Elza's neighbor in Greenwich Village, Elisheba Frisha, retired colonel of the Israeli Army, appeared on the street without her red wig, without her false curled eyelashes and sea-blue eye shadow. Elisheba was hardly recognizable. Like a gray, punished dog she dragged herself to the greengrocer, her leather bag knocking against her gaunt legs. On her way back, pushing a cart with her heavy vegetable and fruit bag, Elisheba stopped to catch her breath in front of Elza's house. Elza waved from her wheelchair and asked Elisheba what had happened. Elisheba smiled and said that the previous night, on taking her prescribed pills for the third time that day, she had encountered God for the first time. It had happened as follows. She'd sat up in bed, taken two tablets in her palm—one white, the other red—picked up a glass of water with the other hand, thrown the pills into her mouth, drunk a mouthful of water, thrown back her head to better swallow the pills, swallowed the pills, washed them down with water, put down the water glass, got up to go to the bathroom . . . But then, contrary to her intent, Elisheba had gone to the window instead. A slanting beam from the streetlight outside had stolen into her room and had fallen directly on the shotgun leaning in the corner. Everyone knew that Elisheba had a gun. She wanted to be able to put an end to herself when the right moment came.

"When the cognac starts to spill over your lip, it's time to stop drinking," Elisheba used to say.

She had looked at the ray of light reaching from the lamppost to the gun, and then it had happened. God had found her. She had not seen Him, had not heard Him, had not smelled Him, but He had been there. Simply put, God had been there. Elisheba felt as if she had been thrown out of a boat. She asked Elza what she should do now. Elza told her to put the shotgun in the cupboard and to throw away all her bright makeup. She wanted to tell Elisheba in English that in Latvian there's a saying that goes *Dievam nepatīk, ka nabagi trako*—"God doesn't like the poor to make a scene"—but somehow it all came out wrong. Quite offended, Elisheba protested that she had more than enough money, thank you very much. The next day Elisheba was back in to her usual form.

"Forget it," she called out brightly, as she passed Elza.

God had wandered into Elisheba's place by accident. That's what she decided. God is also getting old, and such things can also happen to Him.

Elza looks on as Nabuco rolls a yellow maidenhair leaf in her two-toned fingers. The inside of Nabuco's palms are rosy white, while the other side are blue-black. In Elza's memory the realization dawns that white is supposed to signify good, while black signifies evil. If she said this aloud, Nabuco would object. Different houses, different gods in different sacred corners. But somewhere there is only one door, one threshold for all. You must wait until you are invited to step over it. You have to live in ignorance. Blessed are the ignorant for they shall inherit the kingdom of heaven. One could give all living creatures a medal of honor for living in such ignorance.

The squirrel scatters leaves while burying a large nut that some gourmet has generously thrown to her. In doing so, she releases the scent of earth. Elza breathes it in deeply. The earth is the earth is the earth. Scent is scent is scent. A large pile of fallen autumn leaves is burning on a cleared field. The whiff of smoke needles through the pre-frost, invigorated air. A soul crawls through the eye of a needle. The past is darned and the present must be worn carefully so that the future does not become threadbare.

"*Ma-as.*" Nabuco draws out the vowel sound.

"Miesa."[2] Elza knows well what to respond. She gazes at her deeply veined, arthritis-crippled hands. Her stiff fingers play awkwardly with her small yellow flower. It seems to Elza that she does not recognize these hands. But these are her hands, just the same as the yellow flower is the yellow flower. Trying to squeeze by, the shoulder of the past grazes Elzas's thoughts.

Making love in a bunker at the front. Elza's young skin feels the fingers of her lover playing on the keyboard of her neck and her breasts. She responds the same as a musical instrument newly created by a master craftsman. Her flimsy dress slips down over her shoulders and puddles on her dusty refugee boots. Her lover's hand on her hips, a breath of warm air touches her smooth skin.

"You are so beautiful," her lover whispers to the sound of thunder.

With his fingers he traces the outlines of Elza's eyebrows, her nose, lips, eyelids, forehead, chin, cheeks, the contours of her ears, neck, collarbones, breasts, her solar plexus, stomach, belly button, lap, hips, knees, ankles . . . How wonderful reality is!

Elza has observed the changes in her body without regret or distaste, only with bewilderment. Once, when Nabuco is washing her, Elza, naked, asks to be taken to the mirror. Nabuco obediently holds Elza up under her armpits and politely stares out of the window while Elza looks. Nabuco thinks that this particular exchange too needs to happen without witnesses.

Elza gazes into the mirror. Her thin, splotchy skin is like wrinkled, unfitted linen. Empty breast coffers, a knotted network of veins, the fine wrinkling at her joints. Elza sees on her flesh hundreds of imprints left by time, like the hundreds of imprints on a fossil turned to stone. Time, which has been playful, merciful, ferocious, tender, crude, contained, irrational, sensitive, proud, cynical, polite, deceitful, honorable, unfair, merciless, thoughtful, surprising, patient, unpredictable, real . . .

2 "Flesh."

Elza gazes at the imprints left by time. All coming to naught. Elza allows her flesh to go the way of naught. She will not stretch herself upon the rack of eternal youth. She will not follow all the latest scientific discoveries about the gene that controls aging. It seems to Elza that her journey is timeless. Elza waits for that moment of silence. Her arthritis-crippled fingers will touch it the same way they touch the yellow flower.

At night Elza can't sleep. She weaves her thought shuttle back and forth on the loom of time.

Back and forth, back and forth. But Elza's thoughts aren't weavers, they don't know what patterns to make. Elza's thoughts are like party snappers. When someone pulls them open, they pop and bang into the air, afterward settling down once more in an eternal, silent, painless universe.

When Elza's thought shuttle again stumbles over the small yellow flowers on Horatio Street, for a moment it seems to her that she knows the reason why. When she smells them, her timeworn memory hears an echo.

Always holding a bunch of yellow flowers, Father is leading the tiny girl to her mother's grave. Father wants his little girl to forever love the woman who bore her and whom she never met. The girl gazes at the white marble dove, head bent, on one side of the monument. She pats the motionless bird. It seems so alive. It might flap its folded wings and fly away at any moment. But the stone dove remains where it is. It gazes down at the gravesite, always; a bunch of yellow flowers laid on the earth.

"*Dvesele*," Nabuco rasps.

"*Dvēsele*," Elza draws out the sound.[3]

The color of the leaves in the garden is a sign that it will soon be All Saints' Day or Halloween. On that one night there will be laughing about death in the city. Since no one knows yet how to exchange souls, there will be an exchange of material things. Sweets will rain down on the crowd. Children will go from house to house, collecting goodies. Elza will sit at

3 "Soul."

her windows and look at how the happy, excited people in monster masks run to the death-games field. All night long drums will beat, horns and trumpets will sound, and laughter will resound in the streets.

Year after year Elza will remember herself dressed as Ice Queen with a chalk-white face, wandering away from the crowd to sit all night on the riverbank. The ant-hill of thousands of lights, the splendid humps of bridges, stars that break out from the haze to be counted on your fingers. Each year anew she will dress up for the death joke parade and each year, having gone once again, she won't know how to take part. Her soul will drag her away from the happy, colorful crowd. Her soul will sit her down in loneliness on a bench by the riverside under a golden maidenhair tree. She will feed the late pigeons with sweet bread and feel how souls gather— right here in the reflected lights, right here in the fallen maidenhair leaves, right here under the wings of the pigeons. Elza will be Elza will be Elza. She will touch the hair of the mother she never met—hair like the smooth, nearly living marble dove's wings on her mother's grave. Father's warm hand will pat her comically tousled head. Her lover will dip his hands in the city's river and will wash her chalk-white face clean. Right here on this lonely bench he will kiss her. And above his lips a tiny white powder mark will remain.

Elza will sit almost frozen, afraid to make a move that might frighten the souls. Just the quiet, rhythmic beating of her pulse in her cramped hands, only the throaty gurgling of the pigeons and the rustling of their nails in the golden maidenhair leaves.

"*Yuga-a*," Nabuco calls out almost in victory, because she senses the lesson coming to an end.

"*Jūgs*," Elza drags out the reins of her words.[4]

Elza's soul is a horse. Patient and loyal. It has been harnessed for a long journey. It has moved slowly and resolutely past both short-term resting

4 "Yoke."

places and comfortable, long-term camps. Elza's soul is a deported refugee's cart. It knows where the beginning of the road is but not where the road leads. Elza's soul is a constant yoke, a gift from God, whom she has never met. Not even for a moment, not even by chance, not even at night washing pills down with water, like Elisheba. Elza is still waiting for a sign showing her where the road is leading. Without this, her soul cannot be unyoked. Elza thinks that the long and lonely journey of her soul has all been in preparation for this time of waiting. Elza's soul is a yellow earth flower in the kingdom of today. It has its own way of growing, its own way of marking time—a yellow flower is a yellow flower is a yellow flower. It grows by itself by the roadside, horse-drawn carriages race past her, not realizing that a sign can be so insignificant. Insignificantly, it points out that the road upward and the road downward are one and the same.

"That's all for today." With the precision of a stopwatch, Nabuco closes the little book. She puts it back in Elza's hands, once more organizes the blanket around Elza's knees. Then she pushes Elza's "coach" homeward. The same old frames speed up past Elza's eyes.

... people, buildings, dogs, sidewalk cafes, squirrels, the golden-coin leaves of the maidenhair tree, pigeons, short Puerto Rican flower vendors, faded rose petals in gutters, discounted book piles on sidewalks, antique tea services, fresh chocolate cakes, mannequins—transparent virtual lovers with shaved heads in shop windows ...

Elza hurries by. Elza is Elza is Elza. When the horse-drawn carriage stops at the insignificant sign, Elza and her soul will understand, without the need for words.

TRANSLATED FROM LATVIAN BY MARGITA GAILITIS AND VIJA KOSTOFF

MARCO CANDIDA

Dream Diary

Now, however, I want to get back to what I was talking about in the first place, before I interrupted myself with all these dreams and ideas, meaning I want to explain, if I can, how these dreams I'm writing about come to me, where and how I'm sleeping while I dream, my sleeping positions, and what I eat before going to sleep.

First off I'll talk about my room, so to do that, I'll describe a dream I had on April 6, 2006—or I should say a dream that I wrote down on April 6, 2006, but I could have had the dream before midnight, so—obviously —on April 5, 2006. I say *could have* because on April 6, 2006, I wrote down *two* dreams that I very likely had at two different times during the night. I don't think I've ever heard of someone having two dreams during the same sleep. So more than likely I woke up but didn't write down my one dream and then I went back to sleep and had another, woke up again, and I wrote down both dreams one after the other *as if* they were part of the same sleep cycle. This must be how it happened, and it's the only time it does happen in my entire dream diary.

In the first dream from April 6, 2006, my room is a very normal seven-by-four meter room with a wooden dresser to the right of some French doors off the back balcony. On top of the dresser, there's a fifteen-inch television and a CD case with fifteen CDs—there's mostly 1970s music in my room. The dresser has six drawers, with the bottom three full of files of A4 paper, manuscripts in Times New Roman or Book Antiqua, and the top three full of underwear, socks, and the shirts and T-shirts I only wear around the house. There's a white computer keyboard, black letters stamped on the keys, and clippings from books and newspapers are taped to the back of the door: a Dante poem, Aphorism 84 from Nietzsche's *The Gay Science*, an article on Pablo Picasso, a couple of paragraphs from works by Martin Heidegger.

I think our dreams are often fragments from the furthest reaches of our imagination, and that's why, even with the dreams that seem the most normal, the most real, there's also the feeling that something's *wrong*. Take a landscape from a dream: maybe the bridge over a river running through some fields and hills is the same bridge we saw four days ago in some movie on some TV channel, and the river running through those fields and hills with the bridge across it might be a stream instead of a river, the Ossona Stream, to be exact, which runs through Tortona and flows into the Scrivia River, and the two banks of the stream might not be the banks of the Ossona Stream, which runs through Tortona and flows into the Scrivia River, maybe they're the sides of that pit that was dug out some five years back for the foundation and plinths on the building site you were supervising for your firm, meaning, the place you used to work, and that landscape of fields and hills with the river running through it and the bridge across the river might be a landscape of fields and hills from an impressionist painting in a show at the Palazzo Ducale in Genoa that you happened to catch a few weeks back, and the stars reflecting off the water, the stars in the sky, might be the drops of condensed milk that landed on your blue pajama top when you had that attack of hyperphagia in front of the TV at two in the morning, and . . . even so, that dream from April 6, 2006 seems to include, down to the last minute detail, everything you'd see in my room, my very own room, without any feeling at all that something's *wrong*.

Aside from the fact that in the dream room everything is *breathing*.

Yes, that's right, I can't think of a better word for it: in the dream room, every single thing breathes in and breathes out. Every object in the room is swelling and shrinking, swelling and shrinking, systematically—swelling and shrinking every few seconds . . . and something else is happening besides: everything is oozing some sort of fluid that's—how to put it?— that's *greasy*. It squirts out, spraying the entire room with its greasy drops, it's on the walls, the bed, the floor, on a book, on my wallet. And with the *breathing, greasy* floor, you can't stay on your feet, you need to hold onto something, but that something's also *breathing* and *greasy*. And because the ceiling light is raining grease, I slip and fall on my face. But before falling on my face, I try to hook the table with my right hand, but I only manage to grab onto a book, my small 1987 *New Abridged Zingarelli Dictionary*. There on the floor, the *New Abridged Zingarelli Dictionary* disintegrates in my hand, and that's when I see it.

First, the *Zingarelli* hasn't disintegrated. What's really happened is that at the center of the cover there's now a hole with some kind of pudding inside—a sunken pudding—and this pudding is sending out a silver light. I see *things* in this light. Inside the soft *Zingarelli* pudding, there's a ballpoint pen—the pen I use for underlining my books. I have no idea what my pen's doing in my *Zingarelli*, but there it is. I watch it bobbing around a while in the glowing pudding before I reach to pluck it out. Right away, something else takes its place: the yellow notepad I use for scribbling down ideas and stories, and right beside the notepad there's my old wooden globe from when I was a boy that wound up in the trash after my brother chucked it at my head and gave me a lump almost as big as the globe itself. I can't imagine what the globe's doing in my *Zingarelli Dictionary*. And I try to pull the notepad and globe out, too. But I realize the globe is much too large to come out of the hole that's opened in the cover of the *Zingarelli*, and it's also a little *deeper* in the pudding than the pen or notepad, so I have to insert my whole hand, almost up to the elbow, *inside* my dictionary. I'm wiggling my fingers around trying to figure out how to grab hold of the globe and pull it out, when I realize the book's turning into a sticky sack—and inside the book it's hot, like a hot-water bottle—and the deeper my arm goes, the more the book stretches, widens. The hole in the book cover's growing, and I pull out the globe, and then the hole shrinks up again with a sound like a creamy cake going splat against a wall. As soon as the globe's out, there's another object, a yellow sweatshirt with a white star sewn on the back. Of course I recognize it: it's the sweatshirt I always wore from ages twelve to sixteen whenever I sat down to read or write. I put it on every time, maybe thinking that star on the back would help me. So I keep this sweatshirt tucked away in the dresser or in a box in the closet—and once in a while, I'll look for it. When the sweatshirt's out, I see something else rising to the surface that's important to me, or used to be. And I'm beginning to realize that if I don't stop, I'll just keep pulling things out of my dictionary, and then I have an idea. I set the *Zingarelli* on the floor and I take down the stuffed toy dog that's hanging on my wall. The dog swells and shrinks in my hands and oozes grease. I can't figure out how it's taking in air: maybe its grease-soaked fabric is really porous; still, I feel like I'm holding a *live thing*, a *living object*. I poke the stuffed dog and my finger sinks into something like putty or Plasticine. I scrape out a furrow then make an opening and once again a silver light comes pouring out. Inside there's a red rubber ball like the kind from the toy store down the street that my brother and I would buy when we were little to bounce on my *nonna*'s balcony.

Behind the ball there's a human hand.

It's wrinkly, with long, red fingernails, and it's covered in *caffelatte*-colored spots: it's the hand of a lady who's getting on in years. I start pulling on the hand, but there's an arm attached and a shoulder and a neck and a head; I feel them though I can't see them. There's an entire human being in this stuffed dog, and I'm pulling with all my might, trying to drag her from an opening some ten centimeters wide. And while I'm pulling, the person inside the dog starts saying, *Stop that bouncing, you little monsters! You're destroying your* nonna's *plants! And my geraniums! You rotten little boys!* I know that voice. That's the voice of the lady who lives above my nonna's apartment, and whenever my brother and I bounced our rubber ball around on our *nonna*'s balcony, she'd go out on her own balcony (which was tiny in comparison to ours) and she'd start in with her *Stop that bouncing, you little monsters! You're destroying your* nonna's *plants! And my geraniums! You rotten little boys!* Who knows, I tell myself, maybe if I get her out, the lady upstairs—Signora Iolanda—will still be gripping that bamboo rod in her left hand that she always used to beat her rugs, and she'll start chasing me around with it, whacking at my back and behind. Even so, I tear the stuffed dog open some more, stick both arms in and, straining quite a bit, I start to pull her out. First her right arm. Then her whole head—and as soon as her head's out with her eyeballs all dirty and those mint-green curlers in her iron-gray hair, she sputters, *Stop that bouncing, you little monsters! You're destroying your* nonna's *plants! And my geraniums! You rotten little boys!* Then her chest pops out, those big, fat tits under her flowered housecoat, then the rest of her. Once she's out of the stuffed dog—which makes a noise like a creamy cake going splat against the wall, then just like that is back to normal—Signora Iolanda starts pacing up and down the room with all of its *breathing, greasy* things just like she used to do years ago, pacing back and forth on her balcony every time she heard my brother and me bouncing our red rubber ball on our *nonna*'s balcony, and every six or seven steps, saying exactly what she used to say: *Stop that bouncing, you little monsters! You're destroying your* nonna's *plants! And my geraniums! You rotten little boys!* Pulling Signora Iolanda out of the dog has made me realize something: every time I pull something or someone from something in my room, I'm literally pulling out something or someone that makes up the memory that this thing in my room (for reasons I can't always explain) stirs up in me.

Then, at the end of the dream, I'm searching for the things in my room that hold the memories of my grandfather. *Nonno* died some years back. I miss him terribly. Maybe he's in my guitar, I tell myself in my dream, or in the television or the stereo or the mirror or the door to the closet. Or maybe the memory of my *nonno*—who was actually born on April 6—is in one of his gifts: the binoculars he gave me, or the saber, or the coin collection. In the dream—and also right now—I want to hold him, hug him, and even if he's only like Signora Iolanda, even if he's only restricted to my memories, it goes without saying that my memories of him would be vast by comparison.

My dream on April 6, 2006 reflects a thought of mine, though turned upside-down, a ghost I've had running back and forth across my mind ever since I lost my job, and that's made me think that all of us, we human beings, we mortal beings, all of us, so even nonhuman beings, we're all *living things*. Maybe this ghost first showed up when I took to spending my days in bed or on the couch, waiting to fall asleep, to dream, and I lay in a position more like a thing, more like an inert body than a living one. I started thinking that just because we breathe doesn't mean we're any different from things. Some people might say this is just the foolishness of a depressed mind and aside from everything else—meaning, aside from the fact that we can move and blush and go pale and reproduce and lose blood and make feces and grow fat and grow thin—aside from all of this, what really makes us different from *things* is we can think. On the other hand, that ghost crouching in the crevices of my brain tells me that there are things that move automatically (robots), and there are things that blush and grow pale (dolls), and our blood's not so different from gasoline and other fuels, and as for thinking—are we really so sure that we think? Aren't we more like stones falling and accelerating at the speed of 9.1 meters per second who think of nothing but wanting to fall at 9.1 meters per second? Or more like trees that only think and say the word "tree," or leaves that only think and say the word "leaf"? In the end, aren't we simply *living things* that breathe and move and feel, but we're still things, and so, sooner or later, aren't we destined to go back to being things exactly like a leaf, a stone, a doll, a robot, or gasoline? And really, won't we grow obsolete much faster than many of the things I've mentioned?

Maybe this is why—because we're growing obsolete much faster than other things—that we worship God with a symbol that's just a thing. We kneel in veneration before a thing that resists the erosion of growing obsolete—that doesn't wrinkle, doesn't break, doesn't change; or, if it does, then slowly, much more slowly than we things do. We observe things, we want them, study them, buy them, learn how to use them, and maybe all because we really want to be like them: we want to be the guitar hanging on the wall of our room, one of the pens in the penholder, pages full of words on philosophy—we want to be a book, probably. We're things that revere other things, that look at other things with love, with envy, because we're living, breathing *things* and when we become things like any other thing we'll have crumbled into a million bits and won't even have the dignity of a chair, a table . . . a book. Of things that *survive*, and I mean this *literally*.

On the other hand, while I lay stretched out on my bed thinking about these things, that ghost crossing from one side of my brain to the other, I was also thinking that //time// of all our words is the one most founded on superstition, that it should be removed from every mouth and every dictionary—from every physics formula. Time, I thought while lying in my bed, doesn't exist. What exists is the movement of matter—or better—matter in motion, because //motion// doesn't exist any more than //time// and //space// exist; it's just the word we use to describe matter in motion. Time is not a thing. When asked what time is, we can't point to some specific object, the way we can if we're asked what a chair is, a column, a lancet window, hemoglobin. Time isn't tangible, just as space isn't tangible, and the idea that we could turn these artificial (yet useful) terms into something tangible, into something that heals, or something you can kill, or something you have to fight against, this might be one of our last great myths.

Time is even more nonexistent than space: consider how often we speak about time with words about space: //a stretch of time//, //an expanse of time//, //a length of time//, and so on. Or else we personify time; faced with time, we become animists: we say //time passes//, //time flies//, //time heals//, and so on. Or else we turn the things that represent time into time itself: the hands of a clock, a stick's shadow on the sand. If a clock exists, we tell ourselves, then time exists. If a moving shadow exists, or a rising and setting sun, then, we tell ourselves, time exists. But time doesn't exist. It's like saying that because we hear something in the attic, because we hear chains shaking, a violin playing every night at midnight, our house must be haunted. Yes, maybe these ways of referring to space and time are useful, though I didn't think so while I tossed and turned in bed and so-called time went by; those terms are useful like having a god to pray to is useful, or a Santa Claus to wait for, or a spirit to guide us, or a truth to believe in: sure, these things might be useful, but they don't exist. And so the notion of a space-time continuum, which is actually curved and permeable, is only the result of believing that time's a thing, which it's not; time is just a word, a word that absorbs every movement of every last particle in the universe. Most of all, time is useful for constructing the universe according to physics, which, along with mathematics (much more than philosophy and literature) is our best method, our most useful method, for representing the world—but even physics has its limits. It's not an all-powerful, all-inclusive explanation of existence.

And so the claim that //everything is relative// is certainly inspired, but probably no less false than Socrates' statement //I don't want examples of courage but the definition of courage//. If we think about it, these statements are complete nonsense that have influenced our ideas for centuries, because you can't find a definition for an abstract concept, for a word that's just a word and not a thing, and we can't really know that everything is relative; it might sound good, but it's also an incredibly confused bit of reasoning, because it generalizes the specific and specifies the general; it subsumes the particular in the universal and the universal in the particular; it induces and deduces at the same time, //everything is relative//, //relativity is everything//, the greatest possible hasty generalization and *reductio ad unum* that man's come up with yet. And, even so, stretched out on my bed, staring at the things in my room, thinking, I still couldn't help but feel that I myself, yes, I was everything and relative.

TRANSLATED FROM ITALIAN BY ELIZABETH HARRIS

ÉILÍS NÍ DHUIBHNE

Trespasses

Clara reaches the footpath just as the bin lorry turns the corner and drives out of the estate. Now her rubbish will be festering away in the bin for the best part of a month because she's going abroad the day after tomorrow and she doesn't feel brave enough to ask her neighbour, Bubbles, to haul out the bin next week. She's already asked Bubbles to feed Soots the cat, and you have to draw the line somewhere. So it will be there for her when she comes back home. Stinking like a fish graveyard.

C'est la fucking vie.

She drags the bin back up the garden and through the house and out the back with a certain ease, even though it's heavy, and there are three steps to negotiate. But Clara's arms are as strong as a weightlifter's. You wouldn't think it to look at her. She's a petite woman, with a certain smart quality to her, even when dressed, as now, in an old faded dressing gown. (She was in bed when she heard the drone of the bin lorry.) Clara would look chic in a sack, some of her friends say. Gamine, is what she is, with her trim little body and spiky short hair, colour changing with her mood— it's purple and blonde at the minute. She looks a bit like what she is, namely, a beautician. It's her job that explains her physical strength too— most of her day is spent removing hair from women's legs, faces, and other body parts. You need to be strong, as well as dexterous and sure of yourself to rip off the waxed paper so swiftly that the client doesn't realize it's happening until it's all over.

She puts coffee in the coffee machine as soon as she's stowed the bin out in the back garden and lets it filter while she's throwing on her clothes. There's a hectic day ahead even though she's closed her salon, as she calls the front room where she zaps unwanted hair off her clients. Before you go on a trip there's always a load of things to do. Maybe if you were better organized it would be different, but Clara, who looks as neat as a knife, isn't organized at all—she tends to put things on the long finger, to dump an important letter on the kitchen table and say, "I'll file it away later." And *believe* she'll file it away later. As a result she spends half her life looking for mislaid items, usually of a financial nature. Today, when she has plenty else on her plate, she has to dash off to her accountant with the P60s and the other tax stuff. All those forms in that horrible shade of Revenue red. It's Halloween next week. Which means, in Ireland, tax time.

Naturally, she always leaves it till the last minute.

The rain is still bucketing down as she makes a dash for the car, pulling her collar up around her neck. Such disheartening weather. It makes the suburbs of south Dublin (and this is supposed to be the *good* part of the city) look bleaker than they really are. All those pebble-dash walls turn grey as wet knickers. If there's anything Clara can't stand it's pebble-dash. The hard little nipples just make her puke, always did, even when she was a child. One of those irrational aversions. The way some people are allergic to peas, or pineapples.

But they don't bother her right now. Nothing can really dent her happiness because in a few days' time she will have left this place behind her and be with her son, Eoin, in San Francisco, for three blissful weeks. He's been over there for two years, working in a hotel—he's head bellboy now. She had to pretend to be pleased when he got promoted from being something else—junior bellboy. She doesn't even know what a bellboy is, but it's not the career she had in mind for her only son, who got a First in Greek and

Roman Civilization and looks like a film star. Well, who is she to complain: her Two-One in Philosophy didn't prepare her for her career as a beautician, although it wasn't the worst preparation she could have had. And Eoin is happy is the thing. He likes America, even though it's a drag that he can't come home because he's undocumented. Clara hasn't seen him since he left Ireland. She didn't realize how much—how very much—she missed him until she was filling in the form online for her air ticket. Then, as she keyed in her credit card number, she started crying and she didn't stop for twelve hours.

But that was ages ago. In two days she will be with Eoin and therefore everything makes her happy. She is playing "San Francisco" on the CD player—she's been playing it for two and a half months, nonstop. There's a tinned fruitcake, a porter cake, from Bewley's lying on the passenger seat, ready to go into her case the day after tomorrow—Eoin's favourite cake. She loves to see it there, waiting to be enjoyed. By him. Oh yes, today everything is wonderful. Even this boring suburb that she's had to live in since her relationship with Alan ended, which wasn't today or yesterday, and where she never felt at home. Such a haphazard sort of place. It looks as if all the roads and houses fell out of the sky and just happened to land on these unremarkable fields, miles from anywhere that makes sense. Miles from the city and miles from the mountains and miles from the river and the sea. Who would live here if they had a choice?

If you come to San Francisco
Be sure to wear some flowers in your hair.

Watermill Grove. That's where the accountant is, in a semi-detached house with pebble-dashed walls and a picture window looking out directly on other semi-detached houses with pebble-dashed walls and picture windows. His office is around the back in a wooden shed—the neighbours kicked up when he had it erected, but you don't need planning permission for those wooden structures, Shomeras. Clara has considered getting one herself, and moving her salon to the back garden.

She parks her car in the first free spot she sees, which as luck would have it is just opposite the accountant's house. *You're gonna meet some gentle people there.* She turns off the motor and grabs the big brown envelope. Off she dashes across the road.

The accountant is not in the office.

But his wife is.

His wife is a woman with soft creamy skin and a big warm smile. She is padded and comfortable looking, in a baby-pink jumper made of cashmere or some smooth wool. A fawn skirt.

"Michael had a bypass operation two weeks ago," she says, cheerfully. Michael is the accountant.

"What!" Clara says. What will happen to her tax returns now? She gives the office a furtive glance. It has a reassuringly worked-in look: papers are stacked in wire trays and a few letters are scattered on the desk. And there's the smell of work: coffee and computer and sweat. "That's terrible! How is he?"

"He's fine," the wife smiles. "He made a really fast recovery."

"Oh, good, good," says Clara. Only four days to the deadline. After that they'll start shovelling on the fines. Heart surgery will be no excuse. "I'm really shocked. I didn't know."

"He didn't know himself until three weeks ago," the woman says, and she laughs, proudly.

"Really? Didn't he have pains . . ." Clara fiddles with her brown envelope. "Angina or whatever?"

The accountant's wife shakes her head.

"Not a thing. No pain. Apparently when the blockage is on the left side you feel nothing. If it's on the right you get shortness of breath and chest pains and so on."

"You get a warning . . ." Clara nods, interested. Her mother, who died two years ago, a month after Eoin went to America, used to have angina. She had pains on the right side. She got a warning. But she didn't get a by-pass because she was on the medical card, so she got some pills and then she died. Eoin couldn't get back for the funeral. If he'd come home they'd never have let him in again.

"But on the left, not a thing. No warning. I never knew about any of this until now," the woman laughs.

"No," says Clara. "You only learn all the complicated details when something happens."

She gives the accountant's wife the envelope with the tax documents in it.

"He wants me to take files in to him already!" the woman says, pleased. "Can't wait to get at them!"

"Oh don't, it's much too early for that," says Clara. "He should rest." He could probably do her returns, sitting up in bed, on a laptop. Pass the time for him.

"Don't worry," the woman smiles. "Most of them are done. It's only a few of the stragglers that are left. I'll do them myself, they're the little ones."

"A woman's work is never done!" Clara says. It's so great not to be made to feel guilty, even though she's ridiculously late.

The woman sighs contentedly.

"If there's a problem, I'll give you a ring."

■　■　■

While Clara was in the accountant's shed the sun came out. Now golden light washes the houses, so they glow softly in their frames of autumn shrubs and trees. In the driveway of one of them, just beside where Clara parked her car, a woman is raking leaves. Light mounds of golden foliage are lined up along the sides of her drive, like a range of tidy little mountains. It is a pleasant sight. *All across the nation . . . there's a whole generation . . . people in motion.* Clara smiles at the woman as she is about to say, "Isn't it a lovely day?"

The woman looks up from her sweeping.

Venomous.

That's the only word to describe the expression on her face.

"Are you the person who blocked my driveway?" she hisses.

Clara glances at her car, a twenty-year-old Mercedes Benz, the only luxury—near luxury—she allows herself. It *is* parked very close to the edge of the gateway. She hadn't paid much attention to how she was parking because she was so glad to be getting the tax papers out of her hair.

"Oh gosh, I'm really sorry!" she says in dismay. "I didn't notice I was so close to your drive." She smiles then and adds, "But not to worry, I'm off now anyway!"

The woman is not placated. Instead her face grows angrier.

"You parked illegally," she hisses. "You broke the law. Do you always park like that?"

"What?" Clara is puzzled. "I'm sorry!" She looks carefully at the woman. Elderly. Her clothes are verging on the shabby: grey pants and an anorak in a drab shade of yellow old women often wear. The clothes are ordinary but her face is not. It is contorted with rage, like the face of a witch.

Clara wonders if the woman might be a little disturbed. "It was only for a few minutes!" she shrugs, dredging her keys up from the chaotic depths of her handbag.

The old woman snarls. "It was not a few minutes! It was not a few minutes! You broke the law. Are you always breaking the law?"

Are you always breaking the law?

Clara inhales deeply. She feels like a child, in her tight jeans and purple leather jacket, her high boots. She feels like a child although in fact she is probably not that much younger than this angry old woman.

"You broke the law," the woman says again. "I couldn't get into my drive."

Clara glances at the car parked behind hers and assumes several things without thinking about them. One of those assumptions is that the car behind hers, a red Yaris, is the woman's. She must have arrived when Clara was in with the accountant's wife and had to park on the road, instead of on her driveway. But would that be so irritating that you'd eat the face off a complete stranger? Not being able to get into your drive is not quite the same as not being able to get out of it.

"You're overreacting," says Clara, frowning. She glances at the house. It has a name, carved on a piece of fake wood: "Assisi." Probably holy statues all over the place inside. She shakes her head.

She should go now, before she says things she'll regret. One part of her is urging her to leave. But some emotion boiling up inside stops her doing that. She's getting drawn in.

"You're crazy," she can't stop the words erupting.

"And you're a criminal!" the woman's voice rises to a real scream.

Then Clara makes a supreme effort, suppresses her annoyance, and climbs into her car.

■　■　■

She has to retreat down Watermill Grove, do a U-turn, and come back up to get out onto the main road. As she drives back towards the corner she sees that a small crowd has gathered at the old woman's gate. There's a young woman, with a pram, and an old man, with a face as angry as the old woman's. The old woman is pointing at Clara and the others are looking at her accusingly. There's something unreal about the group. It looks choreographed, like a scene from an opera or a ballet.

The old man beckons Clara over, crooking his finger and gesturing menacingly. With his big hooked nose he's the evil count. He could be wearing a black cloak and three-cornered hat, shiny pointy-toed boots, a dagger in his belt. But his clothes are as ordinary as his wife's. It's the eyes that belong to the other dimension, as they splutter and sparkle with rage. The two old people glare at her. The house and driveway are like a backdrop on a stage. The faces are like masks, not like real faces, which change expression in response to what people say. She wonders, seriously, if this is some sort of reality TV hoax. But Watermill Grove isn't the sort of place where they do reality TV hoaxes. It's too far from town. It's too boring. It's too real.

Clara could decide to ignore him and drive away from this farce. She's calmer than she was; she's distanced herself. Discretion is the better part of valour, that she knows. But something holds her, some dark spell. She stops the car. The evil count stalks up to her and she rolls down the window.

"Show me your driving licence," he barks.

"What?" she wasn't expecting this.

"Do you have a driving licence?"

"Of course I have a driving licence," Clara says.

"I'd like to see it," he snarls.

Naturally, Clara hasn't a clue where it is.

"I'm not showing it to you," she says.

"In that case I'm going to report you to the guards."

She laughs in surprise. "Okay," she says, with an elaborate shrug. "Go right ahead. Report me to the guards!"

Now he's taken aback.

"Go on," she says, encouraged. "Report me! Report me to the police!"

Repetition is the name of the game.

"I will," he says, uncertainly. "I will. I will."

He ambles off across the road and into his house.

The young woman moves away and pushes her pram down the road, her head bent towards the contents of the pram. The old woman picks up her rake and begins to work at the leaves. The scene is beginning to lose momentum; everyone senses it's time to draw the curtain. But the old man hasn't made his final exit. He returns with an old envelope and pencil and makes an elaborate show of taking down the registration number of Clara's car. He gives a last grunt, scowls at her and returns to his garden.

Clara's mobile phone rings.

Eoin.

"Hi Ma," he sounds as if he's next to her in the car. "Just checking that everything's on track."

"Yes, sweetie," she says, glancing out the window, which is open. "Everything's on track." Her heart is thumping. Thump thump thump. There's a shake in her right knee. "I'm just leaving in the tax returns, you know, with Michael." The old woman's head is bent over the leaves, her rake is raking. The old man is gathering up the heaps of leaves and putting them into a green bucket. He clamps them down with his foot, to compress them, squeeze more in. "Someone is reporting me to the guards, for illegal parking. Some crazy people," she says this very loudly, hoping they'll hear.

"Oh," Eoin sounds alarmed. "Don't worry, Mom. Don't mind them. Just drive away. Okay?"

"Okay." The old man looks over at Clara and spits, in her direction. The glob of spittle lands far from her, on the footpath outside his gate. He picks up the bucket and shuffles into the house with it, stooping under the weight of leaves.

Eoin says, "Promise me you'll drive away as soon as I ring off."

"Yes yes," says Clara.

There's a pause.

"Have you sent in your ESTA form to Immigration?"

"Yes, yes," she says, again. "I did that weeks ago." All those stupid questions. Do you suffer from a contagious disease? Are you a drug addict? Have you ever been convicted of an offence by the police? *Offense. Felony.*

That's not a word Clara ever uses. It's not a word used in Ireland. "I did it. I got an email back. That's all okay."

"Okay," there's a pause and he adds, "Ma, wear something ordinary, for the flight. You know what I mean?"

She smiles.

"Just makes it easier at Immigration," he sounds sheepish.

"I'm not a complete eejit," she says. The last time she saw Eoin his hair, red, was down to his waist, and he was wearing a T-shirt saying "FCUK." "Don't worry. I'll put my hair in a nice little bun." She'd already planned to dye out the purple bit of her hair before travelling. "I've got a nice black suit all ready. I'll look like a plainclothes nun."

"That's the spirit," he says. She can see his grin but wonders if he's cut his hair? It's curly. It's beautiful. He looks like a poet. "See you on Friday then, nine-thirty P.M.? Twenty-one thirty, right?"

"Right! Twenty-one thirty," says Clara. "What time is it over there, now?"

She always asks this even though she knows perfectly well that it's eleven hours ahead; in her head she has one of those clocks you see behind the reception desk in hotels. Hers gives the San Francisco time, so she knows what Eoin is likely to be doing, at any hour of the day or night. She asks just to prolong the conversation. But he's already rung off.

■ ■ ■

All across the nation . . .
There's a whole generation . . .
People in motion . . .

She flicks off the CD player and goes over to the radio.

There's a report of a court case on the news. John Murphy, a farmer in the midlands, died after being assaulted by Dan and Robert Ryan, his neighbours. John Murphy's heifer strayed into Robert Ryan's field and John went after the cow to make her come back to his own field, her own field. A row broke out about property and trespassing and the men fought. John Murphy sustained head injuries and died almost a year later, never having come out of hospital. The question was, was it murder or homicide or neither? The jury would have to decide. The men were forty years old and this happened in 2008, although it sounded like the plot of a play you couldn't put on because it is so dated and old fashioned.

■ ■ ■

When Clara comes home after the encounter with the people on Watermill Grove she sits down at the old blue table in her kitchen, which is filled with stuff she's collected from skips and second-hand furniture auctions, and writes a letter to them. The letter says, "I have never encountered two old people whose faces were so uglified by anger." It adds that she had reported them to the police.

She tears that letter up and writes another one.

The second letter says she had not blocked their driveway, that their behaviour was antisocial, and that they were a public nuisance. She adds that they would be hearing from her solicitor.

That one gets torn up too.

Then she thinks she could shame them by using a bit of reverse psychology. She gets a thank-you card and signs it with a false version of her name—Ellie Murphy is the pseudonym she selects—puts it in an envelope, and addresses it to the Residents, Assisi, Watermill Grove.

But she doesn't post that either.

Clara has plenty to do—she should be packing, making lists, preparing for the long journey she must soon take, the day after tomorrow. But instead she sits and writes letters to two cranky old people whose names she doesn't even know.

She can't get them out of her head.

At six o'clock, when it's dark, she takes the thank-you card and the porter cake—she can get another one tomorrow, or even at the airport, although it'll cost more there. She drives back to Watermill Grove, parks around the corner and walks to "Assisi."

A small blue Micra is parked in the driveway—even in the dark she can see it is a very bright blue. That wasn't on the road this morning. It's such a screaming shade of blue, she couldn't have missed it. She wonders where their own car is, the red one. No sign of it. Then she wonders if they have a car at all. The Micra looks like the kind of car a grown-up daughter living at home, a schoolteacher or a civil servant, might have.

The curtains are drawn and there is no light at the front of the house, so she guesses they're in the kitchen, eating their evening meal. Their tea. Rashers and sausages, sliced pan. Something like that. She walks quietly up to the door and leaves the card and the fruitcake, in its plastic wrapper, on the porch. A pot of geraniums catches her eye. Through the glass in the front door she sees a crack of light down the hall. She imagines she hears the sound of voices. The old woman's she thinks, and a younger voice. The daughter's? Maybe it's just the news on TV. Almost without thinking what she's doing, she roots in the flowerpot. Her fingers find a key ring, buried just half an inch below the surface. Exactly what they're always warning you not to do. Two keys, the Yale and the long one for the safety lock.

Her hand opens the hall door.

Inside, exactly what you'd expect the old farts to have. A crucifix on the wall, a horrible paper with a pattern of some sort of sharp, unnatural looking grasses, like swords, all over the walls. The yellow anorak is hanging on one of those old walnut hallstands. Brown lino on the floor. It's cold. They are too poor or too mean to keep the heating on.

A door at the end of the hall opens and the old witch comes out. She is still wearing the gardening trousers. But she has an apron on—a surprisingly nice apron, white with pink flowers and frills. A present from some-one, obviously. It's one of those aprons with a huge pocket all across the skirt and the old woman is carrying something, clothes pegs perhaps, in this pocket.

What?

Her face falls, falls as if it is an egg which has been hit with a fork and smashed. All the sharp cross features collapse into a puddle of shock.

It's me, Clara says. She's shy again, subdued by this old woman, just as she was this morning before her temper erupted. Feeling silly, she holds out the fruitcake, proffering it: the peace offering. She can't find any words to go with it.

The old woman's face becomes rigid. She doesn't smile. She has never seen this woman smile, it occurs to Clara. And that is an odd thing, even for someone you've met just twice. The old woman lifts her hand. Clara moves closer, to hand over the cake. The old woman does not take the cake, however. No. That is not her plan at all. She dips her hand into that big pocket of hers and pulls out what she has hidden there. Which is a knife.

Now it's Clara who gasps: What?

The witch lunges and stabs Clara in the chest.

It's quite a good quality knife she's got there, with a sharp point, and she does manage to make a dent in Clara's leather jacket. But there's no way she could injure Clara, given her own feebleness and the thickness of that purple leather.

It's quite a good quality knife she has in her hand. And when that knife is in Clara's hand, strong and deft and skillful, it slides easily into the old woman's scrawny throat—it slices through the bulging blue veins as smoothly as it would into the white flesh of a boiled potato.

A puddle the colour of a cheerful red flower spreads over the brown floor.

Clara is already out the door, down the path. She is in her car, driving down Watermill Grove, before the old woman has realised what's happened, before the old woman realises she's going to die, on this ordinary autumn night, a few days before Halloween, while her daughter is down at Tesco's getting a barbecued chicken for their tea and her husband is down at the chapel, at evening Mass.

■ ■ ■

It's dark as Clara gets up but by the time she's made the coffee morning has broken and another bad day begins. Rain spits against the window and turns to tears on the cold glass. A blast of wind ruffles the palm tree in her patio so badly that it looks like the tossed hair of some garden giant.

When she's washing up, though, the sun creeps out from behind a cloud and casts light on the west side of the garden, shining on the heaps of leaves that lie in big drifts under the hedges. She'll have to rake them up before she goes, if she gets a chance, if the rain holds off, if all goes well. Alan used to do that sort of thing, before they broke up, ages ago when Eoin was five. Eoin has never raked leaves, or done anything much in the garden. Your children know the garden is not their responsibility, whatever about the inside of the house.

A wild gust sends the leaves charging down the garden like a cavalry racing through the sleeping grass.

It's then that she sees the old woman, in her mind's eye, raking the leaves off her driveway, making those neat hillocks of golden light along the edges, and her husband helping her. She sees them there, moving together rhythmically, old people clearly accustomed to working together, raking leaves or washing dishes, hanging clothes on the line. They look like characters in a soothing pastoral painting, with a title such as "The Reapers," or "The Gleaners." They look like a couple working together making hay, or footing turf, or gathering seaweed, on a golden morning in a blessed landscape in the west of the country, miles and miles and miles away from this cold suburb, which looks as if all its roads and houses fell out of the sky and just happened to land on these unremarkable fields, miles from anywhere that makes sense. Miles from the city and miles from the mountains and miles from the river. Miles and miles from the silver sea.

TRANSLATED FROM IRISH BY THE AUTHOR

KEVIN BARRY

Doctor Sot

Late in January, Doctor Sot felt the bad headaches come on again and he drank John Jameson whiskey against them. The naggins slipped pleasingly into a compartment of his leather satchel but they needed frequent replacing and he thought it best not to replace them always from the same off-licence in town. He aimed the car for the twenty-four-hour Tesco on the outskirts of the town. A cold morning was coloured iron-grey on the hills above town—brittle and hard the winter had been, and it was such clear, piercing weather that brought on the headaches. The heater in his eleven-year-old Mégane juddered bravely against the cold but inadequately and his fingers on the wheel had the look of a corpse's. Steady nips of the Jameson, he found, kept in check the visions of which these headaches were often the presage.

The Mégane had a personality. It was companionable and long-suffering and he had named it Elizabeth for his mother. Car and mother had in common a martyr's perseverance and a lack of natural advantages.

"Small devil loose inside my head, Liz," said Doctor Sot, "and it's like he's scrapin' a blade in there, the little bastard."

As he crossed the humpback bridge over the White Lady's River he whistled the usual three-note sequence for luck, a bare melody that rose once and then fell. He sucked in his cheeks against the pain and reached for the satchel on the passenger seat. He groped inside for a naggin. He wedged the naggin between his thin thighs. He unscrewed the top and fate dug a pothole and the pothole caused the Mégane to jolt. The jolt splashed whiskey onto the grey trousers of his suit.

"Oh thank you very much," said Doctor Sot.

He checked the mirrors before raising the naggin. Clear. And just his own eyes in there, which was a relief. Mirrors were more troublesome earlier in the mornings. He drained what was left of the whiskey and great vitality raged through him and he tossed the empty naggin in back.

"Another dead soldier, Liz," he said, and with his grey lips he bugled a funeral death march.

The Tesco at eleven this weekday morning was quiet and the quietness for Doctor Sot had an eerie quality to it. As he walked the deserted aisles, wincing against the bright colours of the products, he felt like the lone survivor in the wake of an apocalypse. What would you do with yourself? All the fig rolls on earth wouldn't be a consolation. So taken was he with this grim notion he walked into a display of teabags and sent the boxes flying. He was upset to have knocked them and got down on his hands and knees to remake the neat triangle they had been stacked in. He felt a hot seep of urine against the inside of his thigh. He summoned his deepest reserves to staunch it.

"This is a nice bag of sticks," he said.

The seeping was slight—a mercy—and the boxes of tea were at least in some manner restacked. He proceeded with as much nonchalance as he could muster. From the bakery counter he picked up a chocolate cake for his wife, Sal, who was the happiest woman alive. Also in his basket he placed mouthwash, a family pack of spearmint gum, and eight naggins of the John Jameson. A patient, Tim Lambert, appeared gormlessly from around an aisle's turn with a duck-shaped toilet freshener in his hand.

"Tricks with you, Doctor O'Connor?" he enquired.

Doctor Sot put his basket on the floor and went into a boxer's swaying crouch. He jabbed playfully at the air around the old man's head.

"You're goin' down and you're stayin' down, Lambert!" he cried.

Lambert laughed as he eyed, for the full of his mouth, the contents of the doctor's basket. Doctor Sot picked up the basket and primly moved on, the humour gone from him. The consolation was that Lambert's lungs wouldn't see out the winter—he had told no lie. Oh and he knew full well what they all called him behind his back. He knew it because another of his elderly patients, Rita Cryan, was gone in the head and had forgotten that the nickname was slanderous and meant to be secret.

"That's not a bad mornin' at all, Doctor Sot," she always croaked when he paid a house call now. He tended with Rita to strap on the blood pressure monitor a little too tightly. There was temptation to open one of the naggins before he got it to the counter but he denied himself and bore the small devil's caper.

"You'd want a good class of a pelt on you," he said to the girl at the till. "Brass monkeys."

But she was an Eastern, and as she blankly scanned his items, he realised that pelt was perhaps a little rich for her vocabulary, not to mind brass monkeys.

"Pelt like a bear," he said. "For the cold, I mean. Look it! Here's Papa Bear inside in his lovely warm pelt!"

He flapped his arms delightedly against his sides to indicate Papa Bear's cosiness.

"Fifty-three euro and eighty-nine cent," she said.

In the Mégane, he opened a naggin and took a good nip for its dulling power. He saw a distressed van come coughing and spluttering into the car park. The rainbow colours it was painted in could not disguise the distress. It was driven by a young man with braided hair. Many small children, all shaven-headed, wriggled and crawled along the dashboard and against the windscreen. The man climbed down from the van and slid back the side door. More shaven-headed children poured out and more braided adults. These, Doctor Sot realised, must be the new-age travellers the paper had been on about. They were camped in the hills above town. On Slieve Bo, if he recalled. They were colourful and unclean and wore enormous military boots. There were bits of metal in their faces. They made a motley parade as they went across the car park. The driver remained at the side door of the van and gave out yards to someone inside. A young woman poked her head out and spoke to him. He huffed and he gestured and he followed the rest of the travellers across the car park. She remained. She stepped out and leaned against the van and rolled a cigarette from a pouch. Doctor Sot's breath caught as he watched her. She was remarkably beautiful and vital. Her hair also was in braids and piled high and she wore striped leggings tucked into her boots. She felt his stare and returned it. She smiled and waved at him. He slugged hard on the naggin and took off.

There are wolves in our valley—this is what Doctor Sot knew. We do not know when they will attack us but attack us they surely will, with their hackles heaped and drool sheering from between their yellow teeth. The only illusion of permanence is that which is finagled by love. The careful study of sickness had taken a great toll from him but a moment's connection with this young woman had lifted him, had in an instant remade the illusion, and Doctor Sot wasn't back across the White Lady's River before he had a plan formed.

The tinkers, those older travellers, held that the river's crossing was here auspicious because on the bank by the hump-back bridge was a maytree hundreds of years old and Doctor Sot, who would take all the luck from the world that he could get, whistled again his three notes as he crossed back into town. His home and practice was on a neat terrace of greystone that was of some prestige in the town. It had been bought cheaply in the long-gone heyday of his practice. Having come from less— his persevering mother had put him in the university out of a council house—Doctor Sot enjoyed still the mild grandeur of his address. The three stone steps that led up to his door, the nine-panel fanlight above it, the fine parquet blocking of his hallway's floor, these were details that he greatly enjoyed and all the more today, so elevated was his mood—the guilt of the mood's provenance had not yet begun to seep.

Details were important to Doctor Sot. The likes of a Doctor Sot doesn't get to fifty-nine years of age without grasping the trick of it, the trick of it being that we must move out and back from the foreground of things, occupy our minds with the fine details, paint in the far corners of the view. Happy Sal was all foreground.

"Oh adieu! Yes adieu! Oh adieu all my false-hearted looooves!" sang Doctor Sot as he tapdanced through to the back kitchen, one hand flapping a minstrel's wave, the other clasping the satchel. Sal flushed and chortled at the sight of him. She threw down her serial killer novel and bounced up from the small pink sofa by the stove.

"You'll never guess!" she cried. "He's only taken the head and buried it in the desert!"

"This is the prostitute he met at the truckstop?"

"One and the same," she said. "Had the head in his fridge but it started to stink."

"Neighbours might be alerted, Sal."

"He's making a move to be on the safe side," she said. "He's headed for Tulsa. Ham sandwich, lovie?"

"It would fill a hole, Sal."

"Your glass of beer with it?"

"Might take the fear of God off me."

They embraced. Sot was stick and bone, Sally was hot and pink and fleshy.

"Mind you," he said. "I've a bit of a rush on. I need to make a call before surgery."

"Oh?" she said. "A call?"

She was already slicing the batch loaf. There weren't many calls these days.

"Health Board," he said.

She opened the fridge for the ham, the butter, the can of Smithwick's. Happy as a duck she was, unshakable from her good humour, and of the opinion that her husband, if anything, grew more marvellous with every passing year.

"They givin' you gip again, dear-heart?"

"Not at all," he said. "It's just I've had a think about this Outreach programme."

He sipped from the glass of beer she handed to him. He raised his eyes guiltily over the foam of it.

"But they can't force you, Carl?"

"Of course not, babycakes. It's just I've thought maybe I was a little quick to rule it out . . . Maybe I should, you know, give something back?"

With his bloodshot eyes and his hammering heart! Doctor Sot hurried the beer, and he would leave the sandwich uneaten on the plate. He needed five minutes before surgery for the business with the mouthwash and the gum. His hurry would carve out another five for the call to the Health Board. As he downed the last of his beer, pain ripped the back of his skull. He went to the sink to block the wince from her. He squinted out and up to the white sky. Great wingéd creatures were taking shape up there. He turned quickly again to Sal.

"Service!" he cried. "What ever happened to the notion of serving the people?"

"You know what, sweetness?"

Sal's mouth shaped with awe as she grasped the brilliance of his idea.

"It could be just the thing for you! Take you out of yourself!"

Whatever this heroically complicated husband came up with was fine with Sally. She soon enough forgot the details of his adventures. Before he had even reached the phone in the hallway's nook, she was deep in the pink sofa and in the tale of her Tulsa-bound maniac. He was snacking on innards as he zoomed along the blacktop.

"Obviously, Carl, we're delighted you'd volunteer."

"I'm sensing a but," said Doctor Sot.

This Mannion fella at the Health Board was easy enough to read. All he wanted for Outreach was the young guns with the big grins and the surfer hair. Sot raged:

"Thirty-five years of experience! And I offer it up to you! I am offering, Mr. Mannion, to take part in your bloody Outreach programme! Just like you asked!"

"Carl, it was just a circular. Just a general call for volunteers. This was three months ago and really we're sorted now. All the halting sites are serviced. The seminars for the community centre are looked after. I've a couple of lads who've . . ."

"What about the new-age travellers?" said Doctor Sot. "Who's providing Outreach there?"

"You mean the crowd above on Slieve Bo?"

That had him. Mannion had to admit that the new-age travellers had not, in fact, yet been added to the Outreach list.

"Animals, are they, Mr. Mannion?"

"Oh I mean they'd qualify, I suppose, if they're receiving benefits but . . ."

"But but but, Mr. Mannion!"

It was agreed by sighing Mannion that the new-age travellers would be assessed to see if they qualified for Outreach.

"In the meantime," said Doctor Sot, "it'd be no harm, surely, to go up there and show a friendly face? Just to introduce oneself? Maybe a few leaflets about nutrition? About chlamydia, that type of thing?"

"Whatever you think, Carl," said Mannion.

It was Doctor Sot's experience that the longer he stayed on the phone to people, the more he got what he wanted.

"And what'd be my best road up Slieve Bo, Mr. Mannion?"

His surgery ran from noon until two. It was as slow as it always was now. Only the old and fatalistic still patronised the O'Connor practice. The lady of the Knotts whose twin had died in the winter was in about the voices again but the voices had turned benevolent and she was less disturbed than she had been. Ellie Troy had that grey, heartsick look but she was seventy-two now and she'd had the grey, heartsick look since she was forty: it was a slow death for poor Ellie. It was the weather for sore throats, Doctor Sot told Bird Magahy. His own headaches weren't so bad during surgery and he was careful not to gaze out toward the white sky. Last in was Tom Feeney, the crane driver.

"It's the man below, Doctor O'Connor."

"Do you mean, Tom . . ."

"I do."

"He mightn't be doing all you'd require of him?"

"It's not that."

"No?"

"It's the opposite of that."

"Oh?"

"I'm in a state," the sixty-year-old crane man said, "of constant excitement."

Doctor Sot prescribed a week's Valium and the taking up of a new hobby. He was in the back kitchen by five past two, kissing Sal, and telling her he was away on a mission.

"Outreach, Sal!"

"Bloody hell they've snapped you up quick enough!"

"I'll be back for the tea surely."

"Careful how go, honeybob!"

Over the bridge, a three-note whistle, and the main road he turned off for a side road. The side road became a boreen. The boreen as he climbed became track. Track became narrower track, and it turned onto a rutted half-track. It was like a path that animals had trampled down. Suddenly space opened out on all sides and Doctor Sot steered his Mégane through the high air but she laboured, Elizabeth. The high country had its own feeling. Ascending into the iron-grey of its colours as the afternoon light fatted up, Doctor Sot was alerted to the different intensities of these greys and shale tones. Austere from below, they were radiant when you were up and among them. The high reaches were now everywhere open to him, the valley below glistened its turloughs, and the gorse was seared to a winter bronze. The half-track hairpinned, and the travellers' camp was announced by a sudden assault of skinny dogs. Which was all the Mégane needed.

"Easy, Liz," said Doctor Sot, as he steered the old girl through the dogs.

The camp was sheltered from the west winds by a great outcrop of shale. There were as many shaven-headed children as there were skinny dogs. The grown travellers skulked in the rearground, and were watchful; they came nearer. There was something that resembled a teepee. Inside it was a generator, juddering. Hooded crows stomped all around. There were rough shelters made with lengths of tarpaulin and these were strewn around a copse of trees by the outcrop's base. There was a horse trailer with a smoking chimney. The distressed van of rainbow colours was parked up on blocks beside it. There was a pair of old rusted caravans. Children and dogs surrounded Doctor Sot as he climbed from the Mégane. The ground was hard-packed underfoot, brittle and flinty, the frost wouldn't think to lift up here for months at a time. The children were pin-eyed and unpleasantly lively. The dogs might have been alien dogs, so skinny and yellow-skinned and long-headed they were, like bad-dream dogs.

"Ah down off me now please! For the love o' God!"

Five portions of fruit and veg daily seemed immediately beside the point. He might have landed in far Namibia such was the foreignness of things. The young fella who had earlier driven the van came through the barking children and the laughing dogs.

"S'about?" he said.

"Doctor Carl O'Connor!" cried Doctor Sot. "North Western Health Board!"

"Oh yeah? I'm Joxie."

"Outreach!" cried Doctor Sot. "Welcome to Slieve Bo . . . Joxie?"

Languorous, the young man, as he swept back his mass of braided hair. He arranged it away from his face with a lazy hand. He was sharp-featured, sallow, bemused.

"I'm here about the nutrition," said Doctor Sot. "I'm here about the sex diseases."

"You jus' piss yerself?" said Joxie.

More adults came forward. They swatted the children and kicked the dogs. The beautiful young woman was not among them. A forest of braided hair sprang up around Doctor Sot. He shielded his crotch with his satchel. Indeed there had been a little seepage.

"Aim of the Outreach programme," he explained, "is to bring the, ah . . . the services . . . to . . ."

He should have boned up on the stuff in the leaflets. He should have learned some of the lingo. But the travellers smiled at him regardless. They were not unwelcoming. Their accents were mostly English, the lilt of them specifically southwestern.

"Devon, so happens," said Joxie.

He poured for Doctor Sot a cup of green tea. They were in back of the horse trailer by a turf-burning stove. The young man's full title, it emerged, was Joxie the Rant.

"Rant, Joxie? Why so?"

"Coz I get a rant on," he said. "A ranter, yeah?"

"Do him a rant, Jox!"

"Bit early, is it no?"

The adults of the camp were greatly taken with Doctor Sot. There were a half-dozen of them packed into the horse trailer around him. He was a break from the boredom. Boredom was bred into them by suburbs and by drab English towns. Doctor Sot found it difficult to tell them apart, even to sex them, but he knew well enough that the beauty was not here. They were entertained by him. There was muffled hilarity to the brief silences that yawned out between them. To fill these, he spoke of the importance of five portions daily of fresh fruit and veg.

"Your broccoli is a powerful man," he said. "Handful of florets? There's a portion, there's one of your five."

He spoke of oily fish, such as mackerel, for the sake of its omega-3.

"Ground control to Omega 3," said Joxie.

The travellers smoked their roll-ups and drank green tea. As this was not an official Outreach session, as it was more a break-the-ice visit, Doctor Sot saw no reason why he shouldn't offer to strengthen their tea. He opened the satchel and with a wink produced a full naggin.

"Nip of this lad?" he whispered. "Greatly medicinal."

"They do know yer out an' about, yeah?" said Joxie.

By the time a second naggin had gone around, the travellers had in their civility produced tins of own-brand supermarket lager and flagons of cider. They questioned Doctor Sot as to what pills he might have in his satchel. He laughed them away.

"It's the six, just, is it?" he tried. "Just the six of you, for grown-ups?"

"Well there's Mag an' all, ain't there?" said Joxie. "Mag's in her bender."

"Oh?"

"She got one of her spells on, don't she?" said Joxie.

Quickly it was as if Doctor Sot had become part of the camp. The travellers largely forgot about him. They were in and out of the horse trailer, attending to children and dogs. They smoked their roll-ups with a resin crumbled in. They sipped at their lager and cider. They didn't say no to a nip of the Jameson—Doctor Sot had fetched extra from the Mégane—but their conversation was no longer centred on the visitor. They talked drowsily about making some turnip mash. They talked about how they were going to get the van fixed. They talked, at some length, of the significance of the number 23.

"Why have the children no hair?" asked Doctor Sot.

"Nits," said Joxie.

Joxie rolled up the sleeves of his army shirt to show Doctor Sot the abscesses that had formed around old needle holes. Doctor Sot said that he'd be as well to come down to the practice and there they could have a closer look, there would be no charge for it. Joxie eventually agreed to rant. One of the hanks of hair battered some tom-tom drums, and Joxie launched into a half-sung, half-shouted diatribe. It was all Greek to Doctor Sot, though he recognised that there were repeated references to "Jah Rastafari," the number 23, and, more aggressively, to "George Bush."

Night came among them. Doctor Sot was entirely painless as he sat back in the trailer and he dreamed of this woman named Mag. A hand placed before him a saucer of curried vegetables.

"Really I should be making a move," he said.

He ate the food. It put sense in him. He picked up his bag. The dogs and children and adults were all around him in the dark as he climbed into the Mégane.

"Been an education," said Joxie.

They all laughed, Doctor Sot as hard as the rest of them, and indeed until he wept. His eyes were full of the happy tears as he started up Elizabeth. He immediately drove her into a ravine. He sobered at once, with the impact, and the travellers helped him from the car. It was the end of the eleven-year-old Mégane. He brought out the rest of the naggins and the chocolate cake that he had bought earlier for Sal but had forgotten to give her.

"Poor Liz," he sighed. "Poor Sal."

He sat on the hard-packed soil of the camp, with a handkerchief held to his bleeding head. There was some of the relief that accompanies an old parent's death.

"Hell we gonna do with you?" said Joxie.

The van was out of commission also—it would be next morning before he could be brought down the mountain safely. He would stay the night. The travellers found their way around the camp's darkness by the lights of their mobile phones. Each was a pinprick of light against the mountain black. He used his own phone to call Sal. He told her he was caught above on Slieve Bo, of all places, that it would be morning before he could get back. Sally was not at all worried. She was used to his adventures and disappearances. Often Doctor Sot was gone for days at a time. Many was the ditch of the northwest he had woken up in. Once he woke beneath an upturned rowing boat on the shore of Lough Gill—one leg of his trousers had been entirely wet, the other entirely dry. He had never quite pieced that one together. Tonight's accommodation wasn't bad at all. He was shown into one of the rusted caravans. The travellers turned out to be early-to-bed types: the boredom. By nine, there were no lights at all but those dim cold ones hung in the sky above. Bald children and alien dogs stretched around the caravan with him and they all slept sweetly. Doctor Sot drew on a naggin and looked out to the camp. The chocolate cake, uneaten, was on his lap in its white box. His eyes adjusted to the night shapes out there. The beautiful young woman appeared from the trees by the shale outcrop, oh adieu all false-hearted loves. She squatted on the ground and urinated, with her striped leggings bundled around her boots. Doctor Sot waited for her to finish, and then he climbed from the caravan quietly. He eased the door closed behind him. She heard him come towards her and she turned her eyes to him and smiled. The serenity in her smile it was clear at once was that of a psychotic.

"Ya wanna see my bender?" she said.

"I'd love to, Mag," said Doctor Sot.

"Knows my name 'n' all," she said.

The bender was on the one side a length of tarp stretched over a run of willow branches staked in the ground. The other side was walled by the shale outcrop and on this Mag had sketched drawings of great wingéd creatures and a series of mathematical equations.

"Soon's I get 'em right," she said, "I paints over an' I start again."

"You're bringing forward knowledge each time, Mag," said Doctor Sot.

The bender was warmed by a tiny potbelly stove, its flue extended through a hole in the tarp. The bender was lit by a battery lamp and it had pallets for flooring.

"Ya wan' yer pallets down," she said. "With yer pallets down, the damp it don't get up."

"The way to go, Mag, unquestionably. We don't want the damp getting up."

"Thing is," she said. "Soon's ya get yer pallets down, get yer rats run under, dontcha? So what I've done?"

She stuck her head out the bender's slit and tugged at Doctor Sot's arm so that he did the same.

"Chicken wire," she said. "I've closed off space between pallets, haven't I? Means no rat run."

"There's peace of mind in that, Mag."

They had cake. She showed him her equations. Mag was involved in divining the true nature of time and memory. She believed that each of these ungraspable entities ran in arcs, and that the arcs bent away from each other. She had concluded this after long study of her staked willow branches. The diverging nature of these arcs was the source of all our ills. She might be onto something there, thought Doctor Sot. He wasn't sure, at first, where she was getting the figures for her equations from. Then he realised that they were being carried to Slieve Bo in the talons of the great wingéd creatures.

"Do you take medication at all, Mag?"

"Poisons? Hardly," she said.

"Nip of this, Mag?"

"Nah," she said. "Don't agree with me."

They sat beside each other with their backs to the shale. She drew up a blanket over her striped legs and offered him some of it. He took a piece and raised it to his face to smell it. It was the smell of a child's blanket: stale rusk and hot milk.

"Do you sleep, Mag?"

"In daylight more so," she said.

But after a time her eyes did close. Doctor Sot slid a hand from beneath the blanket and lightly, very lightly, he laid it against her face. He felt the tiny fires that burned there beneath her skin. Her lashes were unspeakably lovely as they lay closed over her light sleep. If Doctor Sot could draw into his palm these tiny fires and place them with his own, he happily would.

Down in the valley the blackbirds were singing against the winter dark. The White Lady's River ran calmly beneath the humpback bridge and past the maytree whose blossom would in late spring protect us. The town slept, but in the back kitchen of the terrace house Sally was on her pink sofa yet. She shaped her mouth harshly and sounded an animal's cry, as if she meant to devour the night. For fear that he would get back early, she would go and lay cloths now over all the mirrors of the house.

KRISTÍN EIRÍKSDÓTTIR

Holes in People

1.

It was Sunday and on Sundays Dad relaxed, sat the whole day in the living room in his mottled sweat suit, listening to records and reading science fiction or hi-fi magazines. He didn't want to be disturbed.

I remember his hair, he dyed it black. In the mornings he combed it with gel and mousse; he mumbled as he stroked his glistening raven-black mane. His skin was white and flabby as if he ate nothing but sponge cake.

On this Sunday my brother and Mom were home. He sat in the living room, ungroomed in overalls, listening to records and flipping through the newspaper. Suddenly he called out to me. I was sitting on the floor in the foyer playing with my button collection, which I kept in an oblong tin box with a picture of Egyptian mummies on it. He startled me. I went to him in the living room and he stroked my hair.

Let's go out to the garden, he said.

It was summer, the grass bright green and freshly mown, the sprinkler sprayed water in a circle, the fence beautiful with a new coat of paint. In the parking lot between the houses someone in a helmet rode a BMX bike all alone. Dad went into the garage and got a shovel, he began digging a hole in the middle of the yard.

Are we going to dig for treasure? I asked and suddenly became a little worried for my button collection, but he didn't answer me.

Watch me dig, he wheezed and I waited as Dad vanished deeper into the hole, the shovel swinging and dirt raining down.

I was confused, I didn't know what Dad planned to do with the hole, what we would be putting into it and why.

When the hole was as deep as Dad, as long as a grave, and the dirt pile as tall as me, he climbed out. He was sweaty across the chest and red in the face, between gasps he told me that I now had to fill in the hole myself.

But Dad, I asked, aren't we going to put something in it first?

He shook his head and folded his arms; I began shoveling dirt into the hole.

I remember wondering why I needed to fill an empty hole with nothing but dirt and worms.

Loose dirt takes up more space than packed earth and once I finished filling it in there was a burial mound in the middle of the yard.

We went back inside, Dad sat back down in the living room to browse through his magazines, and I played war with the buttons from my box.

That was the day before Dad disappeared. No one figured it out until late in the evening, after Mom phoned his work friends who told her that Dad hadn't even shown up that morning.

I was only six years old and didn't understand what was happening right away, didn't understand why anybody would leave, why vanish like that. But I remember all of us searched for Dad—first for him, then for clues. Someone ripped up the garden. I remember that. The lawn was all torn up.

Some people stalked through the swamp near our neighborhood. It was at night and they held flashlights and lanterns, I saw them through my bedroom window. No one called out Dad's name, which I thought strange. All these bouncing lights in the darkness and silence.

■

A month after Dad disappeared my brother found the first clue. I don't know why he stuck his hand in the pipe under the kitchen sink. Maybe he had a hunch, maybe the sink was stopped up.

But he put his hand in the old, disgusting plastic water pipe; it jutted out, cut open and useless.

The clue he found was a small container that Dad had bought when he was a kid, when he went to Morocco with Grandpa and Grandma. It was as small as a bottle cap and made from thin polished wood; the picture on the lid had peeled off and no one knew what it might have been. My brother opened the box and inside it was a note. On the note Dad had written one word in block letters: *EITUR*—"poison."

Mom began crying again. She hadn't been crying as much as she was after Dad first disappeared.

But after my brother showed her the box, she closed the drapes, locked herself in her bedroom, and let out those painful sobs that my brother and I couldn't stand.

We sat on the swings next to our house and inspected the note, held it up to the sunlight to see if Dad had written something on it with invisible ink, but there was only that one word. *EITUR.*

My brother was almost ten years old. And after Dad disappeared his personality changed a lot. He stopped teasing me, which I thought was wonderful, but I missed his smile, his stupid jokes.

Now he became serious, as if he was pretending to be a grown-up, and if I tried to tease him he never got mad, he would just say to me in a low voice that I should stop misbehaving and leave him alone.

Could Dad have taken poison? he asked, turning pale. I shook my head.

No, I said. He got on a boat and sailed into the Bermuda Triangle, fell into a quagmire and piranhas ate him alive.

I was getting bored with all the seriousness around my father's disappearance; after he left there was nothing but darkness at home and I wasn't even allowed to play. My brother slapped me hard across the face, stood up, and headed quickly in the direction of our house.

I found the second clue. My brother was depressed because he searched all over the place for more clues but never found anything.

I was toasting a piece of bread and looking for the preserves when I saw a piece of tape.

The tape was wide and the same color as particleboard. I pulled back one edge and peeled it off, behind it was a small hole in the veneer, the size of a thimble. I put my finger in the hole; there was something inside that I tweaked out. It was a tiny blob.

I snuck the blob into my bedroom, put it down on my desk, and brought out a magnifying glass that I stole from Dad's den. I directed the lamplight onto the little blob, which was speckled just like a gold nugget, and raised the magnifying glass to my eye.

I saw it was probably dried up glue, but there was something inside it. I began kneading it with my fingers and discovered a tiny, hard pellet. Under the magnifying glass the pellet was blue and green and white and brown, a globe. Poison, the earth. I tried to understand the connection between the two clues, but got nowhere.

When my brother came home I showed him what I found. He studied the clue with the magnifying glass, then looked at me, seemed unsure, and looked even more depressed.

The next day, after he had recovered from his mood, we put the globe inside the Moroccan box and my brother went pale again:

Could Dad have taken poison in Morocco? he asked. I decided to keep my mouth shut.

■

We put the clues inside a shoebox and hid it behind some old cloth and sewing things that Mom kept on a top shelf in my brother's room. We didn't tell her anything about the clues, we didn't mention them at all.

They would be our secret until we were through collecting enough to figure out what had happened to Dad. We realized that no one would take them seriously, or that's what my brother said.

People didn't understand how Dad thought, he said, and I wondered what that would be like, how our Dad thought.

Before he disappeared he spent most of his time at work; he worked for a large collection agency. He would come home tired at night and my brother and I tried not to bother him or make him angry. If we forgot and were loud or began fighting—like we did sometimes before he disappeared—he would raise his voice, slam doors.

He shoved my brother once, swung at him thoughtlessly, and my brother locked himself in the bathroom. I stood outside the door, knocking lightly. I didn't know what to say. I just knew my brother was sad and when he was sad I automatically became sad too.

Often there were long stretches between finding clues, and then sometimes we might find several in a row. The next year we began finding them again—in a chink of the wall, in the creases of the furniture.

The very last one was securely taped inside a broken lampshade that I found in the garage. I tore off the tape and a photograph fell into my lap. It was taken at Thingvellir Lake; it was of my brother and mother.

In the photo, they're standing on the veranda of the summerhouse that Dad's company rented out to employees in the summer. With serious faces, squinting against the sunlight streaming straight into their eyes and creating sharp shadows. My brother is wearing only underwear with his baby belly popping out, and he's clinging to a stuffed animal.

Mom is skinny, her straight hair put up in a knot and light bangs falling across her forehead. She has a tender look on her face, wearing a pale pink summer dress.

When I saw Mom in the photo I became very sad, I felt almost like she was fading out into the sunlight. I was guilty. We were often so difficult, my brother and I, and Mom so powerless, as if she didn't have the energy to care for us, to yell at us, to discipline us.

I stuck my hand back into the lampshade, felt around, and found another piece of tape, another photograph.

At first I couldn't make out what was in the photo. Eventually I finally figured out it had once been a picture of me in my crib. Dad had drawn along the outline of the baby's body with Wite-Out and filled it in. I turned the photograph over and on the back was written, in Wite-Out, white on white: *EITUR*.

Now the word jumbled around in my mind and changed. Inga Rut Elliða-dóttir—my name. *EITUR*. My name. I curled into a ball and cried. I finally understood that *I* was the reason that Dad left, because I am *POISON*.

Many days passed before I showed my brother the photographs.

One night he came home from band practice, was in such a great mood, made himself a sandwich, whistling loudly.

He sat down at the kitchen table and began eating his sandwich. I sat across from him, laid the photos down in front of him, told him where I had found them and he stopped chewing.

He lifted them up, felt along each edge and tossed them down on the table. I felt another pang of guilt, for ruining his good mood.

Don't you understand? I said. It's my name. *EITUR*.

My brother's eyes opened wide. Forget it, he said. The old man went to hell, he's probably getting drunk somewhere in Thailand, he doesn't care about us, he can eat shit.

2.

A long time after Dad disappeared I stood in the living room of my house, holding a kitchen knife and pointing it at my boyfriend.

He knocked the knife out of my hand, kicked it into a corner, lifted me up and threw me across the room; I landed on the cocktail table.

Glass and bottles exploded, shards flew everywhere, and our neighbors called the police. They came fifteen minutes later. I was covered in blood and my boyfriend was winding a rag around a bad cut on my ankle.

As they were trying to decide what they would do with us, one of them snooped around in the kitchen cupboards and found a stash of Ketamine that we were keeping for a friend of ours who was serving a short jail sentence. We were arrested.

My boyfriend was found guilty for various minor infractions but I was ordered by the judge to enroll in an alcohol treatment program and I was still sober a few months later. The social service agency offered me a referral to a psychologist at a discount and I met with the woman once a week. I would begin crying as soon as I entered the waiting room and the first visit I did little more than sob unintelligibly, blowing my nose in the tissues she offered up immediately and with great sympathy.

She was very interested in Dad, the clues, my brother, Mom, and I laid it all out, telling her everything that I could remember.

I drank practically every day ever since I was thirteen and did a lot of bad things. According to the psychologist I was, at the time of my arrest, in some kind of shock and lacked the will to live.

I felt I didn't know anything or couldn't do anything and had nothing to live for.

The psychologist asked me to think this over and come up with a list of things that I was good at, but nothing occurred to me.

Finally I told her that I would make a good hooker, I was good at getting men to feel that they were important.

She didn't reply. She only scribbled in her little book and continued talking about Dad. She had Dad on the brain, it was as if she believed that in the end the answer to all my problems lay in thinking about why my father left.

Slowly but surely I got better and with the help of the psychologist I developed an interest in photography. She told me that my language was full of imagery, that I had a unique way of looking at the world, and she proposed that I get myself a camera. She was absolutely right, I have a keen eye for light and color.

My brother and I began communicating again, after years of having no contact whatsoever. He lived in Denmark, was married, had children, and worked as a web designer. He was the exact opposite of me, he did well in school, was the responsible sort and full of ambition.

After two years of sobriety he encouraged me to apply to a photography school in Copenhagen.

I was accepted and moved in with my brother and his family, went to school, and looked after my nephews. Mom came for more and more visits, and finally rented herself a small apartment near my brother's house. We became a family again.

We never spoke about Dad. After all this time we still couldn't bring up the subject. The man-sized hole between us three.

I was the one who found him. Our meeting was one of those unexplainable, chance events, just like the time my fingers rooted around a hollow in the wall when I was little and found something that he had left behind him. A word or a camel the size of a grain of rice.

The camel stood half buried in chewing gum under one of the kitchen chairs and I came across it when I was dragging a chair nearer to the table a whole five years after he'd disappeared.

■

I walked aimlessly down to the harbor to take some photographs. A large ship was unloading cargo containers, on one of them was a picture of a camel and the ship was marked as sailing out of Casablanca, Morocco.

I photographed the container and the ship without thinking back to the Moroccan box and rice-sized camel. Then I saw the men on the dock open the container and cover their noses.

I crept closer and smelled it too.

It was the odor of a space that had been undisturbed for many months. Dad's smell. I knew it right away.

The sailors stood at the container hatch and retched. I went over to them, covered my mouth and nose with my hand, and walked right in. They didn't try to stop me, they probably were too surprised to react.

The container was outfitted like a house, full of cans, food wrappers, empty bottles, leftovers.

On the walls hung photos of naked women and newspaper clippings from all over the world. The body lay on a mattress in the corner of the container, the features had sloughed off and maggots covered every inch.

The funeral was in Copenhagen. We wanted to put him into the earth as quickly as possible, where he could continue to rot in peace.

When I saw the coffin in the ground it triggered something in my mind and I remembered the day before he disappeared, when he asked me to come outside with him into the garden and dig a hole.

The event was so fuzzy in my memory I wasn't sure if it even happened. Mom stood between my brother and me, she cried but we were dry-eyed, held her, didn't hear a word the minister said to us.

A few days later we went to the container. Mom refused to come along. She didn't want to hear anything about Dad and I understood that, in her heart, Mom hoped that he wasn't dead, the idea that he chose to disappear like he did was still too much for her.

In the cardboard boxes set along the wall were souvenirs. They were wrapped carefully in newspaper and sawdust.

We examined a shrunken head, ivory from Africa, Incan statues from Peru, geisha dolls from Japan and all sorts of strange relics whose origins were a complete mystery to us. We didn't know if Dad bought these things as investments or collected them simply for his own enjoyment.

Alongside the mattress lay a stack of notebooks. We looked through them and saw that they were crammed full of his attempts at writing fiction. They were numbered from one to one hundred, some chapters he had rewritten many times, always in those awkward block letters.

The novel was titled *Freedom* and dealt with a man who cut himself loose from a gray, monotonous existence and traveled the world. The narrative was unsophisticated and concerned a certain protagonist, a tall and well-built Icelander who was known only as "The Viking" in every port, always getting into trouble but saving himself with his cunning.

Amid these escapades were accounts of sexual conquests. Stories of Congolese black girls with big asses, submissive Asian beauties, promiscuous Inuit girls, and teenage Ukrainian prostitutes.

We read one of these episodes and my brother threw the notebook down and grabbed his forehead.

I can't do this, he groaned and got himself a beer.

It was the middle of the night and we sat in the dining room. I kept on reading and with each word I was grateful that I didn't know the man who wrote them. I could tell from the narrative that he had an unbridled love for himself.

A love that destroyed everyone who came near him, and made him oblivious to its consequences. Blind love.

I asked myself why that was. Whether something at his core might really be beautiful, something that others couldn't perceive but that he alone knew he possessed. Maybe this hidden *something* gave him his ever-renewed justification to seek out love and admiration.

My brother buried his head in his arms on the table. I stroked the back of his neck to comfort him but then realized that he was laughing.

TRANSLATED FROM ICELANDIC BY CHRISTOPHER BURAWA

LÁSZLÓ KRASZNAHORKAI

The Bill

FOR PALMA VECCHIO, AT VENICE

You sent to us and we knew what you wanted so we sent Lucrecia and Flora, sent Leonora, sent Elena, followed by Cornelia, then Diana, and so it went on from January through to June, then from October through to December we sent Ophelia, sent Veronica, sent Adriana, sent Danae, then Venus, and, little by little, every plump, sweet whore and courtesan on our books turned up at your place, the important thing, as for every male Venetian, being that their brows should be clear and high, that their shoulders be broad and round, chests wide and deep, that their bodies should open out the way they would under a deep-cut chemise, and that your eyes should be able to dive, as from a cliff, from their tempting faces down to their fresh, sweet, desirable breasts, just as you described to Federico who brought us your order and who then described it to us in turn, saying yes, just as before, just as wide and deep as the valley, the valley of Val Seriana, where you yourself come from, Federico grinned, because, according to him, that was what you were really after, that valley in Bergamo where you were born, and he went on to tell us, and the others confirmed this, that nothing else concerned you, that you weren't in the least interested in the dark secrets of the flesh, only in waves of blonde hair, sparkling eyes, and the slow opening of the lips, in other words in the head, and then in the prospect that opens from the chin down and spreads below the broad round shoulders to the landscape of the scented body, not the rest, and that you were always asking them to slip their straps to below the shoulder because, you told them, you had, as you put it, to see the shoulder utterly bare but at the same time to see the lacy white edge of the chemise on its concave arc from shoulder to shoulder, that arc just above the painted nipples of the breasts, which reminded you of the horizon above your village in that deep valley, the valley of Seriana, though you didn't make that perfectly clear to them at the time, that idea being something that occurred to Federico, and only after a while, though he didn't explain it either, and, in the end, it proved impossible to discover why it was you painted so many not exactly fat but extraordinarily large women in your pictures, because you wouldn't answer a single question about that, and were, in any case, known for your lack of patience, and how, impatient, you would often expose their breasts entirely, so they said, only to cover them up again most of the time so they never really knew what you wanted, and some were scared of you because they'd heard all kinds of rumors and were ready for anything, their chief fear being that you, in your *bottega*, might demand something of them that they were not able to do; but, as they went on to say, you didn't really want anything anyway, and, what's more, it often happened that you paid in advance, and, once you stopped painting for the day, sent them away immediately without even a bunch of grapes, never allowing those enormous women to take you to bed, they just had to stand there, or sit on a sofa, stand or sit for hours on end without moving, it being just a matter of the hourly rate and the fear of what might happen, because you pretty soon got a reputation, people said that the Bergamo man, as they called you, was not in the least interested in fucking, and wouldn't even touch, merely instruct his models in his quiet polite way, how she should sit or stand, and then he'd just look, watching how she looked back at him, and then, after an age of waiting, would ask her to lower the left shoulder of her chemise a touch, or to ruffle up the folds of her dress a little more, or say that she should uncover one breast, though he was always standing a good distance away, beyond touching distance, and, so the ladies would tell us, you'd be sitting in an armchair as the two servants led them back to the pier so they might return by the waiting *mascareta* and that you never actually came anywhere near them nor would allow them to touch you, unlike those, they giggled, who just wanted to stare while they themselves mounted some man from behind; because you weren't like that, the girls told us, that wasn't why you hired them . . . you just looked at them and they had to stand there for hours, which was impossible, or sit, though of course they were fully prepared, there being painters enough in Venice able to pay for the visit of a whore or a *cortigiana onesta*, and they'd stood or sat for every kind of artist, some having served you before, and some, from time to time, even having posed for the great Bellini, only to face the universal ridicule of seeing themselves depicted as the Mater Dolorosa, or Mary Magdalene, or St. Catherine in S. Giovanni e Paolo or the Scuola di S. Marco, which gave everyone a good laugh and, boy, did they laugh! though in your case, Signor Bergamo or Seriana, whichever you prefer, when you'd finished with them they didn't, for some reason, feel like laughing, and when one or the other of them told the others what it had been like with you after a couple of visits, they kept saying they had no idea what you were about, and, above all, couldn't understand why you turned them into such vast mountains of flesh, since, said Danae, my shoulder is nowhere near as enormous as that, nor am I anywhere near as fat as that, said Flora pointing to her waist, and, to tell the truth, there was, after all, something incomprehensible about these disproportionate figures because, despite the exaggerations, they remained lovely and attractive, and no one could understand how you did it, nor, more importantly, why, but then your whole art was so peculiar, everyone said, that it seemed it wasn't exactly art you were aiming for but for something about the women or in them, which led to ever greater confusion because the filthy way you looked at them was quite intolerable, they said, so even the most experienced whore felt nervous and looked away, but then you'd snap at them and tell them to look you straight in the eye, though otherwise you treated them well enough, it was just that you never laid a finger on them, that being something they could never understand, the reason they were scared of you, never looking forward to visiting you, although you paid them well enough, giving even the lowest of them at least a few miserable escudo, and as for the freshest youngest whore or *cortigiana onesta*, you paid well over the going rate for her, despite the fact that, for all your fame, you're far from the wealthiest of them and, they say, all those pictures you painted of Lucrecia and Danae and Flora and Elena are still stacked up in your store, the religious paintings being the ones that sell, the ones in which Danae becomes Mary, and Flora becomes St. Catherine, one under some tree with the baby in her arm, the other in a pretty country scene, these all having been purchased, as we know, while the ones you painted for some lecher wanting a picture of his whore, well, you couldn't always convince the customer that what you'd given them was exactly what they wanted, since their lovers remained stubbornly just Lucrecia, or Danae, or Flora, or Elena, so most of those pictures are still in the *bottega*, all stacked up on top of each other, because, despite having sold a few, you sometimes couldn't hide your own dissatisfaction with them and went back to them time and again, which was why you occasionally sent word with Federico for the same woman, albeit in a different shape, and we could see why you'd want that because we've had a thousand, ten thousand, indeed a hundred thousand such requests in the Carampane, and ever since you first moved into Venice it was obvious to us that it was always the same woman you wanted, and so we supplied you with Lucrecia and Flora and Leonora and Elena and Cornelia and Diana from January through June, and Ophelia and Veronica and Adriana and Danae and finally Venus from October through December, though all you wanted from January through June, and from October through December, was the same woman, and only after giving considerable thought to the question of why you painted our ladies as fat as you did, did we at last figure out the secret of why these enormous women looked so fiendishly beautiful on your canvases, or at least one of us figured it out, meaning me, figured out that what you wanted, beyond any doubt, was precisely the same thing each time, which is to say, that valley in Seriana, you filthy reprobate, that is to say the valley between a whore's shoulders and her breasts, that is, the valley where you were born and which might perhaps remind you of your mother's breasts, which is not to deny that you're a handsome man with a fine figure, though the most attractive part of you is your face as everyone who's met you knows, because all the whores notice that and they would have done it for you for nothing but you didn't want them, no, all you wanted was to stare at their chins, their necks, and their chests, and they quickly got to hate you because they hadn't the least idea what you wanted and we had to tell them to calm down and just go along with it if you asked for them because they'd never make an easier escudo and, what's more, you'd dress them up in fine clothes as always, which, by the way, makes us all the more suspicious that you really are searching for something, and, as the years passed, there were new Floras and Lucrecias and Veronicas and Ophelias, and they were all different, but all the same to you, and they had to take their high-heeled shoes off as soon as they got to the door, in fact had to take off all the clothes they'd arrived in, because you had them strip naked down to their underwear and you had your two servants give them a lacy chemise and anything else necessary, inevitably some gorgeous robe embroidered with gold thread, or a dress or sometimes just a blue or green velvet jacket, then you gently asked if they would expose one breast, to pull the chemise down a little, and then gazed for hours at those soft, wide, round shoulders, the innocent-corrupt smiles on their faces, and it was as if you hadn't even noticed the hot perspiration on the fresh skin of those naked breasts, took no notice at all of what they had to offer you, because you had no use for narrow waists, milk-white bellies, those ample hips and the soft hair between their legs, were uninterested in the ways their lips, knees, and thighs might open, in their warm laps and those clouds of intoxicating perfume, and however one or the other tried with words and looks and sighs, with everything she knew of the thousand different ways to seduce a man, it all left you cold, you just waved them away, told them to stop all that nonsense and that all you wanted them to do was to stay absolutely still, to sit quietly on the sofa and look at you, to keep their eyes on you and not look away, not even for a moment, and insisted on this to the point that all of them, every single one from Lucrecia through to Venus, became quite annoyed at this idiotic and pointless game of you-look-at-me-I-look-at-you, because what after all are we, they complained, raising their voices, looking furious, child-virgins from the lace factory? though we, of course, knew that what you needed was not them, not as people, but what you could get at *through* them, and I, personally, always thought we should stop talking in terms of any specific model and concentrate on what lay behind the model, some idea like the female figure being La Serenissima, and the male being Le Carampane, though from all I've said so far it will have been clear to you for some time now where I'm coming from, I mean who it is telling you what an unusual man you are, a man uninterested in women as such, more in what might be found *by way of* a woman, someone who is looking to perfect the most scandalously refined, satanic sensation, to whom, from that point of view, a woman is just a body, a notion I can understand and agree with, because I myself think we're all nothing but bodies, end of story, though there's so much you can tell from these bodies, if you catch one in a moment of desire, at the moment when the body is most alive and burning with lust, how deep and mysterious and irresistible is the desire that forces you to want—to demand—possession of some object for which you are willing to sacrifice everything, even though it's nothing more than a small patch of skin, or a faint flush on that skin, or just a sad little smile, maybe the way she drops a shoulder, or bows her head, or slowly raises it, when a tiny blonde curl, a maddening strand of hair accidentally falls across her temple and this strand promises something, you have no idea what, but whatever it is you're willing to give your whole life for it, and maybe it's precisely because of this that I feel convinced—and you too will be aware of this—that it's not at all the way they peel off their clothes that drives men crazy, oh no, quite the opposite, the way a breast pops out, the revelation of a belly or a lap or an ass or pair of thighs, because any such revelation means the end of unfettered illusion, no, it's the moment when the faint flickering candlelight reveals the animal in their eyes, because it's this look that drives us crazy, crazy for that beautiful animal, this animal that is nothing but body, that's what people die for, for the moment, that splinter of time, when the animal appears, beautiful beyond comprehension—and that's the light you sometimes catch in the eyes of Cornelia and Flora and Elena and Venus, while all the time being fully aware, since you've lived long enough, of the fact that this is just how Cornelia, Flora, Elena, and Venus happen to look today, that they are already old and wrinkly inside and out and that nothing interests them except their bellies and their purses, though most of the time both are empty, and so you call them again and again, and we keep sending them in new and different shapes, so off they go: Cornelia and Flora and Elena and Venus and their eyes might do the trick and hit the perfect spot, because clearly that's what you yourself want and that's why you forbid them to do anything that otherwise you would probably indulge in, so you don't let them take off their clothes and completely reveal their breasts or anything else they've got because you know that the animal essence is a matter of deferred pleasure, it exists only in the act of deferral, that the promise in their eyes is just that, a promise, a promise that something will happen later, or maybe sooner, or indeed in the very next moment, just as we are unbuckling our belt, when all our clothes drop away at once, the way their eyes promise, which is the look you are searching for and which you clearly want to immortalize in your painting, and, on a good day, you find that look right away, and it perhaps promises satisfaction now, yes, right now, but only perhaps, for deferred pleasure is the very essence of this essentially infernal arrangement, the cage in which you too are imprisoned, as is every man in Venice —in the world at large—and though you might always be wanting to paint the moment pending, the moment the promise is fulfilled with all that this entails, the whole process recorded in color and line on your canvas, you can buy the whole process inherent in her look for one escudo, if you get what you paid for anyway; this painting you so desire to paint is, in fact, about something else that no one could ever paint, because that would be a picture of stillness, of stasis, an Eden of Fulfilled Promises where nothing moves and nothing happens and—what is more difficult to explain— where there's nothing to say about this immobility, permanence, and absence of change, because, in fulfilling the promise you have lost the thing promised, it's what vanishes in the fulfillment of itself, the light in the desired object goes out, its flame quenched—and so desire limits itself, for however much you may desire there's nothing more to be done, because there is nothing at all real about the desire, desire consists entirely of anticipation, that is to say the future, because, strange as it is, you can't go back in time, there's no returning from the future, from the thing that happens next, no way of getting back to it from the other side, the side of memory, it's absolutely impossible, because the road back from memory inevitably takes you to the wrong place, and perhaps its whole purpose is to make you believe that there once was a real event, something that actually happened, that the thing once desired did indeed exist, and all the while your memory is shepherding you away from this object and offering you its counterfeit instead, because it never could give you the real object, the fact being that this object doesn't exist, though that's not exactly your way of perceiving it, since you're a painter, meaning someone who inhabits desire but can reject it in advance, consoling yourself with the thought that there will come a moment when the chemise drops away, though believing the promise of that thought makes you a guilty man, a miserable sinner, a man condemned to sinning miserably until the Day of Judgment arrives, though that day is still far off for you; so, for now, you can carry on believing and desiring, and you need not think, you can go crazy, you can rage and thirst until you can hardly breathe—and then you can remember Federico and send him over to us, and we can send you Danae, Veronica, Adriana, and Venus, the lot of them, and we can carry on sending them as long as Federico arrives to tell us what you need . . . but there will come a day when we draw a line under it all, the day when we call it a day, adding up everything you ordered, and then, there will be no more Palma Vecchio, no more Jacopo Negretti, then it will all be over and we'll send you the bill, you can be sure of that.

TRANSLATED FROM HUNGARIAN BY GEORGE SZIRTES

INGO SCHULZE

Oranges and Angel

Last weekend, the third Sunday in Advent, I finally unpacked the angel. We spent almost two hours picking it out in Naples last year. That is, we hadn't actually wanted an angel. We wanted a couple of those figurines you find in a *presepe*, the manger scene set up at this time of year in almost every Italian church, where they then grow into whole cities and landscapes, like the ones we build for model trains. During a previous visit to Naples I had bought a figurine of that sort, a market peddler with her fruit stand. Holding the woman in the palm of my hand, I thought she looked lovely and lost, like the sole inhabitant of some planet. In the girls' room, however, first her melons and oranges turned up missing, then her head. We had told Ralf what had happened, and he reminded us about it when we got to Naples. Ralf was not to be deterred from presenting us with a large angel—the good ones cost around two hundred euros—as a thank you for our hospitality, as he put it.

Ralf visited us in Rome twice last year, and both times he vanished again with no warning. In retrospect the angel seemed like a kind of security deposit. He had hailed a taxi in Naples to take off in pursuit of a car full of women, and the first sign of life we'd gotten from him then was the Christmas card I received yesterday, asking if there was an angel hovering above us.

At that point I would have been hard-pressed to describe the angel: large, a good fifteen inches high, baroqueish. Removed from the soft wrapping paper, it appeared to have shrunk remarkably—until I discovered the two wings packed with it.

Now I saw before me the wrenched face of the vendor as he strained to remove the angel's wings, while his wife explained that we needn't worry about transporting it. They sent entire manger scenes to Canada, Australia, and Japan every year. Urging her husband on, she spread her arms wide to demonstrate how easy it was to pull out the invisible angel wings and then reinsert them. "*Si fa accussì!*"—that's how it's done, she cried, "*Si fa accussì.*"

It's amazing to me now that we ever took the angel once its wings had been ripped off and screwed back in again. But Ralf insisted—just look at those hands, so lifelike, as if they were playing a harp.

Determined to treat the angel better than its vendor had, I first sought out the holes in its red bib apron and long robe of bright, shimmering olive green, then threaded the nail carefully through—and immediately lost my place. Wielding the wing like a hunting knife, I poked around again with the nail in search of the hole, which couldn't have disappeared. I went at it more vigorously, and the fabric tore. That is, I heard it rip, but could see no sign of the tear. I had almost given up when the nail slipped into place. I now held the angel up by the eye screw between its shoulders, and the first wing did a marionette's flap on one side. The second was also reddish blue and just as much trouble. Maybe Ralf's card and my difficulties with the angel have nothing whatever to do with this story. But it's not really a story either, more a postponed diary entry from our three-day excursion to Naples. Because time and space are the only things that connect what happened. I believe, however, that the first experience made me more receptive to the second, so that suddenly everything took on a meaning that, from a more sober perspective, probably isn't there, at least not for other people.

It was purely by chance that Ralf came with us to Naples. Ralf is a friend or acquaintance—depending. In September 1988, as a graduate of the Ernst Busch Acting Academy, he joined the theater in Altenburg, landed a couple of good-size roles, and kept out of politics. But then, in the spring of 1990—I was already working at the newspaper—he started drinking. He was fired a year later, went into rehab, returned to Altenburg, and supplemented his unemployment checks by delivering our free paper. His new passion was computers, the Macs in our office. Ralf made friends with our two typesetters and evidently learned the trade simply by watching. When we decided to add a third typesetter, the two women wanted Ralf. He stayed on until our bankruptcy in 2001, set out on his own designing websites, and has muddled through ever since. Although we no longer had much to do with each other—I left the paper shortly after he was hired— he was the only person from those days that I still heard from with any regularity.

Last year Ralf asked if he and his new girlfriend could spend two nights with us at the Villa Massimo. I agreed, although in Berlin we hadn't seen much of each other except when he just happened to drop by.

His visit at the end of June—when he showed up all alone—proved a blessing at first. A few days previous I had torn an Achilles tendon, and surgery had left me with a cast on my right leg, so that I could walk only on crutches. On his first day with us, Ralf managed to locate a wheelchair and pushed me wherever I wanted to go. He quickly made friends with the kids, including those of other fellows at the Villa. They adored him, even though he did little to court their favor. But Ralf could yodel and draw and do headstands, and he knew magic tricks. He could snatch his self-rolled cigarettes apparently out of thin air, sometimes already lit, and make them disappear just as suddenly, so that the kids assumed he was capable of any miracle. He was also more relaxed around them. With us he thought he had to talk about books or art, which proved fairly strenuous.

Since Tanya didn't like to drive in Italy, ten days later Ralf was our chauffeur for a jaunt to the shore. It turned out to be a beautiful day. Where the real beach began, he grabbed me around the hips, I threw an arm over his shoulder, and we made our way across the sand. At first it didn't bother me to talk about the women standing along a stretch of the road right before it entered a pine forest; almost all were women of color wearing short gaudy dresses or snug-fitting pants and keeping their backs turned to the road. Ralf interpreted this as modesty, I guessed it came from a different tradition—the courtesans of antiquity are said to have also enticed their clients with buttocks rather than breasts.

But they were all Ralf could talk about the day after as well. Did I know where these women came from, where and how they lived, if they had documentation, how much they charged, how much their pimps deducted, if they ever washed themselves nearby, and did they ever actually get to see the sea, and plenty more along those lines.

"How should I know?" I finally protested.

That afternoon Ralf asked me for the car. He didn't return until early the next morning, slept till noon, clowned around with the kids, wolfed down a couple of jelly sandwiches, and borrowed the car again early that evening. This went on for several days. I found his behavior embarrassing and puerile and rude—if only because of the kids. Tanya, however, suggested that the women probably found Ralf more pleasant than the sorts of guy we had spotted moving in packs along the shoulder of the road. "Main thing is, nothing happens to him."

"I find him disgusting," I said, putting words to what had only become clear to me at that moment. Just seeing his toothbrush next to mine revolted me, and suddenly it was a real effort to use the same toilet he did.

Ralf must have sensed this. One morning, there he was, sitting on his suitcase. He said good-bye to the girls, told us thanks, and left. The car was standing in the parking lot, tanked full and sparkling clean, inside and out.

When I heard from him four months later in November, he sounded embarrassed by his escapades, or at least he apologized on the phone, without saying what for. By then I had admitted to myself how cranky and unfair I had been during my crutches-and-wheelchair phase, and didn't want to refuse him a second visit. It was sort of a mutual making of amends.

When Ralf arrived in Rome on December 6th, the girls were thrilled. The first two evenings he gave to us entirely. One of Ralf's new quirks was an inordinate consumption of oranges. I was suspicious at first; he had read Seume's *A Stroll to Syracuse,* and I remarked that I found it comforting that Seume could at least fill his belly with oranges for a few weeks. But Ralf's appetite showed no sign of abating. He would schlep several kilos of oranges from the market every day, doling some out like advertising freebies and stuffing himself with the rest. You ran across orange peels almost any time and anywhere, and he always peeled them in a spiral, leaving shapes you could balance on your fingertip or on top of a bottle, something I hadn't seen since childhood, when oranges were still a rarity—we called it "making monkeys."

Ralf made himself as useful as he knew how, worked on my website, showed Tanya how to edit and cut digital video, and downloaded a lot of children's cartoons. Our orange man never said a word about his summer excursions. When we asked him if he wanted to drive us to Naples, he was raring to go.

I was happily anticipating Naples, even though I had reluctantly agreed to write something about the Tadema exhibition at the National Museum. Even the girls, who had had enough of our excursions and were no longer impressed by our promises, could hardly fall asleep the evening before we left.

On the morning of December 12th, however, it looked as if an escalating truckers' strike would spoil our lovely plans. I dialed one taxi number after another, to no avail. Gas stations were running out of gas, supermarket shelves were emptying fast, fruit and milk had already vanished from many of them. With suitcase, shoulder bags, and two girls, we hurried to the Piazza Bologna. The metro, usually crammed full at this hour in any case, was pure hell—or perhaps what people like us call hell. Without Ralf we would have missed our train with reserved seats. Tanya and I had our hands full just keeping the girls from being squashed, so Ralf took charge of our baggage, but didn't make it onto our metro car. He showed up at Termini just before our train pulled out—with our suitcase balanced atop his head, bags slung over his shoulders, and a blue plastic bag of oranges dangling from his right wrist.

I'm always fascinated by the fact that it takes only two hours to get from Rome to Naples, and another two, in the opposite direction, to Florence. For me it's always as if Rome lies at the equator, and Florence and Naples are overarched by two entirely different skies.

It may sound like wild enthusiasm or at least an exaggeration when I claim that I had already wholly experienced the uniqueness of Naples two years before, when for the first time I climbed out of a taxi on the Piazza San Domenico Maggiore. This city has its own peculiar density—I know no other word for it than density. The volume of its squares, streets, alleys, courtyards is so supercharged that Neapolitans seem to me more mature than other city-dwellers. And warmer, and maybe a little nastier too, depending on who you run into. They have neither energy nor time for illusions.

Naples is a city that squanders its beauty, and not just in criminality and decay. All of a sudden the most splendid church emerges, but you can barely see the façade, let alone get a sense of it in its entirety. Its real splendor is often first visible from a back courtyard. Nowhere is the air so saturated with smells, and the air changes with every step you take. You are given the once-over, patted and jostled, silence doesn't exist. The rattle of *motorini* demands a continual glance over the shoulder. But this density would be nothing without the vastness that accompanies it. All it takes is to climb a couple flights of stairs or to move from one side of the street to the other, or simply to turn around, and you're dizzy from the *vista sul mare*, which I experienced the first time from the windows of the Hotel

Britannique, where we were staying this trip too. With its '70s décor, it looks pretty rundown. Only the high ceilings hint of its old *grandezza*. Even now a shiver passes over me when I recall my first visit—pulling open the casements in the darkened room, pushing the wooden shutters out, and closing my eyes as the light crashes in. Despite all the descriptions I'd heard or read, despite all the paintings, photographs, and films, I thought I'd be prepared for that moment. In those few dazzled seconds of trying to orient yourself, it's as if you have wandered into a painting or movie—it's all so familiar, nothing is familiar. It's never a repeat view, if only because the light and the color of the water generate a different space each time. Each time I'm terrified by how close Vesuvius is, each time it seems unreal that Sorrento and Amalfi are located on that peninsula, that that island out there is Capri. The vastness is the other side of the coin, the counterpart to the density so surprisingly and intimately related to it. The view across the Gulf of Naples embraces all that we are: from Virgil to Nietzsche and Wagner, from Benjamin to Malaparte to Saviano—seemingly random names chosen from so great a number.

That was my lecture once the girls had fallen asleep on the train, while Ralf peeled his oranges and divided them into thirds. I also said that I was well aware of the dubiousness of such generalizations, that they probably revealed more of my own ignorance than any real knowledge, and yet also represented my best attempt to get my bearings in the place.

Of course other cities are louder, more fragrant, more foul smelling, narrower, faster, wider, more unpredictable—Calcutta, Sanaa, Cairo, Tokyo. I either love or hate them, but they remain foreign cities. Naples, however, is the black sheep in the family who is more annoying than some lunatic at the train station, or a gorgeous aunt or niece who sets your head spinning faster than any pin-up girl.

Apparently there were no strikes in Naples, or at least no visible signs of such caught our eye. At least there were enough taxis. We took our luggage to the hotel, rode back into the city, met up with the rest of the group from the Villa Massimo—who arrived late because truckers had blocked the highway with their rigs—in the Pizzeria del Presidente, and then headed up to the National Museum. Just to describe our walk through the narrow streets—the rich dark colors of the façades, the lights strung for Advent, the mild air, the bright streaks of sky between roof gutters, the clotheslines, the gulls and pigeons you might have taken for handkerchiefs that the wind had ripped free and set spinning into the sunless blue—a real description of that walk would require far more time and space, and still not come close to capturing the happiness I felt with every step I took, a happiness that seemed as unfounded as it was perfectly natural.

Once inside the National Museum we stood for a long time gazing at the *Farnese Bull*. Paula wanted a story to go with each work of art. We puzzled over the *Alexander Mosaic*, wondering who the man behind the mounted Alexander might be, and felt sorry for the soldier left to lie in the dust while the fleeing Persian king's chariots rolled over him. Ralf carried Anna piggyback almost the entire time.

I was in a hurry to get upstairs to see the Tadema exhibition. The few paintings by Sir Lawrence Alma-Tadema that I was familiar with had always left me more amused than anything else. As a master of his craft he was without parallel. Every detail, every shifting shadow across polished marble, every ornament of a robe draping the knee of a seated figure, was perfection. A pile of Tadema's pomegranates is so three-dimensional you think they may fall out of the painting. And yet I found him infinitely boring. And not just because the faces of his idealized figures all look alike. I saw his paintings as the epitome of a zeitgeist—the various academies of the late nineteenth century had fought tooth and nail to win Tadema's membership—that found his glistening sidetracked processions a cause for celebration. I find it an interesting phenomenon that in the era of photography someone held fast to a version of *veduta* painting and populated his canvases with his own salon guests—who had probably arrived by train —clad in classical garb. In the case of a man who was born in 1836 and died in 1912 one might plead mitigating circumstances for this attempt to flee the ever-accelerating world of modernity into one of ostensibly eternal classicism. And yet: Weren't such paintings already an anachronism by the date of Tadema's birth? Or had I missed something? I wanted to find out from his paintings.

Arriving on the second floor the first thing I saw was Vesuvius. Staring at it from the same room where the model of Pompeii is displayed, you realize what others may smile at as a commonplace: Without Vesuvius there would be no Pompeii, no Herculaneum, but then also no mosaics and no *Alexander Mosaic*; this museum wouldn't exist either, and even a Tadema would have painted differently.

No wonder then that we also think of Vesuvius as a museum piece. Distance and the museum's higher elevation might save us from the lava. But death from the air was a possibility too. Herculaneum had been buried by billowing small chunks of lava and a rain of ash, while toxic gases, which are said to make excavation risky even today, did the rest. The wind would only need to be from the wrong direction, and a new eruption would claim far more lives than the one of two thousand years ago.

"Actually," Tanya said, "people shouldn't be let into the city without a reserved seat on the evacuation train."

That might have served as a good lead-in for my article: "Tadema—Under the Volcano." But the exhibition was closed. At first we didn't understand and assumed the cord dividing the hall—one half of which was devoted to various painters of *vedute* set in antiquity and the other half to Tadema—was a precautionary measure to protect the paintings. Once we realized our mistake, we presented our tickets for the special exhibition. But the uniformed women and men sitting beside the barrier turned away from us. "*Chiuso, chiuso!*" cried the one seated closest, and without so much as a glance at our tickets.

"I've paid," I said, "and now I want to see the other side of the hall." They were silent. "I'm going to write about it, it's really in your own interest." No response. Only when I reached out to remove the cord did those ladies and gentlemen spring to life. One *signore* grabbed me by the arm. He was trying hard to keep his voice down. Tanya translated. Unemployed workers had barricaded themselves on the balcony up ahead, where they had unrolled their banners. No one knew how they would react if anyone got too close. The police had been notified, we would have to wait. "How long?" I asked. "Just a few hours," came the answer, then he let go of me.

I didn't know what to do. The uniformed guards realized at once that I had capitulated and returned to their seats. "Then I can't write about it," I said. "So you're free to go," Tanya said.

For my reading that evening we entered a side street off the Piazza San Domenico Maggiore and then descended a set of stairs into an artist's studio. Camilla Miglio, a professor at L'Orientale, introduced me. The audience consisted almost exclusively of female students, most of them barely over twenty. I kept staring up at the window that looked onto the piazza. Last year, we were told, when Terézia Mora had given a reading here, they'd come close to having to shut down because of the sirens and shouts and the blue lights of police cars. The son of a Mafia boss had been shot dead very nearby.

On our return to the hotel we were greeted with a shock. The girls were sleeping and Ralf lay stretched diagonally across our bed, an empty bottle of red wine with its cork replaced was on the little table by the window, plus a saucer full of cigarette butts, and beside it a stack of orange peels. It took Ralf a while to come around. At first he didn't understand why we were whispering.

According to him he had been drinking again for a good while, but in moderation, only in moderation, he said, no harm in that. That was beside the point, Tanya said, whether in moderation or not, and a whole bottle isn't really "moderation" in any case. Why was he drinking in secret, I asked. But he wasn't being secretive about it. He hadn't drunk anything in our company, I replied. "You two don't drink," Ralf said. "On your account," I said.

I found his red-wine breath insufferable. I just wanted him out of the room quick.

The next morning Ralf joined us at the breakfast table in a sunny mood. If we didn't mind he'd like to accompany us to Pompeii.

Tanya went on with her story about the dogs there and how they had chased my mother in the summer of 2001. At the exit from the ruins she had turned around without a second thought and opened a bottle of water she'd bought from a street vendor, then poured the water into the cup of her hand so that the dogs could drink. Ralf said that without the eruption Pompeii would be a totally insignificant town nowadays, worth a look at best because of an old church with walls decked out in provincial baroque, a phrase taken verbatim from his guidebook.

The girls were bored by Pompeii—except for the corpses in glass display cases. It occurred to me that this was a town first colonized by Greeks and that Greek had held on as the preferred language well into the first century BCE. But then former Roman legionnaires donated money to build an amphitheater, and bit by bit gladiator games replaced performances of tragedies. Although the Greeks were no less cruel in war than the Romans, I was overcome with a strange sadness by the realization of how everyday life can undergo such brutalization within a single lifespan. The reconstructed amphitheater was closed; bars now blocked the entrances through which those doomed to die had been forced inside. It stank. It seemed to me an eternal stench, as if the fear of death had lived on, had seeped into the stones as urine and shit.

Vesuvius stood out clearly against the afternoon sky. What would we do if it suddenly erupted? I wondered if Ralf would lend us a hand as he had in the metro the day before? And what about us? Would we leave him behind wounded, just so we could save the girls and ourselves? And what would that moment be like, when—with the children in our arms—we understood that there was no escape? I thought about the scene in *Kill Bill* where Uma Thurman is buried alive. She turns on her flashlight and works her way out of the coffin and up through the soil. Even though I knew better, I couldn't imagine our fate to be any different: We too would dig our way up and out, over and over again.

We had crossed paths with several young Asian women a few times— our last encounter, just as dusk fell, was in the Villa dei Misteri. The mural was painted in perspective, but with the focal point shifted slightly off-center, lending it a feeling of modernity that provoked our speculation. What else would have been lost to us if this work of art had not adorned one of the few intact houses of a provincial backwater? One of the Asian girls entered the room, cast a glance at the mural, and vanished again. I couldn't control myself. "There is nothing better than this," I shouted in English and ran after her a few steps. Whether her vacation was short or long, she would not see art like this again. Look into the eyes of these women, I wanted to say, look at these gestures, the raised arms and the little basins in their hands? Doesn't it seem as if this were only yesterday?

The young Asian woman turned around in fright, hesitated briefly. I waved for her to come back, but she scampered away like a nymph fleeing Pan.

Tanya said that it would be charming to go on a trip that left out all the major sights, as Roussel is said to have done, who let himself be driven everywhere, but never left the car, not even in Egypt, just pulled the window curtain back a bit. I said that I couldn't see anything charming about that, really couldn't. Ralf was evidently trying to decide which side to take. But suddenly, for no obvious reason, he spread his arms wide, traced circles with his hands, and began to dance in small steps across the stone floor in front of the barrier. With eyes closed, he slowly raised his arms, his fingers intertwined, his head nestled first against one bicep, then the other. Then he snapped his fingers and did a couple of spins, arms outstretched at his side and making snaky motions.

His dance lasted no longer than thirty seconds. After a final tippety-tap with his feet, he opened his eyes again.

"Where did you learn that?" Tanya asked.

"At the beach," he said, "last summer."

Not even the girls could talk Ralf into a repeat performance, but he promised to dance with them in our hotel room.

Nothing came of that, however, because after we returned home, he said good-bye and took off to see something of the city.

We planned to have dinner that evening at L'Oca, where we were to meet Valentina and Carmen, who had invited us twice now to visit them in Naples. Valentina said that three men had been shot dead the evening before, halfway between the studio and the Cappella Sansevero, not a hundred meters from where I had read.

The next morning we packed our things and rode with Ralf to Raimondo's bookstore, Dante & Descartes, where we could leave our baggage until time for our train. I briefly considered trying the museum again for the Tadema show, but this was to be the girls' day. And they wanted to see manger figurines and visit the aquarium.

The Via S. Gregorio Armeno has row upon row of shops, every single one with nothing but crèche figurines. As I said, it was Ralf who gave us the angel as a gift. What he probably would have liked best was for us to buy another angel too, so we'd have one for each girl. Anna and Paula were each allowed to pick out a statuette, but both chose a shepherd with a lamb over his shoulders. Ralf bore the big green box ahead of us on the walk back to the bookstore.

Raimondo had made coffee, and for the adults there was baba. The children got cocoa and cookies and the inevitable oranges.

Ralf had stepped outside to smoke. I told Raimondo about our failed attempt to see the Tadema exhibition and said that it was in fact true what the guidebook said: that in Naples everything is put to immediate use, it all happens in the now. Not even the museum, I said, is a place for the past, because there too the present triumphed in the form of a protest by the unemployed, just as Vesuvius would likewise triumph again someday. My final words were mixed with a shout in the street. I heard it but paid no attention. In Naples someone is always shouting, and no one was to be seen at the door that opened onto the Via Mezzocannone.

Later we tried to reconstruct what we had actually heard. We had all definitely heard "Stop!" but we couldn't even agree on the name. "Felice," is what I thought I'd made out, but neither Tanya nor Raimondo could recall that.

Tanya was the first to react. "That's Ralf shouting," she said, "it's Ralf." She said it very coolly, as if she didn't want to upset anyone. We got up and went outside.

Ralf came running up the street toward us, waving and shouting that name, Felice, or at least that's what I think. He had seen her in a car with three other women, he had recognized her. "And they didn't have any clothes on," he cried. A car was heading down the street, its brake lights flashed, a silver-colored car—middle-sized, nothing special. Ralf hailed a taxi, which drove on to the taxi stand at the upper end of the street, maneuvered back and forth to turn around, and came back down. "Call the police," Ralf said, leapt into the taxi, and slammed the door. We could see him leaning over the front seat, gesticulating. The silver car turned left.

"We have to call the police," Tanya said.

"And what are you going to tell them?"

"That there was a car with naked women sitting inside."

I called Ralf's cell-phone number. I got his voice mail. I tried again, until we realized that there was a ring coming from his shoulder bag, which he had stored behind the counter. In it were—in addition to two oranges— his wallet, toothbrush and toothpaste, and his guidebook. We waited for the carabinieri above the bookstore in a room painted green. All we could do was provide them with Ralf's description—that, and what he had shouted. Tanya said that it was evidently one or several of the prostitutes he had made friends with last summer, at the beach south of Ostia. Had he been a client, the carabinieri asked. "Probably," she said.

The short carabiniere was pokerfaced; the tall one stared at me as if I was the offender. They took down Ralf's cell-phone number. Tanya reviewed Ralf's recent calls, but it looked as if he had made none since December 6th, the day he arrived in Italy. He had received only a few SMS messages from Vodafone promising "low-rate travel calls." I didn't find any Italian area codes in his stored numbers—except for ours. Toward the end I gave the carabinieri our address at the Villa Massimo and was in turn given a number to call as soon as Ralf got in touch with us again.

When Raimondo offered to cancel our visit to the aquarium, we both rejected the idea almost in the same breath. Nothing in the world seemed more worth the effort than to head off to the aquarium with Tanya and the girls.

During the short taxi ride I caught myself constantly staring into other cars. But why would pimps want to smuggle naked women through the city in broad daylight? The carabinieri had asked no questions along those lines, whatever that meant. We had to drive back through the long tunnel, since the Stazione Zoologica Anton Dohrn—its official name—lies on the far side of the mountain, in a little park.

There was an unpleasant fishy odor at the ticket counter. But that didn't bother me, on the contrary, anything that put distance between Ralf and us made me happy.

Christiane Groeben, the Stazione's archivist, who has lived in Naples for over thirty years, led us upstairs to the hall with the frescoes by Hans von Marées. For the girls the attraction was the fish, but we wanted to give the frescoes a look. I tried as best I could to concentrate on her comments.

The building had been erected over the course of eighteen months in

1872–73, right on the coast at the time. Today a wide coastal highway separates the Stazione from the sea. The frescoes were painted in the summer and autumn of 1873. They have been restored several times since then, most recently in the '90s.

Although the girls began romping about almost immediately and could barely be kept under control, eliciting the immediate and repeated apologies to our guide we felt were her due, for me the frescoes were both a discovery and a gift.

I admired the tension Marées created merely by the placement of figures and how his faces are a blend of the individual and the abstract. Nothing is more alien to his work than the theatrical gesture, the narrative episode, or the snapshot effect of a Tadema, who was only one year his senior. The individual frescoes stand on their own, and enhance one another. They emerge in relationships, each to each, but without telling a story. And of course I was also amazed by the concept behind the enterprise. The interplay of art and science—the room balances the large laboratory on the opposite side of the building and was originally conceived as a concert hall, which soon became a library—was augmented to a triad by the addition of the aquarium. It was intended both as a way to offset costs and popularize scientific knowledge.

The exceptional part was that here in this space I felt the mood of panic enveloping me since Ralf's latest escapade ebbing away. I cannot say why this was so, but it wasn't that the frescoes had taken my mind off him. On the contrary, I saw Ralf everywhere. Not in any sense of similarity, even though the arbor trellis at the head of the room to the east, a fresco in which Marées painted himself together with friends, was also a pretty fair depiction of my, or our, relationship to Ralf, of both its comity and antagonism. But that analogy wouldn't have been necessary.

The seascape with oarsmen on the north wall, the fishermen with their nets at the rear of the room, or both frescoes of orange groves between the high doors of the balcony opening onto the sea—each individual fresco would have done the job; yes, I would be content even with a detail of the gull gliding just above the water behind the boat, or of the hand reaching for an orange. Marées could transform the everyday into art. That was my simple discovery. In his work a gull was both a gull and a messenger sent out over the waters. His oranges were oranges and at the same time the apples of the Hesperides and the forbidden fruit of Paradise.

Each minute I stood among the frescoes seemed to lend me strength. My eye moved between the groves of orange trees and out into the Gulf. I couldn't say whether what Ralf had done made any sense, maybe it was the wrong thing to do. I didn't even know if I ought to hope that he caught up with the silver car or lost it from view. My only wish was to see Ralf again as soon as possible. The rest would work itself out.

Finally we descended to the aquarium, where the odor wasn't nearly as penetrating as on our arrival, and came to a halt before a large octopus stretched inert across the stones.

The claim that his pose was that of someone in a chaise longue is not some after-the-fact invention of mine. Yes, in some way he reminded me of Tischbein's portrait of Goethe, because the massive head and trunk— it's difficult to exactly tell the two apart—was draped a little to the left, whereas it had extended all its arms to the right. I found it odd to see its suckers, more familiar to me from *insalata di polpo* or *frutti di mare*. Anna asked whether the octopus was alive. It did indeed look more like a splotch of algae. We would probably have soon moved on had it not been for Frau Groeben's commentary. She told us it had three hearts, plus blue blood. It was a creature of nobility, since if you compared its brain mass to its body weight, it was more highly developed than Homo sapiens. "And in terms of elegance," she added with a twitch of one corner of her mouth, "it was in any case an evolutionary mistake for life ever to have left the water."

The tips of its tentacles began to display some movement, although I did wonder whether the animal itself or water currents were the origin of those gentle curlicues. But then there was no mistaking a wavelike motion that passed along the arms, growing stronger and stronger, like a motor slowly revving up. Although its tentacles were all wriggling in much the same way, they were anything but in synch. Didn't it seem incredible that the motions of this configuration should all belong to the same creature, were all an act of its will? Some of the tips were curling up, others unrolling, some lifted, others sank, some thrashed about a little, others hardly at all. The effect of this polymorphic and yet unified animation was hypnotic.

The girls had already had enough and moved on to the next tank. Tanya followed them. Frau Groeben said that, given their intelligence, octopi are of great significance in research. And then she told an almost unbelievable story. A fore-forerunner of this current specimen had been teased in the research lab by one of the employees. The man had kept splashing the water, something that these creatures evidently do not like. He startled the octopus over and over. The next morning as the man stepped into the room, a surge of water hit him in the face. Before he realized what had happened, another volley landed square on the bib of his overalls. When he told his colleagues, at first they didn't believe him. But they later discovered that the door was also wet and that the puddle before it could not have come from just those two shots. The octopus, they concluded—and our guide shared their opinion—had been taking practice shots at the entrance the night before.

I was paying such close attention to her story that at first what I was seeing didn't even register. The entire octopus was now caught up in the motions of its arms. It had raised itself from the stones, and now swam headfirst to the right, dived, swam back, tugging its arms like a bundle of garlands along with it, rose up again, and repeated the process. "It's doing somersaults!" I said.

As if I had spurred it on, it increased the tempo and at the same time reduced the radius of rotation. It was now executing one continuous forward roll, making it impossible for me to say to which cycle its rotating arms belonged, this one or the one previous. Several of them seemed to have taken on a life of their own, twisting and turning through the water according to self-imposed laws.

"It's doing this for you," Frau Groeben said as she turned away. "These are the calamari." She was now standing in front of the tank opposite, a few steps behind me.

"So you're saying it's really doing it for me?"

"Squids," she said, "don't live long in captivity, they barely last two days. We keep them alive for two weeks at any rate."

"So in two weeks all these will be dead?" I asked, turning to look at the tubular squids skittering through the water. Their lurching movements reminded me of bats, but in slow motion. I may be mistaken about this too, because I didn't want to risk taking my eyes off my octopus for more than a few seconds.

"Look at that," I said, "now he's doing backward somersaults!"

I applauded, I called out to the girls, who shouted back. Tanya sounded excited as well. Frau Groeben walked on ahead to join them. Left alone now, I pretended to go on clapping. "Bravo, you're great," I whispered, as if this were a dog or a horse before me.

The forward and backward rolls must have tired it somewhat, because it now took brief time-outs, during which I thought it would sink back onto the stones and I would finally have a chance to move on.

I used its next time-out to take my departure, after first applauding one last time and whispering something stupid.

I slinked away, passing by other tanks without paying them much attention—or I've just forgotten in the meantime. All I remember is a stuffed turtle by the name of Marlene, because it had died on the same day as Marlene Dietrich.

Other visitors had entered now and were lingering in front of the octopus tank. I admitted to myself a twinge of jealousy. It was now displaying its talents for them.

When I checked back in their direction they still hadn't moved on. I waited another minute. Then I walked back toward them, well-aware that I wanted to catch my octopus *in flagrante*. But it was sprawled out on its chaise longue, and didn't budge. I held my distance. Once the others set on their way again, I stepped forward as if to apologize for my behavior and at least say my good-byes. "You were great," I said, *"grazie mille."*

In that same moment the octopus raised its head from the stones—and what it now did shocked me. Within a few seconds it had mobilized all its arms and flung them out, it was a veritable explosion of tentacles, the head of Medusa awakened to life—for what is more apt than a comparison of tentacles and snakes? It took only a moment and they were extended from one end of the tank to the other, while at the same time the white underbelly was turned toward me. I gazed into its mouth, stared at every single sucker. It was no longer a Medusa head, it was beautiful, magnificent. The simultaneity and randomness of its motions were an inconceivable miracle. Yes, a miracle, and somehow obscene. A dog will suddenly thrust its muzzle into your crotch or clamp onto your legs and whimper with arousal —even at its worst that's merely unpleasant. This was different. It unnerved me and I sensed I was on the verge of losing my self-control and breaking into tears. Of course under normal circumstances nothing would have happened, but in this moment I too stretched my arms wide and pressed my hands against the glass, the way I sometimes do against a train window when Tanya and the girls are leaving for a visit with her parents.

That was our farewell.

By the time we got back to Raimondo's, Ralf had picked up his things. I called him. He was at the train station. He thanked me for our having notified the police. He sounded tired and just kept saying that everything was okay and we needn't worry. I assumed he would wait for us on the train platform and bought two kilos of oranges at the station. I called his number several times from the train, only to be told over and over by the same woman's voice that unfortunately my call could not be answered at present.

I walked the length of the train twice, from the last car to the first. Even when we got off at Termini we kept an eye out, but there was no sign of him.

We walked with our luggage to the taxi stand and joined the long line. There was still just enough daylight to see the starlings, hundreds maybe even thousands of starlings above Rome. Swarms of them in flight are beautiful, but eerie too, as if they're tracing some message of doom in the sky. One theory says that, instead of flying south, these birds perform dances, metamorphosing into indescribable shapes, now a dance of seven veils, now spirals and banners of smoke, comparable in elegance only to the movements of tentacles.

I asked myself whether the octopus shared my mood, whether it perhaps thought of us, its visitors, and what shape its image of us might take —a question I still ask myself today, with the angel hovering at last in the girls' room, the angel of Ralf the orange man, who had danced the women's dance for us, in the middle of the Villa Misteri in Pompeii.

TRANSLATED FROM GERMAN BY JOHN E. WOODS

ZURAB LEZHAVA

Sex for Fridge

The clumsy old Apsheron refrigerator, which had been handed down through the family as though it were an heirloom, together with a single, lonely kitchen chair, was all that was left in Albert Karbelashvili's kitchen. Why the chair? Because it was a weird-looking piece and the guy who bought the four matching chairs wouldn't take it with him. Albert was stuck with the ancient monolithic Apsheron fridge for the same reason—no one would buy it. Like an evil spirit, the old fridge would follow him around forever. It had been in the family's first apartment—one that had four rooms. Karbelashvili's parents sold it a long time ago and traded down to a three-roomer. Then they moved to another three-room apartment in a poorer neighborhood. Eventually, Karbelashvili's parents moved even farther away, now inhabiting another country entirely—the undiscovered one. But their offspring continued their tradition—buying and then selling rooms, furniture, and other household items. Every so often, Albert would exchange his apartment for a smaller one and sell all sorts of things that he'd inherited. Then, for a while, he would live on the money he made from these sales. This way of life didn't entirely satisfy him, to be sure, and he would wonder sometimes how long he would keep it up. But he was never able to answer his own question.

All the time he was living in his tiny one-room apartment, he wasn't in any position to change his lifestyle. His place was on the outskirts of the most miserable part of the city—an area people called "Eve's Asshole," because it was so far away from the world of men. Half-wild starving dogs and half-domesticated packs of jackals roamed the streets attacking each other around the filthy dumpsters and just causing havoc. The local human population loved to fight as well, and seized every opportunity. The majority was unemployed and God only knows how they supported themselves. In summer they hung around the streets in front of their houses all day and night, and in the winter, well, God only knows where they went or what they got up to. Eve's Asshole was the last inhabited part of the town before the fields and tiny villages began. There was no way Albert could move any farther out. He would rather live under a hedge in the city than move to a village. In a village he would have to work and he avoided work like the plague.

All that was left in Karbelashvili's apartment was the solitary chair in the kitchen, a rusty, peeling iron bedstead, an ugly wardrobe in a style that had vanished long ago (made in the Khashuri factory), an out-of-tune piano, and the thirty-year-old Apsheron refrigerator. All things no one would ever buy. But the most irritating was the fridge. Purchased by his parents before he'd even been born. Something in its works would periodically kick in with an exploding sound that came with no warning whatsoever. This would set the fridge motor working—whirring and shaking. The thing would vibrate so vigorously that the kitchen cutlery would rattle in their drawers. The force of the vibration had been increasing over time, in fact, so that now, when the motor came on, the fridge would begin to move, and eventually do laps around the kitchen. Albert's father had put a barrier of heavy silicate bricks around its base so that its mobility was restricted to one small area. Eventually, however, the fridge managed to escape. As if by magic, it would cross the brick perimeter and stand vibrating away right in the middle of the kitchen. Sometimes, summoning amazing strength and with an almost-human desperation, the fridge would make a dash for the nearby hallway or hurl itself against the walls. With its dangling electric cord, it looked like a big white dog on a leash—a dog that sometimes barked and ran in circles but which would then calm down and sleep peacefully for a while before waking up to bark again . . . as if someone was teasing it. Yes, it would be impossible to sell the fridge, but Karbelashvili couldn't convince himself to throw it away either. In spite of its bad character, it did in fact keep things cold. It still had value.

So Albert went over the want ads in the newspaper. With his pen at the ready, he scanned the page for someone who might want a used fridge. To his astonishment he found such a person. The ad informed him that the buyer's name was Zhuzhuna and she would buy any cheap used fridges. There was a telephone number as well. Albert circled the ad, went to the bedroom, picked up his phone, and dialed. After several failed attempts, the receiver eventually made the appropriate sounds and Albert knew he'd gotten through. He heard a woman's calculatingly high-pitched voice. There was something very peculiar about her pronunciation.

She said, "*Hull–ooooooooo?*"

Karbelashvili cleared his throat and said, "Hello—may I speak to Mrs. Zhuzhuna?"

"This is *Zhu-zhu-na* speaking," the woman answered in her piercing voice.

"I'm calling regarding your ad, Mrs. Zhuzhuna! I have a fridge for sale."

"*Ahhhh!* What kind of fridge?" Zhuzhuna asked cheerfully.

"It's an Apsheron!" Albert shouted.

"An Apsheron? How *muuuuuuch* do you want for it? Apsheron isn't a very good make, you know," the woman half-shrieked, half-squawked.

"They're fine! They're great!" Albert said, trying to sound like a wholehearted Apsheron fan.

"How much do you want for it?" the woman asked again.

"Not much at all! A hundred laris."

"One hundred laris?" she asked, as though this was a fortune.

"Eighty, then!" Albert conceded.

"Eighty? That's still a lot," the woman said.

"Seventy then," Albert conceded once more.

"What about fifty?"

"No!"

"Why not? Apsheron is a terrible make," the woman said.

"Good or bad, the answer's no," Albert retaliated. "I won't take less than seventy."

"Is delivery included?" She'd found a new escape route.

"What do you mean, delivery?" Albert shouted. "No, no delivery."

"Is the motor working?" the woman asked. "Is it in a good condition?"

"The motor's fine and it's in excellent condition," Albert answered.

"I'll come and have a look at it," the woman announced.

"Yes, come and look at it," said Albert.

"Whereabouts are you?" the woman asked.

"Eve's . . . End," answered Albert.

She repeated "Eve's End" thoughtfully—"That's so far away. Hard to bring a fridge back all that way. No, forget it."

Karbelashvili shouted in desperation, "Okay, look, I'll knock off another ten laris—you can have it for sixty."

"What about getting it into the car?" the woman asked.

"I'll help carry it down."

"But what about carrying up at the other end?" Zhuzhuna asked, getting greedy.

"No way—I'll only help to carry it down and put in the car!" Albert said.

Zhuzhuna took down Karbelashvili's address and promised to come in the next hour or so. She said good-bye for now and hung up.

After an hour and a half, Albert's doorbell rang. The noise was so loud, it sounded as though his caller wasn't pushing a doorbell but squashing some screaming insect into the wallpaper so hard that it would end up being absorbed into the pattern. Albert opened the door and saw a tall, hefty, red-cheeked woman with a big head. Yes, women of this type—tall, fat, red-cheeked women with big heads—often affect high, piercing voices. They think a thin voice will offset their bulk. If a tall, fat, red-cheeked woman with a big head also had a deep, husky voice, life would be simply hopeless. And it is true that to some extent an artificially high-pitched voice, a bit like a pig squealing, does balance things out. Bald men behave in a similar way. Having no hair on their heads, they often grow bushy moustaches, sometimes tropically abundant, to offset the absence of vegetation above.

To cut a long story short, this Zhuzhuna who approached the door with her characteristic shrieking and squawking carelessly brushed her feet on the mat like a horse cantering in place and entered Albert's apartment. Albert showed her into the kitchen and pointed out the fridge.

"This is my fridge," he said instructively.

"Oh!" And the red-cheeked woman started nattering on in a loud, demanding voice. She was looking for faults in the fridge. Probably she enjoyed finding fault. She couldn't see anything wrong with the thing but took careful note of its contents—an opened bottle of Minimo vodka, a piece of salami, and some mustard in a miniscule plastic container. With barely concealed pleasure, she examined this excuse for a delicatessen and began to quiz Albert about his marital status. As soon as she learned he had no wife, she told him the story of her life. According to her, she had a husband, a small apartment, and a job in some unspecified kind of office doing some unspecified kind of work. Zhuzhuna's husband, according to Zhuzhuna, was an uneducated, insensitive man who only knew how to spend money. Creditors would come by their apartment, trying to track him down. He had all these schemes and plans and would invariably get into debt trying to bring these plans to fruition. Creditors would come more and more often and track dirt into Zhuzhuna's home. Her husband would sneak out in the morning and return late at night and poor Zhuzhuna, as she referred to herself, had to endure everyone's continuous whining, complaining, and grumbling, not to mention their threats. She didn't love her husband and didn't respect him and dreamed only of making him suffer—but she didn't know how best to do this yet. Their apartment was on the top, ninth, floor of their building and when it rained, water came through because the roof was so terrible. Her useless neighbors, who shared the same staircase, refused to contribute any money to get it repaired. Her no-good office job, where Zhuzhuna was simply wearing herself out, didn't pay her or any of the other employees anything close to a living wage. In fact, it was no longer paying any wages at all. There was no work to do anyway, and even when there *was*, well, why bother killing yourself over it? Really they came to the office to drink coffee and gossip. Not that Zhuzhuna came right out and admitted this. She didn't care for being criticized, especially when this was justified. Everything and everybody around her was in the wrong, whereas she was right in every way about everything and everybody. In that respect she was the same as Albert. They were soul mates. Though they differed in at least one important respect. She had most qualities in excess, but she was missing a vital ingredient in her life—love.

Although, actually, Albert was the same on that point too. Forget that bit about them differing. They were soul mates.

Mrs. Zhuzhuna had one dream. She very much wanted to find an elderly, rich lover who owned a car. He would, by necessity, be married to someone else, and would provide her with money and presents. They would have a regular meeting place and he would be, to quote Zhuzhuna, hygienic and discreet. This large lady of forty-plus couldn't understand why she hadn't found such a man—or, more generally, why such men seemed to have become such an endangered species. Yes, such men are few and far between and there is no shortage of women younger and more beautiful than Zhuzhuna.

She drank like a man—she could drink any man under the table. She enjoyed long witty toasts, particularly if accompanied by the recitation of a little poetry. Red-cheeked and fluttering her eyelids, she would explain to her drinking companions the meaning of brotherly love—for example—and how siblings can love each other best of all. She liked to talk in more or less the same terms about family love and motherly love and about all the subjects that might come up over a night of drinking and toasting. She could sing, and if there was a piano nearby, she would bang the keys and shriek out a song, overwhelmed by emotion. When she could get away with it, Zhuzhuna liked to use strong language. She liked rich food and had a prodigious appetite, about which she'd make apologetic jokes. Then she'd start eating away. Especially anything made with pork. Zhuzhuna liked pork.

Somehow—almost imperceptibly—between Albert, who had just turned forty, and Zhuzhuna, who was over forty, a very lively conversation developed, which Zhuzhuna directed quite deliberately toward her own indirectly expressed and simple suggestion. This consisted of Zhuzhuna and Albert consuming the vodka and sausage in the fridge, then frolicking in bed together until such a time that Albert, with a feeling of gratitude, would hand over the fridge free of charge.

To put it briefly, the fridge would be exchanged for sex.

But Albert, like all men, wasn't too clever, and didn't understand what this strange woman was up to. This was partly because he was worrying about an embarrassing possibility that had only just occurred to him. While it was true that the fridge kept things cold and its light came on when the door was opened, he realized that the motor might start up at any moment. He had no idea what to expect if the woman saw it happen. Would she still want to buy the crazy thing? A fridge that every so often decided to take out its frustrations on the tiled floor around it, jumping over its brick fence and lurching around the room like a mad animal?

Still, Zhuzhuna was, as they say, gently, gently, bit by bit and step by step, leading their stilted but sociable conversation toward her desired conclusion—the exchange of sex for the fridge. But she wanted the owner of the fridge to think it was his own idea; she wanted him to be the one to suggest such a transaction. And, naturally, to suggest it in a form acceptable to a respectable woman such as her. Finally, after much persuasion from Albert Karbelashvili, and many demurrals on her part, she would yield at last to temptation.

"If my husband was good for anything, why would I be here?" Mme Zhuzhuna speculated aloud, wondering now at Albert's failure to take the hint and offer her some vodka and sausage. "Why would I be buying such a terrible fridge if I had a man to buy me a decent one? Besides, if my husband were a real man would he have allowed me to come to Eve's Asshole to buy this fridge? The only thing he brings home is creditors. He creeps out of the house early in the morning and comes back at midnight so I have to deal with them. Just the other day I had to take our fridge to the repairman myself. It was broken for two weeks and I had to pay for the repairs with my own money. I don't know what to do with him! Is he a real man? Is he a real man?" She paced the kitchen, like a queen giving orders, or like a snorting broodmare. As she did so, she repeatedly—"accidentally"—brushed against Albert.

And Albert in turn lifted his hand in a tentative way. Then he mustered his courage and suggested punishing her husband a little.

"Really, he can't be a very responsible man, your husband," Albert said uncertainly, smiling at Zhuzhuna in an appeasing way. "Men like that deserve whatever's coming to them. They should be made examples of! And of course the best way to do this is to make a cuckold out of him. Yes, adultery! You must be unfaithful to him."

"Adultery! Be unfaithful?" Zhuzhuna raised her innocent eyebrows. She didn't seem to be offended by the suggestion. It was a surprising idea, that's all. One that had never occurred to her. Be unfaithful! "Yes, but is it worth it? And with whom? Nowadays men just don't appreciate a good woman like me."

"Why not me? Be unfaithful to your husband with me! Believe me, I'll appreciate you." Albert reached out for Zhuzhuna's big, wobbly backside.

"Hey!" Zhuzhuna pried away his sweaty hands with her strong stubby fingers. "How can you appreciate me properly if you're more of a beggar than my husband? All you have in the world is a fridge and you're selling that!"

"Well, so what? You can't measure everything with money." With a smile on his big-nosed face, Albert looked down at his pants, at what can't be measured with money but only with a ruler. Then he looked up and reached out again for Zhuzhuna's big wobbly bottom.

"Leave me alone, for heaven's sake!" Zhuzhuna tried to remove his hand. "Who needs a poor man? If only there was a rich old man who wanted to support me. Do you know anyone like that? Perhaps you could introduce someone like that to me . . ."

The woman was greedily bustling around the fridge. She opened and closed its door, poking her head inside as if really trying to gauge whether it would be worth buying. In reality, she was hoping that her host would finally take the hint and offer her some vodka and sausage. Albert didn't, however, take the hint, because he wasn't entirely certain that a little vodka and sausage would really be enough to convince this woman to be unfaithful to her worthless husband.

This delicate situation would perhaps have been diffused by the fridge's motor, but the fridge seemed to have no intention of switching on. It was impossible to predict when it might next want to stretch its legs. The thing would only switch its motor on when it felt like it; it didn't follow any set schedule. But then, just when Albert began to forget to worry, the motor *did* kick on with its usual explosion, and the fridge, making a neighing sound, began to shake as though it were having an epileptic fit. It tried to jump out of its brick corral, but couldn't manage—Albert had added more bricks as a precautionary measure. Still, Zhuzhuna shrieked in terror and threw herself into Albert's arms. Then she pushed him away again and yelled:

"My God! What is it? What was that?"

"The motor's a little noisy, that's all," Albert said soothingly.

"It certainly is! It'll drive my neighbors crazy if it starts working at night."

"No, they'll be fine," he said. "Really."

Eventually the motor switched itself off and the woman calmed down a little. Then she tried to use the noisy motor as a way of reducing the price of the fridge, but Albert was determined to dismiss this defect as minor and not really worth their consideration. Zhuzhuna had decided she'd pay no more than twenty laris, but Albert was demanding at least forty.

"Twenty!" Zhuzhuna shouted and put her foot up on the only chair in the kitchen, which wobbled slightly. Having done this she caressed her own plump thigh, making her dress fabric cling to it, and with a twinkle in her eye repeated: "Twenty."

Albert slid his hand under her thigh. "Thirty-five," he said, voice trembling. He felt her bare skin.

"Twenty . . ." she whispered and nibbled his ear.

"Okay, thirty." Albert moved further up her thigh. Zhuzhuna took his weak hand in her two strong hands and began to move it up and down along her leg as though it were a sponge.

"Damn it, let's go!" Albert said through gritted teeth, succumbing to his fate. He plucked at Mrs. Zhuzhuna's substantial waist with his frankfurter-like fingers and guided the devoted family-woman out of the kitchen into the bedroom. He tried to push her onto the bed, but she refused to move because they hadn't settled on a price. Help me take it downstairs and load it on the car as well, she asked in a whisper.

"Yes, okay!" Albert agreed and then tried again to push Zhuzhuna toward the bed.

"Let's drink first," Zhuzhuna said. She steered Albert back into the kitchen and made him open the fridge. As there was no table in the apartment, Karbelashvili put everything on top of the fridge. He then went into the bedroom and opened the wardrobe where he kept all his other possessions, including his groceries. He brought out a half-eaten loaf of stale bread and stained dirty glasses and put them on top of the fridge as well. Then he took everything off again, blew the dust off the top of the fridge, and put it all back. He still wasn't satisfied and so pulled out a plastic bag that had been stored behind a redundant radiator. He moved the food out of the way, put the plastic bag on top of the fridge, then laid the food out for the third time.

"Come on," he told Zhuzhuna, inviting her to the feast. Zhuzhuna protested and made some sarcastic comments about having to stand at a fridge in order to eat. First she asked him to move the food onto the windowsill, but since they had only one chair, which wobbled, Zhuzhuna made another suggestion. On her initiative, they moved the only chair into the bedroom and put it next to the peeling bedstead. It was good timing, because the moment Albert took the vodka and glasses off the fridge, the motor started up again. The once white but now yellowish, preternatural fridge shook its frame with such strength and persistence that the bread, sausage, and mustard were thrown onto the floor. The vodka and glasses had had a lucky escape. Zhuzhuna and Albert picked up the groceries and put them on the plastic bag on the wobbly chair together with the vodka and glasses. They sat side by side on the peeling rusty bed. Albert poured Minimo vodka.

"You forgot the salt," Zhuzhuna muttered, her mouth full of bread and sausage. She pinched Albert very hard on his backside.

Albert got up and brought some salt. They were drinking vodka, eating, and touching each other. More precisely, Albert was caressing Zhuzhuna while she was pinching him as if she wanted to tweeze off bits of his flesh. Occasionally, they listened to some music from a small cheap radio. The radio's plug was burned out and its batteries were almost dead. This meant that Albert couldn't plug the radio into the mains, and since he couldn't afford to replace the batteries, he could only turn it on for short periods of time. After that you had to switch it off to allow the exhausted batteries to recover their strength. Zhuzhuna could play—or, more precisely, bang— the piano, but she couldn't do so here because there was a meal set out on the only chair, and anyway, the terribly out-of-tune piano lacked a key. Not that Zhuzhuna was too interested in playing. She was knocking back her vodka faster than Albert and composing a toast as well, a toast that included quotations from famous poets and a lot of cursing into the bargain. She cursed out her husband, her neighbors, her colleagues, her bosses, her elected officials—everyone. The whole world was her personal enemy. There was a conspiracy to keep her miserable. They were all criminals. Albert more or less agreed.

When the vodka began to take effect, Karbelashvili pushed his hand into his pocket and said that he would go get another bottle of Minimo. Zhuzhuna demurred, reluctant to let him spend money—but it was obvious that she wanted more herself.

"Can you afford to be so generous?" she asked him in a soft voice and went back to sponging her leg with his hand.

"Money? No, I don't have money," Albert answered, tipsy. "But you owe me twenty laris and I'll buy the vodka out of that twenty."

Zhuzhuna, unlike Albert, was not the least bit tipsy—she just wanted more to drink. She weighed up the situation and decided against this course of action, because to be honest, it was impossible to buy an old fridge at that price and still come out ahead.

"No, it's not worth it, don't bother," she whispered to him, continuing to rub his feeble hand against her thigh. "No, you don't need it. Don't bother."

"What do you mean? I want to," Albert said. He was completely lost in pleasant thoughts, thinking himself rich and consequently omnipotent. "Give me the money."

"No, I won't!"

"Give it to me!"

"No!"

"You know it'll be great to have more vodka."

"No, it's not worth it!"

"Give it to me now!"

"Fine, but only ten for now, you lunatic."

"Fine, first give me ten. What's wrong with you—don't you trust me?"

"Yes, I trust you—ooooooh." Zhuzhuna neighed like a horse and handed over the money.

Albert tidied his rumpled clothes and went down to the shop, adopting what he considered the bearing of a businessman. Scowling at everyone he saw, he bought bread, one bottle of Minimo, more sausage, and some batteries for his radio. He asked the shopkeeper to put everything in a disposable plastic bag and took the change, five laris and thirty-five tetri, and went back home. There, Zhuzhuna was making a racket playing the piano and singing a love song in her high-pitched voice. She had moved what was left of the food to the bed and was sitting on the chair. Albert put the bag of groceries on the piano, took out his new batteries, and swapped them with those in the radio. He turned up the volume to check whether it was working, then turned it off and listened to Zhuzhuna. She had already been singing for a long time, though, and was getting bored. She got up and pushed her chair toward the bed and put the food back where it was. They sat down and continued their feast. The woman was talking, the radio was playing, and finally they finished eating, cleared away the leftovers, took off their clothes, and got into bed.

Albert didn't like the sight of naked Zhuzhuna. When dressed, she had seemed tall, plump, somehow appetizing. When she removed her clothes, she just sagged. He also caught sight of a big sanitary pad when she undressed. Yes, this woman was large and very unhealthy. Sure, Karbelashvili was also unhealthy looking: frankfurter-like fingers, huge feet, skinny legs. After they had both undressed, there was a strong smell of feet. But look, to cut a long story short, as a result of the above-mentioned details, and more besides, Karbelashvili did not enjoy their encounter too much. Besides, unlike Zhuzhuna, he was quite drunk, and as we know, this can put a damper on a man's abilities. Albert no longer had any desire for this woman, and he was sorry for having wasted his money. He was sorry too about the fridge, the fridge of his fathers, which he had let go for a song.

Zhuzhuna kissed Albert, vigorously. There was no emotion in her kissing—she was simply wiping his face with her wet lips while brushing his hand against her body as if reapplying soap after rinsing. Thus did Albert reach what would have to be defined, in medical terms, as orgasm. At precisely that moment, with the help of his female partner, he accidentally touched a mole the size of a big currant, somewhere high between the woman's thighs, close to her pubic hair. This finally made him feel disgust. He pulled away from Zhuzhuna's body and reached for a damp cloth he kept under the mattress. He wiped himself off and then threw the same cloth across to the woman. They lay still for some time. Zhuzhuna tried to kiss Albert on occasion, but he wouldn't let her. They lay still for some time. Albert smoked. The woman stroked his head, not caressing him so much as consoling him.

Then they dressed and Zhuzhuna phoned her husband and told him she'd bought a fridge. She made him write down the address and asked him to come over. Forty minutes later, he arrived in a van, shook hands with Albert, and then shyly stepped aside. For some reason Albert liked him at once. Zhuzhuna took out a ten lari note and gave it to Albert, telling him to go into the bedroom. She gestured to her husband that he should stay in the kitchen. In the other room, Zhuzhuna embraced Albert once more and kissed him on the lips like a horse. Then she let him go, but gave him one last small, "graceful" kiss before tiptoeing to the doorway.

Albert and Zhuzhuna's husband, with a lot of effort and groaning, brought the fridge to the stairs and, because the elevator was out of order, carried it all the way down while Zhuzhuna shrieked out useless advice, got under their feet, and generally made a nuisance of herself. When they were halfway down the stairwell, the light went out.

Finally, the fridge was in the van and Albert climbed back up the dark stairs, locked his door, laid on his bed, switched on his radio, and reached for the leftover bread and sausage. He began to chew and fell asleep among the crumbs. After a while he was woken by a headache and an unpleasant dryness in his mouth. He got up, drank some water, undressed, and laid down again. When he laid down he felt dizzy and a wave of nausea forced him to rush barefoot to the bathroom, where he threw his arms around the toilet bowl and vomited several times. In spite of careful aim, he made quite a mess on the floor. He then carelessly washed his face and hands, poured some water on his feet—because there was vomit on them—and staggered out of the bathroom. He drank some more water and threw himself onto the bed. It still smelled of Zhuzhuna's perfume, which turned Albert's stomach even more.

Albert dreamed he was going into his own kitchen and up to the old fridge. The motor was on and shrieking, the fridge was shaking and trying to jump out of its corral. Albert opened the door and reached in for a bowl, jumping around from all the vibrations. There was some stew in the bowl and also a spoon. Karbelashvili stirred the stew and was pleasantly surprised when he discovered that it was still warm. He slurped a spoonful and stirred it again, in order to get some meat this time. He caught a piece but when he saw it, he screamed. The meat was a part of Zhuzhuna's fat body—a big chunk with a mole like a currant on its boiled skin, and even a little tuft of hair. Albert woke up terrified, but calmed down a little when he realized that this dream, like all others, would fade in time, and soon only exist as a vague reminder of an experience that had left an unpleasant taste in his mouth. On the other hand, he could look on the bright side: Life was possible because Albert Karbelashvili still had the money that he'd gotten for the fridge of his fathers—fifteen laris and thirty-five tetri.

TRANSLATED FROM GEORGIAN BY

VICTORIA FIELD AND NATALIA BUKIA PETERS

ERIC LAURRENT

American Diary

LOS ANGELES, CALIFORNIA.
SATURDAY, MARCH 14, 1998.

The Venice Beach Cotel, where I've just spent my first night on American soil, is a modest hotel, situated on Windward Avenue, barely a hundred or so meters from the Pacific Ocean. Built no doubt several decades ago, it's a three-story building, the main façade of which, with its windows vaulted in ribs, its facing of white and golden bricks, in a diamond-shaped pattern, and its archways, all pointedly pastiche, it seems to me, the late Gothic style of the Doge's palace. A long mural fresco revisiting Botticelli's *Birth of Venus* adorns the whole lower section of its occidental façade: while he might have his Zephyr, Flora, and Hora virtually indistinguishable, the artist has, on the other hand, outfitted the Goddess of Love in a pair of roller-skates and clothed her in an indigo monokini and royal blue thigh-high socks; he's also put a harpoon in one of her hands, which she clutches against her breast, ensuring that the Anadyomene has metamorphosed under his brush into just another summer tourist: half skater, half huntress. To be comprehensive I should add that the sea conch of the original has been made to disappear, while the sea itself, upon which she once rested, is here completely paved over—a choice justified, I imagine, by the goddess's new gear: it's rather improbable to go roller-skating in the water, and even more so in a scallop shell.

Right now I'm sitting at a table in a bar on the premises, drinking a too-watery coffee, closer to tea in color, against a background of conversations held by ten or so youths of every nationality as they eat breakfast, and of pop music too, in this case exclusively Anglo-Saxon, played quietly through four speakers suspended in the corners of the room.

Through the sash-window opposite, I can see the street below, both sides of which are lined with basic stalls, made of simple, white plastic tarpaulins, held up by iron poles with banners stretched between them that bear, if not a company name, at the very least the name of the articles in which this particular stall specializes (bikes, incense, blades, jewelry, etc.); then, in the background, there's the beach whose sand, a grayish yellow, is bristling with palm trees, their tufts swaying limply in the wind; and finally the ocean, on the murky water of which slide the large shadows of several clouds.

Hanging on a wall to my left is a canvas painting representing, in a vaguely impressionist style, a view of Venice, no doubt the way it was half a century ago, before they discovered oil and ripped it open to bore into the ground, with a charming lacework of canals spanned by bridges and lined with houses of a ... Venetian inspiration; the glass plate protecting this painting reflects my face with an imprecision that seems to me to perfectly allegorize the semi-conscious state in which I find myself, thanks to the time difference.

SAN FRANCISCO, CALIFORNIA. MONDAY, MARCH 23.

Many times along my way I passed neon signs for massage parlors. My senses stirred by abstinence, as well as from chatting with a certain young woman, I decided in the end to step inside one of these establishments, which I imagined were a sort of whorehouse. So I went down a few steps that led to the basement of the building and rang the bell at a door with frosted glass, which was opened immediately by an automated system. A few steps later I was standing in front of a kind of counter, similar to a hotel reception desk, except that the place was dark, deserted, and silent. A black and obese woman, with alarming features, her hair in braids, wearing a black dress and wooden sandals, appeared before me and asked me for forty dollars before handing me a folded towel and showing me to the showers. I went into a stall, which was faintly lit with a green wall light, and undressed. After drying myself, I came out, the towel tied around my hips, and took a few steps in a dark corridor without bumping into another living soul.

The colossal black woman then found me and directed me into a massage room, windowless, with a kind of examination bed, on which she invited me to lie down. Before my incredulous eyes, she gave me to understand that if her person wasn't suitable to me, I could be massaged by another woman. I informed her that I'd prefer that. She left the room, impassive. I remained standing close to the bed, wondering what sinister joke was being played on me.

You can imagine my terror then when, a minute later, a woman with the same build and an equally upsetting face—though white-skinned—joined me. I didn't dare utter any recrimination, lay down without saying a word, and, tense and knotted, let myself be palpated by the enormous hands of this matron, praying that she wouldn't indecently assault me in the process.

When the creature left, I dressed again swiftly and left that crypt, less frustrated by not having been able to enjoy the charms of a lady of the night than relieved to have escaped safe and sound from that terrifying ordeal.

LOS ANGELES. WEDNESDAY, MARCH 25.

Tonight I had a long phone conversation with Martine, telling her in great detail about my life since I departed Paris—a way of sharing my experience, to a certain extent. I miss her company, and her body too. In order to contend with the continence imposed on me by the distance between us, I bought a copy of the magazine *Hustler* yesterday, the American version. Flicking through it, I was struck right away by the extreme anesthetization of the bodies displayed in its pages, which were not only perfect in their proportions, but appeared refinished, made-up, hair done, almost completely waxed, including the men, whose torsos were bare and scrotums smooth—even the vulvas and anuses seemed to be made-up, offering their folds and creases in the tones of pale and tender roses. This overwhelming banishment of any corporeality seemed to me to reveal a puritan approach to pornography.

LOS ANGELES. FRIDAY, MARCH 27.

I was awoken, as I had been every morning since taking a room in this motel on Sunset Boulevard, by police sirens. Their wailing comes at such a high volume that its only function seemed to be forcing other drivers to move to the side of the road, or to stop; quite obviously, there's a political design behind this resounding ostentation: that of asserting the omnipresence of the forces of law and order, a way of reassuring the citizen—and perhaps, who knows, of dissuading an offender from doing anything too sinister.

Yesterday the hotel cleaning lady threw out several copies of *Le Monde* that I'd managed to get hold of here, which made me furious, as I hadn't read them all yet. With the help of the little bilingual dictionary I'd brought with me, I carefully put together a few sentences in order to convey to her my desire that she spare herself such enthusiasm in the future—I rehearsed my lines several times to get them right in my mouth. When I passed her at the bottom of the stairs, I reeled them off in one go. *No comprendo inglese*, she replied when I'd finished.

The little old couple staying in the room next to mine must be deaf as posts. They turn on their TV at daybreak and set it at such a volume that I can even hear the actors of the shows they're watching breathe. When this noise ceases, that means they're going out: I hear them speaking then as far away as the street corner, as they express themselves just as loudly, without a doubt intending to be heard.

LOS ANGELES. THURSDAY, APRIL 2.

On Wilshire Boulevard there's a monument commemorating the conquest of the West: it's an equestrian statue depicting the actor John Wayne, whose pedestal is sculpted with bas-reliefs featuring battle scenes with cowboys and Indians. Can you imagine, in France, a monument commemorating World War I being adorned with an effigy of Jean Gabin, on the grounds that he starred in *Grand Illusion?*

Los Angeles abounds in places of worship to such an extent that it's not impossible that everything on this planet which might be considered a religion, from the most ancient to the most recent, the most widespread to the least known, the most serious to the most harebrained, has a home here. There's no one building manifesting any sort of spiritual heritage, like Notre Dame in Paris. They all seem to be equal.

While the city is equipped with multiple areas where you can let your dog defecate, you can't find, on the other hand, any public toilets in Los Angeles. This is no doubt due to the fact that people only get around here by car, rarely on foot. In the event that some pressing need should take you, you have no other choice but to go into a snack bar or a restaurant. Most of the time, the toilets there are designed so that it's impossible to have any privacy, the stalls not being separated from one another except by thin partitions which don't go down to the ground or up to the ceiling, consequently allowing all kinds of smells and noises to circulate. This doesn't seem to perturb the natives, who relieve themselves there with great casualness: burping readily, farting amply. This relaxation is all the more surprising given that, in everyday life, Americans are very civilized people—these places of relief thus seem to have for them, over and above their customary purgative function, the function of relieving stress as well.

Americans, or at the very least Los Angelenos, display an excessive preoccupation with prophylaxis. In bars, in restaurants, in nightclubs, in cocktail bars, it's striking to observe that, for fear of contracting some malicious virus, nobody puts their glass or tumbler down; should the case arise nonetheless, they never take their eyes off the vessel in question; and if they aren't certain, having retrieved it, whether they reached for the right glass, they simply won't take another sip: or, worse, they'll go and empty their container, then wash it; ideally, they'll change it for another.

In the same vein, there isn't a single place in California—stores, supermarkets, shopping malls, post offices, restaurants, nightclubs, and I forget where else—where you won't see a janitor permanently pacing back and forth, brush in one hand, dustpan in the other; not a one either where you won't catch sight, placed in the middle of an aisle on a shiny floor, of one of those yellow cones—it's sometimes a sort of trestle-shaped sign—on which the following warning is written: "Caution wet floor" (often accompanied by its Spanish translation: *Precaucion piso mojado*), a warning intended, one assumes, to prevent any lawsuits in case of a bad fall, Americans having become for some years the most litigious people in the world. (I have, on this point, read recently that some people, victims of a road accident driving back from a very alcoholic dinner, had sued their host on the grounds that he'd gotten them drunk during the meal.)

MEXICAN HAT, UTAH. THURSDAY, APRIL 9.

We were hungry in Tuba City. By a stroke of luck a little market was being held there in a vacant lot, barely amounting to twenty or so stalls, above which a delicious aroma floated. We stopped and immediately headed toward the stand where the smell was coming from: there we fed on pancakes of fried maize filled with red beans, green chili peppers, and other ingredients simmering in tin-plate stewpots resting on gas burners, and mutton too, which was cooked on a grill placed over a wood fire. We ate standing up, among Indians who were doing likewise. We were quickly approached by an old, mangy dog, whose watering eyes and hanging tongue implored us, and whose master, a miserable Navajo with a weathered face, brown complexion, and long braids, didn't take long to join him, and very politely beg us for a few dollars. "Marc, you make more than I do," I said, while removing a few pieces of meat from my taco. "I'll take care of the dog, you take care of the gentleman."

Martine and Stéphanie wanted to buy stamps to send some postcards. So we pulled our car over somewhere on the side of the road to Cameron, under a sign that read: "Historic Post Office." As soon as we'd pushed open the door of the presumed post office, we realized we'd been fooled: it was a souvenir shop. Hundreds of stamps were offered to the shopper, all inspired by the conquest of the West, in an endless glorification of the cowboy figure. The most tragic thing was that Indians were running this shop, in other words the descendants of the victims of said conquest. Relatively speaking it was a little as if, forced by necessity, some Jews undertook in two or three centuries to establish a trade in Nazi weapon displays at Auschwitz.

There's no other country on this planet that gives such a feeling of privatization of space. You have to ask yourself sometimes if there's still any land that doesn't belong to anyone here. The country roads are perpetually lined with fences that don't open onto any passing track for miles, which results in giving you the impression that you can only brush over this continent, can only touch it with your eyes.

Moving eastward at dusk we were able to watch the darkening ultramarine blue of the night in the frame of the windscreen and, at the same time, scaled down in the rearview mirror suspended on it, the oranging nightfall behind us, as though by way of that cinematographic effect called split screen, which enables the division of the frame so as to show two actions simultaneously.

SALT LAKE CITY, UTAH. FRIDAY, APRIL 10.

One rarely pays attention, it seems to me, to the common origins of Salt Lake City and Las Vegas, both founded in the nineteenth century by the Mormons. Their two atmospheres couldn't seem more opposed, and yet, these two cities remain absolutely linked, all you have to do is visit the Mormon Temple in Salt Lake City to be convinced: it's lit up during the night like the hotel-casinos on the Strip and, like them, built with an ostentatious design that pastiches every known style—in the image, as it happens, of the religion in whose name it's consecrated: syncretism of all the practices, reformed or not, of Christianity. Salt Lake City is in fact only the mystic version of Las Vegas, its puritan reverse: here, marriage "seals the spouses for eternity"; there, prostitution is almost legal; here, the night completely empties the streets; there, it fills them; here, the consumption of alcohol is banned; there, they serve you free drinks.

But where the two cities coincide is in their ideology. To rechristen the lost, as the Mormons do, really proceeds in the same spirit as winning the jackpot: in both cases, it's a question of raising the curse bound to original sin, either by assuring the eternal salvation of the soul through a new purification or by liberating oneself, through rapid profit, from the divine retribution that followed the Fall, requiring that man live from the sweat of his brow. (And if, behind this, there is the unconscious desire, quite simply, to free oneself from God entirely? In any case, to this day, the only hotel rooms in the U.S. where I didn't find a Bible in my nightstand drawer were those that I occupied in these two cities.)

Salt Lake City gives the impression of not having any homeless; the pavements there are spotless; you never hear police sirens; the people passing express themselves in low voices and their cordiality is such that it's not at all rare to be greeted in passing; at night, as I wrote earlier, the avenues are empty, just like the lobbies and offices—often still lit up—and everything's quiet. A permanent curfew seems to reign here. If Las Vegas is a puppet town, Salt Lake City seems, in many respects, a ghost town.

PANGUITCH, UTAH. SATURDAY, APRIL 11.

We noticed earlier that the roads in this country are patrolled by scores of campers that stop frequently on the shoulder of the highway; it's always a couple of retirees who get out, who you'll then see photographing or filming the countryside before taking off again. They seem for the most part to be heading west, idle and doddery modern incarnations of the former pioneers, for whom conquest now consists of an exhaustive but exclusive appropriation of territory through the image.

America is so vast that you find a type of place there that Europe has lost to the point of completely forgetting: the relay post. The increase in means of transportation being a factor, each of these stopovers now extend to the dimensions of a hamlet, always developed with the same layout: a main street lined on either side with single-story or sometimes two-story dwellings and a succession of motels, restaurants, and service stations. The activity of these small localities revolves entirely around the refueling and relaxation of the traveler and his vehicle, respectively. They're a little like the geographical equivalent of those beings Flaubert wrote about, if memory serves, who only exist to serve as bridges between men.

We ate earlier in a kind of saloon. Several tables were occupied, clearly by locals who'd come in couples; the men were for the most part dressed in jeans and checked shirts, wearing Stetsons; the women wore colorful dresses made from thick fabric; they were all plump, and their flesh overflowed the hemispherical armrests of their wooden seats. They were digging into huge, thick filets of beef and piles of French fries, which were served to them on enormous plates, while they listened attentively to a country singer with a nasal voice, barely filtering through an abundant handlebar mustache, performing in front of them on a makeshift platform. They requested extra helpings of fries, ordered desserts, all the while bringing frequently replaced half-liter glasses of beer to their lips. Barely had the singer finished his set when they all got up from their table and exited the premises, as if the music had had some kind of aperitif effect on them.

ZION VALLEY, UTAH. SUNDAY, APRIL 12.

We spent the night in a motel in Springdale, run by Mormons. Before leaving, in the early morning, we asked for some coffee. The polite response we received was that the house didn't serve any, on the grounds that Mormonism prohibited this drink, something we hadn't known. On the other hand, continued the employee we'd spoken to, it would be the house's pleasure to offer us the Book of Mormon, which is, after a fashion, the Bible of this religion. "We asked for a stimulant," Marc replied to him in French, "not a soporific."

Unlike that day last March when I'd come here with Philippe Durand, Zion Valley was now overrun with tourists, to such a degree that the red tarmac road which passes it for thirty or so kilometers was sometimes congested like a Los Angeles street at rush hour. Luckily, American tourists seem to abhor walking, which ensured that we didn't pass anyone as we strode alongside the Virgin River between the tall pale rocks, leafed like the edge of a book and pleated like fabric, placing our feet on the virgin ground, where only animals, including a puma, had left their mark.

LOS ANGELES. TUESDAY, APRIL 14.

Los Angeles never gives the impression of being turned toward the open sea, as coastal cities usually are. For all that, it doesn't seem to turn its gaze inland either. In fact, the city appears to look at itself, to feed on its own image. It's perhaps for this reason that some of the biggest movie studios are found here.

I recently read in a paper that the American pornographic cinema industry produces approximately 10,000 films per year, 95% of which are shot in Los Angeles, notably in the San Fernando Valley (by way of comparison, Hollywood produces no more than four hundred a year). The taboo on the explicit performance of the sexual act in mainstream cinema has, quite obviously, created a gap.

Advertisements are ubiquitous in this city. Thus there isn't, just to give one example, a single public bench that hasn't been covered in them. Should you wish to avoid their visual solicitation by raising your eyes to heaven, you'll then be regaled by the plane overhead pulling a promotional banner, or a zeppelin bearing some name brand in large letters. Every surface here seems to be considered first and foremost as a potential advertising venue, from public benches to the sky.

However stubborn or hermetic one is in this regard, there's no way these days of avoiding pop music, which is broadcast in every last public space—and in Los Angeles more than elsewhere, where certain streets even have music played through loudspeakers. Also, it isn't unusual to end up knowing by heart, and despite yourself, certain hits—it even happens that you surprise yourself by liking some of them. While traveling, this phenomenon is even more noticeable, without a doubt due to the hypersensitivity into which our constant attentiveness plunges us. In this way I discovered I'd developed a weakness here for the song "Frozen," by Madonna (a singer to whom I was completely indifferent till then), which all the radio stations played over and over again and of which I've just now, at a record shop located on Sunset Boulevard, bought the single; on the sleeve is a photo of the artist's face: her long hair, in wild, wavy locks, dyed a strawberry blonde, slipping along her cheeks and falling over her shoulders in chaotic arabesques, which can't help calling to mind Venus's hair as painted by Sandro Botticelli, that same goddess who had welcomed me here, exactly one month ago, on a Venice fresco—I've come full circle, as they say.

TRANSLATED FROM FRENCH BY URSULA MEANY SCOTT

ANITA KONKKA

The Clown

1.

It's been raining for a week. Nature seems to have decided on my behalf
that I shall write my memoirs, because on a rainy day you can't do anything
but write and drink wine. I remember that when I was a child, rainy days
at the dacha were unpleasant, my brother threw tantrums, Father complained, Grandmother clattered the dishes angrily in the kitchen, and
Mother cried and drew princesses, from underneath whose hoop skirts a
yellow trickle flowed, forming a puddle on the floor. The princesses stood
stiffly like paper dolls, they had fans in their hands and golden curls. I had
no talent for drawing and not for much of anything else either, but I was
a great liar. I told stories about things that had never happened, neither on
the moon nor on the earth, but I told them as though they were completely
true and I even believed them myself. I got beaten for telling lies, even
though without lies we couldn't manage in our country. My father told lies
every day and was very successful. He became a Party member and a high-
ranking official in the Ministry of Culture. But my grandmother, who considered lying a sin, landed in a concentration camp in Stalin's time. She
managed to get out of there alive, thanks to her temper. It was she who
taught me that people are already full of sin when they're born and that sin

must be beaten out of a person, like dust from a carpet. When she'd given me several sound beatings I stopped telling lies if there was any chance of her overhearing.

I just now went outside to see how it looks. The rain is sneaking slowly along the leaves of the orange trees and the sky is dark gray, but there's hope of something better, because gaps have appeared in the cloud cover, where a yellowish light gleams through. The rain will stop by tomorrow, I'll manage till then, because I still have a couple of liters of wine and some bread. I drink wine and consider how I could begin my memoirs. In order to refresh my memory I've attached a picture to the book shelf. It was on the cover of *Der Bild* during my days of greatness. In the picture I'm looking up at the sky, as though I'd again committed some terrible sin and was expecting a brick wall to fall on me, or else the voice of Yahweh to thunder down in reproach. There's a sad look in my eye, like a dog's when it's just been kicked by its unpredictable master. My face is pale and narrow, my lips are red, there are dark patches under my eyes, my nose is sharp, its pointed shadow falls on one cheek, the other cheek rests on my hand, I look worried, as though I was thinking of the world's natural resources being exhausted, or the population explosion, or the fate of the rain forests or endangered species. Every morning the picture looks different. It's begun to live its own life. Sometimes there are more, sometimes fewer, wrinkles on my forehead, and one morning I could even see the trace of a smile in the corners of my mouth. On some mornings my face looks really miserable, as though I've got a severe toothache, and then the shadow of my nose is longer than usual too. What can a person do about her nose, when Grandfather's name was Israel and Father's was Isak? They thought of naming me Hannah, but they came to their senses in time.

In the picture I'm wearing blue work overalls, with an old, worn-out hat on my head. I remember those clothes well, because I was playing the part of a workman who's afraid of his boss, so afraid he ends up doing everything backwards. It was one of my best performances, because when I was playing that role I brought together all my experience from the twenty-five jobs I'd held down before my career as a clown started gaining momentum internationally. The audience laughed until their sides ached, not only the children, but also the adults, when they saw me making all the same mistakes they themselves were afraid to be caught making at work. The audience also laughed a lot when I appeared as a woman. Perhaps that routine was so popular because I was basically playing myself, Albertina Vinniyeva. No one knew that I was really a woman, you see—they thought that I was a man playing the part of a woman. Probably that's why I was such a good clown. I didn't have to act—I was honestly terrified of failure. And the more afraid I became, the better I failed, and the more the audience enjoyed it. When I became world famous, I stopped being afraid, and that's when I lost myself, stopped being a good clown, because my genius was really in my fear. I knew that my performances were poor. In spite of that, the theaters were full and everyone laughed at me because I was the famous Milopa, and because the newspapers had said I was a good comic. People don't believe their own eyes and ears, they believe the newspapers. That's the reason it's so easy to cheat them.

I was funny only as long as I was just being myself. Fellini asked me to appear in one of his films, but he had to cut my part because I was boring and stiff like a wooden horse; it was all clear as day on film. That's when I was at my most popular—the critics went on praising me and never noticed I wasn't doing good work; they never could tell good from bad, and only loved me the more when my act went from being based on real experiences of failure to becoming a failure in itself.

My vanity grew along with their praise and I began to imagine that I was the world's greatest clown-artist, a sort of Picasso of the clowning world. I no longer listened to myself; I just tried, in my desire to please, to satisfy the critics, who always just wanted to see something new. As a failure, I was a success, but as a success, a failure. I completely abandoned my original act, making each one of my performances fresh and different, but now, being a celebrity, I found I was only able to imitate my former, funny self, and my performances became so mechanical that I got tired of hearing my own jokes. Everything that I said and did seemed hollow and affected. Nowadays that's called "burning out," I suppose, but I think it's more accurate to say that I had become a sort of prostitute of the spirit— I didn't burn out so much as whore-out. I did it both on and off the stage for various boards of directors and committees, the ones that manage variety shows and give out grants to magicians, trapeze artists, trick riders, lion and tiger tamers, and other people in the field who have demonstrated promise. I had power, money, fame, and two competing circus directors as lovers. They loved my fame, not me as a woman, but then there wasn't much about me as a woman to love, since I didn't even have breasts.

I was on a German tour, in Berlin, when I had a breakdown just before a performance. I lost my voice and couldn't move anything except for my eyes. I couldn't even lift a finger. A doctor came and gave me a tranquilizer, but this didn't cure the paralysis. My body was wiser than I was. It refused to continue the pretense. I was carried to the ambulance like a chunk of wood and taken to the hospital, where I lay in a near-catatonic state for a month. I took sick leave after I was released from the hospital, and after that started collecting a temporary pension, being listed as physically unable to work. I never went back to the ring. I was an incompetent clown, nothing more. I'd never learned any other profession.

2.

Gallimard has asked me to write a memoir about my life as a clown, because apparently there's an audience for that sort of thing. I still don't know how to get started, even though I've thought the matter over for another week. Maybe I should go into therapy. They say there's a good analyst on the island named Pere Calsina. Of course, I wouldn't know a good analyst from a terrible one, in Spanish. My Spanish is so terrible I could hardly bare my soul to anyone around here. Maybe Pere Calsina could explain to me in Italian or French why it was that even as a child I wanted to be a clown? What's so funny, really, about a circus clown's pants always falling down, or his getting hit in the head with a brick or a ten-ton weight dropping on his foot or a pole whacking him in the face and knocking off his nose? My brother wanted to be a streetcar driver when he grew up. He didn't get his wish. He became a lawyer.

I asked Mother to sew a clown suit for me and she sewed a Harlequin outfit out of varicolored scraps of cloth and made a hat with bells on it. I went as a clown to a class costume party, but nobody laughed at me. When I tried to be funny, I failed completely. When I tried to be serious, people laughed. It was almost as confusing as trying to remember which stories of mine were lies.

When I was fifteen, I still wanted to be a circus clown. Mother didn't tell me not to, but she did suggest that I learn some proper profession as well, since a clown's career is very uncertain—there's a lot of competition, and directors tend to be suspicious of female clowns, since they're all men themselves, and men tend to think women can't become great clowns, because they have smaller brains, or whatever excuse might be fashionable at the time. Besides, I might fall in love at some point, which could end up meaning children. Children, for their part, were the main reason for my mother's saying she thought it would be worth my while to learn to become, say, a librarian, because an itinerant life would disrupt my children's attendance at school. She knew this from experience, since she was the daughter of a fire-eater, after all.

"I'll never fall in love and I'll never get married. I'm not that stupid."

"I thought exactly the same thing when I was your age," she said.

She was a former trapeze artist who'd given up her career when she married my father, who had begun his career as a lion tamer, advanced to being a teacher at the Moscow circus school, then rose through the Min-

Anita Konkka 343

istry of Culture to become the Republic's coordinator of vaudeville arts. After Mother stopped working on the trapeze, her legs hurt all the time. First she got varicose veins, then her bones began to break all by themselves, as though her legs couldn't endure life on the surface of the earth. Most of the time she lay in bed, humming wistful songs and reading people's fortunes in tea leaves, though she never consented to tell what sort of future awaited me. She just looked at me sadly with her hand on her cheek and sighed deeply. What could she do about the fact that the circus was still in her blood too, even fifteen years later? She really wasn't suited to normal life. She pined away and died before her time.

After high school I applied, and was admitted, to the Moscow circus school. Father knew the principal and arranged for me to get in.

"There's nowhere else for you to go. You don't know how to prepare food and you can't get married—you're too ugly," he explained.

He was right. Before I became famous, I only had one lover—a bear tamer. He was so drunk that anybody would have been good enough for him. I happened his way and he held me in his arms and pressed me against his hairy chest. He smelled of vodka, onions, and bear piss. Not really such a bad smell, once you get used to it. I went to bed with him because I wanted to know what it was like, what all the women murmured about, why they were so eager and had such great enthusiasm about getting married. But in my opinion it wasn't worth the bother. It felt stupid to lie in bed with my legs spread while a man lay groaning on top of me. Maybe it would have felt different if I'd loved him. The rubbing began to bore me. A copy of *Pravda* was on the night table; I thought that I might as well get some reading done, so this time wouldn't be completely wasted. I reached out to grab the paper but I couldn't quite reach it. The bear tamer was furious—he almost knocked my head off. He grabbed me by the shoulders, threw me back against the bed, and said, "I'll show you *Pravda!*"

He squirted some liquid between my thighs as he said this, then slumped down to lie on my stomach, wheezing so heavily that I thought he'd had a heart attack and was about to die, since he was so fat. Fortunately, he pulled through. Afterward he asked whether he'd been good and wanted to kiss me on the mouth. I didn't want that, and I couldn't answer his question either, since I had no one else to compare him to.

I was the only woman in the clown course and probably the worst student in the history of the school, but because of my father's position, I wasn't kicked out. For my graduate thesis, I only barely managed to throw together the required Marxist study on how class distinctions are enacted in the art of clowning. I didn't mind the subject matter: clowning has always been a proletariat art, by and for the oppressed. The problem was doing research. Without filling my thesis with the requisite quotes from Marx and Lenin, I'd never get my degree—but whenever I opened their collected works, I began to feel terribly drowsy. Even in the classroom, hearing either of those names triggered a yawning reflex and made my ears close up. As such, I yawned constantly in school, and nothing of what I heard there made the least impression on me.

3.

With Father's help I got through my thesis and graduated with a degree in the art of clowning, after which I was sent to the Murmansk area as a third-class circus clown. I had to be a red-nosed, stupid, fat clown, which wasn't really my style, because I was more the small, thin, sad Pierrot type. The director of the circus said that the people didn't understand elitist French-type comedy, however.

I was a great idealist in those days and believed that the public's taste could be developed, but the director was a realist and kept me on a very short leash. When I performed as a fat clown, only the sympathetic young girls laughed at me out of pity, not wanting to offend. What could I do about the fact that the people didn't find it the least bit amusing when my pants fell down, I banged my head, and stumbled over my own feet? I didn't find it amusing either.

After half a year the director said that I had no talent for the clowning profession and offered me a post as a ticket taker and concessions girl, but I took offense, packed my things, and went back home. After that I had many jobs. I was an assistant in a mental hospital, an export chocolate quality controller in a candy factory, a guard at the Pushkin Museum, a janitor in a detox center, a nursing assistant at a children's daycare, a ticket seller at the ballet, an assistant at the Lenin Library, a food server in Cafeteria Number 3, and a floor assistant at the Peking Hotel. I'm good at languages: I know English, German, and a little French. But I got fired from the hotel because I didn't understand that I was meant to inform on the guests and my coworkers.

Through his connections, Father finally got me a job as a rabbit keeper at the Moscow Grand Circus, and then a promotion to clown's assistant. His last good deed was organizing a foreign tour for me. He'd been diagnosed with cancer of the liver. He was dying. He wanted me to go abroad and stay there, though of course he never said aloud that he hoped I'd defect—he was a cautious man. I decided to do as he wished, because after his death I had no other close relatives in the Soviet Union except my brother, and, as a lawyer, he would know how to worm himself out of any difficulties my defection could cause for him.

I defected in Milan. I said to my roommate late one night that I was going out to buy cigarettes around the corner. Annoyed, she crawled out of bed to accompany me, since we weren't allowed to go out by ourselves. We were all under orders to report everything that our workmates did to the circus political instructor, except for going to the toilet. In addition, we'd given assurances to the official who'd issued our passports for the trip that we wouldn't indulge in any conversations with foreigners, and that we'd be especially careful with members of the opposite sex. I told my roommate, who was a magician's assistant, that she didn't need to trouble herself on my account: I'd be back in a minute or two. When I left, she was sitting on the edge of the bed with her hair tousled, yawning like a hippopotamus. The last I saw of her was her pink tonsils.

When I stood around the corner from the hotel, waiting for a bus, and looked at the Café Dante's green flashing neon light, I had a strong feeling that I'd stood in the same place and lived the same moment before. I was strangely calm, as though I knew there was no reason for nervousness or fear. I can't explain why. Perhaps I was calm because I was only doing what was proper for me at the time—fulfilling my destiny, as they say. When the bus came, I rode to the train station and bought a ticket for Bologna, where some old acquaintance of my father lived. Clearly fate was on my side, because I got to Bologna without any mishaps: no one paid any attention to me and the train wasn't even late, as they usually are in Italy.

I consider Italy the country of my spiritual rebirth, because that's where I became the clown Milopa, naming myself after Milan—and because that's where I parted from my former homeland and circus comrades. For the first time in my life, I was able to breathe freely and be my own self. The Italians liked my sense of humor and received me well. They got to see my best performances, because of that. Spain and France understood me too, whereas Germans prefer the red-nosed, drunk type of clown. It was in Germany that I discovered people tell lies in the West too. I was very surprised. What on earth do they have to lie about? They don't get into trouble if they tell the truth, as they did in my country.

I'm out of red wine, so that's all I can say about lying today. Besides, the typewriter platen moves so slowly, like a louse in tar, and the letters all stick to each other. Are the batteries low? I have to go to the store to buy red wine and new batteries before I can start writing my memoirs in earnest.

TRANSLATED FROM FINNISH BY A. D. HAUN

Anita Konkka **347**

TOOMAS VINT

Beyond the Window
a Park is Dimming

In my dream, behold, I stood upon the bank of the river: And behold, there
came up out of the river seven kine, fatfleshed and well favored; and they fed
in a meadow: And behold, seven other kine came up after them, poor and very
ill favored and leanfleshed, such as I never saw in all the land of Egypt for
badness: And the lean and the ill-favored kine did eat up the first seven fat kine:
And when they had eaten them up, it could not be known that they had eaten
them; but they were still ill favored, as at the beginning. So I awoke.
[GENESIS 41:17–21]

Dusk. Someone quite obviously turned the light down, put out the lamps,
or pulled a thick blanket over the daylight. That's what the end of the Estonian year is like: with disconsolate haste the days get shorter—one's eyes
haven't yet gotten used to the light when darkness takes over again. A mea-
ger afternoon flurry had covered the parkland with a thin veil of snow, like
a stain, had annihilated the green, turned the roads ashen-gray. Only the
limestone pavilion on its island, reflected in the seemingly bottomless wa-

ter of the pond, struck the eye with an unreal whiteness. It didn't seem to belong to the gray-black crepuscular landscape.

Vilmer, a relatively well-to-do businessman of fifty-eight, was gazing at the park from the window of his home, as he had looked at hundreds of times before, with hundreds of different feelings. Now he was studying the change of the delicate greens, from daylight brightness back to black and white as the months passed, until they were almost colorless. Even in a winter thaw, when there was nothing remarkable to strike the eye, he could watch a car laboring through a snowdrift and make a bet with himself as to whether the driver would get through without help.

Outside it was getting dark, and in the room the electric flowers growing on the ends of delicate chromed stems were taking on a yellowish light, which allowed them to be reflected in the window-glass, and the gray-haired man too, thrown against the background of the darkening park. It was like an artistically composed portrait, nature providing the background.

A splash of water was unexpectedly heard in the little apartment, possibly coming from a radiator, or possibly from the bathroom. I should have put some music on, thought Vilmer, but his mouth distorted into a wry smile as he imagined himself selecting a piece of music and lighting candles. That sort of romantic behavior would make me look ridiculous, he thought. At our age it's no longer appropriate to put on trivial performances simply for the sake of making love.

The splashing ended as suddenly as it had begun. Vilmer calculated that it would take his visitor a minute or so to dry her hands and comb her hair. She might, after a pause, take lipstick from her handbag as well, so as to appear especially beautiful when she finally reappeared in the doorway of the living room; her smiling host, waiting by the window, starting at once to caress her ears with words, despite the fact that they would surely sound ridiculously false.

The thought that had struck him, that he might make himself appear ridiculous, made Vilmer cautious. He called to mind a ramble in a thicket of juniper bushes—every step making escape more hopeless, whether one pressed on or tried to turn back.

"The least likely route is always the best option," Vilmer told himself, and he remembered the liberating relief that had come over him—that time in the thicket—when he had decided at last that going back the way he'd come was after all the most sensible solution.

The woman had still not reappeared, and Vilmer reflected: it was chance, coincidence, a whim of fate that brought us together. She is only a woman, just like dozens of others in my circle of acquaintances.

Vilmer was himself a little dismayed by this turn in his thoughts. What had looked at first like a pleasant interlude now appeared in quite a different light. In a dimmer light, he told himself with a chuckle, and looked back outside, where at that moment the streetlights were coming on, and before his eyes appeared the memory of hundreds of little lamps being lit in the dusk of a spring evening by the Eiffel Tower.

Like a Christmas tree, thought Vilmer at the time, but this ironic allusion was meant to suppress his doubts. He was about ten years younger then, and then as now a new relationship seemed to be flaring up, and then as now Vilmer had been afraid that emotion would make him ridiculous. Then the woman with him had squeezed his hand, clearly moved. Around the steel tower, against the background of the evening colors of the sky, there had appeared a noble aureole, and the couple felt that some part of that celestial halo must have descended upon them too.

Vilmer recalled that the married woman whom he'd befriended on that trip to Paris had finally yielded to him in a flood of tears, but after that had developed the presumptuous notion that Vilmer owed her something. Rude would be a good way to describe the way Vilmer broke off that relationship after getting home. Rudeness seemed the only possibility at the time, but it had been an unpleasant situation, and it continued to depress him when he thought of it. He had always tried to keep away from emotional women, but the fact that this one had raised a real hue and cry in pursuit of him, was, at the time, obviously Vilmer's own fault. One must never sing the same song as a woman. There has to be some palpable difference in key, or at least in the lyrics.

When Vilmer was flying home from Toronto a week or so ago, a woman happened to sit next to him who, without ceremony, started chatting to him as they waited for take-off. At first Vilmer was reticent—after exchanging a few polite words he retreated into the thicket of his own thoughts, but the woman skillfully lured him out again. By the time their plane left the ground, Vilmer was happily and openly talking away, something that, given his nature, was rare—a downright peculiar way for him to behave.

The ice was broken, Vilmer concluded happily, observing himself sitting next to the woman, and it was strange that throughout the whole long journey he didn't worry once about the future course of his life.

But he should have worried about it. More precisely, he should have admitted that his twenty-two year marriage to Kristi was coming to an end. Everything good in this world must surely come to an end sooner or later. But once you stand face to face with the facts, such endings are hardly uncomplicated.

Vilmer dwelled now on a bitter memory: Kristi hadn't even gone with him to the airport on his way out.

He'd gotten a ride from his son-in-law, with whom he didn't have a close relationship, and couldn't have had one, because how can you get close to a person whom you've only ever seen a handful of times? Vilmer's poor knowledge of English restricted their conversation still further. The only real point of contact between the two men was that this person was the father of Vilmer's daughter's children. Being with his son-in-law made the sense of alienation Vilmer had felt throughout his visit all the more acute.

All around him in Toronto they had jabbered in a rapid English that Vilmer couldn't follow. His six-year-old grandson had wondered how his Grandad could have gotten so "stupid."

When Kristi had visited their daughter a couple of months before, her primary concern was to get their grandchildren talking Estonian. But now she agreed with their daughter's cynicism on the subject: "There's no sense in teaching the children Estonian. In ten years' time they'll have no more use for the language."

When the woman sitting next to him on the plane started talking in pure Estonian, he, after a brief reluctance, felt a sense of pleasure and even of intimacy in being able to pour out everything that had been contaminating his soul over the past few days.

"Just imagine," complained the woman, "*five* of my friends' grandchildren don't speak a word of Estonian!"

At first Vilmer didn't like the woman, whose name—strange to say—he still didn't know. She gave the impression of being a superficial babbler, an impression that deepened at the moment when, searching for something in her handbag, she simply tipped most of its indescribable contents onto her lap and the floor. When Vilmer was helping her retrieve her belongings, their hands touched for a moment; he flinched at this, but the woman just smiled, and that smile, somehow, managed to win Vilmer over, despite his numbness and recalcitrance.

Vilmer now let himself get embarrassed over the fact that he still didn't know the woman's name. Or, rather, that he still couldn't remember it. Surely the woman would have introduced herself when she sat next to him? Slid her name along his earlobe?

But what good would it do to know her name anyway? wondered Vilmer. Maliciously, he found himself wanting to go on referring to her as "the woman."

He imagined what it would be like to stay involved with the woman for weeks at a time and still manage to avoid learning her name. Vilmer smirked.

Then he pretended that their intimacy, what had not yet happened, represented a lasting, indefinite commitment. Vilmer chuckled at first, but soon his expression turned sour. He realized he had assumed all along that he and the woman would sleep together today. And, indeed, the sheer unequivocal nature of the situation seemed difficult now to deny.

"How ridiculous!" he muttered, but his muffled voice unexpectedly climbed in volume, winged its way beyond the bathroom door, and reached the woman within as a risible vocalization.

Vilmer pressed his hands to his ears, as if afraid to listen to himself, and said: "I must have had precisely this in mind when I stuffed my business card into her hand at Helsinki Airport."

"Nature abhors a vacuum," he added callously.

On the day of her arrival in Toronto, Kristi had said: "I've found *feelings* in me, unexpectedly. I understand now that I've been given only one chance to live, and if I don't live it to the fullest then I'm a fool, plain and simple."

"Well," said Vilmer. He would have liked to say something smart, something so biting that it would break Kristi's heart. Instead he shut his mouth.

"Nothing I can do about it," said Kristi, and it seemed that at that moment she was sincere and just a little bit unhappy—as if a cheap cup had fallen from her fingers and shattered into pieces.

Now Vilmer was looking solemnly at the blurred reflection of his portrait in the window, behind which he could see the dimming prospect of the park. What did the man reflected in the window want to say? What sorts of feeling had been inside *him* when he heard that the woman with whom he'd shared half his life was leaving for good?

He couldn't remember anything but the crushing sense of being insulted, and then the desire to rise above his own reaction, to on no account appear ridiculous in his wife's eyes.

All this had taken place some time ago, and now instead he had to content himself with the knowledge that he was no longer alone in his apartment, that in a moment or two there would emerge from the bathroom a woman whose name he didn't know, a strange woman with whom he was meant to begin an affair. It seemed to him that he was now like a novelist who has dozens of possible plot twists available to him—any one of which would let him go on writing for hundreds more pages—but who, unable to pick a suitable one, decides instead to conclude his story right where he left off.

How ridiculous, thought Vilmer, and he couldn't or wouldn't explain to himself what it was that felt so ridiculous to him at that moment.

This woman had called him one morning, a week after he got home. "I've got a suggestion for you . . . but I can't talk about it on the phone," she added after a short pause. There was a weepy disappointment audible in her voice, as if she had staked everything on one card and was already sure of losing.

They agreed to meet during their lunch hour, but a few minutes later Vilmer was already beginning to realize how much the telephone call had disturbed him. Hundreds of thoughts and speculations fought for ascendancy as they ran through his mind, and the woman's body and smile hovered in front of his eyes. He suspected that he had been too indiscreet about himself when he'd first met the woman—that garrulousness felt now like a severe cold he'd since recovered from. Vilmer thought that the woman would find him entirely different this time. With a trace of sadistic pleasure he was even enjoying the woman's anticipated incomprehension, amazement, awkwardness.

As the lunch hour approached, however, he felt again the strange mood that had caused him to give the woman his card in the first place. A gesture she couldn't help but interpret as an unambiguous desire to continue their acquaintance.

Vilmer would have been glad to erase the whole flight from his mind. He wasn't interested in any woman, much less in dealing with a person who had once blurted out so many personal things about herself, like . . . Vilmer searched now for an apt and exact comparison, and happened upon the image of those very intimate items she had strewn about on the plane after upending her handbag, but this excellent simile was accompanied by the memory of the fleeting touch of her hand, and so the woman's smile appeared before his eyes again, an echo reverberating inside his soul.

A curse, really.

But then, why "soul"? What precisely is a soul? Just another metaphor? Or something real that simply can't be touched?

You're really the ultimate fool, Vilmer reproached himself in the restaurant during their "date," but despite this, he carried on talking and talking. The woman joined in their chat enthusiastically. She kept repeating his words, taking such pleasure in them, until Vilmer heard himself inviting the woman back to his place for a glass of wine.

For some years now, Vilmer hadn't been thinking of women as women. His body was no longer in the habit of prompting him to indulge in wild fantasies. His fellow citizens had been retired to their assigned places, all taking on the same sane and balanced proportions. Women were women, they did their work and that was that. Women weren't special anymore. This was important for Vilmer's peace of mind.

Kristi's breaking up their marriage was nothing more than an offense to his pride. It didn't mean anything more. And the wound would heal soon enough.

This change—which he'd always associated with old age—had set in some time ago for Vilmer. Like a pinwheel, his last outburst of extramarital emotion had thrown off some sparks, then smoldered and died, and

Vilmer had realized that he would have an easier time of living if he completely withdrew into his shell. He didn't want to get involved with anyone. It seemed to him that whatever internal erotic cinematograph had once tormented him with its images all day and night had now broken down. The bodies of women caused him only a strange disquiet.

Yet, there was that fleeting touch on the airplane, which made him flinch and withdraw his hand as though scorched.

Their meeting had just been a coincidence, Vilmer assured himself. It meant nothing. And if he had invited the woman to visit him, it was only because she seemed to expect such an invitation. I have nothing else in mind but taking advantage of her, he told himself.

Not that it would do any harm to keep seeing her, really, Vilmer thought. Her company seemed to suit him. They could have lunch together from time to time, go to the theater or a concert. They might even share a seaside holiday in the sun? As long, that is, as he could keep his mouth shut. That would make things easier.

Vilmer looked at his hands, which seemed too big, and he imagined his gigantic fingers groping the woman—an unpleasant picture. These hands were nothing like his own hands. Somehow alien, borrowed from somewhere, maybe even hired—to do heavy, dirty work. I should take better care of my hands, he thought, staring at his splayed fingers. And then: I should take better care of my skin, and so forth, in that vein.

Then it occurred to him: What would his guest think if she came out of the bathroom and saw him staring at his extended hands? He folded them behind his back.

What the hell is she doing in there anyway? Vilmer wondered, annoyed. What if he went and knocked on the bathroom door? "Everything all right?" he would ask, like they do in American movies, and through the closed door he would hear that everything was all right and then some grunt-filled love scene would follow—likewise pilfered from some American movie.

Vilmer smiled bitterly. He imagined a scene with them lying naked in each other's arms in the marriage bed, her whispering sweet nothings in his ear. At first he dismissed the image with a shiver of disgust, but then it started to interest him—how their love scene might look. He viewed it in his mind's eye like any voyeur, but then he recoiled—he'd never imagined himself married to someone else before. His whole love life to date had been bound up in marriage, which he valued in his own way. His terror of damaging that marriage was what had first conditioned so many of his strict rules regarding other women. The marriage bed was sacred, after all.

But not anymore, Vilmer remembered.

"Why the hell am I even bothering?" he asked aloud. A vision of a dog chasing its own tail loomed before him, and it seemed to him that he was the tail. "My life is like a rerun," he said at last, pacified, and then it occurred to him that *The A-Team* would be on TV soon. It ran every day in the early afternoon, and Vilmer did everything in his power—even rearranging his work schedule—to leave time for him to indulge this vice at least once a week. Quite often he succeeded, and it seemed to him that a day when this happened was a success—a well-ordered day.

It takes so little to feel happy, he thought. But then he realized that it would be completely impossible to watch the naïve, ridiculous *A-Team*— so clearly written with an audience of adolescent boys in mind—with his guest in the apartment. Stupid things like that can only be enjoyed as a couple after a long while living together, Vilmer concluded with an irritated sigh.

I've become terribly wrapped up in myself, he decided at last. He couldn't understand why he'd never noticed this before.

"An idiot, you're an idiot," he repeated in a low, malevolent voice, and he realized to his surprise that there was nothing simpler than just explaining to his guest that he no longer wanted to share his life with anyone . . . that being alone made him happy.

Toomas Vint **357**

"How happy?" he wondered. But he wasn't much interested in the answer.

It was quiet in the apartment. No matter how intently he listened, there wasn't a sound from the bathroom.

As if nobody's in there, thought Vilmer, sneaking along the corridor. An impossible thought: the woman had vanished without trace, vanished into thin air, passed right through the walls. Vilmer pressed his ear against the bathroom door, but heard nothing more than the usual hum inside his head. He listened for another minute or a minute and a half, but then something else, worse than the woman's unlikely disappearance, began to worry him—what if she found him spying there? So he hurried on tiptoe back to the living room, where he stood shifting his weight from one foot to the other in front of the sofa, unable to decide whether to sit down or not.

Better to stand by the window, decided Vilmer, though unable to explain to himself why it was better there. The woman's endless stay in the bathroom had upset his plans. Plans? He had to admit to himself, feeling a little ashamed, that in going to meet the woman, he'd seen in his mind's eye how he would ask her in an offhand tone what kind of wine she liked, and, getting a hesitant answer, could then show off his expertise by making his own recommendations. Nothing more than showing off, but why deny himself this pleasure? After all, wasn't that why he had invited her?

In fact, had he really just asked this woman home because he wanted someone to whom he could show off his park-side apartment and splendid selection of wines?

Outside the window, the streetlights were glowing orange around the park. The sky was noticeably brightening and Vilmer felt that the darkening park-scape was slowly being absorbed into the sky.

Vilmer drew the golden-brown curtains. All connection to the outer world was severed. But somehow this didn't make him feel any more secure. The opposite, rather—Vilmer was appalled by the knowledge that he wasn't answerable to anyone. It was this lack of culpability that frightened him most.

"But if I'm not to be held accountable, who am I afraid of?" he demanded in voiceless exclamation   but this was like a voice crying in the wilderness: it neither echoed nor was heard.

"I don't understand why, but I have a feeling that I've reached the end," Vilmer thought, exhausted and still afraid. "But I don't care, really," he reassured himself . . . If he looked the facts squarely in the face, there was really nothing and nobody left to worry about. There was very little left to keep Vilmer clinging to life. He had, without noticing it, played everything out—drawn a metaphorical curtain between himself and the world, just as he had done at his unmetaphorical window a short while before.

But I have a visitor today, thought Vilmer. Who knows, she might just be the beginning of something good. The end need not be the end.

Yet for some reason the visitor was still not sitting with him drinking wine or having a satisfying chat. The lady was still in the bathroom. How long had it been now? Three minutes? Thirteen? Thirty?

Vilmer kept on staring at the golden-brown folds of his curtains. He remembered how proud he and his wife had been when they first put them up. "Now the apartment is perfect!"

It seemed to Vilmer that that had happened a very long time ago. But really "a very long time ago" had only been last spring. Before things had begun to go bad between them. But now Vilmer collected himself and moved again with uncertain steps toward the bathroom door.

Vilmer was astonished to see indefinite little flecks of red on the floor in front of the bathroom door—which to his great surprise did not seem to be locked. He knocked, but got no reply. His heart hammering, he finally pressed down on the handle and opened the door slightly. He saw no more than light reflecting off the bright blue tiles.

In order to see more than this, he would have to open the door wide and step in. He couldn't bring himself to cross the threshold, however, and see where the scarlet flecks of blood were surely washing down from his snow-white enamel bath.

Again, it was rather like a bloody scene in some movie. Vilmer had seen plenty. Perhaps, he told himself, because he had been so well prepared by Hollywood, he wouldn't be too horrified when he at last opened the door the rest of the way.

"Hello?" he called through the half-open doorway, as if over the telephone. Still no reply. He closed the door.

Vilmer surmised—well, he was quite sure—that the woman had died in the bathroom. She'd had a stroke or committed suicide. Vilmer stumbled back to the living room, and stood in front of his television. Then he bent down and picked up the remote control from the incredible chaos of sharp white cup fragments and dark bottle shards. He clicked the television on.

"Nothing I can do for my visitor now," he said to comfort himself.

On the screen, Face was just jumping over a high wall, while the other *A-Team* men had driven their black van into place so that Face could hop aboard and escape his pursuers; at the same time, some homeless people—led by Murdock—were singing "Onward, Christian Soldiers." Then there were commercials, and pink Energizer rabbits started running across the screen.

Vilmer saw no reason, if his visitor had died, that he shouldn't now enjoy *The A-Team* all the way through to the end.

"You win some, you lose some," he thought, rather pleased. But then his mood again swung to the opposite extreme: Why the hell did this woman have to choose his apartment to die in? It would cause no end of trouble. He wouldn't even be able to tell the ambulance people what her name was. And then of course they'd suspect that he'd done her in. He didn't really want to pursue that loathsome thought—but at once it occurred to him that he might indeed, in his confusion, have done something insane, irreparable.

Some movie characters do indeed commit murders they have no recollection of, Vilmer considered. He felt a chill in his bones.

"I have to go in there and see what's actually happened." But his legs would not obey. It's like a nightmare, thought Vilmer. Just like a nightmare . . . perhaps this really is a dream? A comforting thought. He stepped shakily toward the bathroom door once again. Vilmer saw that there were red footprints by the bathroom door. Inexplicable. But it was time now to open the door wide.

There was nobody there.

Blinking his eyes in the bright light, Vilmer saw himself in the mirror. Greasy, messy hair, a week's growth of beard, and a giant, obscene, yellowish-violet bruise under one eye. He was wearing a torn, wine-flecked shirt, and below it a filthy, stained pair of underpants. It was a horrible picture. The mirror wouldn't let him wish it away.

After a long while looking, Vilmer's attention was caught by a bottle with a striking red and gold label that was lying just behind him in the mirror. He turned around and picked the half-full bottle up with a heavy sigh. He drank from it. And again. Clutching the bottle to his breast, he hobbled back to the living room, where he cast an abstracted glance over the confusion that reigned there.

The same commercial was still on TV. Vilmer was seized by the feeling that he'd gotten stuck on the wrong side of the glass.

For him, reality was like an old married woman, too exhausted to nag, sitting on the corner of the settee, staring gloomily at her empty, infinitively wrinkled palms.

TRANSLATED FROM ESTONIAN BY CHRISTOPHER MOSELEY

PETER ADOLPHSEN

Fourteen Small Stories

A DULL FATE

Once upon a time there was a dull baby. Everyone could see it right away. The mother lost interest in the child and sent it to an orphanage. Even there no one paid any attention to it—it hadn't even been given a name. In the beginning, the other children teased it. But that too quickly grew dull. Most of the time the child sat alone in the corner, bored. In this manner the years passed and it began to grow hair on its chin. On the night of its first wet dream, it received a revelation. A glowing angel brought it big news: Your name is Arne and you are God. Arne went out onto the streets right away to preach this joyous message: I am God. But nobody listened to him. Arne repeated it over and over, shouted it from the rooftops, and whispered it into the ears of the clerks in the shops, but to no avail, and Judgment Day was quickly approaching. The dreadful day came when all the other gods waged war against each other and Arne stepped forward into their midst and said: I am God. But still there was no one who listened. They were too busy killing each other. In the end they all died, except Arne. Earth was destroyed, but Paradise remained, as empty as on the first morning of creation. Arne wondered whether he should create something. He began with a subscription to a do-it-yourself magazine. But that quickly got dull, so he decided to stop creating entirely. And so an eternity passed and Arne saw that everything was good.

BUTCHER GOUGH

Once in London, when the plague laid its dark hand on the city, there was a butcher by the name of Hubert Gough. At the beginning of the outbreak he had had a dream that caused him to sell his possessions and purchase beer, dried vegetables, and salted meat, and lock himself in the room behind his butcher shop and seal up all entrances and every crack and crevice. He rationed what he consumed with absolute self-control, but the day still came when there was no more food, and he began to starve. He knew that if he left his hiding place too early, he would die just the same. And his time had not yet come. On the brink of death, he decided to eat his own flesh. With the shop's largest axe he hacked his left leg off under his knee. It required enormous effort to ignore the pain long enough to ensure that only a little blood was lost, to stop the bleeding with a wet cloth, to not pass out, to not scream. But he succeeded and was able to drink his blood and eat his flesh, and lived for a good while longer before he was forced to lop off his other foreleg. When the time had finally come when it was safe to leave the butcher shop, both Hubert's legs had been sawed off at the hip and his left arm at the shoulder. He lived another twelve years in a little box on four wheels.

REPORT ON THE GITII LANGUAGE

Among the many languages to disappear in the Americas during the seventeenth and eighteenth centuries, a particularly interesting tongue is known as *Gitii*, after the word used by the race of Gitii-speakers to refer to themselves. Literally translated, it means "to walk on two legs." This tribe lived in an inaccessible part of the southern Andes Mountains, and thus their language developed along wholly different lines than other Arawakan languages—the linguistic family to which Gitii can be traced, if only with considerable ambiguity.

Phonetically, Gitii had only *one* vowel (except in special circumstances, explained below), that which corresponds to our letter *I*. Thus, their speech must have sounded like a single long tone that, interrupted by breathing, was modulated by consonants, of which there were ten: *D, F, H, K, M, P, R, T, V,* and *Z*. There were four ways to express their one vowel: gutturally, as *Ï*; nasally, as *Î*; rising in tone, as *Í*; or else falling: *Ì*. In addition, the vowel could either be short or long. These phonemes were essential to the meaning of a given word. For example, *rïtí* meant "to sail against the stream"; *rïtï*, "to bathe a child"; *rítîî*, "to turn pale"; and *rítì*, "to eat fish."

As will be evident, these examples are all verbs, and this is because verbs are the only part of speech—excepting a type of preposition—that the Gitii language possessed. It is not, as in the Semitic languages, that other parts of speech could be formed from a root verb; speakers of Gitti were entirely restricted to communicating with verbs. Example: a translation from English to Gitii and directly back to English. "A black bird flies" might be rendered *mídíkí dimïï tí zíkí*—but translating this into English gives us: "to flap with wings," "to absorb light," "over and upwards," and "to fly." Since English doesn't possess the same wealth of verbs as Gitii, it is generally necessary to include a noun in translation that is not literally present in the original language, in order to give the English reader an understanding of which action a speaker of Gitii would have connected to a given word. Gitii included verbs to differentiate between a speaker's washing hair, vegetables, or a child. Indeed, to translate back into Gitii one of the nouns included as a convenience of translation above, you would need a completely different verb. *Gîtíí* for example, as noted earlier, means "to walk on two legs." The word for leg, on the other hand, is *tïzï*, which means "to transport a living creature."

The Gitii people viewed the world in verbs, which is to say in actions; they had no words for what was static and thus had no concept for it, seeing all things as identical with the action they triggered or carried out. One can say they identified an object or a phenomenon with the transformation it went through over time. Enduring things were seen as a chain of events; a person or a tree was always the preceding moment in such a chain.

As noted at the beginning of this report, Gitii did contain, under special circumstances, vowels other than *I*. The vowel *A* had approximately the same function as a swear word might when used to give emphasis to a spoken phrase; depending on how much one wished to emphasize a given word, its vowel would be modulated from *I* to *A*.

The vowel *O* was only used between lovers, and then only during lovemaking, as a type of improvised poetry recited to describe one's partner and the state of the speaker. This "conversation" was an inseparable part of the sexual act and considered a source of pleasure on par with the physical component of the act. The important thing was that the shift from *I* to *O* was smooth.

The only written account we have of this language is from a missionary with the name Bartolomeo Jimenez Ribero, who in his journal wrote about a people whose speech ". . . sounds as though they have a frog in their throat and a fly in their nose."

MADELEINE, OR THE SAD LITTLE NOVEL

Marie Madeleine was born by caesarian back when this procedure was more or less a death sentence for the mother.

As a little girl, she ran over fields and water seeped into her lace boots and most of all she was fond of geography.

Later, she sold flowers at a train station and fell in unbearable love with a soldier on his way to war.

She enlisted as a nurse. One winter night the soldier she had seen was carried into the field hospital following an attack where gas had been used. He was laid near an opening in the tent in order to give some air to his abused lungs, and while a snowdrift piled up by his head, Madeleine tried in vain to find the right words.

Afterward she stole a bottle of morphine and became a whore in a port city. At the end of the pier sat a Belgian man fishing without a hook. He tied a knot around his bait and said that if they were going to get any fish to come up, they would have to hold on tight.

The police doctor treated her for syphilis with arsenic salve.

She became pregnant and at the birth, since the child's head was too large, the doctors decided to crush it, as the baby was more than likely both syphilitic and brain damaged, thanks to the mother's drug habit. Madeleine lost her mind when she heard the crushing sound.

She went to the madhouse and there she lay, bound tight, disinfected nightly with carbolic acid and as happy as could be.

IOTYN

Nearly two billion years ago, on a mist-shrouded planet shrouded at the center of the Milky Way, intelligent beings evolved—beings that didn't possess bodies in any real sense, but consisted instead of invisible gas clouds whose size and movements were controlled by their disembodied minds. Their maximum size was five and a half cubic miles and minimum the size of an atom. They could accelerate from zero miles per hour to the speed of sound in a nanosecond. They couldn't however penetrate solids or in any other way influence their surroundings, and they neither ate food nor generated waste, aged nor produced offspring. Each of the nearly three million individuals of this race possessed a unique consciousness, but their memory was collective.

"Iotyn" was the name they gave each other.

About a billion years ago, curiosity drove the Iotyns to travel out in the galaxy. They first arrived on Earth during the Cretaceous. Soon after becoming part of their communal memory, the little blue planet in Orion's belt became an attraction for Iotyns throughout the galaxy: They had seen life before, but never at such an advanced level of cellular organization.

After approximately a hundred million years on Earth, the Iotyns discovered that they could reside in a mammal by slipping into a fertilized egg just after the sperm cell had penetrated it and had left a hole in its membrane. The Iotyn was then united with the mammal for the duration of its life; a symbiotic arrangement that the animal never noticed and that terminated at its death, at which time the Iotyn was returned to its original, shapeless form. The tactile universe was a revolutionizing experience for the Iotyns, and it quickly became popular to take up residency in earthly organisms.

One million years ago, yet another leap in their evolution occurred, as two Iotyns occupied one egg at the same time and lived together in the host organism; and after this animal's death there weren't two Iotyns that emerged from its body but one. Their consciousness was from then on doubled in depth and intensity, but not in essence. Such amalgamations escalated, and after a period of time, two thirds of the Iotyns became unified, after which the fusion of more than two began to become the vogue: three, four, and even more Iotyns converged to consciousnesses of staggering dimensions.

This development has continued until reaching its inevitable end: The three million Iotyns have now been unified into one massive consciousness, which at this very moment can be found inside a bristly haired dachshund in Lower Saxony.

THE KING OF ENGLAND'S TWO VISIONARY PARABLES

King Edward of England and his first minister had stopped on a little bridge during their daily walk in the castle gardens. Affairs of state were generally the subject of their conversations, but today would be different, as the King thrust his right arm out into the air and stated: "An English yard is the exact distance from the tip of my nose to the end of my ring finger, is it not?" To which the first minister promptly responded: "Correct, Your Majesty, that's what the law says."

"And if we now imagine that this yard represents all the time that has passed since the creation of the earth," the King continued, "how much time would a single file stroke on my ring fingernail then be?" he asked, looking sternly at his companion.

"Oh, ah, I couldn't say, offhand," the first minister said, blinking his eyes and jerking his head backward like a child who hasn't understood a question. "A day, a year?"

"Ha! No," shouted the King, "one single file stroke on my nail would be the entire history of humanity, my good man, all the time that has passed since we evolved from apes!"

"Your Majesty will need to explain . . ." the first minister stammered.

"And if we now imagine that my scepter's golden ball is the sun, and the sapphire in my ring is the earth," the King persevered, taking a ring from his finger and giving it to the first minister, "at which distance should they be placed to represent the actual distance in space? Can you answer me that, my most esteemed first minister?"

"Er, hmm," the first minister coughed and accepted the ring with a deferential little bow. "I must admit that I don't follow Your Majesty's train of thought, if . . ."

"You would have to go on quite a trip, my dear first minister, for my ring would be all the way down with the Pope in Avignon!"

"My dear Majesty, would You be so kind as to explain what it is You're saying?" interrupted the first minister despairingly. "Your humble servant doesn't understand a single word of . . ."

"How could I explain?" thundered the King. "It's just the way it is. Strictly speaking, of course, I can't know any of it! How the fuck am I supposed to know all this when we in this century haven't even developed a heliocentric view of the world, and when we still calculate the age of the universe by adding together the life spans of the Old Testament patriarchs?"

And now the King was utterly dumbfounded. He asked, "What am I actually talking about?"

The first minister scratched his pointed beard and said:

"Don't look at me, Your Majesty. To my ears it was nothing more than what the common people would call devilish talk."

"How peculiar . . ." the King mumbled.

"If Your Majesty would forgive me for saying so, I believe it might be advisable to visit the royal *confessionarius*. Who knows whether this might have been the devil's work, these strange thoughts that have emerged from the royal soul . . . ?"

"Why, my good sir, you're quite right—to the cathedral!"

THE SLOW GIANT

Without reflecting back a single one of the light waves whizzing through the air—and therefore invisible to everyone—a giant as tall as eleven Eiffel Towers stacked on top of one another now stands with his foot raised over a small town in northern Sweden. But it is not standing still, this giant: it's in the middle of a step that has lasted centuries and will last centuries more. The giant is as old as the earth itself and the rhythm of its breaths and its sense of time are of geological slowness: the giant has seen the glaciers glide slowly away, the trees shoot up like small fountains, and experiences the seasons as a continuous, unremarkable tremor. It's only fairly recently that it has noticed the upright-walking ape that has suddenly proliferated across the globe.

THE PERFECT TEXT

The perfect text exists, and anyone who gazes upon this abomination becomes caught, reading it, until he or she dies of hunger and thirst, helpless, unable to let their attention drift, not even after the book's conclusion, when it ties every conceivable thread together in such a mesmerizing way and, at the same time, opens such a wealth of follow-up questions that the reader in his or her quest for answers is immediately sent back to the beginning, which in its inexorable perfection sends the reader's eyes on and on down the pages. The only possible salvation is if another person, eyes averted, removes the text from the reader's field of vision before the end; if not, the perfect words will be indelibly stamped in the unhappy reader's memory. This murderous object, described by a Basque village priest in the eighteenth century as a simple quarto, is stored in the cellar of the building housing the Royal Spanish Academy, which decided upon its discovery to keep the text's existence a secret from the world, and has since renewed this decision every twenty-five years—which is understandable, as only few would believe them, and everyone who might hope to have their doubts confirmed would die reading. So far, dozens of people have met just such a fate. And since the Academy has decided to leave the steel box in which the text is stored unlocked, from time to time a despondent member is found bent over its open lid, at which point there's nothing left to do but put the literary suicide in bed, where his wide eyes will go on scanning from left to right across already memorized letters and words until rigor mortis sets in.

BLOODY LOVE

Once upon a time there lived a man who loved a woman who didn't love him. "I'd rather die than live without you," he said. "Piss off," she replied. "I'll prove it to you," he said, but she'd already gone. That same evening he hacked the tip of his left pointer finger off and put it in an envelope with a note written with the bloody finger: "Love me, or it'll be the hand next time." A month later she received a package with a severed hand, but still she didn't want him. The next step was to slice his whole arm off, but he lost his nerve and he had to live the rest of his life one-handed and alone. They met again as old people and she said: "Look, apparently you *wouldn't* rather die than live without me." And he replied: "Yes, I gradually came to understand that, bit by bit." "Aren't you funny—bit by bit . . ." she sneered, and went on her way.

THE SCATTERED BONES

After Satan had killed God and devoured his flesh, he scattered God's bones across the earth and hid them in inaccessible places, under glaciers, inside volcanoes, under the foundations of tall buildings. Much later, a small boy crawled into a ravine and found one of the nasal bones, which was as big as an elephant's skull. That night the boy dreamed that the entire skeleton was reassembled and God came back to life. He saw the muscles grow from the bare bones, the organs inflate, the veins interweave, and the skin settle softly on the steaming flesh. He dreamed that God rose again and dethroned Satan. The boy grew up and traveled the globe in search of other oversized bones, but he got old and died without having found more than scattered pieces, an anklebone, half a shoulder blade, some splinters and other pieces of the skull not quite substantial enough to form an eye socket. In his will the old man bequeathed his collection of bones to a museum, where they all thought he must have been senile or simply out of his mind. Later, a restorer brought the bones home as a toy for his son. This boy, who was fond of math, measured the collection's partial eye socket with a ruler, putting it at twenty-two inches, and by comparing the 1.5 inches of his own eye socket and his own height of fifty-three inches, he was able to calculate the full height of God to about sixty-two feet. He went to a nearby cemetery and laid out the bones according to the same measurements, as if God Himself had been outstretched on the ground, and he buried each bit of bone in its rightful place. The boy hoped that this fragmentary burial would give some sort of peace to the ghost of a deity who ravaged the earth, but only succeeded in robbing it of an eye, a shoulder, and a heel.

EARTH CONFUSED

One day, for reasons unknown, the Earth dislodged itself from its axis and tumbled pell-mell in its orbit around the sun. As seen from Earth, the sun seemed to have lost all sense of direction and sailed across the heavens like a drunken fly. No longer did it make sense to speak about night or day, summer or winter, as these things changed incessantly and unpredictably. But our confused planet still cast its shadow at regular intervals onto the moon, which thus, in time, assumed the sun's old function as divider of time.

DEUS, LIBER ET PAGINA

Before the beginning of time, God opened the Book of Creation and tore out a page, for if He did not do so, the Book would be perfect and thereby render His existence impossible, since one of His attributes is being the only possible perfect being. Afterward, He started reading and the universe was created as its story passed under His eyes, but when He came to the point where he had torn out the page and simply continued reading, from that moment on there was something He did not know, and therefore His existence was equally impossible, since omniscience is another of His attributes. But being omniscient, He knew from the beginning that whether He tore out the page or not, He would sooner or later be forced to cease existing—ergo, God or the Book or both could not exist simultaneously, which in any case also renders this story impossible. Unless He has not yet reached the missing page.

AT HØJER FLOODGATE

In Højer, the floodgate city in the southwest Jutlandian marsh, a young local by the name of Alfred Erling Larsen stood by the oven in the bakery where he was an apprentice at the exact moment the sea breached the dikes during the flood of 1976, when thousands of sheep drowned, and wanted to hang himself. His particular reason for choosing to end his life comes down to a very short tale: His fiancée, Karen Margrethe Nielsen, the baker's daughter, had that same morning swallowed a ping-pong ball and choked to death. He put the rope around his neck and braced himself to say a few last, well-chosen words, but nothing came to him; he thought about it for a long time, but no words seemed worthy to be his last. This hesitation gave the water in the bakery time to rise, thus saving his life.

A CLASSIC FONT

Suddenly Marcel had the creeping sensation that this situation could appear in a book. Suzanne stroked her hair with an irritated gesture, and he saw it written in his mind's eye: She stroked her hair with an irritated gesture. His first reaction was to grip the armrests in panic. A moment after having also seen this sentence in writing he tore himself loose by changing position on the chair and saying: "It's not my child." The feeling of literature was gone, but it returned the instant she opened her mouth and the words stood before him like a little wall in a classic font: "You're one mean prick, Marcel."

TRANSLATED FROM DANISH BY K. E. SEMMEL AND THE AUTHOR

MICHAL AJVAZ

The Wire Book

There was still fighting going on in some quarters of the capital when old Vieta got into his car and headed out to Cormorant Bay. He wove his way through streets clogged with tanks, armored personnel carriers, and crowds of people. On the northernmost edge of the city he was stopped by guards wearing the uniforms of South Floriana; luckily it turned out their commander was a former student of his. The roads to the north of the city were still quite dangerous, so the commander offered Vieta a lift to the camp in his jeep.

The camp was made up of low barracks standing in a long row on a sweltering plain of sand and rock above the sea. The government troops had by now abandoned the place. Confused and emaciated prisoners were wandering about the scorching sands; they bore witness to the departure of the troops the day before, in a ship that had been waiting below in the harbor. They had seen the troops loading aboard some heavy crates; presumably these contained documents they hadn't succeeded in burning and intended to dispose of at sea.

The professor asked all the prisoners about Fernando. Many of them had met him in the camp. Vieta discovered that his son had arrived there the very day martial law had been imposed. But none of the prisoners knew what had become of him. This was an ominous sign: Vieta was told that prisoners would be driven away in trucks that later returned to the camp empty. Eventually he managed to find a man called Pablo, with whom his son had worked for several weeks in the depot. He had Pablo lead him there. From the outside the depot building looked like all the other barracks, except that it had no windows. Professor Vieta walked about a long, dark room whose floor was covered with battered crates, iron bars, clamps, and large balls of wire. He walked right to the end, where there was a view of wide-open gates, forming a rectangular screen on which were projected the glowing yellow sand and the rock. The sunbeams that penetrated the room carried in a fine, whirling sand. The tin roof over Vieta's head was incandescent; it was incomprehensible to him that anyone could bear the heat in there for longer than five minutes. The prisoner waited in front of the depot. Vieta rejoined him and he explained that Fernando had struggled most with the fact that he was prevented from writing. He never complained about anything else; all those weeks Fernando spent in the sweltering depot he thought of nothing but literature, it was as if nothing else had any importance for him. He once confided in Pablo that in his last weeks of freedom he had planned a novel. Pablo knew that Fernando's only desire in the camp was to write his novel.

But writing was strictly forbidden. The camp guards took pains to ensure that no prisoner ever came by the merest scrap of paper or anything that could be used as a writing implement. Once Fernando managed to steal several blank record sheets, which had escaped the attention of the warders because they were printed on both sides and as such not considered fit for use as writing paper. After this Fernando would get up early, before reveille; guided by the first cold rays of the sun to appear over the barracks, he would use a nail in place of pencil or pen, inscribing his text into the forms. Then he would bury the lacerated sheets in the sand behind the depot. Someone informed on him, however, and an officer forced Fernando at gunpoint to dig up all the papers and burn them. His punishment was a week in the darkness of the solitary-confinement cell.

Fernando without pen and paper reminded Pablo of a narcomaniac whose drugs had been taken away. Often Pablo would catch Fernando in front of the depot with a piece of metal piping in his hand, carving letters in the sand that were immediately smoothed away by the wind; or he would find him scribbling something invisible on a wall with his finger. After a while Pablo was put to work elsewhere; he never saw Fernando again.

Some days later the Conservative Party held its first conference, at which Professor Vieta was elected party leader. Thanks to the work connected with his new position he was sometimes distracted from thoughts of Fernando, but every time the telephone rang he felt sick with fear that the call might bear tidings of the discovery of his son's body. But the body of Fernando Vieta was never found.

Although the leaders of the various radical and partisan parties were in the majority in the provisional parliament, their disagreements ran so deep that they failed to agree on a common candidate for president. Thus it happened that the race was won with relative ease by Ernesto Vieta, the candidate proposed by the Conservative Party, whom no one had taken too seriously to begin with. Vieta spent most of his time in the presidential palace, working long into the night, then pacing the empty corridors and meeting the ghost of his son, or standing on the palace balcony looking down at the sand of the empty square as it shone in the moonlight.

On a yacht at anchor by a belt of small islands off the coast of North Floriana, within view of the mainland, a group of students from the capital saw in the new year together. They had diving gear with them, and on the first day of the new year, after a night of champagne and fireworks, they swam down to inspect a coral reef whose many colors and shapes were illuminated by rays of sunlight that penetrated the warm, shallow sea. One of the students separated from the others and went deeper, into some kind of gorge that opened up before him. In the beam of his flashlight he saw tentacles wriggling about, then big, round, staring eyes and a flash of grooved fins. He was suddenly aware of a dark, twisted line in the water, which continually vanished and reappeared amid the pink and white feelers of sea anemones. The lone diver thrust his hand in among the pulsating anemones and felt the hardness of metal. What he was holding appeared to be wire; lifting it out of the bed of anemones he saw that the twists in the wire described carefully shaped letters of the alphabet. He bent to read, with astonishment, the following: *As Richard's car plunged toward the green hillside of the Chapultepec, a dark figure holding a sub-machine gun leaned out of the back window. There were three flashes and the sound of three short bursts of gunfire.* As the student began carefully to extricate the wire from the stinging jungle of anemones, he witnessed the flight on uncertain little legs of a school of small, translucent shrimp that lived in among them. There were places where he had to tear the wire away from shells that had become affixed to it. The wire seemed to have no end; in the flashlight beam above the rippling anemones more and more words and sentences presented themselves. There in a rift in the coral reef the amazed diver read a story about a car chase through the streets of Mexico City—a fragment of some kind of wire-book thriller. Several meters in he came to a place where the wire was knotted and clogged with aquatic plant life. His touch provoked a soundless, dreamlike explosion—a school of fish of the widest variety of colors and shapes that had made a nest in the tangle of wire, pursued in a dignified march by a hermit crab in its shell. After this the diver followed the wire in the other direction and found another knot; here, too, was a confusion of wire sentences in which fish, sea snails, and small crustaceans had made their home. The wire was fractured in several places; around the knot and in among the anemones there were several smaller broken-off fragments.

The student called his friends, and together they pulled the wire out of the water and laid it on the deck next to empty champagne bottles. Boys and girls in diving kits and swimwear grouped together around the undersea wire text, the words of which were plugged with seaweed, shells, and thrashing fish. The wind had dropped and the surface of the sea was still, like a great floor of smooth blue stone. The students began to tidy up the wire, pulling out aquatic plants whose long flexible stalks had woven themselves into its bends, tearing off mollusks that clung to it. As the debris of the sea was stripped away, the rusty curves that came into view in the radiant sunlight revealed themselves as fragments of wire sentences treating of the torments of love and hate, of ecstasy and humiliation, of demons and man-made men, of despair; then there were sentences describing gunfights and car chases, and others describing the torpid atmosphere of a roadside motel and then a stuffy hotel in some big city. The students succeeded in working free one of the ends of the wire; it comprised the sentence *Diamanta disappeared behind the low rocks that lined the coast*, and a little further along, the word *Finis*. To all appearances this was the end of the text. The students turned immediately to the second great knot of wire and groped about in its damp and greasy innards; it wasn't long before one of the girls pulled out the other end. The students cleaned off the slime to reveal the words *The Captive*, which were written in letters somewhat larger than the rest of the text. After the last letter of the second word the wire ran straight for about ten centimeters before forming the next two words: these gave a name that all the students recognized, that of Fernando Vieta. Everyone was now aware that they were looking at a sort of title page, bearing the title of this work and the name of its author. What they had found in the sea was a book, a book such as had never been seen before, a book written in wire by the national martyr, the son of the President, during his time in the detention camp.

The students decided to stop their work: the wire was so badly corroded they were afraid they might damage it. By evening of the same day the tangle of wire sentences, still scented by the sea and covered with the corpses of tiny marine creatures, was on the carpet of the President's study. Ernesto Vieta sat next to it, running the ends of his fingers along words the hands of his son had fashioned in wire in the unbearable heat of the depot; the father, too, was afraid to straighten out the brittle wire. Fernando had succeeded in outwitting his warders after all: there in the camp he had found something that was at once pen and paper. Ernesto remembered seeing in the dim light of the depot coils of wire scattered about. Obviously it had occurred to Fernando to use the wire as a solid ink, an ink that need not be applied to paper or any other base. The President imagined his son in a corner of the depot, performing patiently the endless task of bending the wire into a long string of words. Perhaps he didn't even bother to hide it, left it scattered about the depot for everyone to see; it would never cross a soldier's mind that this jumble harbored a work of literature. In all likelihood the wire text had been noticed only at the end of the war, by one of the commanders, when all documents were being destroyed. It had been loaded on a ship along with everything else that needed to be disposed of, and thrown into the sea. Professor Vieta imagined Fernando's joy at managing to complete his work in spite of the guards' attentions. He tried to fix in his imagination the expression of bliss on Fernando's face, but it was so many years since he had seen his son that he couldn't guess at what he must have looked like then. All that came to him was the face of a ten-year-old boy.

The wire was entrusted to restorers. For the next three months they tended to it and treated it with oils; painstakingly, centimeter by centimeter they opened it out on the floor of the great hall of the State Conservation Institute. As Fernando's text was gradually revealed, the restorers were taken aback by what they read. But it was not their task to criticize the President's son's novel, so during their regular meetings with the elder Vieta they kept their feelings to themselves. They proposed to the President that his son's work should be cut up into lines, each about a meter in length, making it possible to set it on panels, each of which would form a page of a great book. But the President would not permit such a drastic modification. So the unfolded, restored segments of wire text were placed along the wall of the Institute's main hall, which was circular, and gradually arranged in a spiral which revolved inward and whose outer perimeter more or less matched the circumference of the circular hall, which was thirty meters in diameter. The scents of the sea gradually faded, to be replaced by the smells of conserving agents.

Every day the President made time to have himself driven over to the Institute, where he would see how the work was progressing. On each visit he would kneel and read over and over the passage that had been revealed since the previous day. On some days there would be a whole meter of newly restored text, on others just twenty centimeters. Images from Fernando's work would settle in his brain and then present themselves with painful insistence during governmental meetings; wire sentences would appear with the clarity of hallucination between the lines of the dossiers prepared for his attention. This made it difficult for him to concentrate on his work; with increasing frequency he left the handling of affairs of state to his advisors. Complaints about his idleness proliferated. But at this time all the newspapers wrote daily about the salvage of the wire manuscript of the President's son, a man tortured to death by the previous regime. This moving story aroused great sympathy and love for the President, not least among the lower classes, who until recently had regarded him with perfect indifference. For sale in the markets, in among pictures of the saints and figurines of Our Lady of Guadalupe, there were now statues and color-print portraits of the President and his son. Young people wore T-shirts bearing pictures of both Vietas. Such a groundswell of sentiment was useful for the Conservative Party, and it served to strengthen the government, which in the chaos of the immediate post-war period had been quite unstable. Not even the opposition, composed of members of the radical parties and former partisans, dared challenge too openly a President so beloved by his people.

The nation was impatient for the restorers to finish their work. All but the President and the team of seven restorers were expecting a great work that addressed the struggle for freedom from tyranny—a work that would yield passages for recital on festive and ceremonial occasions and sentences to be chiseled into the plinths of monuments. The President forbade all outsiders from entering the Institute until work had been completed. Although every evening the Institute was thronged with journalists who thrust microphones at anyone departing the building, the restorers were silent about what was slowly emerging from the submarine tangle, thus keeping their promise to the President.

Restoration work was still in progress when Vieta announced he would build a mausoleum with an empty tomb as a symbol of his son's remains. The mausoleum would also contain a room that would be the final resting place of the original wire book. All the publishing houses battled for the right to publish *The Captive*; after long deliberation the President granted permission to the Golden Age Press. The contract stipulated that the book would be published in three forms: the first would be the usual means for reading works of literature; the second a facsimile edition of the wire original, in which the lines of pages would be reproductions of segments of wire; the third a single page in the form of a long strip of paper that would bear a facsimile of the wire text in unbroken flow. The paper strip of the third of these editions would be rolled up and attached at each end to a roller, in the manner of ancient scrolls reading would progress across the page from one roller to the other.

By the beginning of August the last section of wire was restored; on the floor of the hall of the Institute Fernando's book lay in an almost perfect spiral. Its last turn, into the sentence *Diamanta disappeared behind the low rocks that lined the coast,* took it to what was practically the dead center of the room. After the word *Finis,* there was a space in the shape of an irregular circle about twenty centimeters in diameter. Regrettably, the wire was broken in a number of places. The President had three expeditions of professional divers sent to the coral reef, and these succeeded in fishing out from among the anemones a few more sentence fragments. But some of the missing pieces were never recovered. Soon all three versions of the book were published in a print run of many thousands. On the day of publication, lines formed in front of the bookshops before first light. By evening the book was sold out and the publishers began planning the next edition.

But the book was received with disappointment and consternation. Instead of the novel about the struggle for freedom so keenly anticipated by readers, what appeared was a tale so strange that no one could make much sense of it. Indeed, it was no easy matter to establish its genre; it was set in 2001—which was then still the future—like *A Space Odyssey* before it, so eventually the critics decided it was science fiction. Still, the incomprehensibility and oddity of Fernando's novel was in no way detrimental to the Vieta cult of the father and son as it existed among the people: these qualities belonged to the world of the sacral, for the Vieta cult had taken on something of a religious character. In the villages and the slums that skirted the cities, *The Captive* went unread (nor would anyone there have read a novel about the national struggle for freedom either), but newspaper cuttings containing extracts from Fernando's novel were pinned to household altars, next to pictures of the President and his son. When people there read, syllable by syllable, the inexplicable sentences, these were not entirely without meaning: the readers invested them with veneration, love, and hope.

The reaction of the educated classes was far less favorable. Intellectuals had imagined a great personal theme (probably love) woven through scenes from the revolutionary struggle. The motif of subjugation suggested by the work's title was indeed present, as was the motif of love, but the account of the hero's yearning for freedom and the story of his amours had little in common with what the impatient intellectuals had imagined. It was as though Fernando had known what his readers were expecting and was making fun of them. The educated classes would have been perfectly accepting of the work had it been composed of a formless, difficult stream of interior monologue that broke down the contours of things, connections between elements of plot and the unity of character; it would then have been a simple matter to declare the book *a modernist work* and thus assign it to a familiar category. Nor would it have been difficult to ideologize such a work of modernism—by declaring it a protest against the classical forms of art promoted by the previous regime: a representation of the struggle for freedom of expression within the national struggle for greater freedoms. But Fernando's wire was bent into chains of words in classically constructed clauses, in which were set out long, detailed descriptions of characters and places, together forming a strange but fully coherent story. In bending the wire into thousands and thousands of words, Fernando had surely cut his fingers to shreds; the writing of the book must have caused him unspeakable pain. Many of his readers imagined the bloodied hands forming word after word in the sweltering heat of the depot, and they said to themselves, "Why did he suffer so for *such a thing as this?*" Few of them read *The Captive* to the end.

The literary critics were as bewildered by the book as everyone else. But their profession demanded that they be able to write something about anything; polite reviews began to appear in newspapers and literary magazines close to the Conservative Party. Some of these praised the novel for the elegance of its form, others forced on it some underlying message; typically the critic would use his closing paragraph to express regret that the tragic circumstances attending the book's creation had not permitted the author to address its deficiencies in the final version and make of it a truly exceptional work. In this way the reviewers made clear they did not, in fact, think very highly of *The Captive*. And their hypocrisy was founded on a fallacy: to all appearances the work was indeed properly finished and its author had reworked it thoroughly to make it so. It was possible to straighten and re-bend the wire in the act of revision, and the state of the wire testified that Fernando had performed many such rewrites and deletions in the search for expressions that at first escaped him.

Critics of magazines supportive of the previous regime thought it in slightly poor taste to write unfavorable reviews of a book whose author had been a victim of a dictatorship under which they themselves had prospered, so they expressed a hypocritical regret for the fact that the young writer had been unable to develop his talent to the fullest. Typically such a reviewer would make this position clear in his very first paragraph; this allowed him to devote the remainder of the article to an enumeration of the work's perceived shortcomings. It must have been a pleasant task to describe in detail how the son of the current president, whom the reviewer detested and who in turn held him in open contempt, was a bad writer.

So it was that the wire book from the bottom of the sea became first a subject of incomprehension and indifference, then of weary debate that excited no one, not even those taking part. Above all this debate provided a forum for declarations of loyalty, spiteful taunts, the settling of old scores, toadying, exhibitionism, the repairing of reputations, ridicule, and a number of other, similar demonstrations of foolishness and immorality. Perhaps someone could be found who was able to read the book without prejudice—a young person with no interest in the conflicts of his father's generation and no desire to understand them, for example. But young people had no wish to read a work that had become—its incomprehensibility notwithstanding—the official book of the regime merely because its author was the son of the current president and a hero of the resistance. So perhaps the only person in the whole of North Floriana able to read Fernando's book for what it was, to understand it, to realize that the work was a crystalline growth of images born of the borderlands between the realms of nothingness and sense, was an old man who was indifferent to political discord. Such a person, however, if indeed he existed, did not step forward to bear witness to his reading.

But the governing party was loath to give up on the work of a national hero who had died in the struggle for freedom. By the circumstances of its genesis the work was bound to become a tool of propaganda; its actual content was of no great importance. It was necessary only to find in it some sentences and phrases that could be put to use when honors of state were being conferred, that could be chiseled into the plinths of memorials. These sentences and phrases were easily found: any phrase chiseled into marble will take on the meaning we require of it. Fernando's father was not resistant to such interpretations; although he knew them to be a violation of his son's work, he also knew that this violation was of no account; in the depot, Fernando must have foreseen the fate awaiting his book if ever the wire should be found, and without doubt he would have been utterly indifferent to it. But the elder Vieta, like everyone else, was mistaken in his view of the book. Although he knew the text of his son's novel by heart, he read it as a testimony that replaced his lost memories. In the cadences of its sentences he distinguished Fernando's movements, gestures and facial expressions, all of which he had known and forgotten; out of the flow of language there emerged, albeit faintly, other gestures he had never known. Thus, the currents and forces of language begot a false image of the son that he had never known.

TRANSLATED FROM CZECH BY ANDREW OAKLAND

NORA NADJARIAN

Exhibition

Chairs hang from the ceiling. Do not touch. They move themselves, not all the time, not all at the same time. So it's a bizarre effect when a chair, a wardrobe, a bed, seemingly decides to express itself. They hang by invisible wires from the beams and have pencils attached. Their motions write indecipherable messages on blank sheets beneath them: meaningless, desperate, like a memory, or a child's attempt at an alphabet, all over the place. Each one seems to have something to say: the longer you look at it, the more meaningful, the more insistent, the more enigmatic.

The one that spoke to me was the piano stool, the round, wooden, spinning one. I hadn't seen one of those since the days I used to sit next to my piano teacher, the formidably Russian Miss Nina. A red velvet cushion was placed under my little bottom to make me taller, my small fingers concentrated on Brahms's Waltz in G-sharp Minor while Nina repeated, *More! More open! More open! You are playing closed! You are playing like a cage!*

When she left me to pee, always a few minutes before the end of the lesson, I would swirl a full three hundred sixty degrees on the stool until she came back. I tried to play "more open" in the last five minutes just to please her, whatever playing open meant. I wanted to play round and round, open and opener, sharper and Majorer, but it all came out sad, flat, G, Flat, Minor.

And the trace made, on the white sheet, is a circle of lines that criss and cross as the stool spins and my little feet swing in and out.

The exhibition space is like a stage. *I would like to thank . . . I'd like to thank . . .* And the artist's tongue is tied, she can't remember who. The only person who comes to her mind is her father who used to pack and unpack his suitcase, all on the same day, without traveling anywhere. He would put all his clothes in, and his pipe, and his tobacco. Then he'd lock the suitcase and carry it all the way down the stairs, only to carry it back up again, into the bedroom, onto the bed. And open it. It was a ritual that reminded her that her father was alive, that he was there. She often wanted to slip a message into the suitcase when he wasn't looking: *Dad, I love you.* Or: *You have no idea how much I'll miss you.* Or: *Please don't go.*

The spotlight faces her like a full moon. It blinds her. And they all applaud because her exhibition has reminded them of things about their life that they had long forgotten. The piano stool, the table, the gramophone, the suitcase—all part of the past hanging from the ceiling into the present.

Somebody hugs her. It's her father, dead now for almost four years. He tells her he has read the catalog notes, that it finally now all makes some sense to him. *Thank you,* he says, *I packed my whole life into that suitcase, and there is no longer any need to unpack. I'm home. Finally, I'm home.*

The exhibition space is one street away from the Street of the Whores. The whore is cooking a stew with bay leaves, stirring in other spices from her rack, at random. The front door is open and the place smells divine. Any passerby would be tempted. Soon, there is a cockroach scratching its legs behind the gas cooker and there is a man sprawled on the sofa, wearing shorts and a stained singlet, and she is saying, *I'm coming, I'm coming.* They are a romantic couple, the whore, her client. Even a ménage à trois, if you count the cockroach.

She closes the door and starts taking off her clothes. A big, fat lump of nothing, that's what she knows she is. Her feet almost shuffle as she walks toward him in the dim pink light. She wants to tell him something indecipherable, something meaningless, something desperate about her life. But this is business, and business is business.

The whore's mother insisted on her deathbed that she had three daughters, not four. *No, no, the third one died when she was very young, I only have three daughters,* she declared. Her eldest daughter, the one with the perfectly shaped eyebrows, sat on a wobbly chair by her side, holding her hand all the time.

A long time ago the whore was a girl. *You can come and kiss me on a first-come, first-serve basis,* said the girl with fuchsia breath, and she smiled like the bold-colored flower that she was. She breathed onto their faces, watched them turn pink, red, fuchsia, fire, free.

There is always a beginning, and in the beginning, she sold kisses by the hour. Men came, men went. Gradually, slowly, time passed, life passed, they did strange things to her lips, mouth, nose, ears, hair, skin, turned her body inside out, outside in, smiled, swore, broke her, unbroke her, touched her, undressed her, dressed her, told her stories, bought her, sold her.

She is now a ghost of her former self in the dim pink light. She writes her autobiography in her head. The words are all there, the questions, too. *Tell me, did you once love me? No, I mean really love me. Tell me, did you think of me as a woman or as a whore? Do you still dream of me in fuchsia dreams, the girl I was, the girl I became? If you saw me now in the street, would you recognize me?*

She thinks of the man, sometimes. The man without a name. The man she loved. She loved him, but he insisted on paying her. He loved her, but wouldn't leave his wife for her. Long, long, long ago.

After the exhibition, the restaurant is full of literati and glitterati sipping chilled white wine. Snippets of conversation collide in the air. *Yes—*

absolutely incredible—I simply—did you?—purest materials—They couldn't possibly have—No, of course not —the raw one . . .

A mobile phone rings. The zipper of an enormous handbag opens, zzz-zzzzzzip, and then closes again, zzzzzzzzip, somebody talks to the phone and to the party at the same time, a pregnant woman coughs, a glass of water is knocked over.

It is mid-summer and there is a slight breeze. The candle on the table is blown out, the waiter reappears, apologizes, strikes a match, lights the candle, and retires again into the shadow, somewhere to the left of the palm tree. *The baby moved*, the pregnant woman whispers to her husband. *He moved*, she whispers again, and holds his hand.

The morning she finds out she's pregnant, the woman looks at the sky and smiles. It looks almost painted, she thinks. It could have been painted this morning. In nine months' time she will give birth to a son. He will be the most beautiful creature her eyes have ever seen.

But for now she admires the sky. It reminds her of a mural she once saw in Florence. She looks for the photo of the mural but she can't find it. She can never find the photo she wants, in the same way she can never think of the right word to complete a sentence. Instead, in an envelope in one of the drawers of her desk, behind a pile of old letters, she finds five photos. Five photos of her and her husband and a blue sky above their heads. Behind each of the photos, her small, neat handwriting says: Italy, 2005. Behind the sky, she thinks, is a date I had forgotten. On the other side of the sky is a date.

She is not in Italy but the sky is so blue. The sky is so blue, almost a blessing. Five photos of a blue sky, they lift her spirits. She lays them on the table in front of her, plays around with the order, arranges and rearranges her own private exhibition. She takes a deep breath, takes in the past, lets it meet her future.

The baby will grow up to become a man. But for now it is a fetus in the dark. His bones are still soft and pliable, he has not yet been fully formed but his life has started. His mother tells him his life has started, that he will have black hair like his father, that she has given him her green eyes.

There is a sunny spot in the garden, and this is where she stops, like a satisfied tourist, and talks to her unborn son about things he should know about herself and his father. Because we might change, she says, as you grow older. One day we will be different people, we may not even recognize ourselves in the mirror. One day, we may not be able to recognize you. So I want to tell you all this now. I love your father and he loves me. I love you as much as I love the blue, cloudless sky.

The baby moves slightly, it is as slight a movement as the blink of an eye, but enough for her to know that he's listening. *We made you,* she whispers to him, *a long time ago. You were born many years ago, in Italy.*

Days later the artist thinks there is something wrong with her, the way she sees the world all askew, the way she can't balance her feet when she's walking. Like a bird, she can't keep still on the ground. It's almost as if the road she's walking on doesn't exist anymore. But it was here yesterday, she mutters, to no one but herself. But I was here yesterday. Step by step, she thinks she is escaping reality. Her life is a figment of her imagination, playing tricks on her mind. Whenever she passes by a mirror she smoothes the worry lines, she smiles, tries to remember her face when it was younger.

On difficult, unbalanced days, she photographs graffiti or takes found objects home and polishes them like there's no tomorrow. Once she found a pebble. A pin. Part of a sponge, a shell, a broken light bulb, a shoelace, a receipt. She wanted to record the sound a pebble might make under her foot as it clicks against another. She wanted to make an asymmetrical sculpture, one that would inspire longing in people. The feeling of longing, the sensation that only those who have lost something would know about. *Excuse me, have you lost something?*

She wonders how long the road is back to her childhood. *But you can't go back*, said her father, *only forward*. Yet she longs for something. *For what?* asks her father. *I just long for*, she replies. *It's a state of being, longing for. Something.*

The bird lands, and hops. She feels that she is hopping from one place to another in the same city, like a homeless person, a nestless bird. Her father visits her in dreams and tells her: *You're making an exhibition of yourself.* She wants to make sculptures out of things people have lost. *I've lost a pin, a pebble, a coin, an eyelash, my heart, my mind. What are you longing for? What have you lost? When did you last see your heart? Did you pack the suitcase yourself? Please do not leave baggage unattended.* People always want an answer to make them feel good, she thinks. And she knows that when there is no reply to a question, it is considered an asymmetry.

She thinks of her mother. They went to church every Sunday, she lit candles. But her mother was discovered one afternoon, when her husband came home early from work, went up the stairs, and opened the door. The whole neighborhood held its breath. So you've been married to a whore all these years, they didn't ask. So your daughter might not even be your own, so nothing you know is true, so somebody pulls a carpet from under your feet, and you lose your balance. Look out, you're about to fall. And her father lost everything he thought he had, securely, in his hands, his head, his past, his present. Start packing, follow her, change your mind, unpack. You're a loser, a fucking loser, whose wife walked down some stairs and disappeared from his life. He sometimes wishes he'd come home early that night only to find that the lock on the door had been changed. Then everything would have been different. Then nothing would have happened.

The city hides its secrets. If you want to explore, walk in and out of the present, into the past, way back into the past, follow narrow paths and open doors to re-enter the present, to go round cement blocks, in and out of artificial lights.

I, the author of this story, am putting things in the right order or no order at all. I am trying to express in words how I was never able to play the piano openly. My playing was rigid, cemented. Nowadays I prefer to listen to c D s, and write. I am opening up in other ways, I suppose. I've found the key of the cage. I've discovered some words and I'm putting them together and I'm writing and writing.

The exhibition of the hanging chairs is still on. I went to see it again yesterday. There they were, all the seemingly random objects on seemingly random display, hanging from the ceiling. The whore's chair, the artist's father's suitcase, her mother's bed, Miss Nina's piano stool. I stood in the middle of it all, and I didn't know how long I spent listening to their stories, to the silence charged with their unearthly frequency.

Tonight there is a gecko on the wall, a tiny creature with tiny black eyes like beads, a transparent body. I want to keep it there for company, on my wall, forever, to illuminate it with a colored light. But it moves away, runs away from me, hides somewhere in the dark.

Miss Nina plays a nocturne by Chopin. I try to catch the music in my hands, I pretend to be playing it myself beautifully, faultlessly. I am seven years old. For once, Miss Nina does not speak. For once, I long for her to tell me off, to tell me I'm playing it all wrong. I long for her irritated voice, her Russian accent. But she says nothing at all. She turns the pages of the book and plays another nocturne and then another. I swirl three hundred sixty degrees on the stool next to her and finally I lose her, she's gone. All I have is the music in my head. C. Sharp. Minor. There is no book, no piano, no room.

Things shift from here to there and from there to here. The ghosts of the old town write their diaries. Please don't touch the exhibits, they move on their own.

MIMA SIMIĆ

My Girlfriend

My girlfriend is blind. If I wanted to I could fool around, or even have sex, with another girl, as long as we keep it down—with my girlfriend in the same room, boiling the kettle, microwaving popcorn, drying her hair.

When I come home from work she doesn't ask how my day was, she wants to know about the density of traffic, the progression of construction projects in the neighborhood, and what people on the bus talked about. She wants to know if my day was louder than usual.

Sometimes I won't go to work at all. I'll kiss her, shout good-bye at full volume, slam the door—and stay in. I'll hold my breath until she's turned her back to me. There's a good spot in the corner by the window where I can sit for hours; I situate my body downwind, for the draught to breeze my scent away. I synchronize my breath with hers, my chest doubling her chest, my lungs following hers around the room. She talks on the phone, sings along with the radio, dances a little perhaps, swinging her head like a hen pecking up grain in the yard. When she eats, crumbs fall around her like shredded confetti. She touches things to make sure, counts the tiles and her steps wherever she goes.

My girlfriend loves going to the movies. We sit in the love seat, hold hands, chomp on candy, drink soda, laugh as loud as anyone. When the movie ends we hurry to the toilets and listen to people talk about it. This gives her a rounder picture, she says. It's easier to figure out what she thinks about it. And on the way home she wants me to retell the movie, arrange the storyline neatly in sequence, describe it in detail. The actors, their faces, the silences. Especially the silences. She's taught me to watch movies as though my life depended on it. When we first started going out I used to give it my all—I'd bring a notepad, write it all down. Then reconstruct it for her meticulously, like a paleontologist putting together a dinosaur skeleton. This would excite her—we'd make love all night long, and then I'd go over the story again for breakfast.

Lately, though, making stuff up is far more exciting. I'll twist the story around, change the setting, the time, switch the relationships around, make them sexier, platonic, polyamorous, incestuous. Some might say this is cheating, but only the same sort of dull people who're always happy to explain the difference between love and make believe to you. Besides, she seems to enjoy my stories all the more since I've let them run wild. Now she wants to listen to them all night long. Her sex drive seems to have gone down too.

Before me, there were other boyfriends and girlfriends. Dozens, of all sorts. Maybe even black ones. Or a pair of twins, who took turns. Maybe some of the girls were actually boys anyway. I've seen pictures but it's hard to tell who or what these people are. They look pretty ordinary and rather indifferent: they could be her teachers, neighbors, brothers and sisters, or pasted-in cutouts from magazines, for all I know. They don't seem the least bit concerned, bothered, or distressed about posing. They don't need to make themselves pretty for her. Or maybe they too are blind. It's hard to tell when they're fixed on paper, when you can't see them dance, eat, or walk.

I don't know if she was born blind or if she got sick, or if she was in some kind of an accident. She never bothered to explain and the right moment to ask never seemed to come. Now, after four years, it's sort of too late—it would be too delicate to bring it up. Sometimes I could swear there must have been a time when her eyes worked—when I talk colors she pouts her lips as if she knows exactly what I'm talking about. But whenever I see her hen-dance again, I'm back to square one.

Most days, most of the time, my girlfriend stays at home. She likes to cook. She can tell how long something's been frying by the way it smells. They say when you're disabled your other senses get super-developed. When Gandhi was on that hunger strike for thirteen weeks, halfway through he started levitating spontaneously. People would come to him and ask him questions, like what they were thinking about, or what they had in their pockets. If it was food he always knew exactly what it was. My girlfriend's like that. That's why I wear one of her dresses, rub her cold cream into my face, and use her toothbrush whenever I decide to spend my office day watching her from the corner by the window.

When they hear my girlfriend is blind, people usually think right away about all the downsides of dating a blind person, like missing out on some of the best parts of being in a relationship—the exchange of meaningful looks, the foreplay of signals, the silent innuendo. I tell them we skipped that stage anyway. We met at a Halloween party. She was dressed as Daredevil, a visually impaired superhero, and I played along. The next day when I woke up next to her and she wouldn't drop the act, I figured what the hell. It's not like she's missing a limb. We kept in touch over the phone, I got used to her voice. We went for long walks, then a couple of concerts, but the thing really took off when we started going to the movies. Three shows later we were living together.

Even though she can't see herself, my girlfriend likes to make herself up when we go out. Sometimes I get a feeling she's flirting with other men, but I suppose I'm just being paranoid. Most of the time her eyes are as clear as bottled water and never wander around in their sockets—but what do I know.

Sometimes she asks me if I would stay with her if she got paralyzed, or got some rare tropical disease that would make her sleep all the time. Although I can't really imagine how she'd ever get herself into that kind of situation, I always say yes, and I mean it. My girlfriend is really good-looking; I'd be with her even if she was missing a limb.

The other day I found this story about a guy whose faith in God was restored when a blind man made him draw a cathedral. This story got me really excited; I thought reading it to my girlfriend might bring back our sex life. When we got into bed I took the book out, read the story to her slowly, sensually, and then asked her if she, too, wanted me to draw her a cathedral. In my hand I had a pen and on my lap a piece of thick paper that I'd prepared.

But my girlfriend, she just laughed—louder than I'd ever heard her laugh. She took my hand gently and with it drew the most perfect cathedral I've ever seen.

TRANSLATED FROM CROATIAN BY THE AUTHOR

Mima Simić 397

ALEK POPOV

Plumbers

Ich komm zum Glück / aus Osnabrück

The story unfolds in Osnabrück, a middle-sized German town in Lower Saxony, not far from the border with Holland. Dolph and Heidi are in the dining room of their spacious home on Lührmannstrasse. It is Sunday afternoon, sometime in the near future. The couple has been married for twenty-seven years, but have no children, or at least nothing indicates the presence of children. Dolph has just finished reading in the paper that, according to the latest sociological surveys, Osnabrück is the happiest town in Germany. He reads the news again, aloud.

"What does that mean exactly?" Heidi lifts her head. Her gray hair is cut in a severe bob. She has a thin straight nose and pale green eyes. Her breasts are still firm.

"It means, I suppose, that people living here feel happy," Dolph explains, adding with a sneer, "more than elsewhere in Germany."

"I wonder," starts Heidi, "which is the unhappiest place in Germany?"

"They don't say, probably because they don't want to ruin the real estate market . . ."

"Interesting. Do you think prices here are going to go up?"

"I wouldn't be surprised, yes, I wouldn't be . . ." Dolph rubs his hands together in delight.

Dolph is tall, dried out rather than thin, his jaw prominent and rectangular, same as his glasses. Dolph works in the agricultural division of the City Council. Over the years he's risen from a common gardener to a position as manager. At this stage, we have no idea about Heidi's occupation: could she simply be a housewife?

"What could they all be so happy about? Our town is very ordinary, it's not wealthy or even especially beautiful! It never gets very warm out even in summer, and it's always raining. I would understand if it was the people of Munich or Baden-Baden, for example, or . . ."

"But maybe that's precisely the reason. Happiness is in ordinary things."

Dolph gets up, passes behind his wife, reaches out to touch her hair but at the last moment changes his mind and withdraws his hand. He walks to the glass door leading out to the terrace and opens it. He looks outside. The neighboring houses and buildings are submerged in greenery, their balconies covered in flowers, their front lawns freshly mown. The air is full of the soft hissing of sprinklers. Birds are chirping. Dolph doesn't notice any of this, however; he has ears only for the moans coming from the house next door. There can be no doubt about the nature of these sounds. The moans are interspersed with outright cries that seem to reach higher and higher registers of pleasure, almost to the threshold of pain. Noises of this nature are a rarity in this neighborhood. In fact, Dolph realizes that this is the first time in his life he's ever overheard anything like this. The shock he feels is compounded by the knowledge Dr. Zeller had left that very same morning on a fishing trip with equipment and provisions for at least two days. Dolph had seen him go. He slams the terrace door shut and turns around to confirm with one quick look that Heidi too has heard the entire concert.

Her lips form an inexorable question: "How long has it been since *we* did it?"

"It's been some time." He tries the light approach, inside already preparing his defense, running like a hunted animal. "Three, four weeks, something like that . . ."

"It's been three years!" She accentuates every syllable.

"You're joking."

"Why should I joke about it?" Her expression confirms that it would be pointless to argue.

"Three years!" He waves his arm in an especially irritating theatrical manner. "You're certain about that? It doesn't feel like three years—maybe we have different ways of perceiving time. Maybe to you three months simply *feel* like three years, and vice versa. Maybe the truth is somewhere in the middle."

"No, there's a verifiable criterion here. Every year I purchase a new vibrator. I have acquired three since you last touched me. Every new one I buy is bigger than the last, too. I'm not attacking you. It is a simple matter of desire. I can't be mad at you for not wanting me."

A heavy silence follows.

"I'm not seeing anyone else . . . But do you want a divorce?"

"Why? As far as I'm concerned, it's the same everywhere."

"What do you mean everywhere?"

"Don't forget that women tell each other things. Inge, for example, told me that she and Karl haven't had sex for two years. Other couples say the same. Yes, Inge Zauer, precisely! I'm surprised too. They always looked so devoted to each other. So deeply in love . . . Remember the last time we saw them, we wondered how they managed it?"

"How many vibrators does she own?"

"She doesn't need them anymore."

"Has she found herself a lover? Poor Karl."

"Why would she do something like that to herself and her family? No, she's gone and joined the 'Matrimonial-Aid Program'—the so-called

'Plumbers.' I would have thought you'd know about it, it's a program run by the City Council."

"But I'm only responsible for gardening."

"Frau Müller is the coordinator, Johan's wife, from the Green Party, the one who was elected last year. The project's been running for a year already. If I find out you knew all about it and didn't tell me!"

"I swear, this is the first I've heard of it!"

"The program consists of a group of men invited by the local Health and Well-being Commission. They have temporary worker status and their task is to service female citizens in need of sexual attention. No, they are not male prostitutes! Don't be so crude! It's a social project—the service is free except for a symbolic consumer tax of one euro, with all other expenses covered by the Council budget."

"This is some kind of a joke, isn't it?"

"On the contrary, I don't know if similar programs have been started elsewhere, but if you think about it, this probably has something to do with the high level of happiness reported in our town."

"Perversion! Not only that, but a waste of Council funds! No wonder they're keeping it a secret."

"It's not a secret, it's simply not advertised. It's an intimate matter, after all."

"Very intimate, I see! You call, they come, they service you. It's exactly like calling someone to fix the pipes. Are they Polish?"

"Polish? How did you come up with that? I think they're from the Balkans."

"Primitives, then! That's what women like, of course."

"I agree it sounds a bit shocking at first. But if you think about it calmly, it's perfectly logical. If you look beyond the emotional stereotypes, which in practice cause nothing but trauma . . ."

"Never! Maybe I'm not some champion cocksman, but this is beyond the pale—you might as well spit on me here and now. Never! Find yourself an honest-to-goodness lover if you need it so bad. Just don't let me know anything about it! I'd divorce you in a second."

"Pathetic hypocrite!" she hisses.

And now some days have passed. It seems that Dolph has accepted the new situation. He appears to be perfectly composed and in control, despite that slight nervous tic in the left corner of his mouth, which, the marriage therapist has assured him, is completely normal. Being civilized doesn't mean being a robot, nobody expects him to act like a machine. Machines break down, which can be dangerous. On the other hand, people suffer, which can only be cathartic. Suffering is a normal human reaction.

And so, they are in the living room. Dolph rocks gently in his rocking chair with a glass in his hand. Opposite him, not so comfortably accommodated, sits a young, rather dark man, dressed neatly in a black suit, a white shirt, and no tie. He also holds a glass in his hand. The glasses are full of schnapps—a warm, homely drink which helps remove the barriers between people. The man is almost two heads shorter than Dolph, but is otherwise healthy and muscular. His name is Mr. Plumber. He speaks correct but inelegant German with a strong accent.

The two enjoy the following conversation:

"Herr Plumber, I wonder, what's the word for *plumber* in your native language?"

"Plumber."

"Ah, so even your name means *plumber*?"

"Yes, that's correct, Plumber."

"What an incredible coincidence. Did you know that they call people in your line of work 'Plumbers,' here? Plumbers! A bit rude, but quite appropriate, don't you think? So—where are you from, Herr Plumber?"

"From Bulgaria. There's a city called Sliven, that's where I'm from."

"Isn't it interesting, how over the years the actual work changes, but the names of the professions remain? Perhaps you have an ancestor who was actually a plumber?"

"Maybe a distant great-grandfather. My grandfather was a forester."

"Ah, a colleague of mine then. I am also in the green business. And what does your father do? Excuse my curiosity, but I'd like to get to know you better, under the circumstances. Considering what's about to happen, I think this is only normal."

"No problem, my father made charcoal."

"An ancient trade. Might I ask why you are not continuing in this noble family tradition?"

"It's quite simple. There's no more raw material to make charcoal. The woods are completely gone."

"Oh, so your grandfather wasn't vigilant enough."

"On the contrary, he wouldn't let anyone else but my father's family cut the wood. But everything ends one day. So here I am."

Heidi enters, wearing a black see-through nightgown. "I'm ready."

Plumber rises to his feet. "I'm ready too."

Dolph turns the glass between his fingers nervously. "Is it really all so urgent? I have the right to learn one or two things after all."

"Naturally," she says, trying to calm him down, "we're in no hurry."

Heidi sits on the armrest of the sofa, discreetly baring her knee. Dolph shoots a disapproving look in her direction, shakes his head, and continues:

"Are you married, Herr Plumber, do you have children?"

"Yes, I have a wife and four children."

"Four no less! Not that I'm surprised. Is your wife acquainted with the nature of your occupation here?"

"She doesn't mind, if that's what you're asking. As long as I send home the euros."

"You seem to be the responsible type, Herr Plumber. Again, excuse my curiosity, but how did you manage to come by this position? Was it because you were seen to fill a certain quota, or did you win some kind of competition? How was the selection organized, exactly?"

"It wasn't at all simple. One needs to satisfy numerous requirements. My two older brothers were disqualified. Maybe the third would have been selected but he has two more years to serve in prison. Plus, he's uneducated, and we all had to take extensive language tests."

"One last question: How many times a day do you find yourself servicing the pipes of our fair housewives?"

"Now how is that any of your business?" Heidi chips in nervously.

"I don't mind. On average ten times a day, except Sunday, unless there's emergency duty. Of course, there are days when it's quieter. Maybe there's just less interest on certain days, or the men here get more active once in a while. I don't know."

"One thing I don't understand, how do you manage to get it up every time? Aren't there glitches sometimes?"

"I see what you're trying to do! You're unfair!" shouts Heidi.

"Yes, it's happened, two, maybe three times. I'm not a machine after all. I call a colleague to replace me. There's always someone on emergency duty. It's normal."

"Normal? You call this normal? Are you hearing this? You're going to let yourself be seduced by this Balkan barbarian, by this monkey, by this bull who gets it up for everyone in town? You're going to give your body to this man? Give your . . ."

"Please excuse us, Herr Plumber, I'm so embarrassed." Heidi wrings her hands in desperation. "I feel like I'm listening to my great-grandmother. I thought we had agreed."

"Please don't worry, ma'am, I've passed through extensive psychological training. Many husbands react similarly. It's quite normal. The opposite reaction would be rather disturbing."

"You're really too kind. Dolphy, why don't you go and have a beer with Karl, that would be for the best, don't you think? But only if you want to—

I'm not asking you to leave. Inge's told me that Karl is often present when her plumber calls, and even holds her hand. I think, though, that that would be a bit much."

Heidi and Plumber walk into the bedroom. Dolph is left alone. The bed starts to shake. Heidi's moans fill the air and they bear a striking resemblance to those of Andrelle next door.

Ironically, this is Dolph's most sacred sexual fantasy. How many times has he masturbated to the daydream that some stranger is having his way with his wife while he sits nearby, holding her hand? But now, when it's really happening, he feels nothing but helpless rage. The shaking intensifies and so do the moans. Dolph claps his hands. "Bravo! Bravo! It almost resembles an orgasm, darling! It sounds very authentic! You're such a fine actress. You can't fool me, though! I know you don't feel anything. You're completely frigid! How many years did I waste trying to do you some good! In the end, I threw up my hands, I gave up! It's like pouring water into a broken jug—pointless. You're wasting your energy, Herr Plumber, she doesn't feel anything! Nothing!"

Heidi starts screaming. Dolph covers his ears and flees the house. Outside, it's just stopped raining. Thick white mist is rising from the moist ground. Dolph wanders through the haze until he reaches the playground, where Karl Zauer, Inge's husband, and Pastor Farb are playing pétanque. The game is a recent fad, undoubtedly imported from France. At first received with skepticism, it accumulated quite a few, mostly male aficionados over the years. Karl is slightly younger than Dolph. Farb and Dolph are the same age; they may even have attended the same school. Farb has now won several games, which means that Karl has to make a trip to the supermarket to buy beer. Dolph and Farb are soon alone on the playground, an island in the white mist.

"I've been meaning to talk to you for a while." The pastor places his small white hand on Dolph's shoulder. "I know this hasn't been easy for you . . ."

"What have you heard, Father?"

"People have been talking. But I don't believe it. Dolph, I tell them, could not have done something like that. I've known him since we were kids—he has a heart. He's not a cynic, he is not an egotist. After all, all our parks and flowerbeds are his creation. He wouldn't leave his son out on the street . . ."

"What?"

"What do you mean 'what'? Would Dolphy leave Brüno on the street, I ask them? But you know how it is in a small town. We're a close-knit community. Everyone knows everyone. People are interested in each other. Not out of empty curiosity, mind you—they really want to try and understand something about themselves by looking at the lives of others. If for no other reason than to draw useful conclusions."

"Nothing happened, Father. He just left. He moved out immediately after high school. It's quite normal. It's even healthy, I would say. I myself got a place of my own when I was eighteen. No one blamed my father for that."

"No one is blaming you."

"In fact, I have no idea where Brüno might be. Everything happened so quickly. Maybe he's gone to Poland? Though what would he do there? I just don't know. Maybe he's married. He hasn't called even once. Frankly, we've been quite upset."

"I can't believe that you don't know! He lives under the bridge by the river. He's been there for three months."

"He's back? Living under the bridge? Why didn't anyone tell me?"

"He's officially registered at the City Council as a homeless person."

"You're joking, Father, we don't have homeless people in Osna."

"Now we do. It's not such a terrible thing. We can afford it, so long as your boy doesn't start a trend. Social Services are actually rather happy—they have something to do, now. This will keep them from being downsized. Brüno has already been awarded a little financial aid, a mattress, and a sleeping bag. They've also given him a medical exam card. We're also keeping an eye on him up at the church. There's nothing to worry about."

"To embarrass us like this in the eyes of the whole town! As if we didn't have enough worries!"

"I don't believe he's doing it to embarrass you. I had the chance to talk to him—he seems to me to be a remarkably intelligent and responsible man. He has traveled the world, he has experienced a lot. He's seen both good and bad. And he's impressively well read. There's no reason to feel ashamed of your son."

"Why didn't he come back home?"

"That I don't know. Just like I don't know the reason why he left in the first place. I can only guess that he's a typical young man—highly emotional, always wanting to rebel and explore. But the years pass and as one matures one needs a better reason for one's behavior. So in this, maybe you're right to worry; not so much about why he left, but about why he hasn't returned home. The reason must be very serious. I suggest you take a good look at yourself and your family. How are things at home? Your relationship with Heidi? I know it must be difficult, after so many years . . ."

Dolph blinks vacantly. The shaking of the bed and Heidi's moans suddenly rush back into his head. This continues for a few seconds, maybe even minutes, during which he sees Farb's lips moving but hears nothing of what the pastor is saying.

Karl returns from the supermarket with a pack of Heineken under his arm.

"Who wants beer?"

After a few sips, Dolph comes back to his senses. "Karl, why haven't you told me that Brüno's living under the bridge? Why do I have to hear about it from strangers?"

"I'm a stranger now?" Farb is offended.

"I was too uncomfortable to bring it up. It's a private family matter, after all. It could seem one way on the outside but different on the inside. I don't like to stick my nose into things I don't understand."

"The pastor implies that our family situation might have something to do with my son's decision to be homeless."

"I can't believe that—you and Heidi are such a wonderful, civilized, and tolerant couple. How could you possibly have steered him in that direction?"

"Thank you. You and Inge are a wonderful couple too and we're always pleased when you come to visit us. In fact, we've always wondered how you've managed to keep your relationship so warm and close for . . . how many years now?"

"Twenty-three."

"Now, that's worth a toast. *Prost!*"

"*Prost!*"

"So, do you really hold Inge's hand while she's being plumbed?"

The beer goes down Karl's throat the wrong way and he begins to cough uncontrollably.

"Very touching. I myself wouldn't be able to do it. How many times a week does he come by?"

"Who?" Karl continues to cough.

"Your plumber. Ours is actually called Plumber, which also means plumber in his language. Can you imagine? So, what's yours called? Where is he from?"

"I don't know, I don't know! We haven't talked."

"What a laugh it'll be if it turns out that Inge and Heidi share the same plumber."

"What plumber?" Farb is agog. "I don't understand what's going on."

"Really? That surprises me. You've never been too shy about butting in on other people's business."

"Now that's enough, Dolphy, Pastor Farb's wife passed away four years ago! There's no reason for him to know. It's not something people talk about openly . . . Everyone deals with it the best they can."

The mist surrounding the playground seems to recede for a moment.

"Ha, there's one of them over there!" shouts Dolph, pointing. "Do you see him sneaking along the wall? Never looking around? I wonder if he's my guy. Hey, Herr Plumber! Come over for a beer! No, he's not going to stop—they're like robots. Haven't you noticed them, Father? They criss-cross the whole town, tiny but strong, short legs with long bodies, always freshly shaved, dressed in black, quiet, taking long strides?"

"Yes, I have noticed them! I thought they were chimney sweeps. I even thought of asking one of them over to check on my fireplace, it's been smoking terribly all year."

"Ha! Chimney sweeps! Why not? It's just a question of terminology. Somewhere they might be called chimney sweeps. Do you remember the scandal in France? Would there have been so much noise if they were simply called chimney sweeps?"

"Honestly, I don't understand a thing here."

"Karl, why don't you enlighten the father?"

"Why me? Christ, I don't know . . . One day Inge came to me and said, 'My darling Karl, I am so happy with you. I believe we are a perfect match. I could watch you for hours building those little birdhouses of yours. The love you lavish on their decorations! How you elaborate every detail. I wish I was a bird, sometimes, when I see you working, so I could live in one of your fairy-tale homes. Darling, darling Karl . . . I know you would do anything for me. But I don't want to ask anything of you, you've already given me so much. I want you to ask it *for* me, because it's something women badly need. Call it a weakness, an imperfection, whatever you like . . . But this is how we are. Perhaps one day we may be able to overcome this fatal physiological addiction by force of will. We may be able to reach such exalted levels of consciousness that we won't need such things anymore. Yes, I dream of the day when we may stand side by side, free, equal, and pure—

Alek Popov **409**

like brother and sister. Unfortunately, that day is still distant and in the meantime nature makes its demands. My darling Karl, the last thing I want to do is to turn you into a tool, an instrument of masturbation. You go on making your birdhouses, don't worry about a thing. I spoke with Frau Müller, the wife of the deputy, and she shares my feelings exactly.' 'I know,' Frau Müller told my wife, 'that if I demand it of Johan without his really needing it, then sooner or later I will lose his respect. I wouldn't even be surprised if he started hating me, the way one would resent being sentenced to hard labor! No, the ship of marriage should not be propelled by slaves chained to their oars. Let it sail freely, carried by the wind! People evolve, their interests change. Some needs are forgotten, others replace them: this has always been the case. That's why, instead of creating drama, instead of hurting each other, instead of looking for mechanical substitutes or becoming involved in dubious affairs that could ruin our delicate psychological balance, it would be easier if we found some sort of mechanism, came up with a solution—as mankind always has when faced with insurmountable difficulties—that could, once and for all, relieve us of these pressures . . . us and our beloved partners both.' "

"What's on your mind, Father? You're so deep in thought."

"I was remembering my late wife Hedwig."

"Excuse me for saying so, but one could say that you're fortunate."

"You're talking nonsense, as usual. I miss her so much. I remember how we used to sit in front of the fire on cold winter evenings. We would talk about books, theater. At the time there was a young theater director visiting, Sebastian Hirn if I'm not mistaken. A real devil! The liberties he took on stage! But she always defended him. She was very liberal. Sometimes we would just sit quietly and watch the fire. I held her hand. We would sit like that for hours. At some point, she would sigh, she would get up slowly, as plump as she was, and she would bring out some of her homemade kirsch, along with pieces of her plum cake. Ah, that cake. I've still never tasted anything more delicious."

"You don't miss anything aside from the cake, the kirsch, and the conversations?"

"You filthy, soulless reptile! What do you know about warmth, closeness, intimacy? Yes, I performed my marital duties, if you're so interested! But I never let that part of my life dominate the rest."

"If you were telling the truth, your wife would probably still be alive."

"My wife died of cancer!"

"It's either cancer or the plumbers. That's our choice."

"Cancer or the plumbers!" Karl repeats enthusiastically, jumping around like a frog. "Cancer or the plumbers! Cancer or the plumbers!"

"Idiots! You're not only impotent, but proud of it as well!"

"You're no more potent than we are! It's just that you're a widower, so nobody's asking about you."

"Go to hell, the both of you!"

The pastor grabs the pétanque balls and starts throwing them at his friends. Dolph and Karl run in opposite directions. Farb pries another beer from the pack and sips it silently while he too is slowly engulfed by the mist.

Under the bridge over the River Hase, at night. A young man of around thirty sits wrapped in a sleeping bag, reading in the light of a camping lantern. The man is big but out of shape; he wears glasses and is beginning to lose his hair. Next to him is a pair of tall yellow boots blackened by mud. This is Brüno. We hear the voice of Dolph, who appears shortly thereafter out of the bushes lining the riverbank.

"Son! My son! Brüno! Ah, there you are. Why didn't you respond? Look, I'm not here to yell at you. I just wanted to see how you were doing. I heard you were back. You're my only son, after all. I care about what happens to you. I care more than you can imagine. Aren't you going to say something?"

"Good evening, Father."

"Ah, at least that's something. Thank you. As I can see, you've made yourself comfortable here. You're lacking for nothing. The river is rolling, the leaves are whispering, the birds are singing. It's . . . fresh. Osnabrück is a very green town, as you know. I'm not bragging, but I had a little something to do with that! All these paths, bushes, trees, fountains. I gave my best years to this town. So that one day it might be called 'the garden of Westphalia.' You know, according to recent sociological surveys, this is the happiest town in Germany. My home is my garden! Yes, one must always live one's life in such a way that your son always has the option to become homeless! Or even you yourself . . ."

"I think you're drunk."

"Maybe I am—drunk with happiness. While I was walking out this way, I finally saw the sense behind what I've been doing my whole life. When I was looking at all those plants I've cared for, planted with my own hands. I told myself that my effort has not been in vain—now my son can live in a garden. He's who I've been preparing this all for. Only one thing worries me. Aren't you lonely? Don't you feel the need for some company?"

"I have a dog. It's gone for a walk somewhere, but it'll be back soon."

"I mean a human. A close companion. A woman?"

"I'm fine like this. I borrow books from the library and I read."

"Of course. I'm not going to intrude. Live according to your own principles. I only want you to know that you are always welcome back home. If you feel lonely, there's always a place for you with us."

"Thank you, but I wouldn't want to disturb your sex life."

"What?"

"I know that my presence disturbs you. I heard you two talking once, saying that your sex life was never the same after I was born. Is that true? Since you weren't able to shout and make noises like you used to do. You said children are the murderers of sex . . ."

"Nonsense!"

"Do you remember my graduation trip to Munich? I didn't feel like going with those idiots, so I lied to them. I told them I had diarrhea and came back home. I immediately felt that something wasn't right. The house was strangely quiet, the curtains were drawn. Some crazy music was coming from inside. I sneaked through the garage door. You were sitting in the living room with Mother and Karl and Inge Zauer. There were candles everywhere, bottles, Indian incense. All four of you were naked. Condoms were hanging from your and Karl's . . ."

"Enough! Enough!"

"Enough what? At that moment I really did get diarrhea and ran to the toilet in the garage, where I spent the night. And then I spent the next morning cleaning that toilet. Since then it's always been the same for me . . . whenever I'm in a situation where a normal person would start crying, I just get diarrhea."

"I'm sorry. A horrible mistake. Nothing happened though, believe it or not. Karl couldn't get it up, and I thought it wouldn't be fair if I was the only one to profit from the situation. I am so very sorry. Now I understand why you left us, and maybe you were right to. You must have been disgusted. I don't remember quite how we organized that little get-together. Maybe we were looking for variety. You have no idea how family life tires one out. We didn't try to repeat it though. Karl and Inge are, of course, still our friends— we're civilized people, we still invite them over . . . but only for barbecues."

Dolph shakes his head. He dries his face. "What the hell is this, I'm all wet . . ."

"Someone is pissing from the bridge. When they start coming out of Lagerhalle this is their favorite entertainment." The trickle is still dripping down. Dolph steps aside.

"*Scheisse*! Barbarian! Stop that! People live here."

"*Ebi se u glavu!*" says a confident voice from above. "Fuck yourself in the head," in Serbian.

"Not a German, of course! What we're made to put up with! And all because our young people hate working with their hands. It all leads to disgraces like this. I'm not saying anything against you, but what's going to happen if everyone else decides to sit under a bridge all day?"

Loud barking in the distance.

"I think it's best you leave now," yawns Brüno. "My dog is coming back. It's not used to strangers and sometimes reacts aggressively. Don't say I didn't warn you. Come back again when it's gone. I would be happy to see you."

The approaching bark fills Dolph with an inexplicable and almost supernatural terror. He steps backward while looking at the silver face of the moon showing over the bridge. He trips over some kind of a root, sways, and falls into the river. He crawls back out on his hands and knees, wet and covered in mud. He gets to his feet and bolts into the night, leaving a slimy trail behind.

Now we move to the town cemetery. It is a dark, cool morning at the beginning of June. Fresh smell of green and dirt. In the middle of a trimmed lawn gapes a black rectangular hole. Next to it lies a coffin of pale wood. Gathered round it is a small group of mourners. Among them we observe Dolph, Heidi, and Frau Müller the wife of the Green Party deputy. She is a head taller than everyone else and somewhat resembles Marlene Dietrich. She seems particularly distressed, constantly drying the corners of her eyes with an elegant handkerchief. In the coffin are the remains of Inge Zauer, brutally butchered by her husband Karl. The neighbors saw him trying to bury parts of the body in his backyard: an elderly couple who had just officially announced they were leaving on vacation, though they were actually planning to proceed with a joint suicide. Disturbed by what they had just witnessed, they decided to postpone their plans and call the police.

The entire town was stunned by the murder. Despite his pleas, Karl has not been allowed to attend the funeral, forbidden by Inge's sister. Inge and Karl's son, who lives in Hamburg, refused to attend. The humble ceremony is officiated by Pastor Farb, who married the couple many years before.

After the coffin sinks into the ground, the crowd begins to disperse. Only Frau Müller and Inge's sister stay behind. One gets the impression that the two women have different reasons to mourn. Frau Müller's eyeliner is surprisingly resistant to tears.

"Would you like to go for a walk?" Heidi asks Dolph.

Dolph accepts with a nod. The two turn quietly into a side path leading through some trees and follow it to a wide meadow covered with tombstones and bright wild flowers. This is the children's cemetery, for children up to twelve years old, most of them unchristened. Among the stones are perched colorful animal figures cut out of metal, the same figures one often sees at playgrounds— sheep, bears, cows, horses alongside large spotted mushrooms. At the sight of them Heidi exclaims:

"How distasteful!"

"Maybe money from some council program needed to be allocated somewhere." Dolph doesn't fully share his wife's indignation. Deep down he finds the arrangement consoling. Nevertheless, he immediately agrees to raise the subject at the next session of the Environmental Commission, for which he serves as secretary.

While listening to the gravel crunching under his feet, he wonders to himself if he should tell his wife about his meeting with Brüno. He feels the substance of that event is still eluding him, as if the whole thing had been a dream. He's afraid she would ask him about their conversation, and he isn't quite sure what he could tell her.

In the end he simply announces: "Brüno has returned."

"I know. Inge told me, before Karl cut her up."

"And you didn't tell me?"

"I thought you knew."

"If I knew, I would have told you. What do you take me for? Have you spoken to him?"

"No, but I've seen him. He just sits there, under the bridge. There's a bench on the opposite bank of the river. I often sit there and watch him eat or read or wash his feet. There's usually a big dog with him. It doesn't look too friendly. To be honest, that's why I haven't gone up to talk to him."

"I know why he left."

"Yes, I suppose he doesn't like us and will go on not liking us. But does it really matter? We don't like each other either. Maybe that's precisely what he's trying to teach us . . ."

Imperceptibly, it had started to rain. Dolph senses that Heidi is thinking about sex. The tips of her fingers are trembling in his palm.

On their way back home, the two pass by the bus stop at the bottom of Bergstrasse, where they first met many years ago. Every time he passes by this spot, Dolph tries to remember what he told Heidi then, but nothing precise comes to mind. With the years, the design of the bus shelter has changed several times, as often as the schedule of the bus. Today, only the No. 36 stops here, on its way to the train station. On the bench in the bus shelter sits a solitary figure squashed between two enormous suitcases. The couple passes on, but after a few steps Dolph turns back.

"Herr Plumber! Is that you? Where are you headed?"

The man stands nervously, not accepting Dolph's outstretched hand.

"I'm going back home."

"But why?"

"They shut down the program. There's been talk since the incident . . . The others have already left. I waited until the last moment, but today it was officially voted to terminate our contracts. They gave us a small severance compensation, so I can't complain."

"I'm sorry, prejudices are hard to kill off, even in the most civilized societies. Please forgive my emotional outburst at our first meeting. It was human, I know, but after all that's happened, I feel particularly ashamed."

Plumber is awkward, silent. Heidi's figure continues its lone climb up the steep street.

"Were you Inge's plumber? We were close family friends, that's why I'm asking."

"No, it wasn't me. She was plumbed by Fikret, from Pristina. He was the first to leave."

"It really doesn't matter now. Did you buy a present for your wife, Herr Plumber, for when you see her?"

"Well, yes . . ." mumbles Plumber in embarrassment.

"What did you get, if I might ask?"

The bus pulls up just then and Herr Plumber starts fussing with his luggage. Dolph helps him load it on board. Suddenly, one of the suitcases springs open and toys start pouring out—Barbie dolls, Transformers, water pistols . . . and a big pink dildo tied with a purple ribbon. Plumber turns as red as a tomato and rushes to gather his things. The rest of the passengers on the bus pretend not to have seen anything. Dolph leans over, picks up the dildo, and ceremoniously—as if it was a wedding bouquet—hands it back. The doors close and the bus pulls away. Dolph is left standing in the bus shelter, his hand still outstretched.

"My God," he thinks. "This surely is how Prometheus felt when he gave fire to Mankind."

TRANSLATED FROM BULGARIAN BY KRISTINA KOVACHEVA

GORAN SAMARDŽIĆ

Varneesh

In this story, which is simply stifling me in its desire to get out, I see my-self sitting at an enormous table, covered with a waxed tablecloth. The food is virtually pouring off the edges. They've had to squeeze it together tightly to get it all on. There's so much drink and food that it occurs to me that it can't all have been paid for honestly. There is even, in front of me, a bottle of cognac, still in its box, with CAMUS (Produce of France) written on it, and a crisply roasted suckling pig with eyes shut tight, their lashes still in place. This overdone carcass's little legs are painfully contorted, as though the agony of its slaughter has not yet worn off. I pull the pig apart with my bare hands and throw pieces onto the nearest plates. All that will reach the people at the far end of the table, well away from me and there-fore of lesser importance, will be the aroma. The richest foods, the most expensive, have all been shoved toward me, and hardly a minute passes without my being offered something else. I've unbuttoned my shirt and Bermudas to give my stomach room to spread. It's not quite an hour since I started eating. My jaws, canines blunted by evolution, keep on crunch-ing monotonously. They even grind the bones. Everything that finds itself between my two rows of neatly flossed teeth is flattened, crushed, punc-tured. It's like killing that pig all over again as I chew it, I think.

This food and drink piled in several layers onto the table has been brought into the courtyard and set out in honor of myself and my girlfriend, who is seated nearby, gazing at me adoringly. She's afraid that, if she so much as blinks, I'll disappear. The vortex into which I leapt from our balcony and so saved a little life had rekindled her love for me and increased, or rather, restored my value. Stars shine from the sky, and candles from the earth. I was present last month when a workman accompanied by the police cut off the cable bringing stolen power into this courtyard. Three generations of people whose forebears had been brought here from India on the wings of geese crawled out of their basement and stood and watched a thing with a hooklike beak bite into a cable as thick as my little finger. The cable had been cunningly hidden for years, connected to the nearby streetlight. Its camouflage had been removed by crows. The black birds used to fly over our courtyard in clouds. In the end, their actions proved just as sinister as their appearance. They pecked through the cable's covering and revealed it at last for all to see.

I was on the balcony at the time, working out with a punching bag. All sorts of exercise props were strewn about me. The place of honor was occupied by an enormous metal weight that had begun to be devoured by rust. It always amazed me that I didn't fall right through the floor when I lifted it. The explosive echoes of my punches now spread in all directions. In my head I was hitting the workman with the pincers, and then especially that huge enforcer of law and order who'd come along with him, truncheon and pistol buried in his flab. There was still half an hour before my girlfriend came home from work. She didn't like watching me sweating and training and disturbing the order of the house. She liked to think that my figure and my muscles just came naturally, and weren't the result of hard work.

It was no use to my neighbors, however, beneath my feet, buried up to their waists in the earth (in the basement), of whom there was one more every year, that I was rebelling internally and fighting against the state. At that time, when human and civil rights were vaguely intimated rather than known about, any public expression of discontent was likely to end with a rubber truncheon to the head. Unlike today's police, the militia then used less paper and more force.

No, it was something else entirely that changed my relationship with the courtyard-tribe, and it happened one rainy night, a month and a half before the gala feast. For hours before the rain came, my girlfriend and I— each on our own side of the bed—had been melting from the heat. We were trying to breathe our way out of it, panting. Many tenants had taken folding beds out onto their balconies and were hoping to fall asleep under the stars. The sun burned down from above by day and then the moon by night.

We touched each other with the tips of our toes and fingers—closer contact would've been a health hazard: we didn't dare embrace and double the heat! We had pushed our bed toward our balcony so that we were half in and half outside. Our neighbors were babbling, snoring, moaning. There were also these mournful, long drawn-out farts, unbelievably exaggerated by the acoustics of the courtyard. Everything living in the building and around it (dogs and cats) sighed and suffered in the same way.

I conjured up autumn and winter in my mind. An idyll in which I lit a fire and wrapped my girlfriend, my final love (I always think that), into a blanket. My girlfriend was pregnant. My sperm had found a way into her, despite all our highly scientific precautionary measures—as though it were a corrosive acid and not a warm, slimy substance whose surplus I even expel from myself in my sleep, from time to time. Yes, I had somehow overcome all obstacles and managed to swim into the most secret—and, in our case, or so we'd thought, the most secure—chamber of the female body. For me, this was exciting, seductive; for her, alarming. I was truly impressed by my tenacious little tadpole worm: heart no bigger than the period at the end of a sentence. But, in any case: while her stomach was still beautifully flat and attractive, we knew it was no longer empty. The mechanics of our sex, its swaying, riding, rolling, or slow thrusting, had escaped our control, and hidden away a little future surprise for us.

Thinking about winter cooled me down a little and I rolled over to my girlfriend. I found my way into the parting beneath her belly button. The hairs around it were shaved in the shape of an equilateral triangle. They were just long enough to prick me. Her familiar sex accepted me wearily and released thick moisture as though to order. Encouraged by this perfectly slippery substance, whose viscosity could outdo engine oil, I hurried into its depths, and, to this day I don't know how or why, came right away. My girl pushed me off her like some useless sack that had been weighing her down and told me to go to hell. "You can stuff cabbages with that thing from now on—not me, you bastard!" "Forgive me. I'll be right back, just going to have a smoke." "Yeah, you know exactly where you can go!"

We lay naked and crucified on the bed, with our feet virtually in the courtyard, and prayed to God to take us into some other, cooler age. The groans, sighs, and curses from various balconies had merged into a monotonous drone. You couldn't tell who was breathing (or where) or what they were saying. A general mumbling, a dull animal wail for just one breath of fresh air or a single drop of rain, filled the square well formed by our buildings, whose bottom was dry. The bottom of the well was the courtyard.

I smoked and blew the smoke over the balcony from the bed. It seemed to me that the light of the cigarette made the heat even worse. Three meters away, in a niche without a plastic curtain, my girlfriend was taking a shower. The cold water exploded angrily onto her taut, smooth skin. The little drops reached almost as far as me. I watched her indifferently until, inclined to fantasy as I am, I began to imagine that she was someone else's woman. I imagined a man, quite unknown, going into the shower and smacking her naked rump, his hand bouncing off her tight skin, not sinking into it. I just didn't know what to do about the baby in her! She had already entered her third month. A heart like a little signal flare was quivering inside the fetus. That was my child. A knocking on the door of the world to open up—for him, or her. I was old enough to have made myself a replacement me, just in case.

There's no more ungrateful creature than the male, especially if he's human and especially if he's me. Three years earlier I had used every trick I could think of to get her. By the time she woke one morning, warm and contented, her legs wrapped round one of mine, and looked around, unused to finding me beside her and my things scattered around her room, she was mine. I decided not to let go of that little piece of her that I had conquered (a woman gives, apparently, while a man conquers). Afterward, the excitement wore off. Our balloon of happiness began to shrivel. The little piece of her I had taken grew into a great lump, and it began to smother me. Quarrels turned into fights (her hitting, me trying to defend myself), fights into caresses. And so on for years . . . Balkan-style.

As I watched her, imagining what someone who wasn't me would do for her and how much he would love her, the square of sky above our buildings was rent by lightning, confirmed afterward by an immense clap of thunder. A sponge had been spread over our square of sky and it was being squeezed. Water began to pour through the dry gutters, still hot from the day. The heavy rain put out my cigarette butt, thrown through a window, in mid-air. People on the balconies woke up, flustered (those who had managed to fall asleep). I pulled on my underpants and jumped from the bed onto the balcony. I shouted something inarticulate, without any specific meaning, just to announce that I was happy and alive. Something naked came up behind me, out of the dark, and put its arms around me—my girlfriend. "Idiot, what on earth are you shouting about, eh?" she whispered. "Well, it's raining," I said as though no one apart from me had realized. She was fresh. She didn't smell of shampoo, but of herself. I hid her body with mine so that the neighbors hanging over their balconies wouldn't see her naked, and with my arms twisted backward pressed her to me (stuck her to me, that is). I rested my hands, roughened from punches and weights, on her protruding hemispheres. "Oh sweet, naked creature, who is making something in her belly, how could I have thought that you had begun to bore me and that I didn't love you?" I wondered to myself. Tuning into the current of my thoughts, she pushed her hands into my underpants. Everything I had under my navel fit into them. She was touching me. The signal from my brain that I was aroused hadn't reached down there yet. It was only later that down there got hard and peered out of the cage whose bars were her warm fingers.

And so, connected to each other by our hands and wetness, we fell onto the bed again and began to make love. Our two bodies made contact and fused at our mouths and sexual organs. From outside came the scent of soil imprisoned in asphalt. The spindly little tree growing in the middle of the courtyard, where the concrete had broken away to remind us that it was only an artificial deposit upon the earth, and not the earth itself—was bathed in rain. When I told her, just as we reached our climax, that I loved her, she did not hear me through the noise of the rain. The downpour had already reached a tempo that indicated that it would go on raining for a long time. Our neighbors had withdrawn into their hanging caves and were sleeping; cats, dogs and the other creatures that shared our life in the town . . . at the last minute, all of us had been saved by the water.

I woke some time before dawn. To my delight it was still pouring with rain out. The sky was drenching the town with great skill. The relief that the rain had brought had now changed into an enduring pleasure. Conditions in our room, building, neighborhood, town had again become livable. I had fallen asleep on top of my girlfriend. My back was being cooled by the freshness of the air, the little breeze from her nostrils tickled my neck. She was simply stuck to me. Especially to what was inside her. In my sleep my sperm had turned into glue. I thought of ancient buildings, their blocks of stone held together with egg white.

I slowly parted her legs and gradually withdrew from her. A reflex of selfishness, which people call love, woke her and she drew me back. She had interpreted my hardness as early morning arousal.

"I have to go to the bathroom, my love," I whispered as softly as possible.

"Be sure to come right back!"

"Okay."

In my sleepy, tottering state, the journey to the bathroom was long. I stepped into the shower, where my girlfriend had been, where I had imagined her in an embrace with someone else. Something cracked under my foot, followed by two—one after the other—under my other foot. I was already aiming at the hole I knew how to find by heart, when a shower of something dry scattered over my head and shoulders. Each hard drop weighed several grams.

I turned on the light and suddenly saw, in all their vileness, in their incalculable number, the only thing that revolted me in the world—cockroaches. I shrieked and leaped out of that center of repulsion, my wobbling cock still dripping. My girlfriend, immunized against disgust by being in the medical profession, woke up and immediately began to shake and bounce off our bed with laughter. She found it delightful and terribly strange that I too was afraid of something. I wiped my bare feet, filthy with crushed cockroaches, on the carpet and swore explosively. Our building was old and damp. Its inhabitants weren't exactly the cleanest. There was room here for bugs and people both.

The light finally drove away our unwanted neighbors (black, with shiny armor and bare legs), who outnumbered the human variety a hundred to one, and I remembered that I still had to piss. I went out onto the balcony and sent a warm arc down. The liquid from me merged with the water from the sky. The sound of my issue blended into the general sound of pattering, splashing, dripping. And then some devil, or whatever you want to call it, persuaded me to direct my jet onto the roof of the shed, which—though I didn't know this yet—our underground neighbors had taken over and made into a room. So many of them had been born in the basement that they'd run out of space; they had begun to squeeze each other out through the windows and doors. The curtain on the little shed window was a kind of announcement that people lived there, a surplus of them, rather than discarded things. But I hadn't figured this out. Our neighbors had overflowed out of their basement into the shed—but covertly.

I felt an organic satisfaction and (childish) delight in emptying myself so noisily onto the little tin house where (I learned later) that significant curtain had been hanging for three days already, and where they had even begun thinking about how to install some sort of chimney, so they could do their cooking indoors. I was enjoying the sound in my ears, as well as the sensation in my body. My own sound was barely distinguishable from the rain's. Maybe a little louder. I stretched my head back and closed my eyelids. I bent backward at the waist and thrust my suspended organ through the balcony railing. I started swaying and writing something in piss on the roof. I swayed until I was frozen by a yell.

"What the hell are you doing, you idiot? So now you want to piss on my head, goddammit?"

The first thing I registered was that here was this black tattooed phenomenon in a yellowing athlete's shirt—I knew him as the leader of all the courtyard clan, be they children, adults, or elderly—calling me an idiot. Then with the simple tightening of a muscle I stopped my stream and covered myself with my hands. I stepped backward into the room. I didn't want him to see my ass on top of everything. Now, a month and a half later, at the feast table, he keeps hugging and kissing me and begging me with his eyes to ask him for something, anything, and I can't think what—I've already been given everything in the world. I'm young, good-looking, loved, and a hero to boot. My act, spontaneous, snatched from death a life that had barely begun . . .

If I were to roll back the day around which my story revolves, the day that would be crowned with a feast, you might see me in its early moments floating in a bathtub, taking refuge from the heat. It was an immense tub in which generations (some of them already dead and gone) had washed away their dirt—one of the old sort of tub you don't see anymore, standing on lion's paws. It never seems to rust! There I was lying in cold water wondering whether to jerk off or to wait for my girlfriend to get home from work. Sometimes I used to push her up against the wall when she was barely through the doorway, egged on by the pressure built up in me all day thanks to my idleness and youth. As soon as night fell, I would make sure to take the time to repay her for having given herself to me virtually through her clothes.

I splashed myself with the tepid water of the Sava River, feeling bored (perhaps even desperate, who knows). That water, sometimes yellow, sometimes even red—as though it had not yet been cleansed of the last war, during which the people I live among had slaughtered and been slaughtered—reached me through an unimaginable confusion of pipes. Boredom weighed on me with all its enormity. And now I was thinking about the war—the one during which no one could have guessed I would ever come into being. A country full of mountains and rocks, a man weighing barely sixty kilos (including his rifle), who, if he survived, would become my father, either walking toward or fleeing from death (attacking and retreating not by his own volition). My mother was tiny, just a little bundle in flight. There was jewelry hidden in this bundle as well. How much distance spanned between that young man, already lightly injured once, crazed by shooting and hunger, and that little bundle, made heavier by the gold hidden inside it. My own war had not yet begun. It was sending signals from the future. But that has nothing to do with this story. Maybe it'll go somewhere else in my book.

My days were all monstrously similar. They were determined by a certainty so clear it might as well have been filtered, purified, screened. My girlfriend divided up the day. She would decree when I had to get up, eat, study. She was preparing me to be her husband. The only thing that was mine alone in my day (in my life) was working out on the balcony, or running in place. She forbade my friends from coming over. She called them disease carriers. After a few attempts to get close to me and revive the friendships we had forged when I was running free, they all gave up. It was easier that way.

On our street that year the only excitement was when someone stole a side-view mirror or slapped someone. Without fights, killings, even attempted killings, life was dull. As one of the strongest people in our square kilometer, I knew I didn't have any enemies, but no friends anymore either. By force of circumstance, my girlfriend had become everything. I realized then why the lion, king of the animals (not the lioness), was so bored. There was nothing to excite or frighten it. And I thought about all these things one after the other while I lay in the tub. In water which came up over my neck. Another five minutes passed on the clock. It said 12:05 in digital figures.

Then, that afternoon—dreadfully calm till then, if stuffed with thoughts about wars, lions, and jerking off, about the fact that it was more dignified and appropriate at my age (about twenty-five) to come in my girlfriend's arms rather than in the bathtub—was torn to shreds from top to toe by a hideous shriek (atavistic), a shriek which was amplified and seemed to hammer at the sky thanks to the silence that had preceded it, thanks to the implausibility of anything so lively happening in that heat. The scream originated in the courtyard. Instead of dulling the shriek, the buildings all around had magnified it, acting like a gigantic megaphone.

I jumped out of the bath and pulled my Bermudas onto my wet body. As I zipped them up, I accidentally caught the tip of my prick and added my own small contribution (scream, I mean) to the noise from the courtyard. Like all the other inhabitants of the buildings around the courtyard, I ran out onto the balcony to lean over and see what was going on. And what was going on was this:

A woman was running round the courtyard. If she hadn't been shrieking, her gray hair loose to the ground, I would have recognized her at once as the wife of our biggest and strongest Gypsy neighbor, the one who was always smoking. The sun beat down from above, illuminating everything, down to the most insignificant detail. There was no chance at all that the scene below was some hallucination. Then, through that yelling and wailing in a voice hoarse with age and panic, I heard a child's cry. The woman was clutching something to her—that's where the cry had come. "A doctor! Call a doctor! Quick!" was screamed into the pit from some other floor. In the depths of the well the old woman was still thrashing around, her white hair streaming like a banner. "My little pigeon, oh, my little pigeon!" she kept repeating. The bundle was wailing, though the wails were getting weaker.

The courtyard went dark. The black hand of death, or just an innocent cloud? Whichever, I leaped over the railing and jumped down (it wasn't far). There was no time to walk down the steps and out the door that was always locked for some long-forgotten reason. My fall tore my shorts and hurt the soles of my feet. I got to my tingling feet and reached the old woman. I snatched away what she was holding, and, shielding it from the light, unwrapped it. In my arms I held a half-cold baby. A few months old at best. A boy.

"What happened? Tell me!" I didn't care that I'd startled the old woman and woke her from her trance. "My little pigeon, my little pigeon!" she yelled. "Fuck your pigeon, tell me what's wrong!" Half the building had poured into the courtyard by this time. People think they're helping even when they just stand around watching.

I gave her a slap to bring her back to our own dimension, the world of places, dates, hours. There was no time for Gypsy sorcery.

"Why are his lips burned?" I shouted. "What's he been drinking?"

"Juice," said the old woman and burst into tears that were altogether of this world.

"What kind of juice, show me."

"Apple."

"Oh, you old cunt—that's a juice bottle, but it's got *varneesh* in it! Fuck your empty gray head!"

This last was spoken by a young Gypsy girl in a miniskirt, made up and teetering on high heels, the old woman's great-granddaughter perhaps. Her heels were thinner than pencils. It wasn't clear whether she had come from somewhere out in town or was on her way out. Everyone in that poor scattered family worked. Even the children. Nothing was too shameful. Only the baby and the old woman didn't work. One was waiting to grow up and the other to die.

I didn't know exactly what *varneesh* might be, but it sounded dangerous and poisonous. I was already driving to the hospital with the dying child, burning up from the inside. The tires squealed, the engine screamed. I kicked the brake and the accelerator with my bare feet. The child in the back was rolling and bouncing around free and began to snivel more loudly. "Fuck me—if the *varneesh* doesn't kill him I'll certainly finish him off with my driving," I thought. I drove the last kilometer right through the park, rattling over the unpaved ground and avoiding the benches and trees. We popped out into traffic right at the hospital. Nothing that drives on this earth could have gotten him there more quickly.

As though she had just been waiting for me and that stranger's baby all day, my girlfriend, in her white doctor's coat, ushered us in . . . and, in fact, I don't know what she did with us next, that's where my memory shuts down. Anyway, I just knew, as soon as I saw my girl, that the baby would survive. And it did.

When the news arrived from the hospital that the infant was saved and that it would be back home in a few days' time to continue to grow and to be for a little while the youngest tribe member of all, the courtyard exploded with joy. My girlfriend and I were invited to a feast and the old woman who had mixed apple-juice with wood varnish began to be forgiven. When I cooled down from all that leaping, running, and lunatic driving the soles of my feet began to get really sore. My girlfriend gave me some medicine and I soon recovered. Even the pain had been welcome: it reminded me of what I was capable of doing for someone else.

At dusk, when the heat had passed, I was placed at the head of the table in a new armchair. I would never have imagined that it could belong to one of the basement people. The price tag fluttered on the chair. I was the first to try it out.

Out of the basement, in a jumble, dark-skinned people of all genders, ages, and inclinations emerged. They occupied chairs as diverse as themselves. The chairs bore almost no resemblance to one another, so by comparison the people began to show their similarities. They were held together, as a family, by habit, and also by the sense that they were more secure and stronger this way. One thing they all certainly had in common, however, whether old or young, male or female, one shared feature that remained undiminished despite the other traits they'd carried in from all over the world—this fragment of that enormous tribe that had washed up in our courtyard—was that they were, every one of them, natural musicians and singers. On one side of the armchair that was already molding itself to me, a violin appeared, and on the other side a harmonica. At the first scrape of the violin, the first breath in and then out through the harmonica—neither of which were truly being played yet, so much as being warmed up—my soul swelled, and my body tingled. Several women and girls, among whom I recognized the one whose job required that she be made-up and sweet-smelling (which didn't necessarily mean clean) even in her sleep, brought food and arranged it in layers on the table.

And let's repeat, if not exactly word for word, that the table was overflowing with food, that it had to be squeezed together to get it all on, that there were so many bottles with foreign labels that it occurred to me that it could not all have been paid for honestly. There was even an as yet unpacked bottle of cognac, with CAMUS written on the box, and a freshly roasted suckling pig. Its little legs were contorted and its little tail twisted into a question mark. With my bare hands I carved up the pig and threw it onto the nearest plates. I pushed its little head away from me so that its wide open muzzle and tightly closed eyes laughed in someone else's face. The only part of the crispy roast that would reach the people at the far end of the table would be its aroma. All the richest and most expensive foods on the table were thrust toward me and hardly a minute passed without my being offered something more. I had undone my shirt and shorts and given my stomach space to expand. I had been eating and drinking for not quite an hour. The violin and harmonica, now harmonized, led us slowly into the night. The girl (could she still be the same one? did she really play so many roles?) began to sing, and she wasn't bad at all. She placed her hands with their long polished nails on my bare shoulders (I had taken my shirt off) and massaged me. When I tossed my head back to down some cognac, I saw her dark shining face and white teeth. Her tits barely fit into her thin, short dress. I imagined how tight and hot they must be, and how sweat was trickling between them. Everyone was barefoot or wearing cheap plastic shoes, apart from her, still teetering on her high heels because it was her job to be beautiful. From time to time I saw the man that I'd nearly pissed on from the terrace sitting next to me. He was the boss. He was the one directing everyone. He embraced me and his eyes begged me to ask something of him, anything, but I couldn't think what—I'd already been given everything in the world. A child, specializing perhaps in side-view mirrors and windshield wipers, but only from German models, placed a crown on my head made of cardboard sprinkled with golden dust and studded with little pieces of glass. I could not have imagined that I would ever in my life be king for a night. Another child, more a young woman, poured water from a hose over my bare feet, cooling me in the heat. I splashed my feet on the concrete and grinned. This must be how the chief of a tribe must look and feel when his people really make a fuss over him—not out of fear, but love.

Stars shone from the sky and a candle shone on our table. It turned out to be nice that there was no electricity. Upstairs the windows on the buildings went out one by one. Since I was unemployed I didn't care what day, even what year it was. Now in the dark (or rather half-dark), the instruments appeared to be floating and playing themselves. They drew up another armchair beside me and the head Gypsy, with the word KARMELA tattooed in huge letters on his back, sat down. He threw his heavy arm around me, made still heavier by a gold bracelet. It was the first time I'd ever been in a place where such extremes of wealth and poverty existed side by side.

"Well, brother, thank you. That child is my favorite. By the time we all got back from work, he would have been dead. Here's to you! I have a brother in Germany, and now I have you here."

"It was just a stroke of luck that my speed and her brains were able to work together," I shouted, and then was astounded by this combination of words that paper, perhaps, could have borne, but not real life.

I pointed to my girlfriend, who was taking that old granny's (probably someone's great-granny too) pulse with the help of her watch and an extended finger. The old woman's hair was now pushed back under her scarf and she didn't look so terrible. Ever since her peregrinations around the courtyard earlier that day, in the claws of her otherworldly fit, she had not stopped trembling. Maybe we'd saved her life too. Who knows.

"So you slapped my old lady, eh! That's fine, that's fine. She hasn't had a hand laid on her for fifty years! She brought me up and never poisoned *me*, but she was younger and stronger then."

"Well, she's still pretty strong. You should have seen her leaping round the courtyard!"

"That wasn't her leaping around. But you wouldn't understand—you're white."

"So who did I slap, then?"

"Ah, now, better you don't know."

And I never found out. I gave him some of my brandy. Now everyone was stretching out their hands to my girlfriend opposite, for her to take their pulse. Karmela had given her a white T-shirt with a crocodile on it. Having a doctor in the courtyard was a source of amazement for them. Free of charge, and beautiful as well. Karmela put his arm around me again and pulled me toward him. He was drunk.

"Hey! Now you can piss from your terrace to your heart's content. No one can stop you. We all have our little foibles," he said.

"That was the first time! My bathroom was full of bugs, I don't know where they all came from." I protested. "Big as toy cars!"

"It was us who sent them up to you, ha! Come on—drink, eat, everything in front of you is yours, I tell you, you just let rip from up there if you want . . . just don't strip in front of the kids. They wouldn't know what to make of it."

"Are you crazy?"

"No, but I've seen a lot. When I was visiting my best man in Munich I saw a house where people went in on one side normal, men like you and me, and came out women."

I realized that there was no hope of convincing him. This Gypsy had classified me and determined my place in this world.

"So, what else did you see, eh?"

"I saw a man with a branch of boxwood up his ass trying to hitch a ride."

"Ha! And did anyone stop for him?"

"Well, would you?"

Karmela and I had already sniffed around each other enough for him to be able to ask me something personal.

"So you like this girl of yours a lot?"

"Are you guessing or do you know?"

"I know, my friend, you make a racket when you're together, but where are your kids, it's no good to keep running on empty—if that's what you want, here's our Princess, you give her a poke. There'd be a discount for you."

"How much?"

"Free, the first time."

"How about tonight when my girlfriend goes to bed? She goes to work early."

"Come on, I'm not that much of a Gypsy! Have you screw three meters away from her? Out of the question tonight, even if you paid. Why, the doctor's like my own kin now! She saved Tiger! Hang on a minute. Cool down. And look, the rubber's free, thin, German. Guys even forget to take it off."

"Until they need to take a leak."

"That's right. And you know how long I've been offering my own rubbers along with her?"

"How long?"

"Ever since some assholes began puncturing theirs out of spite. You earn a few coins and then pay a hundred for the curettage, is that what it's called?"

"That's right,"

"You see what a lot I know, my friend. Ha!"

At the time, after midnight, I couldn't see anything funny about scraping a child out of someone's womb. It even hurt me to imagine the womb (often just the womb, not the person it belonged to) resisting the extraction of its fruit. My girlfriend came over to me and hugged me. She hadn't taken her eyes off me. She was afraid that I would disappear if she so much as blinked.

"Do you want me to take your pulse?"

"Okay."

"Then come upstairs. You've been a king for long enough, come and be a slave for a bit."

She took off my crown and put it on the table. She said good-bye to everyone with her eyes and led me into the building. Twenty pairs of dark eyes followed us warmly on our way to bed. I didn't really feel like leaving, but something spread from her hand into mine.

Something that must have been love.

P.S. That was the year my girlfriend and I saved someone else's baby, but, in the end, killed our own. We spent a few more together. I bent apart the bars with which she had kept me away from others, widening them, until in the end I came and went as I pleased from my symbolic cage. Once, as often happens, I was late coming back. The apartment was empty. In the middle of the biggest and coldest room there was a bag waiting for me with a folded letter stuck to it with Scotch tape. Snow was coming in through the open, curtain-less window. I figured I would never again light a fire here or keep it going for anyone. When I opened the letter, there was nothing in it. But I still kept it. Even blank letters say something. At least to me.

TRANSLATED FROM BOSNIAN BY CELIA HAWKESWORTH

Goran Samardžić **435**

FRANÇOIS EMMANUEL

Lou Dancing

She took me to the *Santiague*, where people were breaking their glasses to the rhythm of the samba; she took me to *La Maison d'Orange*, where the waiters were wearing lavalieres; she took me to *Screamy*, where the floor creaked under the thud of the house music; she took me to *Pianocktail*, where the Marseillaise was a bitter, tropical delight; she took me to *Cha cha cha*, which wasn't danced there; she took me to *Fin de partie* to finish the set. We ate face to face; we danced, when a dance floor presented itself, in long-drawn-out performances. Very drunk, she'd stagger on the chord made by a sad old piano, bounce up again at the throbbing of congas, or go into a trance to the din of techno. Her dance was often solitary, eyes fixed in her ophidian goddess body, in a state of untouchable offering. Toward two in the morning she had a taxi called and everything ended in an almost chaste kiss, in a hall soaked in red light, under the blasé eye of the bouncer. Before dancing, we'd talked plenty, but what had we said? We'd laughed, but about what? Here and there she'd made distracted movements of her hand, lightly brushing me, saying provocative things, but none of it was anything more than a game, still, of invitations and evasions, of dissimulations. I needed to untangle the truth of something, what was at stake with us, her reserve, her reluctance—unless it was a sinister self-interest. I forced my way with pleasure and anxiety into this love (which dared not, you might say, speak its name). Because I loved her too much already. I loved her spicy little-girl airs, this instinct she had for titillating me, provoking me, catching me, dropping me, taking me up again; for affecting serious, pitiful, charming expressions. I loved the kid in the full-grown woman's body, tiny but bubbling with energy, snug in a pair of jeans or sheathed in a purple dress, and often wearing sneakers. I loved, without daring to touch it, her flecked mother-of-pearl skin.

So what did we talk about? Poetry, Somerset Maugham, W. B. Yeats, the *nouveau roman*. She didn't know much about these things but she flaunted this almost nothing with the talent of a worldly woman well used to literary cocktail parties. She laughed again at my book *Subject Lessons*—an outward manifestation, she said, of my unintentional funniness. I no longer found this offensive. The dialogues of Menelaus and Helen bored us quite quickly. If the music was soft, we spoke of soft music. If we were surrounded by aquariums, we spoke of fish—the fish brought us to sea-floors, the depths brought us back up to islands, from islands we moved to the feeling of insularity that inhabits the English soul, from the English soul we slipped to the Russian soul, or, just as easily, to peanut butter, according to the laws of linear conversation, which makes its way from one word to the other, with certain forks in the paradigmatic axis and certain holes rapidly filled with wine. Over the course of this idle chatter I learned two or three things about her: I discovered that she hated Wagner and Chinese waltzes; that as an adolescent she had done some acting; that she often dreamed of slugs (slugs around her bed, armies of slugs with silvery trails) and that she had a black cat named Chi Salang. The story of an animal ripped apart, recounted in a delighted tone, failed to put me on my guard. I took that for English humor; a nice, childish cruelty which added spice to her charm. For her part, she didn't seem too interested in my life, which deep down was a relief. We lived a sort of holiday romance: her on holiday from Markus Gün and me on holiday from myself. As, inevitably, desire began to take up a little space between us, not to say become awkward, there were embarrassing moments, slips of the tongue, lapses of which we were all too aware, strange conversational shifts, sudden silences. One evening when she was drunk, she offered her throat to me to kiss, her throat and then her lips; said to me in a whisper: Eat me, Louis; then she flinched and stared at me with her dark eyes, sighed: I'm worn out, the taxi's getting impatient; then, several meters on, in a falsely carefree tone: Let's meet tomorrow evening at *Chili and Pepper*.

I must admit she took me by surprise. I'd never have imagined she'd know the place. Fearing that she'd meet Aloïs Stein there, I chose a table buried in the shadows. Behind his sax, Stein pretended not to see me, but as soon as she pushed open the door of the vaulted cellar a strange phenomenon occurred. The old musician caught sight of her, greeted her, improvised an entrance for her made up of caresseses, then played an accompaniment to the long tracking shot of her swaying hips between the pillars and tables. She was dressed that night in a velvety blue, one-piece outfit with straps and wide pants cut mid-calf. Sitting down, she said to me, That sax has the voice of an angel, admittedly a somewhat fallen one, a postmodern angel. All the angels have become postmodern, I answered, they no longer play lutes or harps, you have to ask yourself how God makes head or tail of it all. We ordered a turquoise cocktail with little floating bits of peeled skin, she drank two of them in a row, sighed several more times (God, that sax . . .), then dove by herself onto the *Chili*'s dance floor—a narrow passage between the tables—and it's there everything materialized: Lou Summerfield, her eyes rolling, hips moving, swimming in the warm water of jazz, diving, coming back up, spreading her palmiped hands, opening her arms like elytra, refolding them in complicated contortions, becoming a conger again, eel, garfish, while the light shimmered on the sinuous velvet on her hips, while the sax (God, that sax . . .) came over her, enveloped her at a distance, licked her with delight, slipped notes discreetly under her outfit, through the unraveled, sewn, stretched, endless variations of "Mississippi Sunrise." You could even hear Josephine's voice burping in pleasure. After that moment of rapture, there was "Galloping Mare," then the hot version of "Shanghai Baby," then still others, on and on. The *Chili* clientele didn't have eyes for anyone but her, she was the unending prelude to a striptease number that never proceeded beyond the promise; and the secret complicity they were slowly plotting, she and Stein, when he came to breathe the sliding *wa-was* in her ear. Toward three in the morning those two were still together, but she was showing signs of exhaustion. I went over to her, told her you're too beautiful, this time I'm taking *you* somewhere. It took her some time to understand but she let herself be pulled toward the exit. With his sax, Stein had exhausted her, left her like an old hide, worn out, made malleable. Even in the taxi, then the foyer, the stairwell, the hallway, the bedroom, she put up no resistance to the animality that had possessed me. Of course there were several hindrances: buttons, laces, zippers caught, a whole unsightly battle against the conspiracy of cloth, but at the end of all that the one-piece was at the foot of the bed, her blouse was dangling from the door handle, and she was lying completely naked though suddenly shivering, declaring she was cold, tired, had a headache, and curling up in the fetal position under the covers. Fortunately I had an old Duke Ellington CD, which revived some of her snaky movements. Lovemaking, as they call it, was set off by this languid writhing, but at the height of it, I was forced to recognize that she was with the Duke, not me, and no doubt with Stein even more so; that Stein and his sax had made love to her for four hours already, better than anyone else could, and that I was arriving dead last, like a candle snuffer. In her sleep she was still moaning: God, that sax . . .

She slept until midday. There were, no doubt, other entwinements, moments when, without enthusiasm, she let herself be taken again, but I don't remember them very well; after nights of lovemaking I'm only ever left with a few details in a sea of oblivion. They're the insignificant or fantastic details, like those reddish speckles under her throat that made me think of the Micronesia section on my old, yellowish-brown planisphere; I can also still see her naked body through my translucent shower pane; and then, without laughing, she floats around lost inside the legs of my striped pajamas. Toward four o'clock in the afternoon, she looks me straight in the eyes, says to me somberly: Let's stop telling fairy tales, Louis, tell me about yourself. I told her everything. Soon we'd become submerged in an unshakable gloom, she and I. Toward evening she slipped her blouse and one-piece back on, like any beautiful outfit worn once and suddenly seeming second-hand. So, dressed once more, she kissed me on the forehead. I followed her with my eyes, a small blue patch getting lost in the crowd on the sidewalks. She had smiled, she had said you're the first sometime-poet I've met in the flesh.

Poetry is a difficult art.

■ ■ ■

I loved women so much, ones I'd glimpsed, passed by, lost, those reading on trains or walking in the streets, I loved young mothers with their weary tenderness, slender silhouettes separated by windowpanes, terrified beauties, elegant ones, pensive ones, ones who were lit up, I loved that private secret they guard, the art they have of appearing and then slipping away and vanishing behind the screens of chance. A meeting sometimes took place; a story was sometimes threaded together rendering the initial impression misleading. With Lou Summerfield the initial image was that of dancing face to face while drops of shadow rained down, a solitary dance, the rule of which was to maintain one's distance. Had I broken the rule? For several days she stopped getting in touch with me. The following Saturday, I received this hurried message recorded in a toneless voice on my answering machine: Louis, I've something important to tell you, I'll be at *Vanitie's Fair* tonight.

Vanitie's was a factory that had been transformed into a club, an enormous warehouse where they'd repainted the bridge cranes, pedestals, and other metallic frames in bright colors for crazy nocturnal displays. That's where I had to look for her, there at the back of the bar (a stripped-down machine of some kind, fluorescent yellow) or on the dance floor itself, in the human magma, the steamy anonymity, staring down everyone and no one. My life will have amounted to nothing more than this, then: the unceasing search for a face. And all those bodies moving jerkily in their purple neons around me were miming to the point of ecstasy the disjointed gestures of someone's death throes. Lou Summerfield wasn't there, I circled the dance floor three last times then ended up at the bar, perched on a stool, with some similar types all drinking their heartaches dry. Conversations crossed over and back muffled by the roar of the speakers, one guy mourning his Lorette, the other celebrating his total loss, the third sagging on the counter and waking up at intervals to shout about some minister, and lastly some guy who just kept saying I want to live. Hovering behind his counter, a Mauritian barman lent his tender ear to this chorus of misfortunes; with the unctuous gesture of a prelate, he cast out the white froth from the beer glasses or poured long drops of golden whiskey as though it were the very elixir of consolation. The man who wanted to live let me in on the secret of his life patched with little bits of love, odd jobs, and failed new beginnings. But life is stronger, he pounded this out, and Total Loss agreed, smiling away and paying for another round in honor of his eighteen-cylinder, special series, 117 horsepower vehicle, which had finished upside-down in a potato field. Minister was finally snoring vigorously while the air became blue and hazy and the guy in love with Lorette lifted his head a little, one down, ten to go in this brotherhood of the unfortunate— they always end up looking a little alike. I have no memory of being in the taxi that brought me home, but I awake at midday the next day, pull myself out of bed as best I can, sober up under cold water, find a sheet of paper folded in quarters at the bottom of my pocket:

> *Too much noise, too many people.*
> *Come to the Valparaiso this evening.*
> *It'll be quieter.*
> *Kiss, kiss.*

And so the dance started up again. Those two kisses warmed my heart. The *Valparaiso* was to *Vanitie's* what a fishing boat is to a brand-new cargo liner. Its swaying walls, its corrugated iron roof, its faded signs (*Exotic Cuisine, Full Menu*) were erected on the bank of a sad old canal. Inside there were exactly six tables, the boss, his canary, and me. While waiting for Lou, who, hour after hour, failed to arrive, I chewed on crusty ends of dry bread while scrutinizing a print of a port in browned Technicolor and the slightly greasy poppies on the oilcloth. I told myself Lou was toying with me, that by her absence she was getting back at me for something: winding backward, and in a distorted reflection, the shining demonstrations of the *Santiague* or *Pianocktail*. Then, in my typical, volatile manner of thought, I mulled over melancholia, of which there were at least two distinct varieties: the slightly punishing *Vanitie's Fair* kind, and the bittersweet *Valparaiso* kind. *Valparaiso*: that name of a port town so difficult for me to find on a map being the very paradigm of this dark mood (antique steamships in harbors, sun eternally setting, the oxidized tatters of old Europe, as if time sent all its trash over there, as if they were already reusing the theater sets which had been used as our own backdrop, and worn out much too quickly). The slightly square face of the boss now inserted itself into this meditation. He had to be some kind of mixed-race mountain Indian, with his prominent cheekbones and very black eyes. Leaning very close to me, he pronounced my name—accurately, in his own way—which, however, he had no reason to know. He repeated, Mr. Louis Uccello, someone asking for you on the phone. The receiver was placed beside the canary cage, but there was no one at the other end of the line. The next slightly worrying fact was that the owner claimed it was a man's voice he'd heard. The wait having gone on long enough, he served me some old, burned lamb chops and we made conversation. He dampened his *J*s and stumbled over his *V*s in recounting his life story: a melancholic one. His father was a whaler, his mother an Indian, of the Arayupu tribe, rechristened *Incarnation of the Blessed Sea* by her father, who, after his eyes had met the very human eyes of a mortally wounded cetacean, decided to give up this bloody career. From that point I lost the thread of his story a little, which moved from the storyteller's being detained in an embassy to crossing the Atlantic in the bottom of a luggage hold, the rest of his existence now hanging on this old restaurant-bar whose sign was collapsing like his smile when he served me another tequila which sliced through my mucous membranes. As I'd told him a bit about my misadventures in turn, he suggested there was another man in my lady-story; without a doubt he was thinking about the voice on the phone again. Toward one or two in the morning, when I called a taxi to go home, I was suddenly on my guard. I stared at the dark night on the lookout for something out of the ordinary. No, there was nothing out of the ordinary. An even-tempered driver, blinding headlights, the nighttime smell of my building's foyer, the dull click of my door, then Lou's voice on my answering machine: Too small, too shabby, the *Valparaiso*, let's try the *Rouskelnikov* tomorrow evening. And then after a silence she added: It's important, Louis, it's very important. Aloïs Stein's voice sprang up just after the end of her message; he wanted to see me too: a matter of great urgency. I rewound the tape. Lou's voice was weary, I'd have said, maybe worried; Stein's voice was Stein's voice, heavy as always, a little insistent. I put the two voices on a loop, Lou then Stein, Stein then Lou, barely separated by the beep.

■ ■ ■

Exactly fifteen days ago today, Stein said to me, you were in the *Chili and Pepper* with a young woman who danced on her own all night long. I'd like to know her name. This matter is of vital importance to me. I have the very distinct feeling of having known this woman before. We come across thousands of people and suddenly one of them leaves a special mark. I have a darkness in my life, Uccello, I've a darkness lasting several months ... This woman is dancing in that darkness. She doesn't stop dancing, I'm obsessed by her.

And Stein made an unusual gesture with his hand, as if to dispel the image while at the same time depicting it with his long fingers that twiddled briefly in the air. For the first time with Stein, I had the impression of facing a man like myself. Up till then I'd only seen in him an unusual character, a saxophonist, I hadn't seen him just as himself. Then I answered that her name was Lou Summerfield and that we were meeting that evening at the *Rouskelnikov.*

He let out the yellow collar of his shirt, moving the knot of his tie off center so it started to look like a noose. I'd have been happier if the woman had nothing to do with this story, he muttered. And he turned toward the window for a long time as if to clean out his eyes with the fleecy autumn sky. The door opened several moments later on a decrepit character floating in a pair of trousers with suspenders. The man placed a tray carrying two cups of black coffee on the already cluttered desk. He answered to the name of Bakou, diminutive of Aram Bakoutmezaghian, and must have been linked to Stein by some long domestic-staff history. When Stein introduced him ("my old Armenian associate, my man for delicate missions"), I sensed that we'd be seeing each other again some day in murkier circumstances. Bakoutmezaghian had gray lustrine sleeves and big dumbfounded eyes which were obstructed by the upper frame of his glasses. Stein then took out the telephone directory from the bottom of a pile of files and looked up the address of the *Rouskelnikoff.* Funny name, he muttered, it's almost Raskolnikov, bringing the cup of black coffee to his lips, I saw that he was trembling quite badly, and that made me think of something.

The directory must've been old, because it listed the *Rouskelnikoff* at 106 rue des Péniches[1] and the rue des Péniches sank, after number 40, into a huge excavation planted with concrete stakes and strewn with metallic roofing. At the appointed meeting time, Stein and I were following the fence overhanging the pit. I didn't dare speak to him about the sort of logical continuity that this bitch Lou was constructing, running from *Vanitie's* to the *Valparaiso* then to the *Rouskelnikoff*, and I wondered once again what on earth I could've done to her, other than making love to her one night when she hadn't said no. Stein stared, mesmerized, into the bottom of the excavation. Obviously, he muttered, she didn't reserve a table. We went in search of a more recent directory, consulted it on a bar at the back of a garish tobacconist's where they also served glasses of wine and games of darts were going on. Between the *Rousseboeuf* and the *Rue des Lilas*, there was no longer any trace of the *Rouskelnikoff*, though one of the clients did remember the sign for a little Russian restaurant that had disappeared without a trace in one of the building blitzes which tore open craters in the city later dubbed office blocks or parking lots. With it went the soul of the district, the spirit of the premises, and three quarters of the rue des Péniches, which no longer had any barges beyond those in its name (the canal having gone underground). Rather than staying to dwell on nostalgia, Stein suggested we head for the countryside and sundown; if we'd been near the sea he would've suggested the sea. He was at the wheel of an old black Volkswagen whose roof his head almost touched and which made such a worn-metal meat-grinder sound so that we had to shout to make

1 "Street of Barges."

ourselves heard. When we'd finally left the city, he started driving faster and faster, turned off suddenly onto an asphalt road then onto a narrow track, covered in potholes, which rushed, jerkily, towards the top of a plateau. At the end of the track, a rusted barrier prohibited access to an enormous expanse of concrete paving between which young shrubs sprouted up. It's an old airfield, Stein roared at me before killing the engine; then he jumped out of the car and started taking long strides towards the center of the runway. There he remained at a standstill, motionless, the wind inflating the panels of his open jacket. I come here when I'm thinking of my darkness, he murmured, I sit down on the excrescence, I look south, southwest and I wait.

South-southwest there was a forest and the straight groove of a railroad track. In the foreground stood a square building all of whose windows were broken. It was the control tower, Stein explained, it's overrun with wild pigeons, they wanted planes and control towers; this place plunges us into the depths of time. Then he invited me to sit down beside him on what he called the excrescence, an old metal post right on the runway. You could hear a mournful chorus of crows in the distance making a dimming spark in the dark part of the setting sun. Stein seemed pensive. Sometimes, he resumed, I drive through the gate, I line myself up on the runway—I gradually build up speed and then suddenly cut the engine, first there's the sound of metal, then the noises of the car, then the grinding of the axle and shock absorbers dies down until the vehicle becomes completely still, silence descends on my cockpit then and I feel good.

We left again when night had fallen. He wanted to show me something else. By long detours we arrived at the railroad and took a very narrow trail which, leading toward a rocky mound, climbed away from the train tracks. Stein forced the car up to the summit of the promontory, cut the engine, and opened his window without getting out. Listen closely, he said, at sixteen minutes past eight a freight convoy passes here, imagine that it's the basso continuo. So we waited for 8:16. As soon as the sound of the train could be heard, Stein switched on the car radio, a Miles Davis solo, pure, polished, tragic, drawing out its haughty arabesques on a background of slow, powerful, continuous drumming: freight carriages. Enclosed up there in the black Volkswagen, it was like we were in the cabin of a yacht stranded forevermore on top of a reef, and I thought of that music-mad navigator who had built himself a sailboat around his grand piano for the sole pleasure of making the tragic tones of the *Appassionata* resonate in a storm. Once the convoy had passed, we listened to the end of the piece in a very pure silence. After Miles, growled Stein in a muffled way, after Miles there's nothing left but the scum on things. Not that that woman was beautiful, he went on without transition, beautiful, I mean, according to the canons of beauty, but that she was there, simply there. And in the glow of the interior light he fixed me with a terrible look. He said if the *Rouskelnikoff* no longer exists, if the *Rouskelnikoff* and all the Russian restaurants, and all the canals, the barges, the airports, have been swept from the earth's surface, where should we look for her, Uccello, answer me that. It was a question with no answer, a kind of touching utterance that he wasn't, for that matter, really addressing to anyone. After which he put his head on the back of the car seat, mopped his forehead at length, sighed again, What beauty, what beauty, closed his eyes and fell asleep. An hour later he came to. I'm a little mad from time to time, he apologized. And he started the engine up again.

TRANSLATED FROM FRENCH BY URSULA MEANY SCOTT

VICTOR MARTINOVICH

Taboo

Angela was going out with Grisha. Before, she was going out with Lyama, but Lyama was weird. Freaky. When he drinks, he pukes all over himself. Or he forgets to zip himself up and walks around like that in public. Or he knifes someone. Scruffy beard. Runny nose, he snorts it up. And his eyes —all wild. Who knows how he'll turn out in five years. A daddy for my kids? No thanks. But Grisha is normal. Cool. His cream-colored shoes, yeah, are something else. And how about his white pants—you have to wash them every other day, but Grisha doesn't mind. He washes them, tries to look good for her.

One of Grisha's arms ended in a cloudy, half-liter bottle, the other—in Angie's waist. But Lyama, he always held her a bit lower, and would start feeling her up right in front of people, the moron. She begged him not to, but he thought she was playing hard to get. What Angie liked most about Grisha was that when she asked him not to do something, he never did it. And she also liked that when they met couples with children, he'd hide the bottle behind his back, so the kid didn't see the juice. A good guy. You can't teach that. You have to have backbone to get it.

Today, there weren't too many couples with children, couples without children, or even half-couples—people, lonely people—out, despite the languid May noon, when it's so nice to be out. The path, receding in an emerald green, looked like an empty landing strip, but Angie wanted to escape this solitude into a still greater solitude, to their own shared solitude, and she enticed Grisha onto the trails, where his cream-colored shoes sank in the fresh, moist earth not yet baked by the July heat, where among the bushes of juniper and wild currants, plaster statues of workers showing up for their last shift rose up solemnly, wet from dew, eroded by rain, with the faces of ancient gods.

The passages between the trees here were tangled with a spider web sparkling in the sun; now and then on her cheeks, in the intimate corners of her neck, created only for Grisha's lips, Angie felt the tickle of weightless spider strands. The spiders themselves seemed like creatures with whitish, infinitely long hairs, hung along the trees, and when she and Grisha strayed off into these hairs, the spiders would try to escape, scurrying and gliding down along their clothes.

Here there was a rusty board, "Glory to the Workers of the Ball-bearing Factory," with photographs, faded, of the most glorious workers, now looking like ghosts, who had once toiled in the factory, now abandoned, nothing but ruins, where the park now sprouted with its paths through the tumbledown fence. Here stood swings, horizontal bars, and even parallel bars, straight lines never meant to intersect, which someone's caring hands had nonetheless helped not only to intersect, on one end, but to entwine. Grisha set his bottle down, grabbed onto the bars, hoisted himself up twenty times, and then, catching his breath, in one graceful stroke, executed a full turn.

Angie thought his face was just like those ancient statues of foundry workers and tractor drivers. How strong he was. Yet with all this strength, still a good man. She sipped the frothy, bitter liquid from the bottle, keeping up a slight buzz, woozy with May. Once the bottle was empty, she threw it away.

Grigory tucked in his unbelted shirt and even grimaced reproachfully, as if telling himself he was out of shape, that it'd only been two years since the army and here he's already gone to pieces. Angela was melting. She chucked his chin with a blade of grass. Angela was happy. Angela would have drawn a huge heart on the pavement if only she had chalk.

Yet another moist path opened up ahead, leading into even darker depths of the park's subconscious, and Angie pulled Grisha on, and he didn't resist—he's gorgeous, and lets her lead him around like a bull by its nose ring: so cool. Angie wanted to reach the caves, overgrown with moss —the grottos and pyramids. That was the promise of the incredible, end-less, deserted park. She wanted to reach the place where, among the thou-sand-year-old sequoias with bark red like an Indian's skin, the bison-hunters had camped; she almost hoped that in some remote corner of the park a bunch of thugs would attack her and Grisha, and Grisha would kick the shit out of them, send them running, like in the movies—running from Batman. And then she would embrace Grisha and find that they had broken his nose or lip and a red juice is oozing out, and she'd sit him down on a bench or the roots of the sequoias and would take out a handkerchief, snowy white like his pants, and would pat him with it, and he'd wince slightly and look right in her eyes, oh yes!

They kept walking and didn't talk much. When she asked him to tell her a story, he always told the same one from his army days, about a tank that fell off a bridge, and by now she could reproduce it exactly, with all his in-tonations and pauses intact, with his usual opening, "To make a long story short, there was this incident," and his usual ending, "and like they say, tanks just don't fly." Anyway, they found themselves by a dilapidated wall, crowned with a lace of rusty, sharp wire. And then, from behind a tree, out came Lyama with a knife to quickly and cleanly cut Grisha's throat.

No, of course not, nothing like that happened—but she thought about it happening. Lyama's kind of puny, but if he and Grisha had a face-off, it wouldn't be a foregone conclusion who'd win. Lyama would bite and kick and hit Grisha in the balls. Grigory would fight fair, and that sort always loses.

The lilies of the valley hit them with their smell—almost unbearable, making them dizzy ("Like perfume," Grisha said)—and only a second later, Angie noticed that the grass all around was dotted with someone's scattered pearl beads. She bent toward a plant and, the way they teach you on TV, sniffed it, not touching the stem. The smell was unbelievable. She imagined a tiny bouquet at home, on the night table, by the bed. You would wake up in the morning and everything would smell of lilies of the valley.

"Grish," she whispered. "Let's pick some?"

"You kidding?" He looked around quickly to see if anyone had heard them. They hadn't.

"Oh, come on, who'll notice us here?" Angie hissed.

"It's a crime, Angie. Lilies of the valley have been entered into the *Book of Endangered Species*," he said firmly.

Angela knew there was no point arguing. He'd only cross the street when the walk sign was on, the idiot.

"Oh, Gri-sh-sh-sh," she inched closer to him and snuggled up. Lifted her eyes. Zero reaction. Shit, he's such a square. The only way to win him over was to prove that what she had in mind was fair.

"Look, Grish—I read in the news just the other day that it's good to pick lilies of the valley, because it makes them grow quicker the next year! It doesn't mess up the roots one bit." It was very easy to lie to him—you just had to focus on his wheat-colored lashes and not get distracted by the deep, sweet blackness of his eyes. Or else you'd feel sorry for him. "So carefully, without crushing them. Like this . . ."

Angela squatted, knowing full well that her skirt was inching up in the front and the lily snow-whiteness of her underpants becoming visible. Without taking her eyes off him, with a slight smile and raised eyebrows, she clasped a stalk with the tips of her fingers and pulled it up before he could stop her. Several snow-white beads trembled on the slimmest of threads and here, the whole filament was in her hands. A lily of the valley had been picked. Picked. No matter what, to put it back was impossible. You had to keep on going. That is, picking.

"Are you out of your mind or what?" Grigory chided her gently. "How can we carry them out? Well, I mean, to the dorm? They'll catch us for sure!"

"The main thing is to get to the Metro. There's some old ladies standing there. Like, they sell seedlings. And each one has a packet by her feet. And in the packet are lilies of the valley. If the cops catch us, we'll say we bought them from the old ladies."

"But haven't they shot all the old ladies?" Grisha asked.

"Well, these pay off the cops. So they're allowed." Angie wasn't lying now.

Grisha, naturally, didn't move. Angie pouted.

"Won't you present your lady with a bouquet?"

"I tell you, I'd rather get ripped off buying you some roses," Grigory said nervously, looking all around.

But Angie had already detected a note of hesitation in his voice. She had only to add yet another little note so that the melody of uncertainty, the polyphony of uncertainty, would emerge, and she knew well how to handle the keys of Grisha's piano. She touched her lips to the snow-white pea of a flower. On it remained the bloody trace of lipstick. Angie tore off the pea and brought it to Grisha's cheek, rolling the lipstick along the stubble. Still he hesitated.

"No one can see us here," she whispered in his ear, leaning into him with her hip, feeling his erection.

"And what about the surveillance cameras in all the parks and woods where they grow lilies of the valley? What, you don't watch TV?"

"Oh, come on now, you little idiot! Do you know how many surveillance cameras they'd need to keep an eye on each flower?" She picked another and reached it out to him, then crouched down for the next one.

"Okay." He sat down next to her. "Okay." He pulled up several flowers. "Okay."

Picking lilies of the valley turned out to be easy, even pleasant. There was something in their compliant resistance, when a stem didn't quite want to forsake its bed, something like ... Well, it's like when your eye itches, and you can't scratch it, and you want to, and you scratch, although you shouldn't because then it'll hurt, and it's already tearing, but you keep on scratching.

And so they kept on picking lilies of the valley. At first Grisha picked them one at a time, selecting the ones with the most beads, but then he began gathering them quickly, one after the other, frantically trampling on the plants and dropping the frailer blossoms in the process. The flowers clung to their shoots. Clinging to a shoot—how ridiculous! The same as clinging to life, which is nothing more than a temporary escape from death.

Having picked a handful, he'd give it to Angie, each time shuddering at how many of them—a bunch, and now a little bouquet, and now an enormous bouquet—they had. They had to stop—it was lunacy. The lily of the valley was entered in the Red Book; they should have just bought them from those old ladies, or paid through the nose for the roses, but he, but they ...

"Angie! Is it enough now? Do you have enough?" he asked again and again, but she only waved him away, thrusting her fingers in the hairs of the moss and coaxing out more and more of her beads. And he himself felt that he couldn't stop, that once they started they had to go on, that the price they'd pay would be the same regardless, for a stem, for a bouquet, for a heap. And now they put together an enormous, beautiful, fragrant bouquet for Angie: it looked like the drawing of a bouquet that was printed in his army discharge photo album, opposite the pictures of his relatives waiting for him to arrive, and he loves her and she's waiting for him. Even when he's right next to her.

The bouquet was almost ready, a luxurious shock of hair, a mane, a sheaf. They only had to decorate it along the edges with torn lily of the valley leaves, which suggested hands, a multitude of hands, solemnly bearing a mountain of pearls to the altar for sacrifice. And while Angie was furtively pulling up the last flowers needed for her bouquet, Grisha began searching for bigger leaves. He straightened up, looked around, didn't have time to get surprised, noticed a quick movement behind the tree trunks, in the twilight of the bush, and hushed her, and Angie froze, and that's when both began to hear the crackle of branches underfoot and the muted sputtering of walkie-talkies.

For the first time Angie could remember, Grisha cursed: "Fuck."

"Are we dead?" she asked.

"We should have picked a few shoots and run," Grisha said, calm.

He peered intently into the bushes. Behind them on the path, more quick, random movements, as if the patrols were clearing all the ordinary people out of the park, where now . . .

"But how? How is it possible? Do they really have cameras everywhere? Everywhere we go? In every park? How is it possible?"

But Grisha hushed her. He sat down, feeling his army instincts stirring in him. He looked around. The movement was only behind them, coming from the main path. How many there were wasn't clear. But quite a few. It's been a long time since they stopped coming in threes.

Ahead of them it was as quiet as before. He didn't sense an ambush there. They might also be able to get away to the right, and head down to the streetcar tracks. Five hundred meters through the bushes, dodging between the tree trunks. Out of the park. Jump onto a streetcar and ride off as far as you can, if you get through. Or mix with the crowd, if there's a crowd down there. But we won't get through. And no, there's no crowd. Besides, the park only gets wider on that side. It wouldn't be easy.

"Maybe it's not the cops?" Angie asked. Hoping.

Grisha wasn't about to waste time being ironic, all the more so since irony tended to be lost on him. If not the cops, then what's behind those trees? Dressed in black uniforms? Carrying walkie-talkies? Ha, ha, ha. Well, maybe he would get the hang of irony yet.

Reconnaissance. At eleven o'clock, north, on the left, the factory wall, limiting the search. At six o'clock, the enemy, a firearm, possibly automatic. Number unknown, but no less than a platoon. One and a half kilometers of hard running. The park abuts a busy square in front of the department store. People are heading home from work. Lots of people. Cut into the crowd. Mix in. Go down into the Metro. Jump in the first car you see. Get out the last stop. Wait it out at the dacha. Head off into the woods. Live in a tent.

But first—run. Run. Escape. We all cling with our lives to the idea of escape. What would we do without it.

"So, listen up," Grisha said sharply. "Now. We get up and run. Straight ahead. You go first. Don't look around. As fast as you can and as hard as you can. Straight ahead. I'll run right after you. If they shoot, they'll hit me first. If we break through to the department store, we're only two hundred meters from the Metro."

She raised her lips to him—like, to kiss. "Idiot. This isn't a movie! Come on, move!"

Angie rushed forward, swinging her bouquet, scattering pearls on the moss. Leaving a trail to give them away. The cops will turn up right at the dacha, in the basement, in the dorm, in the tent—there's no way to get away from them, throw the bouquet away, throw it away. Grisha followed her easily. He looked back as he went, not slowing down. Damn! Five, seven, ten silhouettes. They were busy with something over there, probably asking for orders. That's right, guys, keep asking. Meanwhile, we'll get a bit farther away.

To the right came the howl of a siren, muffled by the trees, and the screech of brakes. We did the right thing not running to the streetcars. The right thing. But why so many sirens?

Running's easy, when you're running you don't have to think. Just run. Around the tree trunks. Tree trunks make you hard to hit. Back there, something smacked, thudded, twitched; he instinctively pushed Angie, fell, rolled over and covered her. But it wasn't the crackle of gunfire, not that. They'd just turned on the loudspeaker.

"Attention," an amplified voice roared. "Attention," it repeated, obviously trying to make itself sound more important—how ordinary it was, how plain looking, how easily ignored by its superiors—with its newfound decibels. The park went quiet; even the birds fell silent, as if they recognized, if not this voice, then this same intonation. "Attention. You have violated Article 256 of the Amended Criminal Code . . ." The voice trailed off, evidently trying to recall the exact wording of this Article, but, concluding that a person needn't trouble himself with details when he can speak this loudly, continued, ". . . forbidding the destruction of wild flowers and grasses that have been entered in the Red Book."

The apocalyptic thunder of the voice shackled one's will. It was quite clear that the fugitives needed to run on instead of listening to it, but it was impossible not to listen. The voice was now telling them of their fate. And you could feel that it had in its power to say, "Look, we forgive you, just come out with your hands up, you will be sentenced to ten years of community service, just come out, we won't really hurt you, maybe just knock out a couple of teeth, after all, it's your first offense, since it's everybody's first offense, no one ever gets a second." But the voice, pronouncing each letter of its speech clearly and slowly, did not know mercy. Which was probably why it sounded so loud. The voice kept on: deafening. Not just its volume, but its intent.

"Deadly force will be used against you. I repeat. Deadly force will be used against you. The park has been surrounded. Surrender now."

Grisha raised himself on his elbows and looked out from behind some fern leaves. The police, in chain formation, were coming closer. Each one held a small, gleaming pistol.

The megaphone stood at a distance, hidden by the trees, so that it seemed the stern and slow voice was coming from nowhere and everywhere.

"We have to run," said Grisha under his breath. "We have to keep on running."

From the side of the approaching chain came some muffled noises, crunching sounds. Peeping out, Grisha saw the cops had started jogging, were running straight at Angie and him. You could already see their shoulder straps and bulletproof vests, the cords on their calves, their stripes and buttons.

Grigory jumped up first, grabbed her hand, and dragged her forward, pulling her along, and just then behind them something roared and began to crack-squeal through the tree trunks, hacking branches to pieces and cutting down leaves. Angie jerked and cried out, but no, she didn't drop to the ground—they didn't hit her—she was just terrified, the little idiot; she's never been shot at before, but pistols are hardly Kalashnikovs. They fire like a bull pisses, as his deputy commander used to say. He'd taught his men not to be afraid of bullets. A bullet is stupid, but *dura lex*—the law is severe. That's what's embroidered on the sleeves of these jokers dressed in black. Anyway, since when are cops good shots? It's just that there's a lot of them. Really a lot. Let's say ten, and each has six rounds. And a spare in a holster. That adds up to a hundred twenty bullets. A hundred twenty for just the two of them, him and Angie.

And Grisha had already picked out a clear goal—a broken-down concrete box, probably once a transformer station, transforming something or other, but now simply concrete, through which pistol bullets can't penetrate. If only there was a wall like that around at the dacha. On all sides.

And live like that. Thick concrete. *Dura lex*. Little idiot, what have you done? You pulled on your long pants a little early, kid, and it's not so easy to run in them—they catch on every branch.

They'd almost reached their goal, were circling behind the tons of life-saving, seamless concrete, ricochets spraying the air around them, when suddenly Angie's foot caught on something, *dura lex*, and she fell forward and crawled on her stomach about a meter and then lay that way, and he had to drag her to safety by foot and blouse, to safety behind the concrete, and here she's flapping her eyelids and gasping for air, and is shaking and repeating, "I'm hit, I'm hit," and she points—as if he wouldn't believe her otherwise—points to her blouse, where, by her shoulder, there's a round hole.

"Does it hurt? Does it hurt?" he asked.

Angie shook her head and the leaves were reflected in her eyes. She was breathing heavily. The hole's nowhere near her heart, and it seems her lung is fine too, there's no pinkish froth on her lips. Grisha tore her blouse. Now he sees her bra, and in it such a boring, such an uninteresting—now that they're on the run—breast. But there's no blood. Somehow there's no blood. The entry wound is round, clean, and there's no exit wound. The bullet is stuck inside. In Angela. A bullet in Angela, getting cold, getting warm from her body. A bullet. In Angela. What organs do women have two centimeters below their shoulder? Will she die? Is she already dying? And why isn't there any blood? And why is she breathing so fast? And why are there leaves in her eyes? One hundred twenty bullets for two. Well, that's too many. Too many.

Panting and weak, Grisha threw several pinecones from behind the wall at the police, who scattered in a flash. Grenades, they thought. Imme- diately, in retaliation, came a deep-throated rumble, and the concrete crunched and popped.

He turned to his Angie.

"Can you walk?"

In reply, she fainted. I see. She can't stand. Is it shock? Or did they hit something vital? Shit, what should he do?

He helped her to sit up, leaned her back against the wall. That's it, Angie, my sweet. That's it. Sit a while. I'll think of something. In her hand a fresh bouquet of lilies of the valley, snow white like underwear. Magic flowers. What I'd like to do is keep staring at this bouquet until the police come out from behind the trees, swinging their truncheons.

Grigory ran ahead. Ten, twenty, thirty meters. There was a clearing; it split the park in two. Just a little further. From behind the trees. The sound of distant bells. Pleasant, melodious. There, you can already see the department store. So many people! Sure, it'll be difficult with a wounded Angie. Getting to the Metro. Cover the hole with my hands. The girl's in a bad way. Still no blood. And, looking down to the foot of the hill, where the park ended, he went cold, not believing his eyes, but already resigning himself (after all, they'd picked flowers that were entered in the Red Book!). Near a hillock, at the entrance to the park, dozens of people in black uniforms were already milling about. That melodious ringing, which Grisha had taken for distant bells, came from the clanging of those half-meter steel barriers, whose segments were being unloaded from a nearby truck. Can't jump those, and there's no climbing over, especially with a wounded Angie. They'll see us and open fire. And not with pistols anymore. With assault rifles. Point blank.

He went back to Angie. It was like waking up. The darkness of his despair and then, again, the tree trunks, the park, the concrete, the cops and their pistols. They were closer than ever, of course, already the branches were crackling right by their haven. What were the police waiting for? Were they really afraid of Grisha's pinecones? How beautiful she is. Angela. His Angela.

He stroked her cheeks. She raised her head. There were tears in her eyes. *Dura lex.*

"It's going to be all right." It was easy to lie to her. All he had to do was focus on her eyelashes and not get distracted by the emerald leaves in her eyes. Because there, in those leaves, he'd find himself, and you can't fool yourself for long. "Once you rest a little, we'll run to the department store and jump into the Metro. There's a crowd there now. No one will notice us. We'll get to the dorm. We'll open the balcony door. In the evening we'll feel the coolness from the street and it will be so very quiet. For now, give me the bouquet. Stay here. I'll be back soon."

Grisha grabbed the lilies of the valley. The shoots and blossoms. She'll go on waiting for him even when there's no one left to wait. What a sad song! Angie is wounded, and now that he has the flowers, she's almost not guilty. Maybe they won't finish her off.

He buttoned his shirt. He sniffed the flowering sweetness. In the evening it will be so very quiet. They'll meet once again. But what's an evening, really? Is it worth it to live for an evening?

"Wait for me," he asked her.

Just two steps. The first to the side, the second ahead, far ahead, over the wall, to center stage, so as not to see her anymore, so as to look only at them, the ones still approaching, and you want to take cover behind the lilies of the valley, as if this will stop them, but the flowers aren't guilty, they don't deserve it, at least let them survive. Two or three seconds of silence. Most likely they were taking aim, and then the whole park flourished with incredible, enormous blossoms, which had no smell but sparkled like dew, growing and growing through the sky, through the tree trunks, and through the leaves in Angie's eyes.

When everything was over, they shoved Grisha and Angie into black, opaque plastic bags (someone even joked that they ought to share one, since then they could have one last roll in the hay on the road to their special numbered graves, out in the plot reserved for violators of Article 256 of the Criminal Code). No one knew what to do with the actual bouquet, however, now crumpled and touched by splashes of scarlet lipstick from the bullet wounds in Grisha's body. No one felt like counting the flowers, filling out forms, filing reports for an already closed case, and so they ended up simply tossing them onto the carpet of moss, so that the picked lilies of the valley blended in with the ones still growing, and from a distance you couldn't tell them apart, couldn't tell them apart.

TRANSLATED FROM RUSSIAN BY SYLVIA MAIZELL

DIETER SPERL

Random Walker

DREAM (1)

Something's held on, has adhered to you, has enveloped your body like a film. You've propped up your head, could linger this way for hours. A man is born. A woman is born. A man is reborn. Something is there, is moving. It is a woman, from another life, from many other lives. It is impossible, yet you see her, can see her, are overcome by this love, by this early love. You can see her, not touch her, cannot touch her. You speak with her, she comes next to you. This beckoning has proved enough to prevent you from resting. Are you there? Are you there?

There must be many births from which this culture grows, only to end up in a wooden box again and again. It's a dream, just a dream, nothing more. One hundred thirty-one plastic locomotives in ten colors wait in boxes before your window. Many people emerge, wander up to you, disappear again, you can grow as much as you want to, they wander up to you, disappearing again. You move onto the street, are open for anything, a first love, although you've never kissed her, ever. She is a spirit, to evade the birds.

■

She says: People that don't have any dreams die earlier.

There you are, and pictures, there you are and your pictures.

You say: People that don't have any dreams die, sooner or later.

Sometime or other there's a point where you love all people and all living creatures, a nightmare, because there can't be any desire anymore, because there is no longer any desire in this land anymore, nothing, it crashes in upon you somewhere or other. Are you there? You embrace her before she disappears and lies down in your little wagon. And now? What now? She screams. She bawls, pees her pants, laughs. And you? And now? What?

Nothing. You take her in your arms, throw her into the air. She flies away. No. Now what? Nothing occurs to you particularly. You only know the halftime whistle. The dawn cannot rely on you. A truck, sleeping in the box with little Rottweilers tied on strings. It's not proper to speak with spirits after work. Evolution finds the ways and means of not allowing us to have our peace. Although you haven't kissed her. Never. Ridiculous. No one is there. Only wishes. Not even this much. A woman is stirring her coffee.

SEA

You're sitting on the strand, cannot speak, cannot speak today, you do not hesitate, you just can't. She's sitting next to you. She isn't speaking, she cannot speak today either. You're both sitting a meter apart, have turned your faces to the ocean. She holds her hands around her bent legs, has propped her chin on them. You have stretched out your feet. All around you are many people also staring at the ocean. They look at the ocean, then frequently look at each other, then back at the ocean. Only a very few go into the ocean to swim. You're sitting next to each other, don't touch each other, don't get any closer to one another, don't move, sit next to each other, just this wind and the movements of the ocean. Gulls return again and again, infrequent noises become more noticeable, for whatever reason. You don't move, never toward each other, never away from each other. Perhaps you're not even sitting next to each other. No one here even notices you. From time to time certain movements are put on show. She loosens her shoelaces, takes her shoes off.

You look at her shoes a long time, look at her feet, gazing a long time at her narrow feet. You are summoned to approach the ocean with your surfboard, but you don't hear, cannot obey this call. She too, she doesn't hear it either, can't hear it, still looking at the ocean. You are summoned several times to approach the ocean. None of the people surrounding you know you. Therefore no one can tell the two of you that you must come to the sea with your surfboards. You both remain sitting like this, just so. You remain sitting until evening comes. Shortly before darkness finally overtakes all, you both get up in order to catch the last bus.

She looks back one last time. You two are the last that are going home. You both know that you ought to have been challenged at some point on this day to approach to the sea, you both know it. You both go home now. The sea is nearly motionless at the shore. She moves ahead and holds the surfboard with her right hand, you are following her. You are moving almost in the darkness. Then the bus comes and the last visitors to the beach get in. She presses her face to the glass, otherwise there's just the rumbling of the bus and the streetlights that illuminate the darkness every few meters. Perhaps you'll both come back. Probably not. You move not a millimeter closer to one another. Perhaps you'll be able to distance yourselves from each other, perhaps not.

CLOUDS (1)

A piano is playing before empty music stands, it is late in the evening, a woman stands indifferently, motionless, she is looking at older people, how they glide their bodies across the dance floor with such ease, effortlessly, crossing like clouds, with such ease, for how long?

The bar is called Dubrovnik and before the war was the main place to go in town. I work as head waitress. My name is Ilona. Then I go home. I am waiting for the tram, waiting for Lauri, my husband, and we are going home together. It is autumn. Lauri keeps eye contact with me as we enter the apartment.

He leads me into the apartment, sits me on the sofa, only then may I open my eyes again. Lauri holds the remote control in his hand, he has the choice of twelve stations, it is autumn and our dog is looking for the ball. Then Lauri goes to work, then for the final time Lauri goes to work. There have been layoffs, Lauri, the cards will decide, Kreuz Dreier, that wasn't enough, that wasn't enough, and too much for your pride to go to the unemployment office, it won't take long, a pro doesn't need luck, Lauri, my poor man, the world won't end over it either, even if my boss has forgotten *to modernize*, as she says, no, my boss, people have just gotten older and they can't drink as much as they used to, when they glide across the dance floor, like love, that then disappears again in the autumn, behind the clouds, again and again, only to return again in the spring, on the dance floor, how many springtimes yet, and where will they dance then when the Dubrovnik has closed its doors.

Where does the hot wind blow? And where does love go in winter? And where do the unemployed go with their pride, when they are older than thirty-eight or older than fifty?

■

The lights are off, we're cleaning up, I'm going home to Lauri, I will go home until they've carried the furniture out of the apartment, until they pick up the television again and still before spring has come, Lauri, I'm too old to tend tables at thirty-eight and you, you can't even pass a routine check-up anymore. It's raining against the windowpanes, and we eat soup in autumn, and we eat with the tourists when they wind their way through the country, with their busses and cameras, Lauri, my love, happiness will return, in the autumn or in winter or in the spring, then we'll all work together, all of us that have been let go now. You just have to hold out for a few more crossword puzzles. Four letters, reminds you of needles, and as long as the wallpaper is still hanging on the walls, we won't go hungry. Life is short and sad, wash a few dishes, I don't do anything special, Lauri, it's a filthy hole, where I work, it doesn't even have a name, life is short and sad. Then it snows quite lightly and quite delightfully. And when it snows, our wishes are quite near. I'm opening my own place and I'm going to call it *Work*, and it's noon, and then it's suddenly quite full behind the clouds.

BUS STATION

As a child we once played a game. It had to do with running and looking at people's faces.

I'm bored with him.
I give her my headaches.
I give her my bills.
I'm not coming back.
I want to begin anew.

I'm going to leave everything where it stands and want to begin
   anew.
I'm throwing it all away.
I trust her.
I'm staying overnight.
I'm not afraid of the kid.
I'm closing all doors and windows.
I'm closing all lights and doors.
When one grows old, one no longer wants light.

When one grows old, one searches for darkness.
I still have to wash the dishes.
I still have to change.
I'm bored with him.
I have nothing left to say to you.
I'm buying you.
I'm letting myself be paid for.
I'll give you what you want.
I'm giving you this night.

You move something within me.
I have to wash my face.
I still have to wash my hands.
I really love my husband.
I play golf and pool.
I still want to be young for one more night.
I still want to be desired for one more night.
I still want for a single night for someone to laugh at my jokes, to be
   invincible.
Then I'll give you a list of my maladies,

In order to help you get used to my face,
In order to calm your face.
I am bored with him.

You are too old to go away.
She is too you to notice you.

SNOW

Now you begin to die. The bullet is lodged deep. The rocks have spoken through the fire. You were a poet. Now you are a *killer of the white man.* Now they're following you. In the woods, only the river and the horses, the wind can be heard. Guns replace your poetry, William Blake. They're shooting from the windows of the trains. You're leaning over your cards, falling asleep sitting up. You're playing against yourself. Everywhere are teepees, standing empty. The men in their fur coats shoot at anything that isn't them. They point their guns out the windows. The water running down your head is not dissimilar to the landscape.

It's a long way to the ocean in order to go back. You fall asleep again, have propped your head on the bag. Everywhere there are bones, dead animals. They are following you. The naked bird flies through the river. You've killed a white man. The gun will replace your tongue. The wind will watch over you. You tear up the paper that bears your name. William Blake. One can't stop the clouds by building a wooden ship. Perhaps you'll see more clearly if you don't wear any glasses. Now you're beginning to die. Perhaps then you'll see more clearly. The soul-stealer is made of forest-berries. In the woods lies snow. The birds are wearing lovely coats. You've got a gun now, and it's raining again. You lie down next to a dead deer. The blood is still warm. You taste it, rubbing it on your wound. You sleep next to the deer. From the woods, faces move toward you. You open your eyes a long time, then shut them again. They come upon you. Those that have feathers do not fly back here.

Sometimes the spirits talk like monkeys. You have to return to the mirror, there, where the water meets the sky. The boat has to be strong enough to carry you across. An elk accompanies you. An eagle accompanies you. Then you fall to a knee in order to put the last few meters behind you. Everywhere there are totem poles, these are strange gods. An Indian woman is weighing her child. They place you in a boat lined with cedar branches. You've put on a cap. You're paddling out to open sea. It's raining. The air is damp with voices.

DREAM (2)

My name is Gabbeh. I am at your feet. I am telling a story:
My family lives in the desert. We never stay in one place. Thing is, my father is in such a terrible mood because my mother is so ugly. A rider on his white horse is following us. Sometimes the rider rides across a wheat field nearby. When my uncle has found a wife, then I may marry. The rugs are being washed. Feet hurt. The water is clear. My uncle had a dream about a woman who sings like a bird. It was at the source of a river. We are looking for this woman. If she is evil, she will hide and speak poems. Then, too, may I marry. Mother says, we are the branches on a tree. Sometimes we become more than this, sometimes less. The rider is following us. From time to time I give him a sign so that he doesn't get tired.

During the day, my sisters keep watch over me.
At night, the men do.
I hear the howling of the rider.

I lack courage.

Father would beat me.

Uncle winks at me. I pull the covers over my head. I hear the howling of a wolf. The white rider is following us across the desert. I cry often because I cannot go with him. Then I leave a kerchief lying so that I might be close to him. I look to the distance, how he takes it up close to him, how he smells it. I see myself going with him. My family keeps watch over me. When my mother has come down again, then may I marry. The rugs tell a story of our lives. We move on. Uncle found a young woman at the river that sings like a bird, so lovely. I run as fast as I can. We escape on two white horses. Father pursues us. A shot rings out. You can hear the shot. As clear as water.

This means that my father has broken my neck.

This means that he's killed the white rider.

On Gabbeh one can see a white horse that carries two riders. The man is sitting in front.

CLOUDS (2)

to emerge from a silence to go into a silence they experience the birds when they go with every step when they laugh thus do they pass these thoughts from a distance of ten meters from eleven meters

the loveliest moment has still not begun when they they are addressed in the springtime wind to be hoping to delay to a later life yet quite soon the entry shall come the arrival of longing they don't believe it

with her body and spirit far from home thus do thoughts wander so as not to be here in someplaces or other the dearest people in their head in order to not have to accept the present to endure it in the summer's wind in the face of the saddest events from their childhood at fifteen below zero in the winter during their puberty from within a fatigue for this life at ten below zero

to speak in hate in neurotic blabbering in fury and despair the speaking in order to go on to suffer continually to laugh to laugh with those couple of holes that just beats life because it just can't do any different

only to clothe the seeds of fury when we laugh or to take a leaf in our arms in order to keep it present it's useless to be amazed at or to enjoy solely life this is the agreement in order to be moved by the moment

to no longer be able to have this fear slumber in one's own body finding no desire that wants to hold itself upright uninterruptedly utterly indifferent wherever we look wherever we go when we hear a bell we stand still in order to be with ourselves alone and nowhere else

when a child laughs when they are many bells do ring but it doesn't count for them the children that can be seen in front of the house and they cannot hear them the ears are concealed beneath a cap when the telephone rings when it rings they inhale and you inhale and exhale

they are thinking three thousand years in the future four thousand years and the anger ceases when it rains or the sun shines through the steps like clouds in the sky you think three thousand years they come and go around a continent behind itself

and so they sit on that which was and what was and what shall be

■

the worries and plans for a future for a second in an agreement of ideas to exchange the years yet the longing lies in the distance in a tiredness

in order to return to the true homeland to be with that with all senses that which actually is for example to knead the earth with every step they inhale and you inhale and exhale

RAIN

The cars are driving backward in the rain. Even the people are going backward, when it's raining, and it's already been raining for quite a while. No one can remember exactly when these clouds arrived, the ones that brought us the rain. It's said they will only go away again when people lose themselves in strange new obsessions. And then it's said: Only when the clouds touch the ground can people lose themselves. Every night, in a theater, they replay the events of the rains. Sometimes, two unpaid power bills lead to a power outage. That can happen sometimes.

The man that works in this theater says to a woman: Your breasts are two flashlights.

The woman says: I can't pay the rent. Do what you've promised.

The man says: I will not go. No matter what they say. And even if they take it all away from me. They'll have to drag me away from here. I'm staying. I'm ready.

The man says: Your breasts are two flashlights.

The rain is quite heavy and people are getting drenched to the bone. Passionately they stand in front of the closed shops. And life has to go on, somehow.

∎

The man says: In the dark we are many.

The man says: It is difficult to keep one's balance in light of all that's happening.

The woman says: You're still searching, after all these rainy days, for what

you've lost, to make sure you're not alone when evening comes.

The man says: Who has time to think if one is busy all day and comes home tired at night.

The woman says: You always were in love with two or three women at once.

People who go into the streets in the rain have long since stopped getting paid. They've been living years without money. Since it's been raining, they wander aimlessly through the city only to lose their minds in the end.

The man says: I'm afraid to die. I'm afraid of loneliness and the truth.

The woman says: One can't swim against the current, yet one can't let oneself get dragged away. Only the river itself is an enduring joy.

The man says: If death comes, I'll scream. I'll scream so that I don't choke on my own vomit. I'll scream as much as I can and as loudly as I can.

The woman says: It'll all soon be over.

It's raining the whole time without people ever getting to where they're going. They have become without origin as well. The people don't complain, even if they've long since been compelled to walk backward. The rain has no beginning, and no end. One needn't run away from it. No one bothers to hold an umbrella in their hands anymore. The television and radio broadcast the lives of the rain people.

The woman says: The rain has something to do with hope, that the sun might return again.

The woman asks: How many rainy days do we need to finally give up hope and fill up our holes on this earth?

The man says nothing. He tells the observers about the occurrences of rain. He speaks about hopes that the rain never fulfills. He is afraid.

The woman says: It'll soon be over.

ORACLE

A year ago. In a club. I was there with my cousin. Vacation had just begun. He spoke to me. He said that his name was Kurt. That he was an Englishman. Initially he said that he was Dutch, then that he was English. Both were lies. He was from Italy, as he later told me. From Venice.

We drove around a lot. He always picked me up from school, if he had time. We were often down at the lake and went walking there. We spent a lot of time in the open air. We often went walking for hours.

Yes. Once, in winter.

A cabrio. Initially, a cabrio, then a red Fiat with a smashed window. There were various other sorts of cars. No. I didn't think much of it at all. He told me that he was a dealer.

A hunting gun and a big pistol, a heavy one. I don't know. Sometimes a smaller one, too. I was also allowed to shoot when we were out in the open. He had to shoot. I don't know. Sometimes we made up code names. He killed his parents. Then he was in prison for five years. He couldn't take it there and went to France. He wanted to be free, finally.

No.

■

He always had money. A few trivial things, perhaps, when we were together. Yes. Once he got me an ice cream, and I had to wait in the car, I thought for a second that he'd stolen it. But otherwise. Not much.

At the beginning, no. Sometimes he wanted to tie my hands behind my back, but when I began to scream, then he quickly stopped that. No. Never. It was always voluntary.

We lived in abandoned houses or in barns. I think they were abandoned houses. He just went right in. Nobody was living in there at all. I found that interesting. It was often cold. He was never cold. He also slept very little.

After vacation was over I told him that it was over between us. Yet he didn't believe it at first. No. A few times. Then? No.

He was suddenly standing in front of the school. I was afraid of him. I didn't want to have anything more to do with him and ran away. He said he could kill five of my friends with one hand. Nothing happened. Then, he left. That was the last time. Yes.

One more time. On my birthday. I think he was somewhere on the sea. He called me. He told me that he was a DJ now. Then, no more.

THE FILMS

DREAM

(1) *Don't Die Without Telling Me Where You're Going*,
directed by Eliseo Subiela
(2) *Gabbeh*, directed by Mohsen Makhmalbaf

SEA

A Scene at the Sea, directed by Takeshi Kitano

CLOUDS

(1) *Drifting Clouds*, directed by Aki Kaurismäki
(2) *Schritte der Achtsamkeit* (Steps of Mindfulness),
directed by Thomas Lüchinger

BUS STATION

Faces, directed by John Cassavetes

SNOW

Dead Man, directed by Jim Jarmusch

RAIN

The Cloud, directed by Fernando E. Solanas

ORACLE

Roberto Succo, directed by Cédric Kahn

TRANSLATED FROM GERMAN BY MARK KANAK

ARIAN LEKA

Brothers of the Blade

No one knows out of what sort of stuff we cook up those few joys that nonetheless change from time to time to malice and poison inside us; no one can say why we turn our skins inside out, why we stick the thorns that we meant to reserve for the world deep into ourselves, down to the bone; why we pay such an exorbitant price, meet any cost, to fulfill the irrepressible desire to open ourselves up, to be together, the same as everyone else; why we bullshit; why we sing those things in chorus that we would never have whistled in solitude; why we forgive; why we laugh; why we give string to our kites in days of joy and then afterward feel so empty, seeing that our souls are farther away from ourselves than a ship from its anchor, that anchor which keeps the ship from crashing into the shallows in the doldrums or else in the fierce winter winds. So too thinks the big brother, who has dressed in his black suit today, who's had his hair shorn to a close crop, who is freshly shaven, he who has downed a couple of glasses of raki, no more, just enough to perfume the insides of his lungs, as all men do, because he truly is a man, and he must bear a great burden through the night. At least, he must do so more than his father, whose only responsibility is to beam happily and raise toasts to the health of his sons; at least, he must do so more than his mother, who considers herself to be quite lucky, what with having two sons and all; at least, he must do so more than his sister, dancing with her husband, dreaming of pregnancy, of twins; at least, he must do so more than his wife, who is smirking at all their foolishness. At least, and most of all, he must do so more than all his new in-laws, who want to get him drunk and pin him down on this fresh September evening when he is marrying off his little brother.

Though, really, he has never just been "the little brother." For many years, since the time when their father was no longer good for anything, he has been the man of the house: their mother's helping hand, the bars on their father and sister's cage. It is for this brother that he is, today, wearing a black suit—a unique pleasure.

As day broke on Sunday morning he was shaved by the barber. When he returned, he reeked of eau de cologne and a small bloody weal had appeared over the scrap of newspaper with which the barber had tried to conceal the nick left on his throat. He suffered a moment of overwhelming anxiety as he knocked on the door to wake his little brother—who, in the meantime, had wrapped himself in a white sheet, still in bed, still luxuriating in sleep following the obligatory midnight visit to his future in-laws. The older brother doubted and dreaded lest fate, perverse as always, should serve the bridegroom up into the hands of that same provincial barber—who had, it seemed, reserved for his razor the right of blood vengeance against their family's many generations of sinners, hoping to punish them all in a single moment by spilling the blood of their most exalted son on the day of his wedding. This had all occurred to him in a flash as he stood knocking, summoning his brother to tell him that he must get up and prepare to be married.

He got up, stitched his bones back together by stretching, and, completely unaware of the demons plaguing his big brother, said:

"This feels like a wonderful day to get married. And for everything that goes with it."

And for everything that goes with it. For the potent and viscous coffee that he requested from his mother with a shout. For the homemade curd-cheese donut he demanded hot from his sister. For the tightly rolled cigarette that he had solicited from his father while still supine. For the glass of water "that I want from you, my most legally sororal one," as he put it to one of his sisters-in-law. And then, for everything that goes with being a groom.

"Fine! Beard, locks, and moustache—you can fix them up for me. What sort of goddamn groom would I be if I had to shave myself on my own wedding day?" he'd asked his big brother, after the latter had beseeched him—calmly as he could—not to see the town barber that day.

"Me?"

The big brother's hands began to tremble. He had told the bridegroom not to let himself be put to the blade at the barber's, but still—he had had no desire to carry out the task himself. He felt as though he was standing over a great pit. Then he saw himself surrounded by flames. It seemed to him that some force was maneuvering to undo the good he'd tried to accomplish, was interfering with what had been said and written, forward and backward. He himself no longer understood anything. *Didn't I want to save him from the barber where I myself was cut on the throat?* the big brother asked himself, *Didn't I want to protect my brother from becoming a sacrificial offering on his wedding day, while his bride sits and waits in her parents' house, staring at the walls down to the corners, waiting and longing, reciting between gritted teeth some tuneless lyric, like "When you come to your home, you'll be coming as a guest"?* The big brother had only wanted to strike a little match to shed some light on the path of fate, but he'd forgotten how many people are always waiting in the wings, their guts bursting with the breath they can't wait to let out and so extinguish your little flame. He had also wanted to return to his little brother, in a single day, everything the younger man had done for the family. He had wanted to protect him, to conceal him. But no, it had come out all wrong. In trying to help his brother, he had played into fate's hands, awakening the evil that had slept, like his brother, under a single sheet—hearing himself reminded:

"You will fulfill your brotherly duty by serving me on this one day—one day in return for my entire life, which I have devoted, as you know, to you, to all of you."

Big words, of course, as the little brother's usually were, but as was always the case, true. Arranging the round hand mirror, the bowl of hot water, the soap, and the brush on the well, the big brother raised his eyes to the sky. He'd never had to shave another man before, which is why his jaw was clenched, why he touched and touched again the now dried weal that the village barber had hidden under the scrap of newspaper, while he tried to hone the brand-new razorblade on the whetstone. Meanwhile, the little brother had come out into the yard. He left his half slurped coffee on the throat of the well and took his place in the chair he'd set out, dressed now in a snow-white poplin shirt, stretching his neck out like a lamb, joking and ordering everyone around, father, mother, sister and sister-in-law.

The big brother smiled out of the corner of his mouth. It was the first time he'd ever seen his brother like this. It was the first time that in his head, shoulders, walk, and words, their father, that humble man, the old pillar of the house, was no longer recognizable. Moreover, he could almost hear footsteps. He imagined that all the elders and the wise men of the village were coming out and then beating a hasty retreat, finally leaving his brother alone. His little brother was freeing himself of all those ponderous shadows that had always more dragged him down than they had held him upright, that had prevented him from ever seeing the forest with the eyes of a child who wants the trees for his own kingdom but instead with the eyes of a man whose sole purpose is to sell the wood—so that his father could have tobacco in his pouch, so that his mother could have a black silk headscarf for her head, so that his sister could have a dowry, and so that his big brother could finish school. The little brother was freeing himself of those shadows that had forced him to become a man too soon, he was becoming a boy again as his father and big brother watched. Seeing him laughing, giddy, the big brother squeezed his wrist, lifted the razor-blade, and blessed whatever force was again making the groom into child and brother.

But after this, when my little brother will no longer be the clandestine father and unhappy angel of our household, what will our real father be? What will I be? the big brother asked himself, turning his head toward his wife sadly. He shut his eyes and drew the blade near the little brother's neck, right over the jugular. He swallowed a big gob of spit. He touched the rough skin on his brother's neck before the blade could advance over its quivering fuzz, felt the anxious trot of his pulse. And he abruptly opened his eyes. Nothing could have been more tranquil than his brother's smile.

"Maybe it would be better if you just gave yourself a good combing and left it at that," the big brother said. "It would be easier for both of us."

Only then did he remember to soften his little brother's stubble with hot water and soap. He started lathering the soap as if possessed—as if wanting to fill in and white out the toasted sun color of his brother's face as quickly as possible, as if wanting to hurry on to the rendezvous of blade and flesh, to the thrilling caress wherein metal comes to understand all the divots and scars on our skin, toward that motion that, scraping over stubble, skin, and veins, adds a new face to the world, the face of a new man.

But having done this, the big brother found he couldn't proceed. His eyes were dim, a small drop of spittle was gradually gathering in a corner of his mouth, and a gleaming stream of sweat was dripping from his neck toward his chest. He was entirely spattered and sullied with shaving foam. He knew he needed to get started, get started and finally be done with his gruesome responsibility. But looking again at his brother's face, eyes closed, happy, perhaps dreaming, he couldn't bring himself to act.

"I have a cyst on my neck," said the little brother, "careful when you go around it."

The big brother dropped the brush in the bowl, again took up the razor, passed it twice over the palm of his hand, and pushed up at his brother's sideburns so as to stretch the wrinkles taut where his skin folded under his neck.

"Leave me a little something," the little brother said absentmindedly, "I don't want to look like a little kid."

The big brother sighed. *And after this, when my little brother is not our father anymore, what will our real father be? What will I myself be?* he wondered again, the words ringing like bells in his ear as he got ready to slide the blade down the waiting cheek at last. His fingertips detected a deep scar, about two thumbs under the chin. *This is from the wound he got when he fought a sixteen-year-old boy over our sister,* he thought, and raised his finger a bit further up so as to find a new place from which to begin. *I need to start from the neck, I think, moving the blade against the grain,* he told himself, but when his fingers found another scar there, the big brother pulled his hand away as if bitten by a snake, and remembered that *this* cut had been closed by six stitches and no small amount of suffering, because the tin plate that had opened it, besides being huge, was also rusty all over. *It happened when that neighborhood kid fell into the creosote pit and he jumped in to help pull him out,* the big brother remembered. He lowered the razorblade once again —it glistened in the morning sun—and started to scrutinize his little brother's face. Scars, welts, wens, and lines—a single careless pass would suffice to start a bloodbath. And meanwhile, their entire childhood, the time when they had been inseparable, was mapped right there in front of him, was there for him to touch; and in the space between two wounds he saw that day when they had rubbed each other with shoe polish, under their noses and on their cheeks, so as to look like men a little sooner.

The big brother raised his hand. He placed the razor on the waiting cheek, and while standing rigid, ready to glide his hand down to clear a path—as skiers do, rushing down a snowy pass before jumping into the abyss—asked a question:

"Where do we begin?"

He waited a long time for an answer. So long that he wondered if his brother had been struck after all by the evil he'd sensed early that morning, which he had been dreading since daybreak, when he'd begun to suspect that the vines of fate had crept into the holes in the barber's house and wrapped themselves around the man's hands. But, then again, the odds were that his brother had simply fallen asleep, that he was napping there under the sunbeams, a few hours before he became another person entirely, a husband. *Whatever we cook up our few joys from, it's rare stuff indeed,* the big brother thought. *We change ourselves on account of others, we pay a high price just to be together, until at last the anchor chain snaps and the ship sails off to go about its own business . . .*

The big brother liked to think that his little brother was dreaming something nice, that he was smiling in his sleep—but there was no way to know, we understand very little about the people we share our lives with, and now wasn't the time to speculate, especially after hearing the thick voice of their father call out, "I could have skinned a whole lamb with a piece of glass by now, let alone shaved my little brother!"; a little brother who, by the setting of the sun, will have broken free of his chains to drift away, in excellent weather, to calmer harbors, over untroubled waters . . . smooth like a face without blemish.

TRANSLATED FROM ALBANIAN BY SARA "PËRPARIM" SMITH

Author Biographies

For additional information on the writers and countries
included in Best European Fiction 2011, *as well as*
interviews with the authors, visit www.dalkeyarchive.com.

PETER ADOLPHSEN was born in 1972 in Århus, Denmark. He attended the Danish Writers School from 1993 to 1995. At twenty-five, he made his debut with a collection of short prose entitled *Små Historier* (Small Stories, 1996), followed four years later by *Små Historier 2* (Small Stories 2): pieces from both of these collections appear in this anthology. He has also published two novellas: *Brummstein* (2003) and *Machine* (2006), the latter of which was translated into English in 2008. Adolphsen has since received a three-year work endowment from the Danish Arts Foundation. His most recent book, *Katalognien* (The Catalogued Kingdom, 2009), is a novel in verse.

MICHAL AJVAZ was born in 1949 in Prague, Czechoslovakia. He studied Czech and Aesthetics at Charles University in Prague, and currently works as a researcher at Prague's Center for Theoretical Studies. His novel, *Prázdné ulice* (Empty Streets), was awarded the Jaroslav Seifert Prize in 2005, the most prestigious literary award in the Czech Republic. He was recently shortlisted for the prestigious Magnesia Litera Award for his latest novel, *Cesta na jih* (Voyage to the South, 2008), from which his story in this anthology was excerpted. Two other novels, *Druhé město* (1993; *The Other City*, 2009) and *Zlatý věk* (2001; *The Golden Age*, 2010), are available in English translation from Dalkey Archive Press.

VLADIMIR ARSENIJEVIĆ was born in 1965 in Pula, Croatia. He was the youngest-ever recipient of the prestigious NIN Prize for his first novel *U potpa-*

lublju (1994; *In the Hold,* 1996). Since then, Arsenijević has published four other novels, including *Angela* (1997) and *Mexico: Ratni dnevnik* (Mexico: A War Diary, 2000). In his career as an editor, he founded and ran the RENDE publishing house, and was its editor-in-chief until 2007. He lives in Belgrade and currently runs the Belgrade division of VBZ, a distinguished Croatian publishing house.

KEVIN BARRY was born in 1969 in Limerick, Ireland. He writes columns for the *Sunday Herald* in Glasgow and the *Irish Examiner* in Cork. His short story collection, *There are Little Kingdoms,* won the 2007 Rooney Prize for Irish Literature and was shortlisted for the Frank O'Connor International Short Story Award. His novel, *City of Bohane,* will appear in 2011, and his stories have appeared in many journals and anthologies, including the *New Yorker, Phoenix Best Irish Stories, The Granta Book of the Irish Short Story, The Stinging Fly,* and the *Dublin Review.* He also writes plays, screenplays, and essays, and he collaborates on graphic stories and puppet shows. He lives in County Sligo and in Dublin.

MARCO CANDIDA was born in 1978 in Tortona, Italy. He has published five novels in the last four years: *La mania per l'alfabeto* (Alphabet Mania, 2007); *Il diario dei sogni* (Dream Diary, 2008), from which his story in this anthology was excerpted; *Domani avrò trent'anni* (Tomorrow I'll be Thirty, 2008); *Il mostro della piscina* (The Monster in the Pool, 2009); *Il bisogno dei segreti* (The Need for Secrets, 2010); and he has a novel forthcoming in 2011: *Torneo* (Tournament). Candida is also well-known in Italy for his literary blog at lamaniaperlalfabeto.splinder.com, and for being a great supporter and promoter of the horror genre, which is almost nonexistent in Italian fiction, through his website at www.websitehorror.com. He is currently editing an anthology of stories published at this site.

IULIAN CIOCAN was born in 1968 in Chişinău, Moldova. He graduated from the University of Brasov in Romania. He has published two books of literary criticism, *Metamorfoze narative* (Narrative Metamorphosis, 1996) and *Incursiuni în proza basarabeană* (Foray into Bessarabian Fiction, 2004). He is also the author of an autobiographical novel, *Înainte să moară Brejnev* (Before Brezhnev Died, 2007). He has been a lecturer at the Pedagogical Institute in Chişinău and is currently a journalist for the Chişinău bureau of Radio Free Europe.

KRISTÍN EIRÍKSDÓTTIR was born in 1981 in Reykjavík, Iceland. A graduate of the Icelandic School of Visual Art, she is completing her master's in painting and drawing at Concordia University in Canada. Her first book of poetry, *Kjöt-bærinn* (Chop City), was published in 2004. Two more books of poetry and drawings followed in swift succession. She is a member of Nýhil, a movement seeking to redefine Iceland's literary landscape.

FRANÇOIS EMMANUEL was born in 1952 in Fleurus, Belgium. After studying medicine, he took an interest in poetry and theatrical adaptation. Since the publication of his nonfiction work *Femmes Prodiges* (Extraordinary Women, 1984), his output has been almost entirely fiction. His most recent book, *Jours de tremblement* (Days of Trembling, 2010), won the Grand Prix de Littérature from the Société des Gens de Lettres. His novel *La Question humaine* (2000; *The Quartet*, 2001) was adapted into an acclaimed film, retitled *Heartbeat Detector* by its English-language distributors, in 2007. Emmanuel now spends his time as a writer and as a psychotherapist. Since 2004, he has been a member of the Belgian Academy of French Language and Literature.

ANDREI GELASIMOV was born in 1965 in Irkutsk, Russia. He studied at the Yakutsk State University (Faculty of Foreign Languages), and attended directing classes at the Moscow Theater Institute. His first published short story, "The Tender Age," appeared to great acclaim in 2000, receiving the Best Debut, Appollon Grigoricv, and Belkin literary awards. Gelasimov is considered one of the most popular young Russian writers working today.

FRODE GRYTTEN was born in 1960 in Odda, Norway, which has served as the setting for much of his fiction. A journalist for fifteen years, he developed a reputation for his short stories, which have been collected in such books as *Langdistansesvømmar* (Long-Distance Swimmer, 1990) and *Popsongar* (Popsongs, 2001). His novel *Bikubesong* (Beehive Song, 1999), won the Brage Prize from the Norwegian Publishers' Association, and was a nominee for the Nordic Council's Prize for Literature. His most recent novel, *Flytande bjørn* (2005; *The Shadow in the River*, 2008), won the Nynorsk Literature Prize and the Melsom Prize. His story in this anthology is from a recent collection entitled *Rom ved havet, rom i byen* (Rooms by the Sea, Rooms in the City, 2007), where each piece is based upon and paired with a painting by Edward Hopper.

MERCÈ IBARZ was born in 1954 in Saidí, Spain. She is an author, journalist, and cultural critic and has published novels, short stories, a biography of the celebrated Catalan author Mercè Rodoreda, and essays on film and photography. Her first work of fiction—though as much a work of reportage, autobiography, and travel writing—was *La terra retirada* (The Secluded Land, 1992), about her native village. This was followed by the novel *La palmera de blat* (The Palm Tree of Wheat) in 1995, after which Ibarz did not publish another work of fiction until 2002, when *A la ciutat en obres* (In the City of Works), a collection of short stories, appeared. Comfortable in various registers, her books form an assemblage of personal narrative and poetic prose, as well as evocations of quotidian life both as it is lived and as it is imagined. Her work has been translated into numerous major European languages.

NORA IKSTENA was born in 1969 in Riga, Latvia. She made her literary debut in 1993 with her biography of prewar writer and cultural activist Anna Rūmane Ķeniņa, followed by two short story collections and, in 1998, the publication of her novel *Dzīves svinēšana* (A Celebration of Life), which became a Latvian bestseller. Since then, the author has written a book almost every year—from collections of short stories or fairy tales, to full-length novels and biographies. Alongside her own work, she has edited the collected works of her literary mentor and teacher Dzintars Sodums, an accomplished Latvian-American poet, writer, and translator. Ikstena helped found the Latvian Literature Centre, the International Writers and Translators House in Ventspils, and the annual Prose Readings festival. She is a member and former chair of the National Culture Council. Her latest work includes the novel *Amour fou* and a book of observations and commentaries titled *Šokolādes Jēzus* (Chocolate Jesus, 2009). She is the recipient of the prestigious Baltic Assembly Award, the Three Star Order of Latvia, as well as numerous national awards. Ikstena and her husband divide their time between Latvia, Georgia, and Germany.

DRAGO JANČAR was born in 1948 in Maribor, Slovenia, and is one of the best-known Slovenian writers at home and abroad. After studying law, he worked as a journalist, an editor, and a freelance writer, and traveled to both the U.S. and Germany. As a President of the Slovenian PEN Center between 1987 and 1991, he was engaged in the rise of democracy in Slovenia and Yugoslavia. In 1993, he received the highest Slovenian literary award, the France-Preseren Prize, for his lifetime achievement. He won the European Short Story Award in 1994, was awarded the Herder Prize for Literature in 2003, was awarded the Jean Amery Award—conferred by the Office of the Austrian President—for his contributions to the Central European canon in 2007, and in 2009 was awarded the Premio Hemingway. His novels include *Galjot* (The Galley Slave, 1978), *Severni sij* (1984; *Northern Lights*, 2001), and *Posmehljivo poželenje* (1993; *Mocking Desire*, 1998). He now lives in Ljubljana.

DANUTĖ KALINAUSKAITĖ was born in 1959 in Kaunas, Lithuania. She is a graduate of Vilnius University, where she studied Lithuanian literature. She published her first book of short stories, *Iš jusi šviesa* (The Gone Light) in 1987, after which she retired from the literary world for almost two decades. "I simply lived" was the only explanation she gave, quoting poet and essayist Kęstutis Navakas, who said, "Silence is also an excellent form of self-expression." In 2003, Kalinauskaitė's short stories began appearing in the press, and were finally collected in a book, *Niekada nežinai* (You Never Know) in 2010. *Niekada nežinai* won both the prestigious Lithuanian Writers' Union Prize and the Prize of the Lithuanian Literature Institute. Kalinauskaitė is currently working on her third book.

LÁSZLÓ KRASZNAHORKAI was born in 1954 in Gyula, Hungary. He studied law in Szeged and later Hungarian Language and Literature in Budapest. In 1985, his debut novel *Sátántangó* appeared, which was later adapted by renowned filmmaker Béla Tarr, based on Krasznahorkai's own screenplay. This collaboration between author and director led to three other film adaptations of Krasznahorkai's novels, as well as *A londoni férfi* (*The Man from London*), based on a novel by Georges Simenon. The success of *Sátántangó* established Krasznahorkai as one of the great voices in contemporary Hungarian fiction. A DAAD Fellowship shortly thereafter took him to West Berlin. Krasznahorkai's novel *Az ellenállás melankóliája* (1989; *The Melancholy of Resistance*, 1998) brought him international fame, garnering praise from authors such as Susan Sontag and W. G. Sebald. His most recent novel to appear in English translation was *Háború és háború* (1999; *War and War*, 2006). He now lives in Berlin with his wife.

ANITA KONKKA was born in 1941 in Helsinki, Finland, where she still lives and works. She is the author of numerous novels, radio plays, essays, and articles, and has worked in many professions, including nurse in a psychiatric hospital, typist, public-relations officer, librarian at the Finnish National Office of Statistics, and editor of a history of Finnish civil engineering. Among her novels are *Johanneksen tunnustukset* (The Confessions of Johannes, 1995), *Rakkaus, kestava kiusaus* (Love, The Everlasting Temptation, 1997), and *Musta passi* (Black Passport, 2001). Works by Anita Konkka have been translated into English, Russian, and Hungarian. She won the 1989 Finnish National Prize for her novel *Hullun taivaassaa* (1988; *A Fool's Paradise*, 2006).

ERIC LAURRENT was born in 1966 in Clermont-Ferrand, France. After finishing his studies in literature, he moved to Paris. Laurrent has published nine novels with Éditions de Minuit, including *Coup de foudre* (1995), *Dehors* (Outside, 2000), and *Ne pas toucher* (2002; *Do Not Touch*, 2009). His most recent novel, *Renaissance italienne* (Italian Renaissance), was published in 2008.

ARIAN LEKA was born in 1966 in Durrës, Albania. He studied music at the Jan Kukuzeli Music Academy in Durrës before studying Albanian language and literature in Tirana. He is the founder of POETEKA, Albania's International Poetry and Literature Festival. Among his works are the poetry collections *Anija e Gjumit* (The Ship of Sleep, 2000) and *Strabizëm* (Strabismus, 2004), the novels *Veset e të Vdekurve* (The Vice of Death, 1997) and *Gjarpri i Shtëpsë* (The Snake of the House, 2002), and the short story collections *Ky vend i qetë ku s'ndodh asgjë* (This Quiet Country Where Nothing Happened, 1994) and *Shpina e Burrit* (The Back of Man, 2004). He has also translated the works of Eugenio Montale, Salvatore Quasimodo, and Italo Calvino into Albanian. Leka has twice received the Prize of the Albanian Writers Union and was a recipient of a Heinrich Böll House fellowship in 2006.

ZURAB LEZHAVA was born in 1960 in Tbilisi, Georgia. After finishing Tbilisi Secondary School Number 126, he started to work in the state-run publishing house. In 1982, he was imprisoned and spent the next sixteen years in jail. He now earns his living carving and selling wooden statues. He has published a novel and two books of short stories, and numerous short stories in various literary magazines. Half of his works were written during his time in jail.

VICTOR MARTINOVICH was born in 1977 in Minsk, Belarus. A graduate of the Belarussian State University's school of journalism, Martinovich works as editor of the weekly intellectual broadsheet *BelGazeta* in Minsk, and is head of the political science department at the European Humanities University in Vilnius. His debut novel Паранойя (Paranoia) was published in Russia in 2009 to great critical acclaim, despite being banned in his native Belarus.

HILARY MANTEL was born in 1952 in Glossop, England. She is the author of ten novels, including *A Place of Greater Safety* (1992); *The Giant, O'Brien* (1998); and *Wolf Hall*, which won both the Man Booker Prize and the National Book Critics Circle Award in 2009. She is also the author of a memoir, *Giving Up the Ghost*, winner of the 2006 Hawthornden Prize. Hilary Mantel's reviews and essays appear in the *New York Times*, *New York Review of Books*, and the *London Review of Books*.

BLAŽE MINEVSKI was born in 1961 in Gevgelija, Macedonia. He has worked as a reporter for the Macedonian daily *Nova Makedonija*, and currently writes for the magazine *Focus*. He has published three novels, including, most recently, *Nishan* (Target, 2007), as well as several volumes of short stories, selections of which have been translated into English and numerous other languages.

NORA NADJARIAN was born in 1966 in Limassol, Cyprus. A poet and short story writer who works primarily in English, she is the author of three collections of poetry and a book of short stories, *Ledra Street* (2006). Her work has appeared in numerous anthologies and journals, and has won prizes or been commended in international competitions, including the Commonwealth Short Story Competition, the Féile Filíochta International Poetry Competition (Ireland) and the Binnacle International Ultra-Short Competition at the University of Maine at Machias. Her 2004 poetry collection, *Cleft in Twain*, was one of the books from the new member states of the European Union recommended in an article appearing in the *Guardian* that same year. Her work was also included in *May Day: Young Literature from the Ten New Member States of the European Union*, published by the European Commission. A new book of her short stories is forthcoming from Folded Word (U.S.A.) in 2011.

ÉILÍS NÍ DHUIBHNE was born in 1954 in Dublin, Ireland. Her short story collections include *Midwife to the Fairies, The Inland Ice,* and *The Pale Gold of Alaska.* Among her numerous literary awards are The Bisto Book of the Year Award, the

Readers' Association of Ireland Award, the Stewart Parker Award for Drama, the Butler Award for Prose from the Irish American Cultural Institute, and several Oireachtas awards for her novels in Irish. Her novel *The Dancers Dancing* was shortlisted for the Orange Prize for Fiction in 2000. Ni Dhuibhne is a member of Aosdana and a Writer Fellow at University College, Dublin, where she teaches in Creative Writing.

ALEK POPOV was born in 1966 in Sofia, Bulgaria. He received his MA in Bulgarian Literature from the University of Sofia. His satirical novel, *Missiya London* (Mission London, 2001), was based on his impressions as cultural attaché at the Bulgarian Embassy in the United Kingdom. It became one of the most popular Bulgarian books dealing with the transition to a postcommunist society; a film version debuted in 2010. Popov's second novel, *Chernata kutiya* (The Black Box), was published to great critical acclaim in 2007. He is a recipient of the Canetti Prize and the Helikon Prize for best book of the year

WILIAM OWEN ROBERTS was born in 1960 in Bangor, North Wales. He attended the University of Wales and studied Welsh literature and theater, then turning to an MA studying television plays, focusing on the work of Dennis Potter. From 1983 to 1984 he was writer-in-residence with Cwmni Cyfri Tri Theatre Company, then worked for five years as a Script Editor at HTV. He became a full-time writer in 1989. He is best known for his novels, but also writes for theater, radio, and television. His first novel, *Bingo!* (1985), is a reworking of the diaries of Franz Kafka. His second novel, *Y Pla* (1987) is set in Wales, the Near East, and Europe in the fourteenth century, and was translated into English by Elisabeth Roberts as *Pestilence* in 1991. *Paradwys* (Paradise, 2001) is set during the American War of Independence and the French Revolution and deals with the abolition of slavery. *Paris Arull* (Paris Again), published in 2007, is about the experience of White Russians in exile, following the 1917 Revolution. Roberts's latest novel is *Petrograd* (2008), winner of the 2009 Wales Book of the Year Award (Welsh-language) and the ITV Wales People's Choice Award. He lives in Cardiff with his wife and three daughters.

GORAN SAMARDŽIĆ was born in 1961 in Sarajevo, Bosnia and Herzegovina. He writes poetry, prose, and literary criticism, and is one of directors of Buybook, a popular Sarajevo bookstore. In 2004 he won the annual prize of the Bosnian

Writer's Association for his novel *Sumski duh* (Forest Spirit). Among his other works are *Lutke* (Dolls, 1990), *Otkazano zbog kiše*, (Canceled Because of the Rain, 1995), *Imeðu dva pisma* (Between Two Letters, 1996), and *Leteći Beogra anin* (The Flying Belgrademan, 2009).

INGO SCHULZE was born in 1962 in Dresden, Germany. He studied classic philology in Jena and worked in Altenburg as a dramatic arts advisor and editor of a newspaper. He has been living in Berlin since 1993. He was awarded the Aspekte Literature Prize for his first book, *33 Augenblicke des Glücks* (1995; *33 Moments of Happiness*, 1998), and the Berliner Literature Prize for *Simple Storys* (1998; *Simple Stories*, 2000) both of which are available in English translation. The *New Yorker* has numbered Schulze among the "Six Best European Novelists," and the *Observer* described him as one of "21 Authors to Keep an Eye on in The Twenty-first Century." Ingo Schulze is a member of the Academy of Arts Berlin and the German Academy for Language and Poetry. His books have been translated into twenty-seven languages. His most recent novel to be translated into English was *New Lives* in 2008. *Orangen und Engel: Italienische Skizzen* (Oranges and Angel: Italian Sketches), where the story in this anthology first appeared, was published in 2010.

MIMA SIMIĆ was born in 1976 in Zadar, Croatia. She graduated from the Zagreb Faculty of Philosophy with a degree in Comparative Literature and English Language and Literature, and she holds an MA in Gender Studies from the Central European University in Budapest. Thus far, she has published a collection of short stories, *Pustolovine Glorije Scott* (Adventures of Gloria Scott, 2005), and had many of her stories featured in Croatian and international literary magazines, as well as numerous anthologies. She is a member of the editorial team of *Sextures: A Virtual Forum and E-journal for Sexualities, Cultures, and Politics*, and is on the editorial board of Ekviva, the regional women's web portal. She has translated several books into Croatian and English and regularly translates fiction and theory. As a journalist and film and cultural critic, she writes for various Croatian and international publications.

OGNJEN SPAHIĆ was born in 1977 in Podgorica (formerly Titograd), Montenegro, where he studied civil engineering and philosophy. He continues to live there today and works as a journalist and culture editor for the independent daily paper *Vijesti*. Spahić has published two collections of short stories: *Sve to* (All That, 2001) and *Zimska potraga* (Winter Search, 2007). His novel *Hansenova djeca* (Hansen's Children, 2004) won him the 2005 Meša Selimović Prize for the best new novel from Croatia, Bosnia-Herzegovina, Serbia, and Montenegro, and has since become a cult book in the countries of the former Yugoslavia. In 2007, Spahić participated in the International Writing Program at the University of Iowa.

DIETER SPERL was born in 1966 in Wolfsberg, Austria. He grew up in Zeltweg, a small town in Styria. Later, he studied language, literature, and philosophy in Graz. For several years he was the editor of the experimental literature magazine *perspektive* and founder and editor of *gegensätze*, a theoretical and literary book series. He has worked as a teacher, language coach, curator, and author. He moved to Vienna in 1997, and from 2005 to 2007 he worked for the Wiener Zeitung and ran the literature portion of the art magazine *ST/A/R*. He is the author of numerous radio plays and two novels: *Random Walker* (2005), an elaborate journal of films he had watched, from which his piece in this anthology was compiled; and *Absichtslos* (Unintentional, 2007), a novel in vignettes about Vienna. He is currently Writer in Residence at Bowling Green State University, Ohio.

STEFAN SPRENGER was born 1962 in Zürich, Switzerland. He studied visual art and arts education in Lucerne and Zürich. He lives and works as an author, artist, and teacher in Schaan, Liechtenstein.

VERENA STEFAN was born in 1947 in Bern, Switzerland, and she lived in Berlin from 1968 to 1975 before immigrating to Canada. In addition to writing fiction and nonfiction, she is a translator and poet. A collection of her early works is available in English as *Shedding and Literally Dreaming*. She is also the author of *Rau, wild & frei* (Rough, Wild & Free, 1997), a collection of comparative essays on the figure of the girl in literature. She was co-translator of both *The Dream of a Common Language* by Adrienne Rich and *Lesbian Peoples: Materials for a Dictionary* by Monique Wittig and Sande Zeig. She most recently published the novel *Fremdschläfer* (Unknown Sleeper, 2007), and she has co-edited with Chaim Vogt a forthcoming anthology of Montreal Jewish lifestories titled *Als sei ich von einem andern Stern* (As If I were from Another Star, 2011).

GONÇALO M. TAVARES was born in 1970 in Luanda, Angola. He spent his childhood in Aveiro in northern Portugal, and has written several novels, including *A Máquina de Joseph Walser* (Joseph Walser's Machine, 2004), *Jerusalem* (2005; 2009), and *Aprender a Rezar na Era da Técnica* (2007; *Learning to Pray in the Age of Technology*, 2011), all of which are available or forthcoming in English translation. He is also the author of criticism, plays, children's books, and several volumes of short stories. Tavares has been awarded an impressive number of literary prizes in a very short time, including the Saramago Prize in 2005, and the Prêmio Portugal Telecom de Literatura em Língua Portuguesa in 2007. He teaches epistemology at the University of Lisbon.

LUCIAN DAN TEODOROVICI was born in 1975 in Rădăuți, Romania. He is the coordinator of the Romanian publisher Polirom's "Ego Prose" series, and senior editor of the *Suplimentul de cultură* weekly. Between 2002 and 2006, he was editor-in-chief at Polirom, and he has contributed prose, drama, and articles to various cultural magazines in Romania and abroad, including *Suplimentul de cultură*, *Timpul*, *Dilema veche*, *Observator cultural*, *Familia*, *ArtPanorama*, *Hyperion*, *Discobolul*, *Orizont*, *Evenimentul zilei*, *Cotidianul*, *Wienzeille* (Vienna), and *Au sud de l'Est* (Paris). He has written screenplays for several film projects, including an adaptation of his own 2002 novel *Circul nostru vă prezintă* (2002; *Our Circus Presents*, 2009). His books include *Cu puțin timp înaintea coborîrii extratereștrilor printre noi* (Shortly Before the Extraterrestrials Descended Among Us, 1999), and *Lumea văzută printr-o gaură de mărimea unei țigări marijuana* (The World Seen through a Hole the Width of a Spliff, 2000).

OLGA TOKARCZUK was born in 1962 in Sulechów, Poland. After finishing her psychology degree at the University of Warsaw, she initially practiced as a therapist. Since the publication of her first book in 1989—a collection of poems entitled *Miasta w lustrach* (Cities in Mirrors)—Tokarczuk has published nine volumes of fiction, including stories, novellas, and novels, and one book-length essay (on Bolesław Prus's novel *The Doll*). In English her work has appeared in numerous journals and anthologies, and her novel *Dom dzienny, dom nocny* (1998; *House of Day, House of Night*, 2002) was shortlisted for the IMPAC Dublin Literary Award. In 1998, Tokarczuk moved to a small village near the Czech border and now divides her time between there and Wrocław. For her novel *Bieguni*

(The Runners), she received Poland's top literary award, the Nike Prize, in 2008. Her most recent novel to appear in English translation is *Prawiek i inne czasy* (1996; *Primeval and Other Times*, 2010).

ERSAN ÜLDES was born in 1973 in Manisa, Turkey. He is an avid student of literary theory and writes with a bold, biting humor, pushing the limits of the novel form as we know it. His debut, *Yerli Film* (Domestic Film), received The İnkılap Bookstore Novel Award in 1999. His second novel, *Aldırılan Çocuklar Örgütü* (Organization of Aborted Children), was published in 2004. He has written book reviews for various supplements and literary magazines. His latest novel, *Zafiyet Kuramı* (The Theory of Infirmity), from which the story in this anthology was excerpted, was published in 2007.

MANON UPHOFF was born in 1962 in Utrecht, the Netherlands. She is the award-winning author of four novels, including *Gemis* (Loss, 1997) and *De bastaard* (The Bastard Son, 2004), three novellas, and a host of short stories that are considered among the best in contemporary Dutch literature. She is an editor of the literary journal *De Revisor*. Her latest novel, *De spelers* (The Players), appeared in October 2009.

ENRIQUE VILA-MATAS was born in Barcelona, Spain in 1948. One of Spain's preeminent novelists, he has been awarded the Rómulo Gallegos Prize and the Prix Médicis étranger. He is the author of twenty works of fiction, including *Paris no se acaba nunca* (Paris Never Ends, 2003) and *Dublinesca* (Dublinesque, 2010), as well as several books of nonfiction. His novels *Bartleby y compañía* (2000; *Bartleby & Co.*, 2004) and *El mal de Montano* (2002; *Montano's Malady*, 2007) are available in English translation.

TOOMAS VINT was born in 1944 in Tallinn, Estonia, where he still lives today with his wife Aili. His studies in biology at the Tartu State University were interrupted by a military draft; during his years in the Soviet Navy, he began to write poetry and prose. Upon his return to Estonia, Vint left the university and worked for Estonian television, and was one of the publishers of the underground literary magazine *Hees*. Among his many novels are *Kojamehe naine* (The Janitor's Wife, 1995), *Lõppematu maastik* (An Unending Landscape, 1997), and *Topeltval-*

guses (In Double Light, 2005). Since 1971, Vint has earned his living as a freelance writer and painter. He is renowned for his paintings of metaphysical and conceptual landscapes, having produced twenty-four solo exhibitions and participated in numerous group exhibitions in many countries. Vint's novels and short stories have been nominated for several literary awards; he has won the Friedebert Tuglas Short Story Award twice, as well as the Estonian Prose Award.

Translator Biographies

İDIL AYDOĞAN's English translations of Turkish short stories have been published in various books and magazines. She has co-edited, with Amy Spangler, a special issue of *Transcript Review*, focusing on fiction from Turkey. She has participated in the Cunda International Workshop for Translators of Turkish Literature since 2008.

JŪRA AVIŽIENIS is a Lecturer in the Writing Program at Boston University. She has translated widely from Lithuanian.

ALISTAIR IAN BLYTH translates from Romanian. His published translations include *Little Fingers* by Filip Florian, *An Intellectual History of Cannibalism* by Cătălin Avramescu, and *Our Circus Presents* by Lucian Dan Teodorovici.

NATALIA BUKIA-PETERS is a translator, interpreter, and teacher of Georgian and Russian. She studied at the Tbilisi State Institute of Foreign Languages before moving to New Zealand in 1992 and then to Cornwall in 1994. She is a Chartered Member of the Institute of Linguists and translates a variety of literary, technical, and legal works both from and into English.

CHRISTOPHER BURAWA is a poet and translator. He has received a 2006 Witter Bynner Translation Residency, a 2007 Literature Fellowship for Translation from the National Endowment for the Arts, and a 2008 American-Scandinavian Foundation Creative Writing Fellowship. He is the Director of the Center of Excellence for the Creative Arts at Austin Peay State University in Clarksville, Tennessee.

GWEN DAVIES has published numerous translations of Welsh literature, including *Martha, Jack and Shanco* by Caryl Lewis. Working mainly as a fiction editor, she is the founder and editor-publisher of Alcemi (www.alcemi.eu) and editor of the forthcoming collection, *Sing Sorrow Sorrow: Dark and Chilling Tales.* She grew up in a Welsh-speaking family in West Yorkshire and now lives in western Wales.

VICTORIA FIELD has published two collections of poetry; the latter, *Many Waters*, was based on a year-long residency at Truro Cathedral. She has co-edited three books on therapeutic writing, most recently *Writing Routes*. She is an Associate Artist at Hall for Cornwall, who have produced two of her plays.

WILL FIRTH was born in 1965 in Newcastle, Australia. He studied German and Slavic languages in Canberra, Zagreb, and Moscow. Since 1991 he has been living in Berlin, Germany, where he works as a freelance translator of literature and the humanities. He translates from Russian, Macedonian, and all variants of Serbo-Croatian.

MARGITA GAILITIS was born in Riga, Latvia. In childhood, she immigrated with her mother and two sisters to Canada. In 1998 she returned to Latvia to work on a Canadian International Development Agency-sponsored project translating Latvian laws into English. Her poetry has been published in periodicals in Canada and the U.S. and she is the recipient of both Ontario Arts and Canada Council Awards.

SAM GARRETT is an American who currently divides his time between Amsterdam and the French Pyrenees. As well as work by Frank Westerman, he has translated books by Karel Glastra van Loon, Arnon Grunberg, Tim Krabbé, Lieve Joris, Geert Mak, and Nanne Tepper, among others. He was awarded the Vondel Translation Prize in 2003 and 2009.

ELIZABETH HARRIS is an Associate Professor of Creative Writing at the University of North Dakota. She is currently translating Marco Candida's *Il diario dei sogni* and Giulio Mozzi's *Questo e' il giardino*. Her translations of Candida and Mozzi appeared recently in the *Literary Review, Missouri Review, Kenyon Review*, and *Best European Fiction 2010*.

A. D. HAUN has worked as a librarian, researcher, translator, editor, and English instructor, as well as a volunteer worker with nongovernmental organizations in Germany, England, Croatia, Netherlands, Russia, and South Korea. She has published translations from eight languages including Croatian, Dutch, Finnish, and Korean.

CELIA HAWKESWORTH is emerita Senior Lecturer in Serbian and Croatian at the School of Slavonic and East European Studies, University College, London. She has published numerous articles and several books on Serbian, Croatian, and Bosnian literature. Her many translations include Dubravka Ugresic's *The Culture of Lies*, winner of the Heldt Prize for Translation in 1999; Ugresic's *Lend Me Your Character*, published by Dalkey Archive Press, and Ivo Zanic's *Flag on the Mountain*.

MARK KANAK is a writer and translator who divides his time between Chicago and Leipzig. His translation of Peter Pessl's *Aquamarine* appeared in 2008, and his translations have appeared in journals throughout the world. A collection of his poetry in German, *abstürze*, was recently published by Frohliche Wohnzimmer Verlag in Vienna.

SEÁN KINSELLA is a full-time translator and is currently completing his translation of a novel by Stig Sæterbakken for Dalkey Archive Press. He holds a MPhil from Trinity College, Dublin in Literary Translation, and resides in Norway with his wife and two children.

KRISTINA KOVACHEVA is a Bulgarian native who lives and works in Paris. A graduate of the American University of Paris, she translates between Bulgarian, French, and English.

VIJA KOSTOFF is a linguist, language teacher, writer, and editor. She has collaborated with Margita Gailitis in translating the novels, short stories, plays, film scripts, and poetry of many of Latvia's major writers. Born in Latvia, she now resides in Niagara on Lake Ontario, Canada.

ANTONIA LLOYD-JONES's translations from Polish include novels by Paweł Huelle (whose *The Last Supper* won the Found in Translation Award 2008) and Olga Tokarczuk (whose *House of Day, House of Night* was shortlisted for the IMPAC Dublin Award), short stories by Jarosław Iwaszkiewicz, and nonfiction by Ryszard Kapuściński and Wojciech Tochman.

DUSTIN LOVETT is currently a Fulbright scholar in Austria, conducting research on the cultural aspects of literary translation reception at the University of Vienna. His work as a translator has previously appeared in *Best European Fiction 2010*.

SYLVIA MAIZELL studied Russian Literature at the University of Chicago, in Moscow, and in Saint Petersburg, and has taught Russian. For the past decade she has worked as a translator from Russian, including stories by Vladimir Makanin, Aleksandr Kabakov, Victor Martinovich, Andrei Gelasimov, Emil Draitser, Boris Khazanov, and Dina Rubina.

RHETT MCNEIL is currently finishing a PhD dissertation on Machado de Assis and Jorge Luis Borges at Penn State University. He has translated Machado de Assis and is currently translating António Lobo Antunes, Gonçalo M. Tavares, and A. G. Porta.

CHRISTOPHER MOSELEY teaches at the School of Slavonic and East European Studies at University College, London. He came to Britain from Australia and studied Finland and the Baltic countries. While working as a journalist and translator at the BBC, he completed an MPhil on the Livonian language of Latvia. A freelance translator and editor, he is the author of *Colloquial Estonian* and co-author of *Colloquial Latvian* for Routledge. He has co-edited the Routledge *Atlas of the World's Languages*, edited their *Encyclopedia of the World's Endangered Languages*, and completed the third edition of an atlas of the world's languages in danger of disappearing for UNESCO. He translates into English from Estonian, Latvian, Finnish, and Swedish.

ANDREW OAKLAND has recently translated texts from the Czech, including Michal Ajvaz's *Golden Age* and Radka Denemarkova's *Money From Hitler*. He is currently working on novels by Martin Reiner and Martin Fahrner and a new biography of Franz Kafka by Josef Cermak.

ROWAN RICARDO PHILLIPS is the author of *When Blackness Rhymes with Blackness* and *The Ground*, a forthcoming collection of poems. His translations from Catalan have appeared in the *Review of Contemporary Fiction* and *Best European Fiction 2010*. His poems and essays have appeared in venues such as the *Kenyon Review, New Republic*, and the *New Yorker*. Phillips graduated from Swarthmore College and received his PhD from Brown University. He has taught at Harvard and Columbia and is currently Associate Professor of English at SUNY Stony Brook, where he also directs the Poetry Center. He lives in Greenwich Village and Barcelona.

URSULA MEANY SCOTT is a literary translator based in Dublin and working from French and Spanish. Her translation of Claude Ollier's novel, *Wert and the Life without End*, is due to be published in 2011. She holds an MPhil in literary translation with distinction from Trinity College, Dublin and was awarded a literary translation fellowship by Dalkey Archive Press in 2009.

K. E. SEMMEL is a writer and translator whose work has appeared in the *Ontario Review*, the *Washington Post, Aufgabe, Redivider, Hayden's Ferry Review, World Literature Today*, and elsewhere. He has translated Danish authors Pia Tafdrup, Jytte Borberg, and Simon Fruelund, among others. His translation of Norwegian crime novelist Karin Fossum's next book will be published in 2011.

SARA "PËRPARIM" SMITH has studied at Duke and Oxford Universities and translates from the Albanian.

AMY SPANGLER, a native of Ohio, has lived in Istanbul, Turkey, since 1999. Co-owner of the literary agency AnatoliaLit (www.anatolialit.com), Spangler is the translator of Asli Erdogan's *The City in Crimson Cloak* (Soft Skull, 2007) and co-editor and co-translator of *Istanbul Noir* (Akashic Books, 2008).

GEORGE SZIRTES was born in Budapest in 1948 and came to England as a refugee. He was brought up in London and studied Fine Art in London and Leeds. For his poetry, he has won the Faber Memorial prize and the T. S. Eliot Prize. He has also worked extensively as a translator of poems, novels, plays, and essays and has won various prizes and awards in this sphere. His own work has been translated into numerous languages. He lives near Norwich with his wife.

LISE WEIL received an MA and PhD in Comparative Literature at Brown University. She teaches in Goddard College's Individualized MA program and lives in Montreal, Quebec. She recently published *Beyond Recall*, a collection of the last writings of local painter and writer Mary Meigs, and is at work on a memoir, *In Search of Pure Lust*.

ANDREW WACHTEL is the Bertha and Max Dressler Professor of the Humanities at Northwestern University. He was elected to membership in the American Academy of Arts and Sciences in 2003, and is an acclaimed translator of contemporary Russian, Slovenian, and Serbo-Croatian poetry and prose, as well as editor of Northwestern University Press's "Writings from an Unbound Europe" series.

JOHN E. WOODS is the translator of over forty books from German to English. Among the authors he has translated are Thomas Mann, Arno Schmidt, Patrick Süskind, Christoph Ransmayr, and Ingo Schulze. He has twice been awarded the PEN Translation Prize, and has received the Schlegel-Tieck Prize and the Helen and Kurt Wolff Translator's Prize. He lives in Berlin.

institut
ramon llull
Catalan Language and Culture

 STATENS
KUNSTRÅD
DANISH ARTS COUNCIL

 elic

Estonian
Literature
Centre

 FILI
FINNISH LITERATURE EXCHANGE

 Liberté · Égalité · Fraternité
RÉPUBLIQUE FRANÇAISE
AMBASSADE DE FRANCE
AUX ETATS-UNIS

Service culturel

MINISTRY OF CULTURE
AND MONUMENT PROTECTION
OF GEORGIA

 GOETHE-INSTITUT
CHICAGO

 HUNGARIAN BOOK
FOUNDATION

 Bókmenntasjóður
The Icelandic Literature Fund

J A K

 JAVNA AGENCIJA ZA KNJIGO REPUBLIKE SLOVENIJE
SLOVENIAN BOOK AGENCY

MINISTRY OF CULTURE
Republic of Macedonia

 LATVIAN
LITERATURE
CENTRE

 PRINCIPALITY OF LIECHTENSTEIN

 BOOKS
FROM
LITHUANIA

 N O R L A

 POLISH
CULTURAL
INSTITUTE
www.PolishCulture.org.uk

 DG
LB
DIRECÇÃO-GERAL
DO LIVRO E DAS
BIBLIOTECAS

 M|C
MINISTÉRIO DA CULTURA

INSTITUTUL
CULTURAL
ROMÂN

 SPAIN
FOREIGN
CULTURAL
COOPERATION

swiss arts council
prohelvetia

 CYNGOR LLYFRAU CYMRU
WELSH BOOKS COUNCIL

Acknowledgments

Publication of *Best European Fiction 2011* was made possible by primary support from Arts Council England, with generous additional support from the following cultural agencies and embassies:

The Arts Council (Ireland)

Books from Lithuania

Communauté française de Belgique—Promotion des letters

Cultural Services of the French Embassy

Cyngor Llyfrau Cymru—Welsh Books Council

Danish Arts Council Committee for Literature

DGLB—Direcção Geral do Livro e das Bibliotecas, Portugal

Embassy of the Principality of Liechtenstein
to the United States of America

Embassy of the Republic of Bulgaria, London

Embassy of Spain, Washington, D.C.

Estonian Literature Centre

Finnish Literature Exchange (FILI)

The Goethe-Institut Chicago

Hungarian Book Foundation

Icelandic Literature Fund

Institut Ramon Llull, Catalan Language and Culture

Latvian Literature Centre

The Ministry of Culture and Monument Protection of Georgia:
Program in Support of Georgian Books and Literature

Ministry of Culture of the Republic of Macedonia

Ministry of Foreign Affairs of the Czech Republic

Nederlands Letterenfonds: The Dutch Foundation for Literature

NORLA: Norwegian Literature Abroad, Fiction & Nonfiction

The Polish Cultural Institute in London

Pro Helvetia, Swiss Arts Council

Romanian Cultural Institute

Slovenian Book Agency (JAK)

POLISH
CULTURAL
INSTITUTE
www.PolishCulture.org.uk

THE POLISH CULTURAL INSTITUTE OF LONDON

(http://www.polishculture.org.uk) is a part of the Polish diplomatic mission in the UK, tasked with the aim of promoting and fostering an understanding of Polish culture throughout the country. With offices based in Soho, the heart of creative London, the Institute devises programs of cultural events in the genres of visual arts, film, theatre, music, and literature, in collaboration with the most established as well as cutting-edge British cultural organizations.

THE SLOVENIAN BOOK AGENCY

The Slovenian Book Agency is an autonomous government institution. It covers all branches of the book industry, from authors to publishers to readers, providing different forms of support: promotion of original and non-commercial book and magazine production in literature, science, art, and general culture, as well as youth literature and youth periodicals, and expert and critical works; yearly grants for top literary authors, critics, and translators; public lending rights; promotion of Slovenian books and authors at home and abroad, and promotion of literary festivals, expert meetings, education and training, reading promotion, promotion of bookshop networks; providing information on literary events and books at home and abroad; cooperation with international institutions. ∫ INTERNATIONAL PROMOTION The principal instruments of our international promotion policy are professional advice, grants, and national stands at international book fairs. The Slovenian Book Agency awards subsidies to translators for the translation of works from Slovenian. All the abovementioned genres are entitled to support. A call for applications is made twice a year. ∫ FOR MORE INFORMATION PLEASE CONTACT Slovenian Book Agency, Tržaška cesta 2, 1000 Ljubljana; phone: +386 (0)1 369 58 20; fax: +386 (0)1 369 58 30; gp.jakrs@jakrs.si; www.jakrs.si

JAK

Rights and Permissions

Peter Adolphsen: "Fourteen Small Stories" © 1996, 2000 by Peter Adolphsen. Translation © 2010 by K. E. Semmel.

Michal Ajvaz: "The Wire Book," excerpt from *Cesta na jih* (Voyage to the South) © 2008 by Michal Ajvaz. Translation © 2010 by Andrew Oakland.

Vladimir Arsenijević: "One Minute: Dumbo's Death," excerpt from *Predator* © 2008 by Vladimir Arsenijević. Translation © 2010 by Celia Hawkesworth.

Kevin Barry: "Doctor Sot" © 2010 by Kevin Barry.

Marco Candida: "Dream Diary," excerpt from *Il diario dei sogni* (Dream Diary) © 2008 by Marco Candida. Translation © 2010 by Elizabeth Harris.

Iulian Ciocan: "Auntie Frosea," excerpt from *Tărîmul lui Saşa Kozak* (The Realm of Sasha Kozak) © 2011 by Iulian Ciocan. Translation © 2010 by Alistair Ian Blyth.

Kristín Eiríksdóttir: "Holes in People" © 2010 by Kristín Eiríksdóttir. Translation © 2010 by Christopher Burawa.

François Emmanuel: "Lou Dancing," excerpt from *Bleu de Fuite* (Blueness of Escape) © 2005 by Editions Stock, Paris. Translation © 2010 by Ursula Meany Scott.

Andrei Gelasimov: "The Evil Eye," excerpt from Степные боги (Gods of the Steppes) © 2008 by Andrei Gelasimov. Translation © 2010 by Sylvia Maizell.

Frode Grytten: "Hotel by a Railroad" © 2007 by Frode Grytten. Translation © 2010 by Seán William Kinsella.

Mercè Ibarz: "Nela and the Virgins" © 2010 by Mercè Ibarz. Translation © 2010 by Rowan Ricardo Phillips.

Nora Ikstena: "Elza Kuga's Old Age Dementia" © 2005 by Nora Ikstena. Translation © 2010 by Margita Gailitis and Vija Kostoff.

Drago Jančar: "The Prophecy" © 2004 by Drago Jančar. Translation © 2009 by Andrew Wachtel.

◰ SELECTED DALKEY ARCHIVE PAPERBACKS

PETROS ABATZOGLOU *What Does Mrs. Freeman Want?*

MICHAL AJVAZ *The Golden Age* ▪ *The Other City*

PIERRE ALBERT-BIROT *Grabinoulor*

YUZ ALESHKOVSKY *Kangaroo*

FELIPE ALFAU *Chromos* ▪ *Locos*

IVAN ÂNGELO *The Celebration* ▪ *The Tower of Glass*

DAVID ANTIN *Talking*

ANTÓNIO LOBO ANTUNES *Knowledge of Hell*

ALAIN ARIAS-MISSON *Theatre of Incest*

IFTIKHAR ARIF AND WAQAS KHWAJA, EDS. *Modern Poetry of Pakistan*

JOHN ASHBERY AND JAMES SCHUYLER *A Nest of Ninnies*

HEIMRAD BÄCKER *transcript*

DJUNA BARNES *Ladies Almanack* ▪ *Ryder*

JOHN BARTH *LETTERS* ▪ *Sabbatical*

DONALD BARTHELME *The King* ▪ *Paradise*

SVETISLAV BASARA *Chinese Letter*

RENÉ BELLETTO *Dying*

MARK BINELLI *Sacco and Vanzetti Must Die!*

ANDREI BITOV *Pushkin House*

ANDREJ BLATNIK *You Do Understand*

LOUIS PAUL BOON *Chapel Road* ▪ *My Little War* ▪ *Summer in Termuren*

ROGER BOYLAN *Killoyle*

IGNÁCIO DE LOYOLA BRANDÃO *Anonymous Celebrity* ▪ *The Good-Bye Angel* ▪ *Teeth under the Sun* ▪ *Zero*

BONNIE BREMSER *Troia: Mexican Memoirs*

CHRISTINE BROOKE-ROSE *Amalgamemnon*

BRIGID BROPHY *In Transit*

MEREDITH BROSNAN *Mr. Dynamite*

GERALD L. BRUNS *Modern Poetry and the Idea of Language*

EVGENY BUNIMOVICH AND J. KATES, EDS. *Contemporary Russian Poetry: An Anthology*

GABRIELLE BURTON *Heartbreak Hotel*

MICHEL BUTOR *Degrees* ▪ *Mobile* ▪ *Portrait of the Artist as a Young Ape*

G. CABRERA INFANTE *Infante's Inferno* ▪ *Three Trapped Tigers*

JULIETA CAMPOS *The Fear of Losing Eurydice*

ANNE CARSON *Eros the Bittersweet*

ORLY CASTEL-BLOOM *Dolly City*

CAMILO JOSÉ CELA *Christ versus Arizona* ▪ *The Family of Pascual Duarte* ▪ *The Hive*

LOUIS-FERDINAND CÉLINE *Castle to Castle* ▪ *Conversations with Professor Y* ▪ *London Bridge* ▪ *Normance* ▪ *North* ▪ *Rigadoon*

HUGO CHARTERIS *The Tide Is Right*

JEROME CHARYN *The Tar Baby*

MARC CHOLODENKO *Mordechai Schamz*

JOSHUA COHEN *Witz*

EMILY HOLMES COLEMAN *The Shutter of Snow*

ROBERT COOVER *A Night at the Movies*

STANLEY CRAWFORD *Log of the S.S. The Mrs Unguentine* ▪ *Some Instructions to My Wife*

ROBERT CREELEY *Collected Prose*

RENÉ CREVEL *Putting My Foot in It*

RALPH CUSACK *Cadenza*

SUSAN DAITCH *L.C.* ▪ *Storytown*

NICHOLAS DELBANCO *The Count of Concord*

NIGEL DENNIS *Cards of Identity*

PETER DIMOCK *A Short Rhetoric for Leaving the Family*

ARIEL DORFMAN *Konfidenz*

COLEMAN DOWELL *The Houses of Children* ▪ *Island People* ▪ *Too Much Flesh and Jabez*

ARKADII DRAGOMOSHCHENKO *Dust*

RIKKI DUCORNET *The Complete Butcher's*

For a full list of publications, visit: www.dalkeyarchive.com

⊟ SELECTED DALKEY ARCHIVE PAPERBACKS

CHARLES JULIET *Conversations with Samuel Beckett and Bram van Velde*

MIEKO KANAI *The Word Book*

YORAM KANIUK *Life on Sandpaper*

HUGH KENNER *The Counterfeiters* ▪ *Flaubert, Joyce and Beckett: The Stoic Comedians* ▪ *Joyce's Voices*

DANILO KIŠ *Garden, Ashes* ▪ *A Tomb for Boris Davidovich*

ANITA KONKKA *A Fool's Paradise*

GEORGE KONRÁD *The City Builder*

TADEUSZ KONWICKI *A Minor Apocalypse* ▪ *The Polish Complex*

MENIS KOUMANDAREAS *Koula*

ELAINE KRAF *The Princess of 72nd Street*

JIM KRUSOE *Iceland*

EWA KURYLUK *Century 21*

EMILIO LASCANO TEGUI *On Elegance While Sleeping*

ERIC LAURRENT *Do Not Touch*

VIOLETTE LEDUC *La Bâtarde*

SUZANNE JILL LEVINE *The Subversive Scribe: Translating Latin American Fiction*

DEBORAH LEVY *Billy and Girl* ▪ *Pillow Talk in Europe and Other Places*

JOSÉ LEZAMA LIMA *Paradiso*

ROSA LIKSOM *Dark Paradise*

OSMAN LINS *Avalovara* ▪ *The Queen of the Prisons of Greece*

ALF MAC LOCHLAINN *The Corpus in the Library* ▪ *Out of Focus*

RON LOEWINSOHN *Magnetic Field(s)*

BRIAN LYNCH *The Winner of Sorrow*

D. KEITH MANO *Take Five*

MICHELINE AHARONIAN MARCOM *The Mirror in the Well*

BEN MARCUS *The Age of Wire and String*

WALLACE MARKFIELD *Teitlebaum's Window* ▪ *To an Early Grave*

DAVID MARKSON *Reader's Block* ▪ *Springer's Progress* ▪ *Wittgenstein's Mistress*

CAROLE MASO *AVA*

LADISLAV MATEJKA AND KRYSTYNA POMORSKA, EDS. *Readings in Russian Poetics: Formalist and Structuralist Views*

HARRY MATHEWS *The Case of the Persevering Maltese: Collected Essays* ▪ *Cigarettes* ▪ *The Conversions* ▪ *The Human Country: New and Collected Stories* ▪ *The Journalist* ▪ *My Life in CIA* ▪ *Singular Pleasures* ▪ *The Sinking of the Odradek Stadium* ▪ *Tlooth* ▪ *20 Lines a Day*

JOSEPH MCELROY *Night Soul and Other Stories*

ROBERT L. MCLAUGHLIN, ED. *Innovations: An Anthology of Modern & Contemporary Fiction*

HERMAN MELVILLE *The Confidence-Man*

AMANDA MICHALOPOULOU *I'd Like*

STEVEN MILLHAUSER *The Barnum Museum* ▪ *In the Penny Arcade*

RALPH J. MILLS JR. *Essays on Poetry*

MOMUS *The Book of Jokes*

CHRISTINE MONTALBETTI *Western*

OLIVE MOORE *Spleen*

NICHOLAS MOSLEY *Accident* ▪ *Assassins* ▪ *Catastrophe Practice* ▪ *Children of Darkness and Light* ▪ *Experience and Religion* ▪ *God's Hazard* ▪ *The Hesperides Tree* ▪ *Hopeful Monsters* ▪ *Imago Bird* ▪ *Impossible Object* ▪ *Inventing God* ▪ *Judith* ▪ *Look at the Dark* ▪ *Natalie Natalia* ▪ *Paradoxes of Peace* ▪ *Serpent* ▪ *Time at*

For a full list of publications, visit: www.dalkeyarchive.com

SELECTED DALKEY ARCHIVE PAPERBACKS

Tales ▪ *The Fountains of Neptune* ▪
The Jade Cabinet ▪ *The One Marvelous
Thing* ▪ *Phosphor in Dreamland* ▪
The Stain ▪ *The Word "Desire"*
WILLIAM EASTLAKE *The Bamboo Bed* ▪
Castle Keep ▪ *Lyric of the Circle Heart*
JEAN ECHENOZ *Chopin's Move*
STANLEY ELKIN *A Bad Man* ▪ *Boswell:
A Modern Comedy* ▪ *Criers and Kibitzers,
Kibitzers and Criers* ▪ *The Dick Gibson
Show* ▪ *The Franchiser* ▪ *George Mills*
▪ *The Living End* ▪ *The MacGuffin* ▪
The Magic Kingdom ▪ *Mrs. Ted Bliss* ▪
The Rabbi of Lud ▪ *Van Gogh's Room
at Arles*
ANNIE ERNAUX *Cleaned Out*
LAUREN FAIRBANKS *Muzzle Thyself* ▪
Sister Carrie
LESLIE A. FIEDLER *Love and Death in the
American Novel*
JUAN FILLOY *Op Oloop*
GUSTAVE FLAUBERT *Bouvard and Pécuchet*
KASS FLEISHER *Talking out of School*
FORD MADOX FORD *The March of Literature*
JON FOSSE *Aliss at the Fire* ▪ *Melancholy*
MAX FRISCH *I'm Not Stiller* ▪ *Man in the
Holocene*
CARLOS FUENTES *Christopher Unborn* ▪
Distant Relations ▪ *Terra Nostra* ▪
Where the Air Is Clear
JANICE GALLOWAY *Foreign Parts* ▪ *The Trick
Is to Keep Breathing*
WILLIAM H. GASS *Cartesian Sonata and
Other Novellas* ▪ *Finding a Form* ▪
A Temple of Texts ▪ *The Tunnel* ▪
Willie Masters' Lonesome Wife
GÉRARD GAVARRY *Hoppla! 1 2 3*

ETIENNE GILSON *The Arts of the Beautiful* ▪
Forms and Substances in the Arts
C. S. GISCOMBE *Giscome Road* ▪ *Here* ▪
Prairie Style
DOUGLAS GLOVER *Bad News of the Heart* ▪
The Enamoured Knight
WITOLD GOMBROWICZ *A Kind of Testament*
KAREN ELIZABETH GORDON *The Red Shoes*
GEORGI GOSPODINOV *Natural Novel*
JUAN GOYTISOLO *Count Julian* ▪ *Juan the
Landless* ▪ *Makbara* ▪ *Marks of Identity*
PATRICK GRAINVILLE *The Cave of Heaven*
HENRY GREEN *Back* ▪ *Blindness* ▪ *Concluding*
▪ *Doting* ▪ *Nothing*
JIŘÍ GRUŠA *The Questionnaire*
GABRIEL GUDDING *Rhode Island Notebook*
MELA HARTWIG *Am I a Redundant Human
Being?*
JOHN HAWKES *The Passion Artist* ▪
Whistlejacket
AIDAN HIGGINS *A Bestiary* ▪ *Balcony of
Europe* ▪ *Bornholm Night-Ferry* ▪
Darkling Plain: Texts for the Air ▪
Flotsam and Jetsam ▪ *Langrishe, Go
Down* ▪ *Scenes from a Receding Past*
▪ *Windy Arbours*
KEIZO HINO *Isle of Dreams*
ALDOUS HUXLEY *Antic Hay* ▪ *Crome Yellow*
▪ *Point Counter Point* ▪ *Those Barren
Leaves* ▪ *Time Must Have a Stop*
MIKHAIL IOSSEL AND JEFF PARKER, EDS.
*Amerika: Russian Writers View the
United States*
GERT JONKE *The Distant Sound* ▪ *Geometric
Regional Novel* ▪ *Homage to Czerny* ▪
The System of Vienna
JACQUES JOUET *Mountain R* ▪ *Savage*

For a full list of publications, visit: www.dalkeyarchive.com

...es of Slime Mould: Essays
...des
...TE Fables of the Novel: French
Fiction since 1990 ▪ Fiction Now:
The French Novel in the 21st Century ▪
Oulipo: A Primer of Potential Literature
YVES NAVARRE Our Share of Time ▪
Sweet Tooth
DOROTHY NELSON In Night's City ▪ Tar and
Feathers
ESHKOL NEVO Homesick
WILFRIDO D. NOLLEDO But for the Lovers
FLANN O'BRIEN At Swim-Two-Birds ▪ At War ▪
The Best of Myles ▪ The Dalkey Archive ▪
Further Cuttings ▪ The Hard Life ▪
The Poor Mouth ▪ The Third Policeman
CLAUDE OLLIER The Mise-en-Scène
PATRIK OUŘEDNÍK Europeana
BORIS PAHOR Necropolis
FERNANDO DEL PASO News from the Empire ▪
Palinuro of Mexico
ROBERT PINGET The Inquisitory ▪ Mahu or
The Material ▪ Trio
MANUEL PUIG Betrayed by Rita Hayworth ▪
The Buenos Aires Affair ▪ Heartbreak
Tango
RAYMOND QUENEAU The Last Days ▪ Odile ▪
Pierrot Mon Ami ▪ Saint Glinglin
ANN QUIN Berg ▪ Passages ▪ Three ▪ Tripticks
ISHMAEL REED The Free-Lance Pallbearers ▪
The Last Days of Louisiana Red ▪ Ishmael
Reed: The Plays ▪ Reckless Eyeballing ▪
The Terrible Threes ▪ The Terrible Twos
▪ Yellow Back Radio Broke-Down
JEAN RICARDOU Place Names
RAINER MARIA RILKE The Notebooks of Malte
Laurids Brigge

JULIÁN RÍOS The House of Ulysses ▪
Larva: A Midsummer Night's Babel ▪
Poundemonium
AUGUSTO ROA BASTOS I the Supreme
DANIËL ROBBERECHTS Arriving in Avignon
OLIVIER ROLIN Hotel Crystal
ALIX CLEO ROUBAUD Alix's Journal
JACQUES ROUBAUD The Form of a City
Changes Faster, Alas, Than the Human
Heart ▪ The Great Fire of London ▪ Hort-
ense in Exile ▪ Hortense Is Abducted ▪ The
Loop ▪ The Plurality of Worlds of Lewis ▪
The Princess Hoppy ▪ Some Thing Black
LEON S. ROUDIEZ French Fiction Revisited
VEDRANA RUDAN Night
STIG SÆTERBAKKEN Siamese
LYDIE SALVAYRE The Company of Ghosts ▪
Everyday Life ▪ The Lecture ▪ Portrait of
the Writer as a Domesticated Animal ▪
The Power of Flies
LUIS RAFAEL SÁNCHEZ Macho Camacho's Beat
SEVERO SARDUY Cobra & Maitreya
NATHALIE SARRAUTE Do You Hear Them? ▪
Martereau ▪ The Planetarium
ARNO SCHMIDT Collected Stories ▪
Nobodaddy's Children
CHRISTINE SCHUTT Nightwork
GAIL SCOTT My Paris
DAMION SEARLS What We Were Doing and
Where We Were Going
JUNE AKERS SEESE Is This What Other
Women Feel Too? ▪ What Waiting
Really Means
BERNARD SHARE Inish ▪ Transit
AURELIE SHEEHAN Jack Kerouac Is Pregnant
VIKTOR SHKLOVSKY Knight's Move ▪ A Senti-
mental Journey: Memoirs 1917–1922 ▪

For a full list of publications, visit: www.dalkeyarchive.com

▣ SELECTED DALKEY ARCHIVE PAPER

Energy of Delusion: A Book on Plot ▪ *Literature and Cinematography* ▪ *Theory of Prose* ▪ *Third Factory* ▪ *Zoo, or Letters Not about Love*

CLAUDE SIMON *The Invitation*

PIERRE SINIAC *The Collaborators*

JOSEF ŠKVORECKÝ *The Engineer of Human Souls*

GILBERT SORRENTINO *Aberration of Starlight* ▪ *Blue Pastoral* ▪ *Crystal Vision* ▪ *Imaginative Qualities of Actual Things* ▪ *Mulligan Stew* ▪ *Pack of Lies* ▪ *Red the Fiend* ▪ *The Sky Changes* ▪ *Something Said* ▪ *Splendide-Hôtel* ▪ *Steelwork* ▪ *Under the Shadow*

W. M. SPACKMAN *The Complete Fiction*

ANDRZEJ STASIUK *Fado*

GERTRUDE STEIN *Lucy Church Amiably* ▪ *The Making of Americans* ▪ *A Novel of Thank You*

LARS SVENDSEN *A Philosophy of Evil*

PIOTR SZEWC *Annihilation*

GONÇALO M. TAVARES *Jerusalem*

LUCIAN DAN TEODOROVICI *Our Circus Presents . . .*

STEFAN THEMERSON *Hobson's Island* ▪ *The Mystery of the Sardine* ▪ *Tom Harris*

JOHN TOOMEY *Sleepwalker*

JEAN-PHILIPPE TOUSSAINT *The Bathroom* ▪ *Camera* ▪ *Monsieur* ▪ *Running Away* ▪ *Self-Portrait Abroad* ▪ *Television*

DUMITRU TSEPENEAG *Hotel Europa* ▪ *The Necessary Marriage* ▪ *Pigeon Post* ▪ *Vain Art of the Fugue*

ESTHER TUSQUETS *Stranded*

DUBRAVKA UGRESIC *Lend Me* ▪ *Thank You for Not Read*

MATI UNT *Brecht at Night* ▪ *Diary* *Donor* ▪ *Things in the Night*

ÁLVARO URIBE AND OLIVIA SEARS, EDS. *Best of Contemporary Mexican Fiction*

ELOY URROZ *Friction* ▪ *The Obstacles*

LUISA VALENZUELA *He Who Searches*

MARJA-LIISA VARTIO *The Parson's Widow*

PAUL VERHAEGHEN *Omega Minor*

BORIS VIAN *Heartsnatcher*

LLORENÇ VILLALONGA *The Dolls' Room*

ORNELA VORPSI *The Country Where No One Ever Dies*

AUSTRYN WAINHOUSE *Hedyphagetica*

PAUL WEST *Words for a Deaf Daughter & Gala*

CURTIS WHITE *America's Magic Mountain* ▪ *The Idea of Home* ▪ *Memories of My Father Watching TV* ▪ *Monstrous Possibility: An Invitation to Literary Politics* ▪ *Requiem*

DIANE WILLIAMS *Excitability: Selected Stories* ▪ *Romancer Erector*

DOUGLAS WOOLF *Wall to Wall* ▪ *Ya! & John-Juan*

JAY WRIGHT *Polynomials and Pollen* ▪ *The Presentable Art of Reading Absence*

PHILIP WYLIE *Generation of Vipers*

MARGUERITE YOUNG *Angel in the Forest* ▪ *Miss MacIntosh, My Darling*

REYOUNG *Unbabbling*

VLADO ŽABOT *The Succubus*

ZORAN ŽIVKOVIĆ *Hidden Camera*

LOUIS ZUKOFSKY *Collected Fiction*

SCOTT ZWIREN *God Head*

For a full list of publications, visit: www.dalkeyarchive.com